THE LYTTELTON HART-DAVIS LETTERS

Volumes 1 and 2

THE LYTTELTON HART-DAVIS LETTERS

Correspondence of George Lyttelton
and Rupert Hart-Davis
Volumes One and Two 1955–57

Edited and introduced by
RUPERT HART-DAVIS

There is no transaction
which offers stronger temptation
to sophistication and fallacy
than epistolary intercourse.
DR JOHNSON

JOHN MURRAY

Lyttelton letters
pp 1–198 © 1978 Humphrey Lyttelton
pp 199–408 © 1979 Humphrey Lyttelton
Appendix I and II © 1978, 1979 Humphrey Lyttelton
Hart-Davis letters and notes
pp 1–198 © 1978 Sir Rupert Hart-Davis
pp 199–408 © 1979 Sir Rupert Hart-Davis

First published in paperback 1985
by John Murray (Publishers) Ltd
50 Albemarle Street, London W1X 4BD

All rights reserved
Unauthorised duplication
contravenes applicable laws

Printed and bound in Great Britain
by The Bath Press, Avon

British Library CIP Data
Lyttelton, George
The Lyttelton Hart-Davis letters: correspondence
of George Lyttelton and Rupert Hart-Davis:
volumes one and two 1955–57
1. English letters
I. Title II. Hart-Davis, Rupert
826'.914'08 PR1347
ISBN 0-7195-4246-4

CONTENTS

This double volume is dedicated
by its editor
with gratitude and affection
to the dear memory of
PAMELA LYTTELTON
and to all her and George's
children and grandchildren

INTRODUCTION

The Hon. George William Lyttelton, second son of the fifth Lord Lyttelton (who later became the eighth Viscount Cobham), was born at Hagley Hall in Worcestershire on 6 January 1883. His Eton career was strikingly successful: he reached Sixth Form, played twice against Harrow at Lord's, was Keeper of the Field and of the Oppidan Wall, and President of Pop. At Trinity, Cambridge, he gained a modest third in the Classical Tripos, and in 1908 he returned as a master to Eton, where his uncle Edward Lyttelton was Head Master.

In 1919 he married Pamela Adeane, by whom he had a son, Humphrey, and four daughters. In 1925 he got his own house, which he ran with gusto and success until 1944. Then, after one more year's teaching, he retired to Suffolk.

He taught mostly classics in the fifth form, but his great opportunity came when he persuaded the new Head Master Cyril Alington (with whom he collaborated in the admirable *Eton Poetry Book*, 1925) to allow him to start an optional course of English as 'extra studies' for senior specialists.

It was there that, in my last year at Eton (1925–26), I fell under his spell. His enthusiasm for teaching and for literature was infectious, his taste so sure, his jokes so amusing, that all his pupils on this course were stimulated to unusual efforts in an attempt to please him and to approach his high standards. Any boy who could recite two hundred consecutive lines of English verse to him was excused an early school: I achieved this exemption twice—with 'Love in the Valley' and 'The Hound of Heaven'.

After I left Eton his days dropped out of mine, until we met briefly in 1949, and thereafter occasionally exchanged letters. In 1950 I took him to a dinner of the Johnson Club in Dr Johnson's house in Gough Square; he was elected to the club and we met at its quarterly dinners. In April 1953 he read a lively paper on his eighteenth-century ancestor Lord Lyttelton, whose life was written by Johnson and to whom Fielding dedicated *Tom Jones*.[1] George was somewhat disconcerted

[1] Reprinted as Appendix II on p. 423.

when the occasion was for some reason changed from a dinner in Gough Square to a luncheon at Brown's Hotel:

> To feel hovering about us the spirit of Dr Johnson has, if one may say so, something inspiring about it, but what if we exchange it for that of Dr Buchman, whose headquarters are in Brown's Hotel? That is 'quite another thing', as George III used to reiterate, about almost everything, as far as I remember.

And then on 18 October 1955 we were fellow-guests at a dinner-party given by our dear friends Tim and Rosalie Nugent at their house in Chelsea Square. After a great deal of excellent food and drink George complained that he was lonely and bored in Suffolk, because there was no one to talk to: 'Nobody even writes to me,' he said. Flushed with wine I accepted the challenge.

'I'll write to you, George.'

'When will you start?'

'Next week-end.'

'Right. I'll answer in the middle of the week.'

Such was the origin of this correspondence, which continued unbroken until George died in 1962.

Perhaps, I now think, he had a faint hope that his letters might one day appear in print, but I was always so busy that the thought never occurred to me. Nor would they have so appeared if it had not been for the perspicacity of Diana Murray and the foolhardy courage of her husband Jock, my lifelong friend and another old pupil of George's.

Editing one's own letters is a curious experience, and, when they are to appear on the same list as Byron's, is surely the height of presumption. Luckily mine were written so long ago, and in what seems another life, that I can read them objectively, as though they had been written by someone else. I have resisted the temptation to improve them, and have confined my editing to the removal from both sides of the correspondence of libellous or hurtful passages, repetitions, padding, and references to weather and current affairs which no longer have any point. I have not indicated where the omissions occur. I have split up some of the longer paragraphs. Footnotes I have kept to what I hope is a helpful minimum.

In the first two letters I have retained the opening and signature, which are afterwards omitted, since they are almost always the same: any variation is printed. Similarly I have given our full home addresses in the first two letters and then abbreviated them. From Monday to Friday I lived in a flat above my publishing office at 36 Soho Square.

George was a large man with a huge head and a wide brow, which glistened with enthusiasm in conversation. Owing to some hip-trouble he walked with a stick. When this correspondence began he was seventy-two and I was forty-eight.

Marske-in-Swaledale RUPERT HART-DAVIS
February 1978

POSTSCRIPT

When I wrote the above neither I nor Jock Murray could tell whether any more volumes would be called for. Happily the whole correspondence has since been successfully published in six volumes, and now reappears as three paperbacks, with two of the original volumes in each. My gratitude to my publisher and the hundreds of people who have written to me about the Letters is immense.

July 1985 R. H-D.

Bromsden Farm
Henley-on-Thames
23 October 1955 *Oxon*

My dear George

This not so much the first over, as a gentle limbering up, a few balls off the wicket to see whether the arm will still go over. Sunday is my only day for letters, not counting the twenty or so rubbishy notes I dictate each working day in the office, and I have already scribbled *nine* to-day, God help me. Almost every week I am here from Friday night to Monday morning, so if you write here your letter will gladden my exhausted return. Yesterday, when I should have been reading MSS and compiling endless finicky details for the second edition of the Bibliography of W.B. Yeats (a labour of love, of which more later), I took down the last two volumes of *Ego*[1] (all I have here) and re-read the exchanges between G.L. and J.A. Delicious, I thought again, but pretty daunting too, and not to be competed with. Still, the quality of letters, it seems to me, usually depends on the addressee (forgive that beastly word), and there is clearly something in you that calls for the best one can do—which no doubt partly explains your excellence as a schoolmaster. You will probably find yourself sometimes cast as a mixture of psychiatrist and father-confessor, but you must be used to that. I shan't choose special subjects for you, as Horace Walpole did for each of his correspondents, but simply write whatever is in my mind or your letters suggest. Nor have I time to choose my words as I would for print, so you'll have to forgive many a lame and impotent conclusion.

If I had no family (bless them) or other ties and responsibilities, I should chuck publishing tomorrow, and live in a two-roomed cottage in the Yorkshire dales—don't ask me with whom, though one day you shall know—relying for my livelihood on free-lance literary work. I know exactly how little can be earned that way, but I have few expensive tastes (only books really), I could read all the great books

[1] By James Agate.

which now I have only skimmed or forgotten or never read, and *then* I'd write you letters indeed! But that is a dream which will not be realised for many years, if ever. You must forgive all this egotism, but it's right that you should know who you're writing to. I am in truth some sort of a research scholar *manqué*, but because I have made something of a name as a publisher and am good at getting on with people, it is assumed that I must *like* it, which frankly I do less and less.

Going back to *Ego*, the only question you discussed there on which I have decided views is the definition of genius. This I take to be nothing more or less than a super-normal degree of *energy*—physical, mental, spiritual, or in combination. Or can you at once produce a dozen indubitable geniuses to whom such a definition could not apply? 'Taking pains' to the nth degree seems to me to have nothing to do with the matter.

In bed at night I am reading Alan Ross's *Australia 55*, which you must certainly get hold of. So far as I know, it is the first account of an M.C.C. tour written by a poet and including some account of that repellent continent, as well as the descriptions of the Test Matches which you probably read in the *Observer*. The other day John Sparrow sent me his recent selection of Bridges's poems: I have been reading them slowly, one at a time, and wondering why, with all their technical and verbal perfection, they are not more moving, not greater poems. Was it because his life was too sheltered? Or because the poems came more from the brain than the heart or guts? And yet quite a few of his *lines* stay in one's head, which is surely a good criterion. Goodbye till next week, when I shall expect a whale of a letter to answer.

Yours ever
Rupert

Finndale House
Grundisburgh
Woodbridge
Suffolk

27 October 1955

My dear Rupert

'A few balls off the wicket' indeed! What *will* you be writing when you get your length? It reminds me of Worcs v the Australians when K. Miller terrified everybody with his speed, and their manager told my nephew Charles:[1] 'Of course Keith is only bowling half pace till the weather gets warmer'. I can't tell you what pleasure your suggestion of a regular correspondence gave me on that extremely delectable evening at Tim's. My few regular correspondents are very aged, and between you and I (as, have you noticed, the modern fashion has it?) the difference between what is dull and what is not, is beginning to elude them. N. Cardus once looked like filling the bill, but he petered out. And indeed, except Voltaire and a few others, those who are always writing can hardly be expected to write letters. Now and then, my dear R, you will think 'O damn, I ought to write to G.W.L.' Well, on those occasions you just *mustn't*. The thing must *never* become a burden. It never does or will to me, because I am on the shelf. My only danger is of bursting from having too much to say and no one to say it to. My letters, I suspect, are too long. Only a day or two ago I read in a Lytton Strachey essay on letters that Swift and Carlyle were disappointing, Swift being 'too dry, which is bad, and C. too long, which is worse'. Was L.S. right? He often wasn't. And somehow I think you don't mind length (with reasonable legibility).

How neatly you touch the bullseye: 'I shall simply write whatever is in my mind, or your letters suggest'. Not that dear Maurice Headlam[2] does not do the former; but, alas, his mind is full of Irish politics of fifty years or more ago, of visits to old friends of whom I have never heard, of the novels of Charles Reade in small print, which, if you please, he sends me to read and return. Also a 'Dialogue of the Dead' between Kossuth, Garibaldi, and Michael Collins,

[1] Then the Hon C. J. Lyttelton, captain of Worcestershire, later the tenth Viscount Cobham and Governor General of New Zealand.

[2] Prominent civil servant. Brother of Cuthbert and Tuppy.

composed by himself. The publisher of his *Irish Memories* refused it on the grounds (the tact of you publishers!) that it might stir up feelings better left at rest, leaving M.H. with the gratifying sense of having written something which Mr Lillyvick would have called 'absorbing, fairy-like, toomultuous'.[3]

I knew somehow—perhaps it emerged from your really excellent life of H. Walpole—that of course writing was your proper job. But, dash it all, you airily talk of 'making something of a name as a publisher' and 'good at getting on with people' as if they were easy achievements! You are like Einstein who put his violin above his science, or Mozart who said he would have preferred to be a dancer to being a composer. As to research, who was it who described it as 'that state of resentful coma which scholars attempt to dignify by calling research' (not accurately quoted except for the first five words). Laski produced it—mendaciously—as his own in a letter to Judge Holmes. By the way how *immensely* good that correspondence is, don't you agree? Dr A.L. Goodhart once told me that practically nothing Laski said of what he had done (or read!) was true, but what does that matter? He had the root of the matter *qua* letter-writing in him, and so old Holmes often said. L. said of Horace Walpole 'You are glad he lived, but very grateful that you didn't know him'. And after (as he said) sitting next to V. Woolf at lunch, 'Every phrase and gesture was studied. Now and again when she said something a little out of the ordinary she wrote it down herself in a notebook. *It was like watching someone organising her own immortality.*' Isn't that *beastly* good? Would *genius* be too big a word? Perhaps.

I think I agree with you about energy being the essence of it. Beethoven, Shakespeare, M. Angelo, Keats—yes, the impression I get from all of them is combined speed and intensity, which of course = energy. Which the expression 'taking pains' quite misses. There are so few signs of 'pains' about e.g. *Don Juan* that some quite unstupid people have been blind to its genius. When I was a young beak I praised it in my Extra Studies. A week later J.B.S. Haldane stopped after school and told me he had never enjoyed anything so much. The same day I was scolded for having set half College reading it. And I didn't at the time realise how right *I* had been and how wrong

[3] *Nicholas Nickleby*, chapter XXV.

my stuffy old seniors! Do you realise that in those Extra Studies I had at different times Aldous H., J. Haldane, C. Hollis, G. Orwell, C. Connolly, J. Lehmann, Alan Clutton-Brock, Peter Fleming, Noel Blakiston (I *think*), Alan Pryce-Jones, Rupert H-D.? There's glory for you! But my chief memories of those schools now are of how many opportunities I missed and how much better I ought to have done them. Well, well. It is not what old men forget that shadows their senescence, but what they remember. There is a particularly happy old lady in my home village who says 'Have one of those things—you know, puff, puff'. She has forgotten the word cigarette, but she is happier by far than, according to my cousin Oliver,[4] Winston is. Butler's Budget? What a country cousin you will think me when I ask how does *adding* to the price of everything *reduce* the cost of living? Don't we all know that the only remedy is for *everyone* to have less money? But who dares say so? And so, despairing of human good sense and good will, we leave it to the Ancient of Days to make the next move, which, *more suo* (sorry, it should be *Suo*!), will be an upsetting of the entire apple-cart, after which a still small voice will be heard amid the din and dust, saying 'Well, little man, there is another lesson. Now get up and learn it and try again.' And so *da capo senza fine*.

Bridges? I entirely agree with you. Andrea del Sarto, do you think: 'All the play, the insight and the stretch—Out of me! Out of me!' I have a dreadful suspicion sometimes that artists, if they are really to grow to full stature, mustn't have so much education. Hubert Parry is another example of brilliant promise ending in the merely accomplished and scholarly. 'Dreadful' is too big a word—insincere in fact, because I am no great believer in education—or indeed in democracy or a good many other things. I believe profoundly in what few others seem to nowadays, viz original sin. In fact my favourite text is Jeremiah's blunt assertion 'The heart is deceitful above all things and desperately wicked'. The truth of that seems to me positively glaring.

Well anyhow another thing which is also p.g. is that it is high time I stopped. You will be thinking how right Lytton S. was, and how great the epistolary superiority was of the boy whose letter home consisted of just 'S.O.S. L.S.D. R.S.V.P.' or the gamekeeper

[4] Oliver Lyttelton, first Viscount Chandos.

instructed to tell his employer when the woods had woodcock in them: 'Horned Sir. The kaks becum. Jarge.'

Bless you

Yours ever

G.W.L.

30 October 1955 *Bromsden Farm*

Never did so slender a fly catch such a whopping salmon! When I got home on Friday to find no letter, I sadly feared that mine had misfired or miscarried (if you're going to mix your metaphors, mix them thoroughly like a salad), but on Saturday morning the postman drove up with your delicious budget—so much more acceptable and pointed than Butler's. There's no fear of your becoming a burden: indeed I regard you more as a liberator—and before I read your letter again, let me cover a page or two with details of some of the affairs from which I am so happy, once a week, to be liberated.

Imprimis the publishing business, which in each of its nine years (except one) has produced its yearly, often half-yearly, crisis, has all this year been causing me even more grievous worry. How long can it survive independently? Should I not amalgamate with X, Y or Z? Could I then preserve my independence? etc. etc. Momently all is in suspense till Nov. 21 or so, when doubtless I shall burden you with the next chapter.

In front of this sombre, threatening backcloth, 1955 has dealt me several blows. In February my close friend Humphry House (Fellow of Wadham, English don) fell suddenly dead of a thrombosis. He was 46. His wife and three children were left almost penniless, and as his literary and ordinary executor I had to spend much time on their affairs (I still write to Mrs H. almost daily from the office). Humphry's unfinished literary works consisted of:

(a) The monumental (and would-be complete) edition of Dickens's Letters, which I persuaded H. to take on in 1949. We had already got a grant of £6000 from the Pilgrim Trust to pay for editorial work etc., had engaged an enormous Advisory Board of Dickens experts everywhere, etc. Close on 10,000 letters were already transcribed and checked. When H. died they were all at me in panic, especially the Pilgrim Trust, asking what was going to happen. With a firmness based on nothingness, I said 'The show will go on'. The trouble was that H's knowledge of the nineteenth century in general, and Dickens in particular, was unparalleled. G.M. Young wrote to me: 'He is the only man who knows more of the nineteenth century than I do.' Eventually after months I managed to get the whole cumbersome machine back on the rails with a modicum of steam up. Mrs H. (a remarkably exact, erudite and nice woman) is really in charge of it all, knowing more of it than anyone else, and I have persuaded a very nice Cambridge don, Graham Hough of Christ's, to be nominal Editor-in-Chief, responsible for *writing* the myriad footnotes, for which material pours in from every continent.[1] So much for that.

(b) Have you patience? There's lots to come—the second, revised and enlarged edition of *The Note-books of Gerard Manley Hopkins*. Humphry was the world's expert on G.M.H. and edited the original edition of the *Note-books* twenty years ago. For all H's neatness, the papers in his study were in considerable confusion, but from a quick glance I thought this particular task was near enough completion for me to see it through the press without too much work, so I loaded a car with all the materials and brought them to London, where ever since they have dustily monopolised the only big table in my flat. What I didn't fully realise was that H's assistant in the job, a female ex-student of his, had apparently gone off her head, taking a mass of H's notes and queries to Germany (where she has a job) and refusing to answer letters. [Here my wife gave me some excellent corned beef hash and drove off to play bridge with Celia Fleming. I play only in self-defence—in the Mess, with my mother-in-law, and so on.] So there are the Hopkins *Note-books*: have you ever read them? The most exciting things of their kind since Coleridge's (of which a full edition in many vols is soon to begin appearing). Sparks fly from everything Hopkins wrote, just as, alas, they *didn't* from his friend Bridges. A charming Jesuit called Christopher Devlin (one of his brothers is a judge, one an actor) comes for two afternoons a week to help me with the job, but I am mostly too busy in the office to do more than give him tea and cheer him on. The Jesuits own all the

[1] He soon resigned and was succeeded by Graham Storey of Trinity Hall.

copyrights in G.M.H.'s writings—hence their free supplying of this good helper. There isn't a penny in it for anyone: I just want to get it as good as maybe for Humphry's sake. Oxford are the publishers: I gaily told them the job would be done by the end of the year, but it won't.

(c) A half-finished biography of Hopkins's life up to the time he became a Jesuit. This I have persuaded everyone (Mrs H, Jesuits, O.U.P.) to lay aside till the *Note-books* are done.

(d) A volume of Humphry's essays and broadcast talks, *All in Due Time*, which I had to select, edit, and correct, verifying all quotations etc. It comes out next Friday, and I'll send you a copy tomorrow: there's some first-rate stuff in it. For all my pains, G.M. Young when he got an early copy whipped back a postcard pointing out a howler on p. 16!

(e) A series of lectures on Aristotle's *Poetics*, designed for the English School at Oxford and elsewhere. I got a classics don at Magdalen to vet and edit them, and shall publish next year. That's all for Humphry, whom in the intervals of coping with all his affairs I deeply mourn.

Then, in April—God, why did I start all this? Anyhow it has become compulsive and I must finish. I warned you that you'd get an earful, but perhaps you didn't believe it—in April, I say, a very dear old friend, a cockney actor of great charm, intelligence and wit, whom I met when I was a student at the Old Vic in 1927, gassed himself after two ghastly operations and a year's agony from cancer at the base of the spine. He was 64. Except for shock and sorrow, his death caused me no extra burden: just a couple of journeys to South Devon to comfort his widow.

Then in July Allan Wade died in a split second from a heart attack, without illness and after a full and happy day. A fine death for him, but a fearful shock for his wife, whom I have been trying to help and look after ever since. Allan was 74: she is only 56, and I hope may marry again. He was an actor and theatre-man most of his life (play-reader to Granville Barker for years) but always a literary bloke at heart, collecting his favourite modern authors (Yeats, Max, Henry James, Conrad), digging up bibliographical stuff in the B.M. After the last war I published his edition of Henry James's dramatic criticism, *The Scenic Art*, and then his Bibliography of Yeats. Then I got him to edit Yeats's Letters, which he did beautifully—we worked together a lot on it. Then I persuaded him to edit Oscar Wilde's Letters (never before collected) and he had made a good start when he died. Wilde's son, Vyvyan Holland, a charming chap but unsuitable as editor, offered to take the job on, and the only way tactfully to stop him was to do it myself. So the whole mass of Wilde material came to join Hopkins in the flat of lost causes. Very slowly a devoted colleague and I are stealing odd minutes to transcribe and check the hundreds of letters, write round for more, and generally keep the ball rolling. It's an interesting, and compared with Hopkins a very simple, job—but all my days were busily occupied before this avalanche hit me. Then there is the second edition of the Yeats Bibliography, which Allan was also working on: it's fiddling complicated work, but I know a good deal about the subject, and am repeatedly swamped by lists of new facts and minute corrections from two American professors.

Allan left no money, but a few thousand books (including a magnificent Yeats collection). He told his wife that I would sell them for her, and that I was to keep anything I wanted, thus posing a nice question of conscience. However there are plenty of non-valuable things I'm delighted to have. So as to avoid constant journeys to the Old Brompton Road (where the Wades lived) I've gradually transferred all the books to my flat: they should be gone in a month or two, but just now they are bursting out of the sitting-room. As if all this wasn't enough, six weeks ago my dearest friend Edmund Blunden sent me an SOS from Hong Kong asking if I could find a resting-place for his library, which a kind friend could no longer house. I told him to leave it to me, thinking to find a rich friend with an empty room. None such appeared, and one morning at 8.30 three stalwart Kentish men started carrying the books up to my flat. It took them *eight hours* non-stop—something like 7500 volumes. What used to be my spare bedroom is now breast-high in Eng. Lit. Do you remember Anatole France's old scholar who lived in a room known as '*la cité des livres*'? Well, my spareroom looks like that city after a bad air-raid. If I died tomorrow, as I sometimes feel I shall, the only hope for *my* executors would be to set a match to the building and endeavour to apportion the totally inadequate insurance amongst the various plaintiffs. In fact, directly Allan's books are out of the way I shall be able to get some order into Edmund's, which I fancy are with me for the duration. To complete my tale of woe, in the middle of this disastrous year I lost my pocket engagement-book in which were all my appointments, everyone's telephone number, all my godchildren's birthdays—you know. I've poured out all this, not in self-pity or seeking for sympathy, but just to show you why the thought of writing to you and getting your answers is a blessed one. When you speak of yourself as 'on the shelf', I yearn to join you on that serene and uncomplicated eminence. Your letters can't be too long for me, I warrant you.

Now I shall read the last one again. Where does that heavenly 'state of resentful coma' come from? I haven't enjoyed a phrase so much for ages. I agree with all you say of *Don Juan*, and only wish you had put me on to it at Eton: I didn't read it till I was grown up, and was then bowled over by the wind of its genius. Your tally of Extra Studies pupils is terrific: I can see a future thesis-writer from Dakron, Ohio, submitting a monster on 'The Influence of G.W. Lyttelton on mid-century Literature'. And, oh how I agree about democracy, education etc. Edmund Blunden told me that when he was a boy in Kent the shepherds and farmers talked of crops and weather and seemed so happy. Now they sidle up with a grubby first edition for him to autograph, just educated enough to know they might make a shilling or two that way, and certainly no happier for it.

Now I must read the long MS of an Air-Marshal's autobiography. Forgive this endless stream of egotism. I promise that next Sunday's shall be more cheerful. Do you abominate detective stories? I read two a week in bed at night: can't concentrate on much else then. I've reviewed them regularly under an assumed name in *Time & Tide* for ten years. To me they are a great solace, a sort of mental knitting, where it doesn't matter if you drop a stitch. Goodnight.

3 November 1955 *Grundisburgh*

Your letter is immensely interesting. It is quite clear that for the moment Fortune has it in for you—in that cryptic modernism. You will (probably) crossly rebut as an empty compliment (but you shan't prevent) my saying that only a *good* man finds all that on his plate. How fantastic that *you* should have these publishing crises. Only yesterday a young man—intelligent, literary, foot-on-the-ladder etc.—uttered your name with what I can only call reverence, and he clearly found it heartening that a firm which keeps up such a standard should be so conspicuously successful! That is the reputation you have. You see the world is full of people who are saying 'R.H-D. is the man to get us out of this'. The Archdeacon (probably Archdeacon Chute[1] of Piddlehinton—a fact!) who after some fierce epidemic said in lachrymose terms 'Orphans have lost their props, widows their stays' would now add 'but luckily there is always R.H-D. to look after them'. If you had had the ungracious temper of Hodder, or the cold indifference of Stoughton, there would be a very different picture—a more placid one, happier perhaps, but the central figure would have no halo! How Botticellian I am becoming!

I don't know Edmund Blunden, but I met him once in old C.H. Wilkinson's room at Worcester and liked his quiet, kindly manner. I also liked the expression on his face when C.H.W. was maintaining that there was nothing in the recent exposure of T.J. Wise, whom—only slightly less recently—C.H.W. had been responsible for making a fellow of Worcester Coll. It was a scene of rich comedy and I could see E.B. savouring it like a connoisseur of exquisite vintages, but so demurely that C.H.W. could not be offended.

I can't at the moment place the 'resentful coma' saying; it was Cyril Alington who told it to me and he is now telling it to Marcus Aurelius or the Prince Consort, I hope with success. It is a solemn thought that Queen Victoria and Mr Gladstone must both be there, unless Purgatory has not finished with them for another century or two. But I suppose there is plenty of room. Do you know that deadly little quatrain of Dorothy Parker's (I think) comparing the respective attractions of H and H.

Whose love is given over well
Shall look on Helen's face in Hell,
But he whose love is thin and wise
Shall see John Knox in Paradise.

[1] Previously an Eton master.

I told that to a good parson and challenged him to quote it in the pulpit. He said he would—and they tell me has! Bless you.

P.S. I haven't thanked you at all properly for that House book. I do now, and will write more after reading. Old Boy Dinner yesterday. They were all very pleasant. I was simply Mr Chips (horrible, horrible!! horrible!!! as Henry James said when introduced to an American boy of sixteen and asked what he thought of him).

6 November 1955 *Bromsden Farm*

I have written my weekly letter to my sister in New Orleans and to Edmund Blunden in Hong Kong, so here's to you in Grundisburgh. This is the kind of paper on which I wrote all my Walpole book, but that was a mere 180,000 words, a preliminary knock-up for my letters to you. Yours was faithfully waiting for me on Friday: a noble effort considering your uprooting for the Old Boy dinner. I only wish I was qualified to attend (we abandoned ours when Jelly[1] became bed-ridden), for you have clearly misinterpreted the casting. Indubitably you are the monstrous fine *Fish*, while the Old Boys play the parts of miscellaneous and circumambient *Chips*. I bet you had fun anyhow.

One day last week my son Duff drifted in from Chelsea Barracks and I took him to dine at the Garrick. We chanced to sit next to E.R.T. Holmes and were soon pumping him for cricket gossip. As you'll remember, when he first captained Surrey as a lad, the great Hobbs was still playing. Once Holmes asked him whether he ever paid any attention to the bowler's arm, wrist etc. Hobbs said: 'Never,' and I believe it's true. I'm certain Compton never does either. Do you imagine that all the greatest players have always simply played each ball on its merits as it approaches them, and that it's only the second-raters and below who can be deceived by the googly hand-action?

On Friday I went to Ronald Storrs's funeral. Did you know him? He was extremely kind to me and took the trouble to read the whole of my book in typescript. It was he who taught me never to use 'in

[1] Nickname of E. L. Churchill, my Eton housemaster.

the case of' unless a 'case' is in fact involved. He also begged me not to use 'hectic', which he called 'a silly feminine word'. Except for his learning and wisdom, one might have been talking to a contemporary. Not much more than two years ago my uncle Duff Cooper took me to a dinner of the Horatian Society, where Ronald read a brilliant paper. Now they are both dead. The mourners on Friday were mostly elderly: Charles Tennyson read the lesson very well—from *The Wisdom of Solomon*—and the coffin glowed under Ronald's K.C.M.G. banner of scarlet-and-white. (Have you ever been to a service of the Order in St Paul's? I went to see Duff's banner laid up after his death—very moving and beautiful.) I left the funeral remembering Ronald's telling me how he met my mother at a party in Venice in 1912, and how they quoted Meredith's poetry to each other in a gondola.

My next book, if I ever find time for it (what nonsense—one can always find or make time for something one is *determined* to do), will be about my mother, who was a lovely gifted tragic person. She died aged 40 when I was 19, so the book will in fact also cover those years of my own life. At stray moments, and on the rare walks I take alone, I brood on the problem, hoping that one day the plan or arrangement will manifest itself. In any case it could not be published while my father is alive—not that he is my real father, I feel pretty sure, but he's the only one I've known, and tiresome as the poor old fellow is, I don't want to hurt his feelings. One day, in or out of the book, the whole story shall be divulged to you.

In an American detective story I read the other day a young man was airing a lot of half-baked literary nonsense, and his girl said to him: 'Don't look now, but your Ph.D.'s showing', which I rather enjoyed. Your Dorothy Parker quotation is splendid, and should be sent to the Archbishop of C. Do you know him? Two friends of mine, Humphry House and Victor Gollancz, were under him at Repton and cordially detested him. From afar it's the smugness that most displeases. Humility of spirit is surely a prerequisite of grace.

This must be the last sheet tonight, for I have a French novel to read—all about a dumb peasant and his bloody sheep—and a manuscript to prepare for the printer. Don't think for a moment that this delightful correspondence is solely for your benefit: it is pure self-indulgence. You are the diary I have never kept, the excuse I have so long wanted for forming words on paper unconnected with duty or business. By the way, can you read my writing? Always or only in spots? Yours is superb.

9 November 1955 *Grundisburgh*

In a world where nearly all is dark, as Bishop Gore used to say, two things are luminously clear: viz that your letters are of first-class interest and quality, and that your handwriting is perfectly legible, and, in fact, very pleasant to look on. And the second is very important. Did you ever get a letter from Monty James?[1] I once had a note from him inviting us to dinner—we *guessed* that the time was 8 and not 3, as it appeared to be, but all we could tell about the day was that it was not Wednesday. The late Bishop Brook of Ipswich maintained that all great men—Shakespeare, Napoleon, Brook, etc,—had illegible hands, and conveniently forgot, or more likely didn't know, that Michael Angelo, Henry VIII, Elizabeth (when she chose), Lord Palmerston, all had conspicuously fine hands. But, though I hate to admit it, there is something in what he said—explained by some pundit, apropos, I think, of Napoleon's monstrous script, that where a brain is *very* quick, the hand just cannot keep up. An odd corollary to this is the undeniable fact that in a C or D division the stupidest boys did the best maps, the Collegers always the worst. I wonder why. 'Sir, you *may* wonder.'

Of course you are quite right about Hobbs and Co. Genius doesn't know how or why. I don't think Shaw's 'Those who can, do; those who can't, teach' was only a fairly cheap little gibe at schoolmasters (though he *could* be cheap enough). Surely he meant that e.g. Shakespeare wrote—probably pretty quickly—'You lack the season of all natures, sleep' but it is the Bradleys and the Dover Wilsons who tell us all its subtleties and what was in the mind behind it. I remember an elaborate explanation of a shot of Compton's off a very nasty ball—how swift and masterly was the thought that informed the hand, that any other way would have been fatal etc. Someone asked C. about it and his reply was 'Gosh, yes, I remember; I didn't

[1] M. R. James, Provost of Eton, author of *Ghost Stories of an Antiquary*, etc.

know what to do, so I just had a slam at it'. What a bucolic grin would have widened the mouth of Achilles if he had read Homer!

I met Ronald Storrs once—in the Greek play at Cambridge in 1903. He was some sort of herald. I liked him, but I never met him again. He was not popular as a young man, I suppose because his brains were too obvious, he did not suffer fools gladly, and thought that there were a great many of them about. But my cousin, Archer Cust, was devoted to him, as also, I think, was Alec Cadogan (my fag in 1899!) if anything so strong as 'devotion' can be imagined of 'Sir Icicle' as Diana[2] says his F.O. underlings called him. I have got R.S.'s paper at the Horatian Society and entirely agree with you about its brilliance. I came across recently a glaring instance of 'case' in, of all people, Frank Swinnerton—on Max B's caricatures: 'The drawings, in the majority of cases, are already sold'. But no doubt if some pedant (like me) pointed this out, his defence would be Johnson's, 'that sudden fits of inadvertency will surprise vigilance, slight avocations will seduce attention, and casual eclipses of the mind will darken learning'. (How tediously otiose of me to quote that to you. My excuse, which I have a feeling you will admit as valid, is the pleasure it gives me to write down words which express so perfectly what they mean.)

What interesting forebears and relatives and connections you have. Please say lots whenever thoughts crop up about them, and the pen, like Kempenfelt's, is in your hand and not the editorial blue pencil. Mine, you know, are, on the whole, pretty humdrum. There *was* a 'wicked Lord Lyttelton', but I don't know that his wickedness amounted to much: a sceptical cousin maintained to his pious and scandalised aunts that they regarded anyone as wicked who didn't know how many Sundays there were after Trinity. He was terrified, you remember, by an apparition, though, as Horace W. said, *he* would have thought the appearance of a young woman in his bedroom would have been the last thing to startle Lord L. But some day you might like to hear of my uncle Albert.[3] He was *not* humdrum. He was a missionary. His face, his saintliness, and to a great extent, his clothes and his diet were those of John the Baptist. He was insatiably curious. When moving staircases came in he tried to stop one by holding on

[2] George's eldest daughter, now the Hon. Mrs Alexander Hood.

[3] The Hon. Albert Victor Lyttelton, priest (1844–1928).

to one of the stationary knobs at the side. A moment later he picked himself up from the floor, quite satisfied by the proof that he could *not* stop it. Then he tried (about 60 odd) to go *up* the stairs that were coming *down*, and after a minute or so on what must have been exactly like a treadmill, found out that that too wouldn't do. You would have liked him.

I immensely enjoyed *Old Men Forget* but I never came across the author; good value he must have been. *Talleyrand* too was first-rate. The equivalent to 'the Jordan blood' in your family is in mine 'the Glynne blood' to which the lack of ambition and fundamental pessimism of many of us are always ascribed—also, of course, the comparative colourlessness of the Gladstone descendants. But just imagine if W.E.G. had married someone as serious and intense as himself. 'Aunty Pussie'[4] kept him human. She was the greatest fun, full of surprises, whimsical beyond description, without a grain of self-consciousness. She once expressed great sympathy with Charles Peace, because after all those adventures he must have found prison intolerably boring. The old man glared for a moment, but then broke into helpless laughter.

That 'Your Ph.D. is shewing' is lovely. I see you are agin the Archp. It is curious how much he was disliked by how many at Repton, where also another H.M. told me he really made *no* mark. I have sat under him on a committee and I must say he was not only very good, but we all liked him. Is it possible to make an *ex cathedra* pronouncement on a spiritual or moral matter which does *not* sound smug, especially when you know your chief antagonists are the *Mirror* and *Sketch*, than which organs almost any line you take must be higher and can be made by their clever editors to sound too high? Lang ('Old Lang Swine' as B. Bracken called him to Winston who was shocked and amused in equal measure) *did* seem smug; Fisher is v. genial and friendly. The *Mirror* according to the *New Statesman* has made disestablishment a live issue. To which surely the answer can only be monosyllabic, plural, resonant, and contemptuous.

[4] Mrs Gladstone (née Glynne). She and George's paternal grandmother were sisters.

You've no idea what a joy it is to stagger home on Friday evening after a hellish week, and find a fine witty stimulating letter in your beautiful hand. I never saw Monty James's writing but doubt whether he can have been more illegible than Lady Colefax: the only hope of deciphering *her* invitations, someone said, was to pin them up on the wall and *run* past them! She had known everybody and remembered *nothing*. 'Oh yes, I saw Henry James constantly,' she truly said when I pumped her for Walpole-copy, but not one word or scene or incident could she conjure up for me. Once the lion was under her roof she could start trapping the next one, and they all came because the company was so good. Mrs L. Hunter was an amateur by comparison. I wonder about handwriting. Of the moderns Yeats's was appalling (particularly as he never mastered spelling or punctuation), but Hardy's was good, and Conrad's too. Edmund Blunden's is exquisite: do you know it? If not I'll send you some to see. Shaw's was niggling but clear, Henry James's sprawling and occasionally illegible (I have transcribed a lot of his letters): moreover he often finished his letters upwards over their first page, thus creating a kind of palimpsest in which accents, commas and dashes fly off at all angles like sparks from a squib. All this catalogue reminds me of E.C. Bentley's splendid *Ballade of Souls*, which begins 'The soul of Dante was a white-hot spear'. I expect you know it: if not I shall love copying it out for you next week.

I assure you that your Johnsonian quotations are neither tedious nor otiose. As you say, it's such a pleasure to write down splendid words—almost as though one were inventing them. I'm sure that many of Shakespeare's most staggering lines were just like Compton's most wonderful shots—brought off at the last moment by the instinct of genius, without any conscious preparation or thought. Bradley and Dover Wilson may be right about the mind behind it, but if so they know more about it than Shakespeare did. Have you read the books of my dear friend Leslie Hotson? His detailed knowledge of the period is stupendous, his assiduity in research endless, his gaiety infectious. To the delight of my children he sings songs in all languages, accompanying himself on a guitar. Moreover, he is the only living writer who to my knowledge has a private patron: an enormously rich Englishwoman who gives him $3000 a year so that he can continue his work. Latterly King's Cambridge have given him a research fellowship, so that he can spend half each year over here. He is American, but all his quarry is in Europe—in the Record Office and private libraries. I know you'd love him.

Talking of Cambridge, I spent last Tuesday night there. The Audit Feast at Christ's was quite impressive: 'scarlet and medals' the invitation-card said. I stayed with Humphry House's widow, fought my way into my 25-year-old tails (it's the collar that almost strangles me) and was picked up by my host Graham Hough. At dinner I sat between him and Sir Hughe Knatchbull-Hugessen, an amiable little old man plastered with medals. Unprepared for such an honour, I could remember nothing about him except that when he was Ambassador in Turkey his valet stole and copied all his secret documents (did you read the book called *Operation Cicero*?). This fascinating but delicate subject seemed better unbroached, so I confined myself to Shakespeare and the musical glasses, and we got along very well. Opposite me was Kingsford, head of the Cambridge University Press and an old friend, with whom I exchanged a good deal of publishing shop. Eventually I got to sleep at 2.30 a.m., wondering why I do such things when I don't really enjoy them.

I'm reading the new life of Kipling[1] with much interest and enjoyment. So far little of his inner life or character has emerged (and that little not very sympathetic—his letters are mostly tiresome), but the facts and details of his life (which I knew little of before) are most ably marshalled and set forth. Now, *there* was a genius all right—just that energy we were discussing. I do hope you agree. I should say one of the great literary geniuses of the Anglo-Saxon race, and when time has winnowed away all the vulgarity, lack of taste, jingoism and cocksure brassiness, the residue will be read and enjoyed without end. I'm sure of it. But shall we ever know more of his secret thoughts and sources? I suppose not, for his wife and daughter have managed his posthumous fame as relentlessly as they did his living privacy. He had written almost all his best work by the time he was 40, at which

[1] By Charles Carrington.

age Scott hadn't begun his first novel—I know I'm drooling, but it's getting late and you won't mind.

My frightful Brains Trust is somewhere around 4 p.m. on Monday 21st. I don't know which programme, but definitely *not* TV. Did you hear the story of the overworked law-student who confused arson with incest and ended by setting fire to his sister? I expect it's as old as the *Arabian Nights*, but I heard it only last week. Funny stories are like newspapers: yesterday's is intolerable, one of fifty years ago may be delightfully fresh and unexpected. This coming week may be, should be, fateful for my publishing future, and I can only pray that next Sunday I may have good news to send you. Weeks of suspense and worry have begun to take their toll in headaches, insomnia and intermittent deafness. As I said to my doctor, 'All right, it's caused by worry, what the Americans call psychosomatic. So what?' He confessed himself baffled, since organically all is fine. It will all pass directly my fate is firmly fixed in some direction. Forgive this tiresome clinical intrusion. Better luck next week.

15/16 November 1955 *Grundisburgh*

There are many things I like about your letters and one of the chief ones is they are exactly like good talk—which is really to say all that need be said. You say in one place that you are 'drooling'. And how immensely refreshing and gratifying it is to be drooled to! Surely there is no greater compliment. But your use of the word stirs me to send you a positively majestic reply—not so much mine as Longinus's. He wrote, 'They say that Homer sometimes nods. Perhaps he does—but then he dreams as Zeus might dream.' But all the nice things I could and would like to say to you will not, I fear, counterbalance the felon blow I am dealing you, in sending you the enclosed[1]—when you must be sick at the sight of anything printed. But let me tell you straight; it is simply for you to read in bed or bath or (if I may be coarsely Pepysian) at stool, and then put it away or make it into spills. But you have got to have it—I see no way out of that, and—don't you of all men know it!—an author's vanity tells me that it won't

[1] His talk on Gladstone. See Appendix I p. 409.

bore you. I know it has one unique feature, i.e. that in a 45-minute lucubration there is hardly a word about politics or religion—like the maniac who proposed to write at length about Shakespeare without mentioning his plays or poems. Anyway, like many of those other hideous Xmas presents you are going to get, the only value in it is the kind thought behind it. That at least fears no challenge from even the most doting and devoted of your aunts, if you have such. Many of mine were fairly hard-bitten—no, that gives the wrong impression, but they certainly never doted on me.

How maddening these people are who have had experiences of great interest and remember nothing about them. Lady C. must have been just ticking off celebrities like an American tourist in Italy. Old Ram[2] had an uncle (I think) who wanted to write about Hazlitt and heard of some old chap who had known him well. He went to see this veteran, all agog with excitement. And the old man merely went off into deep, tantalising chuckles at his memories and produced nothing but 'Aha, yes, Wully Hazlitt! He was a queeer, queeer fellow!' and followed up this repeated remark with longer and deeper chuckles. Did you ever read Alfred Austin's conversations with Tennyson. He always addressed him as 'Immortal Bard' but got very little but grunts out of him.

Handwriting. I have seen E. Blunden's, and very good it is, but I only met him once, so have no specimen of his in my collection. And I don't know the E.C. Bentley poem you mention. *Do* copy it for me, if you have a moment of time. I never saw anything of his that wasn't first-rate. That is a fine line to start with. All I know of Leslie Hotson is that fascinating book on *Twelfth Night*. I am enjoying Humphry House greatly. How good he is on Victorianism—that is as far as I have got. (Later) I read him on Thackeray in bed this morning—first-class. And, being almost the only admirer of Carlyle left, I merely draw your attention to his description of W.M.T.[3] at the end and ask you if it is not masterly. But they tell me C's style turns their queasy stomachs, and they hate his 'philosophy'—as if that was his main quality. They don't follow Meredith's advice 'Swim on his pages, take the poetry and the fine grisly humour, the manly independence'.

[2] A. B. Ramsay, Lower Master of Eton and later Master of Magdalene.

[3] Thackeray.

I had a heated argument with some fellow-examiners at Oxford last year. One I silenced, i.e. reduced to speechless fury, by telling him his attitude towards literature was that of a lavatory attendant. Another I at least checked by asking him if he refused to read *The Jungle Book* because he disliked Kipling's imperialism. But he returned to the charge, and it cannot be said of either of us that our manners shewed much of that repose that stamps the caste of Vere de Vere.

I agree with you horse, foot and all, about Kipling. Here again what matters is the genius which I should have thought no reader could miss. But they are put off by his defects—as some are and millions are not by those of Dickens. I used to know *Captains Courageous* almost by heart, and still retain a good deal. My brother, who knew him well, told me it was R.K's favourite. Do you know his 'Proofs of Holy Writ'? It is not easily come by and is not in the 'definitive' collected works.[4] If you don't, I shall certainly send it for your perusal, and if you don't find it entrancingly brilliant, I shall go heavily as one that mourneth.

Look here, my dear Rupert, I do *not* like to hear of these headaches and insomnia (surely the worst of human ills, apart from the mere outrages like cancer, brain-tumour etc.). I look forward to hearing good news in your next and wish I could be seeing you on Friday at the Astleys'. Charles Morgan, I believe, is to be there, but there are those who say that his conversation is querulous, egotistical, unfruitful. And *you* know what I mean by the last, because every sentence you write starts a train of thought or a flight of fancy, so that when I answer, you must be wondering when the *Hell* I am going to stop. And I cannot pretend that letters written on my knee are all that nice to look at—or in my club, where the silence and my nerves are continually being shattered by a harsh croak from a box over the door 'Calling Mr Haemorrhage. Will Mr H. please come to the hall to receive a guest.'

That is a lovely story of yours about the law-student—I can't send the ball back. But, suspecting your soundness about the higher clergy, I think you might like to hear that G. Meredith used to call

[4] Published only in the *Strand Magazine*, April 1934, and in vol XXX of the big Sussex Edition of Kipling's works. It is a dialogue between Shakespeare and Ben Jonson concerning a passage in *Isaiah*.

the Archbishop 'The Mitred Cant'. And in the belief that you are much kinder about the lower clergy I am confident of your appreciating the information that Uncle Albert made a list of conversational openings; this list was found and among the earliest items was this: 'Are you aware that the heaviest eater in the zoo is the gnu?'

There was a peer in the train this morning, in my carriage. What a beautiful blend of splendour and absurdity it is that suitcase and hatbox and dispatch-box should all be merely marked with A. I don't know who he was, but I feel sure he expected us to know—as he will on the Judgment Day, and what a frosty look Peter will get if he *asks*!

(Well, dash it all, who is drooling now?) Do lines stick tiresomely in your head, like tunes, sometimes for days? Not that it always matters. Last Sunday I came across this by Tennyson when a boy, in a poem on Egypt: 'Awful Memnonian countenances calm'.[5] Miltonic echo, no doubt, but better to echo Milton than the *D. Mirror*.

20 November 1955 *Bromsden Farm*

What can I say to thee, O liberal and princely giver? I know exactly what I can say. Your Gladstone lecture is superb: packed and witty and profound, beautifully written and a feast of fun. G.M. Young once said to me: 'The trouble with you, my dear Rupert, is that you will persist in seeing me in "book form".' It's no doubt the effect of being so long a publisher, and the habit continues. This lecture and your Johnson Club paper would fit very happily together between covers, with three or four fellows to keep them company. You must surely have written others? If not, you really must get down to it at once. I don't say we'd sell a million or make our fortunes, but it would be the greatest fun and would enhance my (spurious) reputation for knowing the best when I see it. Please ponder the possibility carefully.

One by one the reasons for your excellence as a schoolmaster are being revealed to me: the latest is a particularly acceptable form of flattery, which must have made your pupils mad keen to please you. When I was still at Eton I wrote Maurice Baring a fan-letter about his

[5] From "a Fragment", first published in *The Gem: A Literary Annual*, 1831.

novel *C*. He sent me an enchanting answer, in which he said: 'You know that George Meredith said that though stolen fruit was sweet, undeserved rewards are the real stuff. I so agree.' So do I, and that's partly why I look forward to Friday evening, and your letter waiting among all the bills and circulars. Your Pepys allusion reminds me that when Winston was privately asked his true opinion of the Graham Sutherland portrait, he is reported to have said: 'It makes me look as though I was straining at the stool'. What fun it would be to make a book of his sayings—but who could disentangle the authentic from the apocryphal? Aunts—there's an absorbing subject. Ask anyone about his aunts, and you will be entertained for hours. Mine all doted on me, but they are all dead—*post hoc*, I mean.

The E.C. Bentley poem goes to you to-day on a separate sheet. Tomorrow I shall send you the other two Hotson books I published. The one about the Sonnets is a beauty. You mustn't protest: I have never been rich in anything but unsold books, and of them I have warehouses full. Back to Bentley for a moment. The *envoi* is a failure, but isn't the rest brilliant in every way? He's still alive, but I fancy writes no more: I see his son Nick the cartoonist quite often. Your words about Carlyle fall on delighted ears: he was a great favourite of my mother's, so I was brought up on him. Early next year I am publishing an 850-page selection of his work in my Reynard Library series: an early copy shall be sent for your, I trust, approval. The selection was made by Julian Symons and vetted by G.M. Young. I finished the Kipling biography yesterday, and am sorry not to have it still to read. The author has done a fine job of marshalling and presenting his multitude of facts, and his narrative carries one steadily on. But—nowhere for a moment does R.K. become likeable, let alone lovable. No letter or phrase or action strikes a sympathetic spark. I imagine the biographer must have felt the same, and I have written him a letter of gratitude and congratulation, asking that and other questions. I don't know 'Proofs of Holy Writ' and should love to read it.

I'm delighted to be able to tell you that, although my affairs are no less entangled, I have now for three whole days been without headache, deafness or insomnia: all vanished as suddenly as they arrived, praise be! When they started I was certain they were caused by a brain-tumour, but my doctor reassured me. It's all most mysterious, particularly since on Friday afternoon I heard that another friend of mine had committed suicide by taking fifty sleeping pills. How could one do it? Two at a time, twenty-five times? I can't bear to think of what he must have gone through. And now there is another widow to comfort—my fourth this year! If my publishing affairs are not settled soon I shall be led away screaming: next week should be decisive, but the whole of the second half of tomorrow will be taken up by this infernal Brains Trust.

I do wish I'd been dining with you and Charles Morgan. I've known him for twenty-five years and am expert at ragging him from pomposity to charming humanity: there are lots of very nice things about him. Yes, I am much more tolerant of the minor clergy, quite ready to be 'preached to death by wild curates' any day, which reminds me, the Kipling biography proves, what we've really always known, that far the most important influence on R.K's writing was the Bible. If more people read or listened to it to-day the level of literary style would certainly be higher.

Other people's dreams are always tedious, but I shall tell you a recent one of mine nevertheless. When we were both twenty-two I married an enchanting actress called Peggy Ashcroft: it was a sad failure: we were much too young to know what we wanted, and actresses should never marry, especially young ones. Anyhow, after much agony we parted and were duly divorced. Nowadays Peggy and I lunch together perhaps once or twice a year in a Soho restaurant and have a lovely nostalgic-romantic talk of shared memories of long ago. She is a lovely person and the best actress living—did you see her Hedda Gabler? Some months ago, when I hadn't seen or consciously thought of her for months, I dreamed that we were lunching together as usual, and she asked me: 'Do you think you could ever be in love with me again as you were when we were young?' I answered: 'The lightning never strikes twice in the same place, but the sun shines on for ever'. Then I woke up. Next day I remembered the dream and wrote to tell P. of it. She was much pleased. I tremble to think what Freud would make of it, but it strikes me as beautiful. You needn't fear a spate of dream-recital, for I scarcely ever remember one. Do you? Now I must go to bed. Goodnight, dear George. You don't know what a godsend you are.

A BALLADE OF SOULS
by E.C. Bentley[1]

The soul of Dante was a white-hot spear;
  The soul of Bonaparte, a thunder-stroke;
The soul of Bismarck was a cask of beer;
  The soul of Blake was roaring flame and smoke;
  The soul of Villon was a tatter'd cloak;
The soul of Washington, a perfect square;
  The soul of Robespierre, a piece of coke;
But Norway has a soul of sheer despair.

The soul of Dizzy was a chandelier;
  The soul of Shakespeare was a greening oak;
And Swift's, a lordly ship that wouldn't steer;
  Carlyle's, a raven of stentorian croak;
  And Chatterton's, a furnace none would stoke;
The soul of Nietzsche was a rotten pear;
  And bluff King Hal's, a reek to make one choke;
But Norway has a soul of sheer despair.

The soul of Goethe was an opal sphere;
  The soul of Chaucer was a chime that woke
The heart of England; Heine's was a tear;
  And Chatham's was a mighty voice—that broke;
  The soul of Calvin, that lugubrious bloke,
Was principally made of heated air;
  The soul of Herbert Spencer was a joke;
But Norway has a soul of sheer despair.

Envoi

  Prince! Royal Haakon! (Did you know I spoke
Norwegian?) *Er De syg af det? Jeg er.*
  You may be happy—though I doubt it, Haak;
But Norway has a soul of sheer despair.

[1] Printed here by kind permission of Mr Nicolas Bentley.

Gosh, this is fun! Each letter from you carries me through Tuesday on wings. And yet—a paradox 'which comforts while it mocks' so to speak—after the second or third reading I am positively *costive* with appreciations, comments, questions; I want to shout, to sing, to laugh, to cry. I have to delay putting pen to paper till Wednesday when all these impulses and emotions have blended into a sort of rainbow over-arching the new day. I won't embarrass you further (like A.M. Goodhart,[1] who once talked rubbish for thirty stricken minutes at Lord's and ended: 'But I mustn't become a pavilion bore'!) by telling you of my feelings, merely reminding you of how old Johnson, hardly able to speak, heard what his friends had done about his pension: 'Sir, this is taking prodigious pains about a man'. How can I help feeling the same, when I think how full your day already is, and of your numberless interests and friends? But I *do* embarrass you! Just let me say once and for all that your letter is the best thing that happens in my week. *Basta!*

I am *delighted* that you enjoyed the Gladstone, and by what you say. But you know, I have a sort of kink (let me not give it spurious dignity by calling it a complex or even a phobia) about getting my lucubrations published. There are half-a-dozen or more, all written, like this one, for some special occasion. Well, I am not in the least modest, and I think they were well enough in their time and place, but I always doubt whether, in Percy Lubbock's phrase about A.C. Benson's diary, they would 'bear the weight of print'. Anyway, my dear Rupert, I promise you that, if a publisher ever *is* approached on their behalf, his name will be R.H-D.

Many thanks for the Bentley poem, which I enjoy hugely. It has many superb lines which would give a kick to any article; the one line you quoted last week, as you know to your cost, made me at once want the whole poem. I like the deliberate 'flop' into bathos, e.g. from Chaucer and Heine and Chatham to Calvin and H. Spencer. You must educate me gently and gradually in modern poetry. I found, not long ago, what *I* thought an excellent little poem by Day Lewis beginning 'Now the full-throated daffodils, Our trumpeters in

[1] Eton master.

gold . . .' and was told by a man, who prays, I think nightly, for the restoration of Ezra Pound's wits, that it was 'twee'. I see that John Wain is producing—editing in fact—a small collection of difficult poems in which the reader is shewn how to understand and appreciate.[2] Do you know of this?

Here is the Kipling thing. I shall be greatly interested to have your opinion. I think it is entrancing, but though an ex-schoolmaster and a septuagenarian I still believe it possible, without any appeal to the bowels of Christ, to believe that I am wrong. I imagine R.K. was not very likeable; the easy sneers aimed at him all have sharp points and edges, e.g. George Moore's—that *perfectly* horrible and repulsive man, and *perfectly* enchanting writer, at least in the three volumes *Hail and Farewell*. Laski met R.K. and described him as being 'like a rather well-to-do grocer . . . his talk has not a sparkle of wit or perception about it'—but I should have liked to hear what R.K. through, say, Beetle, or young Ollyet in that gorgeous tale 'The Village that Voted' etc would have said of Laski. But it *is* odd how dull in talk many witty writers are. A trite remark, I agree. I often make them. However the last laugh went to 'poor Poll' who wrote 'Of praise a mere glutton he swallowed what came, And the puff of a dunce he mistook it for fame,'[3] and carried off the prize for wit and good humour to boot (what *does* 'to boot' mean?)

I look forward eagerly to the Carlyle volume. George Trevelyan compiled a vol. of extracts a few years ago, but I got the impression that he hadn't taken very much trouble over it; it was v. disappointing. I hope J. Symons *has* included the passage in *Frederick* where T.C. likens the previous writers about him, who apparently copied unskilfully from each other, to two dogs who cautiously approach each other, 'investigate the parts of shame, and then depart with a satisfied air as from a problem solved'. I have not seen the passage for forty years, and probably misquote.

It was sad missing you at the Astleys' dinner. We had a really delightful evening. As I hope you know, I never pay any heed when told someone is a bore or a prig etc. I wait—conceitedly!—to judge for myself. And as often as not I find the other judgment was a shallow

[2] *Interpretations*.

[3] Goldsmith on Garrick in 'Retaliation'.

one. I much liked Charles Morgan and should have liked to sit and talk with him for hours. In fact I told him so (what a garrulous old gusher you must think me!). It had seemed to me that the author of those *Reflections in a Mirror* and much else *must* be a very worthwhile man to know and I was right. I do wish you had been there and he would have been at his ease sooner. Tommy Lascelles[4] was there and very friendly and intelligent he was. I sat next to Joan Astley—one of those charmers with whom, at any age, one falls in love without any difficulty or demur. Delightful! That tingling in your ears at about 9.15 last Friday was *not*, as you thought it, incipient shingles, mastoid, or lupus, but the direct result of what she and I were saying. I *hate* your having headaches, insomnia etc. and, as I said, am all agog to hear of your affairs reaching calm waters. I am very glad you told me that dream. Your saying 'The lightning' etc. is *entirely lovely*, and I have no doubt Peggy A. thought so too—and found the next sentence or two rather hard to descry. A wonderful actress, I agree, though I haven't seen her for some time. I maintain I am not deaf and that I don't hear the modern actors and actresses because they haven't learnt how to speak. Do you know that old Beerbohm Tree, whom it was the fashion to sneer at, could say in *Macbeth* 'Which of you has done this' in a frightening little dry *whisper*, and was heard by stalls, d and u circle, gallery, pit, scene-shifters, box office, and half the cabbies in the Haymarket. Old George Chitty[5] once consulted C. Miller[6] about his 'raves'. C.M. told him to tell him a fortnight later about his dreams. G.C. told him he could remember but one, and he didn't think it would help. C.M. heard it and agreed. It was very short—merely that he dreamt his cook had given birth to a zebra.

27 November 1955 *Bromsden Farm*

This delightful correspondence is rapidly turning into a love-affair, and I must confess I share some of the lover's fears lest one day the scales or rose-coloured spectacles may fall from the beloved's eyes,

[4] Sir Alan Lascelles, formerly Private Secretary to King George VI and Queen Elizabeth II.

[5] Eton master. [6] Eton doctor.

revealing the seeming swan as a barnyard goose. One black Tuesday will surely see the end of the affair, but in the meanwhile on with the dance! I shall now read your letter again slowly and comment as the topics come.

First, your reluctance to see yourself in book form. In almost every other direction I bow to your wisdom and experience, but I have spent a quarter of a century deciding what will 'bear the weight of print', and though I've made plenty of mistakes I do know a 'certainty' when I see one. Will you not send me the other 'half-a-dozen or more' pieces? Clearly if the initiative is left to you, the book will be posthumous and you will get no fun out of it. I promise to send you the most candid judgment. Do say yes! I must get John Wain's book and pass it on to you. I know J.W., a *farouche*, ruthless and highly intelligent young man, who has just resigned his lectureship at Reading University to seek his fortune with his pen. In principle I don't think any poem should need notes or laboured exegesis—or at any rate not until its first musical, magical impact has been made. Surely it is the *magic* that distinguishes poetry from verse or prose, and by its very nature magic cannot be analysed or explained. Still, it's interesting perhaps to see what added beauties or meanings the learned can extract for us.

'Proofs of Holy Writ' is terrifically good—brilliant, I should say—and I am most grateful to you for introducing me to it. It (do you remember Cobbett's 'When I see a number of "its" on the page, I tremble for the writer'?) It seems to me to throw rays of light on to the creative use of words by a genius—as exemplified in R.K. himself. He always referred to his own inspiration as his 'Daemon', and he makes Shakespeare do so here. The story reminds me of that wonderful one called 'Wireless', in which the consumptive chemist's assistant gets the Keats poem through the ether. Both are comments on how great poets work.

So glad you liked Charles Morgan: his best books seem to me his shortest (and least pretentious). Some of his essays are fine. I like Tommy Lascelles very much: he is in process of being elected President of the famous Lit. Soc.[1] Joan Astley is an angel: I wish I saw

[1] The Literary Society, a dining club founded in 1807 by Wordsworth and others.

her more often: always so gay and natural and friendly: no effort at all. I'm delighted to be able to report no recurrence of headaches, despite an appalling week: three long business interviews with a sharp accountant (next week *must* see some concrete result) and a harrowing interview with the widow of last week's suicide, crammed into a merry-go-round of other nonsense.

Sorry you wasted your time on that broadcast: I didn't hear it, but I gather that my remarks had almost all been cut (it was only 20 minutes out of 75). The thing itself began with a luncheon in a private room in the Howard Hotel—*assez lugubre* in all conscience. I sat between the BBC man who was arranging the broadcast and Lady Violet Bonham-Carter, whom I had never met before. A simple man of my acquaintance once met G.K. Chesterton and described him as 'quite all there and very spry'. I can't find better words to describe Lady V. We chattered amiably about her father, the art of oratory, the future (God save the mark) of the Liberal Party, etc. With the brandy we were handed copies of the Questions, and there followed a long friendly wrangle as to who should answer which first. I was allotted two—'Are books too expensive?' (which I belaboured so stoutly that no one else dared utter) and 'Which are the two greatest poets of this century?' I said Yeats and Hardy, and eventually they almost all agreed with me. Do you? Hardy can only be included because (a) he *published* all his books of poems save one in the twentieth century, and (b) those uniquely wonderful love-poems, written after his first wife's death and harking back to their courtship, were composed in 1912–13. You must know them: if not I shall come and read them to you relentlessly. Of Yeats's greatness I have no doubt either. I once saw him in the Athenaeum, looking every inch the poet with flowing blue-white hair. Both he and Hardy grew in stature as poets all through their lives: so many sing their little lyrical song in youth, and then dry up or repeat themselves thinly.

Back to the Festival Hall, where we sat at little tables on the stage under bright lights. Away in the darkness were 3000 stodgy schoolchildren, who took some rousing. It was like appearing on the stage in a huge theatre without any rehearsal. We each had a microphone in front of us, but it's difficult without practice to talk as cosily as the BBC like when you can see tiers and tiers of live faces stretching away dumbly into the darkness. Ivor Brown wasn't a very good chairman. Thank God it's over anyhow! My wife and son, who were perched high in a box, claim to have enjoyed it. Afterwards I took them both to a monstrous cocktail party given by W.H. Smith at the Savoy, on to a hurried dinner at the Garrick, and then to a good gripping play called *The Queen and the Rebels*. Phew!

On Tuesday evening I journeyed to Putney (people never think their own home is far away) to dine with the Arthur Ransomes. He is a most delightful and interesting man, of whom I will tell you more another day. My present concern is that he should finish his autobiography, for he has made me promise (as his literary executor) to finish it for him if he dies too soon (he's only 71) and he has left all the most difficult bits to the last. (I am already literary executor for Hugh Walpole, Duff Cooper and Humphry House—also *in posse* for William Plomer and others. It's a thankless and exacting task.) To continue my hideous week—On Wednesday evening I took the chair at the Book Exhibition for an author of mine called 'Elephant Bill' and dined him there after. On Thursday a dinner-party at the Priestleys' in Albany—nine people including Edith Evans and Rosamond Lehmann. All very agreeable, but when does one read or write, rest or think? J.B.P. was at his most amusing, all chips temporarily removed from his shoulder. He told of an American Rotarian who couldn't see half a grapefruit without getting to his feet and starting 'Ladies and Gentlemen . . .' And so back here to the quiet and your splendid letter. Last night my son took Evelyn Shuckburgh's sixteen-year old daughter to a neighbour's dance and brought her here for dinner first. She was very pretty and extremely self-composed, telling us that when she 'comes out' next summer she's determined not to be an ordinary 'deb'. Even her coming-out dance is to be highly select—'You know, Humphrey Lyttelton's Band and as many intellectuals as possible'. So now you know!

30 November 1955 *Grundisburgh*

Yes, of course, you, in strong contrast to the majority of men, do know what you are talking about, and in recognition of that fact, I will dig out my old stuff and send it to you—if I can find 'em. I expect, after perusal, you will think that 'posthumous' is the key-word!

One sentence in your letter brought me in M. Twain's words a 'spell of the dry grins', viz your apprehension that when we meet we shall have nothing to say. My dear, these weekly outbreaks of epistolary elephantiasis on my part—well they are like imposthumes or furuncles (and I shall be disappointed if you don't have to look out *that* one!). They are proofs of over-fulness. The only not *wholly* pleasurable thing about your letters is that after one we can't settle down and tire the sun with talking. Once at Hagley were assembled for the Worcs-Australian match Plum Warner, Charles Fry, Gerry Weigall and Harry Altham. They arrived at tea-time and from then, up to, during and after dinner they and my nephew talked cricket-shop. At 3 a.m. one feebly mentioned the word 'bed'. My nephew with a face of horror ejaculated 'Bed!!! But we've only touched the fringe of the subject!' Them's my sentiments often during this immensely enjoyable correspondence.

I am glad you liked 'Proofs of H.W.', but I knew you would. The speed of thought behind what his Shakespeare says, and the weight and Broadbentian[1] curmudgeonliness behind B. Jonson's are surely masterly. I always wanted to meet R.K. at Hagley and ask him how the *devil* he knew *exactly* how a beak should take a Horace—or any other—construe. 'Regulus'—the rehabilitation of Mr King—is staggeringly good. We in the nineties were taught the Classics by one Craven Scholar after another, but only Arthur Benson got anywhere near teaching like Mr King. *You*, by the way, would have loved A.C.B.[2] and I am *not* referring to the author of *The Upton Letters* etc. That so to speak was the son of Oileus and not the son of Telamon[3]. The other man who filled every bill in the way of companionship was Charles Fisher, who went down with the *Invincible*. I remember him saying much what you do about the *magic* of great poetry.

'You can see how the good things are done, but about the great you can only wonder how the devil he did it.' That was said apropos of

[1] Henry Broadbent, Eton master.

[2] Arthur Christopher Benson, Eton housemaster, prolific author, Master of Magdalene.

[3] Each had a son called Ajax.

'La Belle Dame S.M.' It was impressive to hear a strong agnostic, as he was, say that there was no greater line in all the poetry he knew than 'Through the dear might of Him that walked the waves'. You interest me about John Wain—clearly a good man. But I wonder why he should say anything so silly as that, apart from his knowledge of Latin, Housman was a very stupid man? And Auden said much the same of Tennyson, the only thing *he* knew about being hypochondria! Are you in a temper when reading as often as I am? Leavis on Lawrence, for instance. I haven't read much yet, and so far the atmosphere is that of a clever disgruntled undergraduate with his conceit, dogmatism, bad temper and sneers. Charles Morgan told us he is very popular in the U.S.A. God help us all! Why should we all be bullied into admiring D.H.L.? But perhaps we should be kind even about Leavis. T.R. Henn told me last week that L. had had a very unhappy youth, during which he saw his father killed in a street accident. Like poor Baron Holstein who never saw a well without longing—and usually managing—to poison it. *His* father was killed by a bull, which is perhaps worse than a bus.

Your picture of what must have been rather an appalling affair—that lunch and broadcast—is very vivid. My temperature fell while reading it. I could hear Lady V.B-C's bright, sweetly reasonable, slightly irritating utterance and see those stodgy children. Ivor B. was clearly unhappy. They cut out, of course, 'Are books too expensive?' For the first half of the twenty minutes you said nothing but that you knew nothing (and between the lines didn't care a twopenny damn) about text-books. The B.B.C. is to me like democracy—a good thing that those who run it do all they can to spoil. I don't refer to the grunts, twitterings, banshee wailings, and occasional bellows which diversify East Anglian reception. H.Q. clearly thinks anything is good enough for Silly Suffolk. I am sure you are right as to the two great poets of this century, though I must frankly admit that I am not clever enough to follow W.B.Y. except in bits. As William Cory said in a flat-footed couplet: 'The feelings lose poetic flow. Soon after twenty-seven or so'. I am too old for Yeats, just as I am too old to hear the cry of a bat. Hardy, yes, I am with you all the way. And he put part of my case in 'In Tenebris'. Surely the pessimism and gloom of the Audens and Co in the Thirties was a very poor, thin, *rootless* crop compared with Hardy's undramatic, unegotistical picture of the human situation as he saw it. And what sheer pleasure one gets out of a couplet like:

> Numb as a vane that cankers on its point,
> True to the wind that kissed ere canker came.[4]

Would that have got through the crust of those 3000 dumplings? But *what* a week you had—no time to stand and stare! I imagine you would much prefer the Evanses, the Lehmanns, the Priestleys etc rather more *spaced*? It must have been too like having several rich dinners at once. The present fashion is to run J.B. Priestley down, but I enjoy reading him. No doubt he may grouse and/or preach too much at times but he is nearly always good fun and good value. You too, though less goofy about them than I, enjoy fine phrases. Refresh yourself with J.B.P. on 'An old Bual' in *Adam in Moonshine*. That is writing, if you like. And M. Murry, who disapproves of the style of *Job*, would no doubt think it horrible. I like J.B.P.'s story of the American Rotarian. That passion for after-dinner oratory is very odd. The Ipswich cricket club centenary dinner shewed how infectious it is. There were eleven speeches plus a soprano of tremendous man-power and a humorous raconteur. We sat down at 7.0 and rose at 12.15. I felt very Johnsonian about 'the paucity of human pleasures'. And there was no Lehmann, Evans, or Priestley in the company. One man told a cricket story that I first heard in 1899 and another a risqué one that was the signature tune of the penultimate class at Evelyn's Prep School in 1893.

This very evening my son is being interviewed on TV. A strange affair. He is, I gather, one of a series of 'public' men and the two immediately above him are the Archbp. of C. (your *bête noire*) and Lord Montgomery. All leading comedians you see—though it gives me a paternal thrill that Miss Shuckburgh should class H. among the 'intellectuals'. I must stop. The room is arctic. I am just home from a meeting of the Woodbridge Governors; the main discussion was on whether a certain outside staircase was dangerous through its 'treads' being too narrow. 'What did you do, Sir?' 'Sir, I abstracted my mind and thought of Tom Thumb.'

[4] Hardy, 'She to Him'.

I certainly did have to look up 'furuncle' and am delighted to add such a splendid specimen to my vocabulary. Yes, you're right about our next meeting: we ought to compile a serial agenda for it, or re-read the correspondence just beforehand. One leading item must be A.C.B., and indeed the whole Benson family. I got very interested in them when I was preparing my Walpole book and read a mass of their works. It seemed to me that in biography, autobiography and the like both A.C. and E.F. were very good indeed, but in fiction, and A.C's essays, mediocre and not readable to-day. A.C's life of his father is a *most* interesting book: so much brilliance manifested in the children, and not a single grandchild to carry it on. The pattern is very like that of the Walpole family. By the way, have you *got* a copy of my book? If not, perhaps I might send you one for Christmas—just for reference.

All yesterday was taken up by manuscripts—a goodish biography of the seventeenth-century Margaret Duchess of Newcastle, and a short novel written in English by a Hungarian woman about a consumptives' home in Hungary. Despite all these obvious disadvantages, it has quality and I think I'll publish it, though it won't sell. I wonder you bother with Leavis on Lawrence. Leavis has his points; his writing is at least *alive*, which so much literary criticism isn't, but I much prefer the old-style critics who tried to get inside their authors, find out what they were driving at and interpret accordingly. Nowadays they attempt to force the authors into some preconceived theory of their own. With Leavis it usually takes the form of claiming that one, or possibly two, of the author's books are imperishable masterpieces, of immense 'importance', 'significance' and all the rest of it, while the rest of his *oeuvre* is beneath contempt. Leavis has already meted out this punishment to Conrad, Henry James, George Eliot and others: now it's the turn of D.H.L. At some moment when Osbert Sitwell was particularly annoyed with the Leavises he got through their guard by repeatedly referring to them in print as 'those talented sisters-in-law'.

Why is wireless reception so appalling in East Anglia? I had an aunt and uncle who lived at Aldeburgh, and when I stayed there the old boy and I had to kneel down with our ear to the machine to catch the cricket news. I have their same set in my London flat now, and it works perfectly. Going back to Yeats, I refuse to agree that you're too old to appreciate him, just as I've always understood that the cry of the bat is simply too high for the human ear to catch, regardless of age. So glad you're sound on Hardy. You must know both 'The Convergence of the Twain' and 'An Ancient to Ancients?' I long to know more of your daily life and surroundings. Please describe them for me—house and garden and what time you get up and go to bed. Have you a lot of books in the house? Do you belong to a circulating library or the London ditto? Have you any servants? Is it difficult to keep warm? I imagine you the presiding genius of every conceivable local body. Do you drive yourself from bench to board in a car?—That'll do for this week.

Last Tuesday with pride and sorrow I watched my son Duff march off towards Germany with his battalion (1st Coldstream). He looked enormous (the same size as me) and terribly young, and since tears always spring to my eyes at the first strains of a drum-and-fife band (as at a glimpse of the King or Queen), I was more moved even than I had expected to be. The band continued to play Auld Lang Syne on the platform until all the women were weeping. I left before the train went. On Thursday I attended a gigantic luncheon given by the Paternosters Club, after which Lord Mountbatten made a most able and interesting speech in favour of the Navy. Among other bodies he praised the Royal Marine Commandos and told us the Egyptians had been so impressed that they determined to create some of their own. A hundred picked men from the Egyptian army were put through a stiff Commando course, and did so well that the Minister of National Guidance (who, as Lord M. neatly pointed out, is now no longer guiding anyone) drove to the barracks to congratulate them. The gallant hundred were drawn up in one long line and the Minister went along it, shaking hands with each man and saying: 'Well done', 'Magnificent', 'Bravo', 'Egypt is proud of you' and so on. When he got to the end of the line he found his gold watch was missing.

7 December 1955 *Grundisburgh*

Before all else, '*Yes*' to your noble offer of your Hugh Walpole book. (How *greedy* this looks—it puts me with the man who began on the salted almonds at some big dinner before grace; the dean beside the chairman was equal to the occasion: 'For all that we are about to receive and for all that Mr Jones has already received . . .') And how beautifully *pat* it comes, for the copy I had disappeared over a year ago—a daughter, a guest, a neighbour—we simply don't know who was the culprit. It wasn't even lent—there have always been some of them which don't come back. As I expect I told you at the time, I liked Hugh Walpole very much though I met him only twice. He gave an *admirable* talk to the Eton Literary Society of which I was President. I wrote after it and said how much it had been enjoyed, and got a charming letter back in which he said he was so much pleased by what I had told him that he went out at once and bought a picture. I remember a dreadfully sad account of A.C.B. in the book—all gone to seed with nerves and self-absorption and pettiness. A tragic family really, ending, actually as well as figuratively, in nothing. But, as you say, how good A.C. and E.F. were when describing people. E.F's novels are as dead as A.C's musings, but *As We Were* and *Final Edition* will always be readable. I remember enjoying some of Hugh's[1] novels, *An Average Man*, *The Conventionalists* etc. There were some deadly good pictures of English life, e.g. country house life, the squire, the parson etc.

Do you know 'The Ancient House', Ipswich's showpiece—built so long ago that the medallions on the front representing the continents lack that of Australia as it hadn't been discovered when the A.H. was built? It is the best bookshop round here. I should like to screw them up still further, but the 'still small voice of coins' cramps me. It is odd. All the last eighteen months I meet men who are positively sleek with dividends, glossy with bonuses, but my holdings? No—when I buy some stock, word goes round the Stock Exchange 'Lyttelton has bought. Sell out'. I was delighted to meet a bank director recently who said his experience was the same. He added, what I am sure is true, that people always tell of their gains, but rarely of their losses. Anyway do remember that we should always

[1] Robert Hugh Benson, the youngest brother.

love to see you, and that in the spring, in addition to the reburnishing of the dove, we can do you a very nice line in daffodils and nightingales. As St Paul says (not very precisely) 'If there be any merit, think on these things'.

Not that the diversions of Grundisburgh are very numerous—no huntin', shootin' or fishin', no Morris dancing, nor Knurr and Spell. We could call on Mrs Pizzey, we could talk to Mrs Paternoster—oh no, I forgot, she is stone deaf. Charlie Balls has, alas, left the village. No coarse laughter from you, please. It is a very common name in Suffolk, so much so that at, say, a political meeting a loud shout of 'Balls' is usually not a comment on what is being said on the platform, but merely one of the clan hailing another across the hall. But there is always work of some kind in the garden—not much with the spade with which Wilkinson (*not* Lyttelton) had tilled his land, but with axe and saw. I hate the spade but love the axe. The fare is well enough and those who have tasted my wife's omelettes are convinced that even on the innermost recesses of Abraham's bosom they would find nothing better. We have no resident staff. A good woman comes in the morning; the gardener we share with another, but, thanks be, he lives next door, so lights the stove every day. There is a rather spacious garden with a stream, a revolving summer-house which is warm whenever the sun shines, even in January, and where I spend many hours, writing and reading. I get up rather loosely and breakfast at about 9.15. I never go to bed before 12 or to sleep before 1, though not going so far as Dr J. who said that anyone who went to bed before 12 was a scoundrel. I think it is perfectly true to say that (a) no one is entertained, and (b) no one is made to do anything he doesn't want to. Visitors have got on with their accounts, their income-tax returns, their school reports, their blank verse epics, their autobiographies. Lord love you, what grand talk we should have. You should read aloud to me, and now and then there would be a little Beethoven. There would be no Bartok, Hindemith, or Alban Berg. Your bedroom would have nothing of Henry Moore and still less of Picasso. There would be an *Ego* or two by your bedside, some short stories by Aumonier, and a Thomas Hardy. Gosh yes, that *Titanic* poem![2] I remember the thing happening. I was dining with the

[2] 'The Convergence of the Twain.'

H.M. and Mrs Warre came in, quivering slightly with age and dottiness, and said 'I am sorry to hear there has been a bad boating accident'—an odd but very characteristic way of describing the sinking of the largest ship in the world and the death of 1400 people. How trivial Hardy continually makes the moderns look and sound. *Of course* 'An Ancient to Ancients' hits my feeling in every line, and in fact might have been written by me, if I had had the mind—as C. Lamb delightedly reported Wordsworth as saying about himself and the plays of Shakespeare. You remember of course Hardy's 'Reminiscences of a Dancing Man' in *Time's Laughing-Stocks* and its magnificently innocent first line.[3] Once in a *New Statesman* competition, something about lines or phrases which meant *now* something quite different from what they meant originally, I sent up the last three lines of his 'The Caged Goldfinch' in *Moments of Vision*.[4] It was mentioned but I won no prize.

Yes, that is a horrid feeling at the pit of the stomach, seeing 'The Men Who March Away' to the fifes and drums, and the tears are very close to the eyes. I weep at all sorts of odd things, and a good many old men (who have not dried up) do, e.g. Winston, M.R. James etc. Do you remember how pleased E.V. Lucas was to find another man who, like himself, was chary of seeing the greatest of all jugglers, Cinquevalli, because he always made him cry? I know the feeling. It is something to do with seeing anything *perfectly* done, nothing at all to do with sadness. After all in old days Englishmen wept like anything, e.g. in Parliament when the Petition of Right was presented who was the great man who proposed to make a long speech beginning 'I protest . . .' and got no further than 'I p . . .' and after three attempts sat down?

11 December 1955 *Bromsden Farm*

Gosh, I'd love to visit you at Grundisburgh! My dear Aldeburgh aunt died some years ago, so there is no excuse but the Ancient House.

[3] 'Who now remembers Almack's balls.'

[4] 'And some at times averred
The grave to be her false one's, who when wooing
Gave her the bird.'

Surely the best plan is for you to dig out those essays, and for me to visit you as prospective author in the spring? Say a couple of mid-week nights in April—what fun! I don't hunt, shoot, fish, Morris-dance, knurr or spell, so your suggested programme is just what I'd choose for myself. Meanwhile I'll look out a copy of my book, annotate it with the latest corrections and get it to you by Christmas. How flattering that your other copy should have been stolen! I'm all sympathy for your Stock Exchange calamities, but ignorantly, never having owned a stock, share, or particle of capital all my life: you can imagine how tiresome that has often proved.

I delight in your appreciation of Hardy's poems: taking down *Moments of Vision* yesterday to refresh my memory of 'Almack's balls', I found myself reading happily on. Someone told T.H. about 'gave her the bird' (a phrase unknown to his rustic innocence) and he removed that third stanza from all subsequent reprints of the poem. We haven't mentioned *The Dynasts*. Did you hear the Third Programme broadcast of it? I firmly believe that the old boy, with true poetic prophecy, wrote it for broadcasting, though the thing was unknown at the time. He certainly wrote it for something, yet on the stage it is quite unactable, in the study almost (as a whole) unreadable. Those stage-directions, so tedious to read through, were *thrilling* when dramatically broadcast by several voices. Shutting one's eyes and having the work done for one, it was possible, at exactly the right speed and without the interference of print, to shift one's imagination from the whole of Europe to the field of Austerlitz. They cut it too, to great advantage. If ever they repeat it, you must listen to every moment. Particularly moving was the scene where Napoleon rides back, hopeless and alone, after Waterloo and is taunted by the spirits: some of it might be by Shakespeare:

> Great men are meteors that consume themselves
> To light the earth. This is my burnt-out hour.

I've no doubt the whole work is Hardy's masterpiece. Some fancy it as a film, but I'm sure such treatment would vulgarise most of the poetry out of it.

Tears in eyes—Duff Cooper cried readily, and when the 4th Coldstream paraded before Winston on the eve of being put into tanks, he sobbed at their very perfection, just like E.V. at Cinquevalli. Did you know E.V.? A greedy, and I daresay in some ways unadmirable, man, but he was always charming and generous to the young, *quorum pars minima fui* (is that right? I long to remember more Latin, and indeed Greek, and have insisted that my sons keep them up through school and university). E.V's men's dinner-parties at the Orleans Club with a superb conjuror to follow the dinner, were what the Wine & Food Society would call 'memorable meals'. Have you got the volume of E.V.'s cricket writings which I selected and published as *Cricket All His Life*? If not a copy will fly to you. You've just *got* to get over your scruples at my sending you my firm's books. They cost me nothing and would otherwise languish in a basement. One can't help judging others a good deal by oneself, and (as I've told you before) a present of a book is to me always a joy. I suspect you're the same, and since I am rich in unsold books—let's have no more objections. You're just the chap that many of these books were designed for.

Heinemann are to buy all the shares of my company, at a very generous price. My original shareholders, poor lambs, will lose half their money (which they've long expected to do, for the shares were written down by half some three years ago), the later shareholders nothing. Heinemann will take over most of my travelling, overseas representation etc., but the choice and production of my books will remain completely mine. To the public there will be no observable change. Moreover I shall be able, for the first time, to draw a salary on which I can live. The power behind all this is a remarkable chap called Lionel Fraser, a banker who is chairman of the company which owns 40% of the shares of Heinemann (which is a public company). For some unaccountable reason Lionel thinks the world of me, and is determined that one day I shall be chairman of Heinemann. I've repeatedly told him I don't much fancy that kingly crown, but his backing is all-important. Immediately, as you can imagine, I feel as though the crushing weights were gradually being lifted from my shoulders. There are many details still to be arranged, but the main problem is solved, I pray rightly.

Last Monday evening, while I was making the all-important decision, I had to go with Nancy Caccia and two Austrians (a publisher and his wife, very nice) to a so-called play entitled *Waiting for Godot*, which I had carefully avoided up to then—and rightly, for it proved to be the ugliest, dullest, most meaningless twaddle I've ever had to endure. At the interval I could stand no more and firmly took them all back to the Caccias' for supper, much to the relief of the Austrians. At 11 p.m. I went round to see Lionel and made my big decision. Next day, feeling pretty groggy, I made my annual pilgrimage to the University match at Twickenham, and was rewarded by the best game I've ever seen. The Oxford passing, scissors-movements, 'dummies' and all were so bewilderingly brilliant that even the referee was several times caught looking the wrong way. Great fun.

14 December 1955 *Grundisburgh*

Rather a *de profundis* letter from me this week—in a very mild way. I am in the thick of exam-papers, sick to death of reading secondhand tripe about Henry V, and Prospero, and Chaunticleer. Secondhand, because, except at the good schools, the candidates are merely repeating what their half-baked instructors have been telling them, many of whom I suspect are followers of the man Leavis. Who can it have been who told the boys of Bloxham, or the young papists at Birmingham Oratory, that, except for a few lines spoken by Caliban, there was no poetry in *The Tempest*? The unanimous answer to the question about the point of the comicalities in *The Tempest* and *Henry V* is that both plays would be intolerable without them. That is the only obviously first-hand judgment in over 100 papers! Oh no, there is one other, i.e. that 'orison' is Shakespearean for 'horizon'. The obvious fact that if so the passage would make no sense whatever did not disturb the young scholar for a moment.

And—a further proof of my degraded state of mind—I am writing in an arm-chair with a BIRO of all disgusting implements. But enough of these trivial bunkers. Like John Wesley's friend who said, 'We all have our crosses' when his fire smoked. I am delighted you are in smooth water—free, I hope, of much of what to you must always have been the boring side of publishing, free now to work at length and at leisure in the literary field.

Hardy's *Dynasts* I read through with intense enjoyment at Cambridge, and often *in* since, and one of these days shall re-read *in toto.* In the *Spectator* of Dec. 2 John Wain warns us against re-reading an author we enjoyed when young—e.g. Kipling or Housman. Utter rot! Rupert, you must take that young man in hand. His article isn't a work of criticism; it is a shudder of nerves—and so shrill, unbalanced, and *conceited*, for he tells us *ex cathedra* that this is what K. *is* and implies that we who don't agree are merely adolescent. Do tell him not to be such an *ass*? Because he is clearly very intelligent. Why has he not learnt that a little real humility sharpens the perceptions wonderfully and has other good effects too. What a strong tendency there is today to lay down the law about what one may or must, and may not and must not, admire. These brash young men will think that a change of fashion is an advance in wisdom!

To revert. I am not very good at plays etc on the air. East Anglian reception for one thing, but I think the chief reason is my bad choosing. I remember enjoying Shaw because his dialogue is always a joy, and not seeing what is happening on the stage doesn't matter, as nothing ever is happening. But I dislike that Sunday rehashing of some book I have liked. I have my own vivid image of Mr Pickwick or Soames Forsyte, or Bronwen (in that *extremely* beautiful book *How Green* etc. I do hope you agree) and don't want it disturbed. In fact, as you are at this moment saying, and I have often suspected, I am a senile and hidebound Victorian. But I *will* put on *The Dynasts* on the Third when it is on because you tell me to. Not that my obedience is unlimited. I will *not* listen to Mrs Dale, The Archers, The Goon Show, Vic Oliver, Billy Bunter, Bartok, Alban Berg, or Richard Wagner (except in spots) even if you tell me, as a man in the Club did recently, that he supposed the Archers was about the best thing the BBC had ever done. But I must say he didn't resemble you in mind, body or estate. He buys up all the old *Tatlers* when they are out of date; he is an original subscriber to *Lilliput*, he reckons a day wasted on which he doesn't get his game of 'slosh'. No, I should never take him for you. I suspect him of being one of those who think *Waiting for Godot* superb. How refreshing your comments are! Is Nancy Caccia the wife of that admirable man Harold Caccia? Not that I know him at all well. I have always admired him since a certain house-match in which one or two decisions of mine as umpire deprived him of a deserved victory. They must have been infuriating, but he took them superbly. The great defect of the Eton game always was that *far* too much depended on the umpire. At least a house-match a year went the wrong way—I mean a side knocked out early which *might* have won the cup.

I say, what ignoramuses politicians are. In the *D. Mail*, after Attlee's retirement, Desmond Donnelly gave as an instance of A's fondness for deflating exaggerated reputations his calling Mr Gladstone 'the W.G. Grace of politics'. The poor fool didn't realise this was the highest possible *praise*. Attlee was born in the same week as I was, and to any boy of that age the one and only hero was W.G. My father knew him well, and took my brother and me to shake his hand after a match at Worcester in 1897. He was very gracious in a sort of Newfoundland doglike way—more so than to another parent who had also presented his son to him. The first thing the old man said to the boy, his father standing by, was 'Well, young fellow, I hope yer a better fielder than yer father was; he was the worst I ever did see!'—and went off into a Gargantuan laugh. My father heard of this and said 'Oh yes, W.G. never forgave the wretched chap for missing a catch (off W.G.) which lost the match v Middlesex in—if you please—1870!' He had the memory and the patience, as well as the figure, of an elephant. It was sad to hear the larrikins at the Oval hailing him in 1900 with shouts of 'Kruger!' Not that *he* minded. I don't suppose he had ever heard of Kruger. What line would he have taken about heroin?

17 December 1955 *Bromsden Farm*

I hope this letter will surprise, if not disconcert, you by arriving earlier than usual. I am writing it on Saturday because tomorrow Victor Gollancz and his wife are driving over for lunch and bridge, which may continue until late in the evening. When I told you that I played bridge only in self-defence I should have excepted these family games with the G.s, which take place once or twice a year. V.G. is a man of dynamic energy, most stimulating to see for a while, though I should imagine impossible to work with or for, since he is an individualist of dictatorial intensity. I am very fond of him, and I think he is of me. Your excellent letter arrived this morning, just as I was resigning myself to the Christmas rush's having spoilt my week-end. Those exam-papers sound like a foretaste of Judgment, and I can't imagine how you keep nice enough to give anyone any marks at all. Once during the war, when I was Adjutant at Pirbright, I drove over with two Drill Sergeants to inspect the Corps at Charterhouse—what a task for a middle-aged bibliophile! We were accustomed to putting in close arrest any Guardsman who came on parade with a hair showing beneath the back of his cap, and when our eyes first lit on the Charterhouse lads I thought the Drill Sergeants were going to faint. I drew them aside and explained that since civilian barbers were scarce in wartime we should have to ignore length of hair as an attribute on this occasion. They glumly agreed. All this was suggested by your woolly examinees.

Last evening I was reading in a third-class carriage on my usual Friday train to Henley, when the train suddenly ran off the rails. Mercifully we were moving very slowly and managed to pull up without injury or delay, but there were a few moments of incredulous terror. The carriage was full—an enormous woman, a very small boy, several tired business men, etc. At the vital moment they all woke and sat up silent, immobilised by the unexpected. I remember thinking 'The boy will be cushioned by the fat woman,' 'Are we on an embankment?' (It was pitch dark.) 'What can one hold on to?' (Nothing but glass each side, and the laden rack above.) 'This is what it feels like to be in a smash.' And then the train bumped to a halt, and everybody began to talk at once in the friendliest way, as they used to in the war. After a few moments we (and all the other passengers) opened the nearside door and helped the women and children down on to the track. We were only about half a mile short of Twyford station, towards which we trudged carrying our luggage (I had three bags full of books and MSS and my wife's Christmas present), tripping over sleepers and praying no other trains were due. Just before we got there, two porters arrived with lanterns. They forced us all into a tiny relief train, and we reached Henley only half an hour late.

There's one quite good joke in the *London Mag*, in a review of vol 2 of the life of Freud. One of F's disciples (Stekel) broke away from him, cheekily declaring that a dwarf on the shoulder of a giant can see farther than the giant himself. Freud smartly replied that this does not hold of a louse on the head of an astronomer. Perhaps it's an old joke, but not to me. Your list of radio-hates is exactly mine, though I could add plenty to it. Wagner I positively enjoy in small doses, but not, oh Lord, at full length. I am perhaps one of the few people who have slept right through *Das Rheingold* on two chairs at the back of a box at Covent Garden—but I was younger then and could sleep through anything. Now the three geese in the farmyard shatter my dreams—no wonder they saved the Capitol, noisy brutes. Now take a deep breath—I like Sibelius, and Mahler, and revel in the romanticism of Tchaikovsky, but if you play me Beethoven when I visit you, I shall rejoice. Last week I went to a jolly lowbrow French revue called *La Plume de ma Tante*, which I enjoyed greatly. It is gay, quick, nice to look at and full of outrageous slapstick of the broadest kind—so refreshing after that unspeakable *Godot*.

What else did I do last week? Visited Viola Meynell in hospital, dined with Madeline House and another of our Dickens team, attended a committee of the London Library, at which I was put on to a sub-committee to find a new Librarian (my friend Simon Nowell-Smith is retiring to devote himself to bibliography, and don't I envy him!), a dinner of the Lit Soc at which Tommy Lascelles was confirmed as President and myself (very reluctantly) as Secretary, *vice* Sparrow. I sat next to Sparrow and Cuthbert Headlam, who nowadays is not the easiest person in the world to talk to, though no doubt he means no harm. On Wednesday I shirked a committee of the Royal Literary Fund. On Thursday I went to a cocktail party given by Stephen Potter—the usual screaming mob in a small hot room. I gulped down three glasses of champagne and hurried on to the Athenaeum to dine (as cosily as that forbidding citadel permits) with Wyndham Ketton-Cremer. De Beer sent W.K-C a copy of his new edition of Evelyn, and since Wyndham already has one to review for the *T.L.S.*, he asked me if I'd like the other for Christmas. Yes please, I said. Fancy a fifteen-guinea book—I can scarcely believe it!

If I can somehow dispose of the manuscripts which now surround and haunt me, I plan during the four days of Christmas to read something short, sweet and long-forgotten—*Northanger Abbey* perhaps or *Old Mortality*—that will for an hour or two take the taste of this distressing year from my mouth. But perhaps when the time comes I shall just sleep by the fire!

Do you know anything about graphology? All I remember from two expert friends is that when the left-hand margins of a letter grow wider as they descend, it shows that the writer is moving ever closer to the person he is writing to. Look at the margins here, and brood on the truth of this pseudo-science!

c/o R.M.A. Bourne Esq
The Briary
Eton College
22 December 1955 *Windsor*

I am with my other son-in-law this year—well after your day I think. He is one of the great rowing family; his father had the unique record of stroking four winning Oxford crews—on the same level for impressiveness as George Hirst's 2000 runs and 200 wickets in 1906. I asked G.H. once if he thought anyone would ever do that again (a slightly imbecile question, like many put to the 'Any Questions' team). His answer was, 'Ah doan't knaw; but I can tell you one thing about him. He'll be a tired man in September'. A better answer than one often hears on A.Q. I always listen—usually with a rising temperature—so often the answer ought to be, 'That is a very silly question, to which only an expert can give a sensible answer. The opinion of those like ourselves who know nothing of the subject is worthless'. But I cannot remember hearing that answer. And their self-conscious facetiousness can be very trying. But I suppose that when the man in the gallery's judgment is what matters, all this playing to the gallery is not only excusable but necessary.

I say, Rupert, that train! How vividly you describe it and note that inadequate irrelevance of the human mind when faced with crisis. Half of us will be wondering on the Judgment Day how those haloes keep their position or what shop in the Charing Cross Road that trump came from. Not if you are Henry James of course, who met his first stroke with 'So here it comes—the distinguished thing', expecting the next minute to find himself on the golden floor, where Housman told his doctor he would in a day or two be telling the very funny but improper story the doctor had just told him. How can he be sure Queen Victoria or Edmund Gosse's father won't be listening? Perhaps they are still in purgatory. But won't A.E.H. be there too? Let us put the problem to Ralph Wightman, Mrs Stocks and—of course—Bob Boothby.

Tell me now about X and his book. I find much in it interesting, but I don't like him. I do wish these young—and not so young either—men would realise that their sexual imbroglios and defiances don't *shock* us (which is what with a blend of blatancy and smugness they hope to do) but *bore* us. But imperfect sympathies are not to be accounted for. He wrote to congratulate D.H.L. on *Lady C's Lover*. Well let me come into the open, and say with a strident finality of which John Wain has not the monopoly that *Lady C's Lover* is an extremely dull and portentously silly and pretentious book. After which your comment may well be that of Jowett when a man, who attended his lectures on Plato, brought him an essay attacking with much biting irony etc many of J's explanations and comments. Not a word for a whole minute, then in his piping voice, 'You're a Magdalen man, aren't you? Yes . . . Well . . . Good morning, Mr A.'

That literary club must be great fun. Bernard Fergusson (old pupil) and Tim Nugent (o.p.) are members, I think, and both have only one wish when they attend, viz *not* to be next to Cuthbert. Tuppy[1] used to say all Headlams were severely handicapped by the black blood in them which made them hard to work with and kept them out of positions to which their abilities entitled them and were fully equal to. Old Maurice is the least crabbed and yet he was about the only senior Treasury official who was *not* knighted on retirement.

Yes, of course, Wagner in bits—one must have them—and oddly, all the beginning of the *Rheingold* is a favourite of mine. And some of *Tristan*, but gosh! the tediousness of much. I remember a young man leaving in the middle of the last act, apologising loudly to the owners of the feet he trod on with 'You see I have got some chaps coming to

[1] Nickname of G.W. Headlam, Eton master.

breakfast.' You must educate me up to Mahler. My musical knowledge is very rough and ready. I love the fairly obvious Beethovens because I love hearing 'desperate tides of the great world's anguish forced through the channels of a single heart,' but I think of the symphonies I really like No 8 and the Pastoral best. Do you remember Ezra Pound's referring to him as 'the beastly Beethoven'? How one's toe itches sometimes!

I say, Rupert, Jonah[2] has sent a copy of my Gladstone to—I blush to write it—Max Beerbohm! As I have suggested to J. won't he answer as half-brother Beerbohm Tree did when some chap sent him a play, viz.

My dear Sir,
I have read your play.
Oh, my dear Sir!
Yours etc H.B.T.

I must stop. My last pre-Xmas word to you is (*à la* Sir G. Sitwell) 'Don't get into a railway accident. I am sure it is unwise.' No, it isn't quite my last word. That is from Synge, that you may 'go romancing through a roaring lifetime from this hour to the dawning of the Judgment Day'. *And* of course that you will have an immense Xmas and an incomparable New Year.

Boxing Day 1955 *Bromsden Farm*

It was delightful to hear your voice in the midst of yesterday's Saturnalia, and it seems absurd that we can't meet while you're so comparatively near. You're not bound to read that long book of mine all over again, you know, but if you persist in so doing, look out for errors, solecisms, printer's idiocies, and send me a list of them. I haven't given up hope of a Penguin edition, and if there is one I want it to be right. They asked me if I could shorten the book in any way, but I can't, except by removing Appendixes A and B.

I seldom listen to 'Any Questions' and can't imagine how you keep your temper with it. By the way, I've agreed to appear for two

[2] L.E. (Sir Laurence) Jones, writer.

minutes on Television on January 2. It's the first of a series of book-programmes that Priestley is running. I've no idea what I'm supposed to say, but since I have to reach the studio 2¾ hours before the programme starts (for a 'buffet supper') I shall doubtless find out then. It will be my TV début, and I'm sure a sickening failure. Let's hope the fee is adequate!

Where does that splendid line about the 'great world's anguish' come from? You know and remember such a lot that I don't wonder you sometimes long to give it out. Max will love your Gladstone: three cheers for Jonah!

Last week in London was the usual pre-Christmas scrimmage. On Wednesday I caught the 11 o'clock train to Brighton with a dear friend and spent the rest of the day there, doing Christmas shopping. Brighton never fails to improve my health and spirits. I was a sickly child, always ill with this or that, and my mother inevitably took me to Brighton to recuperate: we must have stayed at *all* those big hotels along the front, and the combined sensations of spoiling and truancy persist to this day, quite apart from the air which I love. There are several good secondhand bookshops too, and a theatre, and the walk to Rottingdean, and the antique shops in the Lanes (now spoilt and expensive)—oh yes, I love it all.

One evening I dined with my old father at White's—mercifully two friends joined us and so prevented his usual complaining, wishing he was dead etc.—the most boring and unanswerable form of conversation. On Thursday I went to a party given by Robert Lutyens (son of the architect) in a big studio in Westminster—quite amusing but nothing to write home (i.e. to you) about. My plans for re-reading an old favourite during the holiday have been thwarted, chiefly by the piles of MSS which I had to bring with me. So far I have dealt with 50,000 words of an exploring expedition to Tibet in 1913 (the public doesn't seem to be as sick of this sort of subject as I am), a melodramatic novel set in the Welsh mountains, a travel book about Jugoslavia (who on earth wants to read about that?), and am in the middle of a selection of the letters written by the first Earl of Lytton (Owen Meredith) to his wife from Portugal in the 1860's. They have been put together by his daughter, Lady Emily Lutyens (a darling old creature whose book, *A Blessed Girl*, I published), but I doubt so far whether they're of sufficient general interest. Waiting for me is an account of a disastrous voyage in a cargo-ship from America to the Philippines, full of horrors. In bed at night I have read with great interest a novel called *Heritage* by Anthony West, which was recently published in America. A.W. is the natural son of Rebecca West and H.G. Wells, and the novel is so much *à clef* as almost to be autobiography. Would it amuse you to read it? It's good.

My son rang up from Germany last night, cheerful but exhausted after much carousal in the Sergeants' Mess. He is off for a few days' shooting near the Baltic coast. Peter Fleming looked in just now, gay and sunburnt after ten days on the Persian Gulf: did you see his two pieces in *The Times*? I told you, didn't I? that he's working on a book about Hitler's plans for invading England in 1940, based on both sides' documents. It should be first-rate. The trouble with Peter these days is that he longs to write something but doesn't know what. He doesn't want to travel as he used to do, has little creative faculty, and is altogether gravelled for matter. Fourth leaders in *The Times* and his 'Strix' page in the *Spectator*, excellently though he does them, are pretty small beer, and this invasion book is a boon.

Hardy in his Notebook (of which I have read a little) says categorically: 'Nine-tenths of the letters in which people speak unreservedly of their inmost feelings are written after ten at night'. I quote him in partial explanation of this dull noonday epistle of mine. Some of his other scraps are good, but you have to dig them out of a welter of editorial irrelevance—not that it would worry T.H. much. I shall look forward to your telephoning.

30 December 1955 *Cambridge*

If this doesn't prove the existence of a personal devil I don't know what does. I am at Cambridge on examining business. I expected your letter yesterday. The postal authorities in all England south of the Trent are all suffering from '*la crapule*' or diridonosis. Your letter has just arrived (9.17 a.m.) At 9.30 I go to the exam-room and remain there on and off till 6 p.m., cooking the marks of candidates from schools of whose names, natures and even existences I had been hitherto unaware. To add insult to injury, on the mark-sheet of the very first three contiguous names were (yesterday) Tidey, Tink, Totty. The silver lining is that we failed them all. Among the first girls' names were Miss V. Po from Ceylon, I believe, and Miss Urritocoechea of (like Attlee) nowhere. I return to Eton to-morrow and ring you up on Sunday—after shedding my sack-cloth and combing the ashes from my hair. I have written this letter in 4¼ minutes. Bah!

New Year's Day 1956 — ***Bromsden Farm***

You telephoned just in time, for our machine has since gone out of action. Thursday will be the greatest fun, and I am much looking forward to it. Last night, for the first time in twenty years, I allowed myself to be lured to a see-the-New-Year-in-party at the Shuckburghs'. Evelyn S. is an Under-Secretary in the F.O., very charming and (unlike most Wykhamists) totally devoid of hubris. His delightful wife Nancy is a daughter of Lord Esher. The party was sixteen-strong, including P. Fleming. We had an excellent dinner (all done without servants) at 9.30, but after it there was still a long hour to be filled in with small talk before midnight struck and we could drive gratefully home. Vague and agreeable social occasions like that simply don't fit into my overcrowded schedule, and as a result I am at least two manuscripts to the bad.

By the way, did I last week mention the letters of Lord Lytton and his wife? They (the letters and their writers) grew on me as I went on, and I've said I'll publish the book if they (Lady E. Lutyens and her daughter Mary) can cut fifty or sixty pages out of it. This will have to be done skilfully, sentences and paragraphs wherever possible: it's much too long now, but when it has been pruned I think it will amuse you in a quiet way. It's like opening a little window on to one family of the upper class in 1865—the year Gilbert Murray was born; I must listen to him tonight. He speaks so beautifully. Why is it that the survivors of his generation (or a little younger) are all such fine broadcasters? Lord Samuel, Bertrand Russell etc, all possess a quiet firmness (*suaviter in modo* I would say if I knew exactly what it meant) together with authority, grace and scope. After them the mould seems to have been broken. There are excellent younger broadcasters, but none with quite those gifts. Is it because they enjoyed more of *les douceurs de la vie* before 1914?

By the time you get this my baptism of television cameras will be over, for better for worse, and since I am to receive ten guineas for two minutes on the screen, I fancy it will be better. You shall have a full account on Thursday. I wonder whether you'd rather lunch at the Garrick or at a Soho restaurant? Here is a rotten map to show you where Soho Square is. The outside of the office is painted in O.E. colours[1] and has my name writ large, so you can't miss it. Carlyle is probably already waiting for you at home. He doesn't burst on the public till January 20, when I have *six* books appearing. What is the news of my old tutor Jelly? I had a very shaky Christmas card from him. I see the fees have gone up again: my second boy goes to Fred Coleridge's (where the other was) in September. How long can dwindling income and non-existent capital continue to meet rising fees? Never mind; it's so long since I was able to see more than a month or two ahead (if that) that I've given up that sort of worry altogether. Forgive this brief and dreary letter, and do not take it as a bad omen for 1956, during which you will be asked to decipher thousands of words from

Yours ever
Rupert

3 January 1956 — *The Briary, Eton*

Thursday is going to be a day marked '*meliore lapillo*'. That miserable lapse on the part of the P.O. has left me an irretrievable number of miles behind in this lovely adventure which is our correspondence. You remind me of old C.H. Blakiston[1] (only in *one* respect!). Whatever village we passed on a field-day it always turned out that C.H.B. once had an aunt there, or knew the vicar, or the *only* tailor in S.E. England who made trousers that never wore out etc. Any name in the literary, dramatic, political world I mention turns out to be well-known to you for years past. I must be careful, or I shall suddenly find

[1] Old Etonian, pale blue and black.

[1] Eton master, later Headmaster of Lancing.

that someone I hate, say F.R. Leavis, was your earliest and best friend.

Yes. *Nothing* is more boring than nine out of ten New Year parties. We went to one once in Grundisburgh, and the hours passed on leaden feet. At 10 the hostess played the piano, not very well. Dry cake was passed round, so dry that my wife threw her bit into the fire—unperceived, she hoped, but alas she suddenly caught the soulful but reproachful eyes of her hostess looking at her from the looking-glass above the piano.

That line 'desperate tides' is from Myers's *St Paul*, once so over-praised, now despised.

Thursday! Anywhere. What P.G. Wodehouse calls the browsing and sluicing matter little. The entertainment will be elsewhere. It will emphatically *not* be a day of 'neutral-tinted haps and such'.[2]

5 January 1956 *The Briary, Eton*

Further proof of existence of malevolent personal devil. Here the fog was the thickest since Toddy Vaughan[1] fell into the river. When I got up I nearly said 'How like you, God', as Sir W. Eden did when it poured on the one day he wanted it to be fine. I hope you didn't curse me, and that you hadn't already killed the fatted calf. And is Tuesday *really* all right? (No answer, of course, if it is.) Busy men always hate changing their plans.

Cambridge was very pleasant, but you know, *dons*—! Somehow they seem less real even than beaks. Perhaps I've become like Carlyle in old age to whom *all* men appeared *spectral*. How I look forward to that book—and to lunching with a publisher on Tuesday—*they* are real men!

8 January 1956 *Bromsden Farm*

In sober fact next Tuesday suits me *better* than last Thursday, for I had been up late the night before (dining with Mark Bonham-Carter

[2] Hardy, 'He never expected much'.

[1] Eton master.

and his new wife) and wasn't feeling very sparkling. When I got your sad fog-bound message I cancelled the table at the Garrick, ate some bread and cheese in my flat and slept by the fire for a refreshing hour.

1956 began for me with all the savagery of its beastly predecessor. Do you remember that splendid opening of a poem by Sir John Denham:

All on a weeping Monday,
With a fat Bulgarian Sloven?

I thought of it when I arrived at Soho Square last Monday to find that my stout charwoman, who has 'done for me' these five and a half years, had left a note saying she had flu, couldn't face the stairs any more and must give up the job. On Thursday the darling old ex-butler who has been coming one morning a week to keep my tattered old clothes in some sort of order was taken to hospital and put in an oxygen tent, where he died peacefully next morning, a victim of smog, no doubt, though Lady Emily Lutyens (81), whom I saw on Friday, says it's nothing to the fogs she knew as a girl. She was deliciously scornful of policemen wearing 'gas-masks' to direct the traffic.

I enjoyed my TV debut (of which more on Tuesday), though my nearest and dearest say they saw little but the back of my neck, and that distorted! I remember C.A.A.[1] quoting from Myers's *St Paul* in chapel, and I bought a copy and was much impressed. Now, if I can find it, I shall read it again.

Yesterday we all drove to the Cotswolds to lunch with my wife's stepmother: unhappily there was enough fog to slow us down and shut out all the views. It took most of the day, and I am behindhand with my proofs and manuscripts, among which is a collection of P. Fleming's *Spectator* pieces, which I plan to publish in the autumn as *My Aunt's Rhinoceros and other Reflections*. Remind me on Tuesday to tell you a pleasing story about two zoologists and a flea.

[1] C.A. Alington, Headmaster of Eton, later Dean of Durham.

8 January 1956 *The Briary, Eton*

It is high time you dropped this fantastic pretence that you are *not* the kindest man in England south-east of a line extending from Plymouth to the Wash (oh no, that was the fog). Two really enchanting books have arrived—Sydney Cockerell's letters and Henry James's. I look at them as Swinburne did at his 'ultimate allowance[1] of one who had erst clashed cymbals in Naxos' when Max lunched at no 2 The Pines, anticipating the utmost relish. There *shall* be a special shelf in my library, and when you come and stay in the spring, I shall think out an inscription for it, embodying some aperçu, aphorism, or even apophthegm from you.

This last week celebrated the birthdays of Lord Attlee and G.W.L. (both 1883) in its usual manner, i.e. black gloom and the dunnest smoke of Hell. The new week has begun with sunshine—probably because *your* birthday falls in it?

Well, à Tuesday. I *had* to write this, or you might have thought these gifts from you had *not* made my heart like a singing bird or even a watered shoot.

15 January 1956 *Bromsden Farm*

There's nothing like a meeting—even such a delightful one as ours on Tuesday—for breaking into a correspondence. Of course we discussed nothing from our old agenda; in fact I can't remember what we *did* discuss, and only know that the time passed in a flash of pure pleasure. I hope for you too.

On Wednesday I lunched with the (female) representative of Metro-Goldwyn-Mayer at the Caprice, an immensely expensive restaurant. Knowing that so unwieldy a corporation will not notice the bill, I always (about twice a year) do myself excellently at their expense, 10/- cigar and all. In the evening I took one of my widows to a play called *Separate Tables*, which I saw a year ago but enjoyed again.

On Thursday I lunched with an agreeable publisher called Batsford at the St James's Club and in the evening presided at my old Society

[1] 'A small bottle of Bass's pale ale.'

of Bookmen. Robert Henriques spoke well about authors and critics, and there was quite a good discussion afterwards, though I find the fostering of such occasions an increasing strain.

Friday was a marathon. A luncheon (250 strong) to John Wilson of Bumpus on his eightieth birthday lasted from 12.30 till 3.35. I sat among a nest of dullards and listened to speeches from Geoffrey Faber (long and dull), Norman Birkett (polished but almost too slick and professional), Michael Joseph (dull), Basil Blackwell (rather moving), Charles Morgan (short and good) and the old hero himself, who reminisced delightfully. Then he was presented with a gold watch (and another speech) and so it went on. I scarcely had time to regain the office and sign my letters (which I must have dictated in my sleep) when my family arrived to celebrate my daughter's twenty-first birthday. We consumed some smoked salmon and champagne, went six-strong to a simple entertainment called *Salad Days* (which delighted the young but left us fairly cold: it was like a gay and well-drilled performance by the Wimbledon Amateur Dramatic Company) and then drove to Hampstead, where my sister had prepared a huge dinner complete with birthday cake and more champagne. It was all a great success, from which we crept to bed at 2 a.m. You'll not be surprised to learn that last night I slept for eleven hours!

And now the piles of manuscripts demand my attention, for next week will be busy too. If I can only work my way back to scratch, I should next Sunday be able to send you more than this fitful scribble.

[Here I was interrupted to play chess with my youngest, who goes back to school on Friday. I just won by a fluke.]

In his speech John Wilson said that every day of his life he had made a point of reading at least one piece of literature, prose or verse, both for pleasure and to help him maintain some sort of standard among the mass of new books he is asked to sell. Excellent advice, I thought, to publishers as well, if only one had the time. I look forward to your comments on the Cockerell and James letters: I did a great deal of editorial work on them, but so long ago that I've almost forgotten it. Directly a book is finally passed for press in all particulars, one gratefully turns to the next, and then months later the original one turns up, almost as a surprise, sometimes an agreeable one. I found Cockerell's correspondence with the Nun most moving and unusual. The old boy is 88, bedridden and almost blind. Let's hope he survives till Friday, when the book appears.

18 January 1956 *Grundisburgh*

The mental, moral, physical and spiritual well-being resulting from that really princely entertainment under the shadow of Sir Henry's dignity, Sir Squire's eyeglass, and Sir Seymour's smile[1] should have been recorded on paper and despatched to you. Let me confess—I *did* think of it, but had a faint feeling that you might think it a trifle fulsome, for you must count such luncheons as nothing. So just let me say quite truly and emphatically I cannot remember ever enjoying two hours more. You won't think that *too* Hugh Walpolean, will you? When we returned here I wanted to look up one or two things in his Life, and straightway re-read it from c to c, and nothing else except the paper for three days. My first impression four years ago was absolutely right. It is a *fascinating* book. And an additional pleasure was that I now know the biographer (some of him, not all!) and never ceased to notice and savour and chuckle over his beautifully deft, humorous, and affectionate handling of that hotch-potch which was H.W's life and character. The book really is rich entertainment, because nearly every page stimulates one cell or other of one's imagination, wonder, respect, derision, and so on. He swings from 'stormy' to 'set-fair' and back like a mad barometer, and his biographer, full of kindness and amusement, accompanies him. How good his insight and comments are sometimes, and how insensitive and commonplace at others (e.g. the Oval scene on p. 273—a boy's description). He is cruel about old A.C. Benson (resenting, I fancy, his own youthful allegiance?). The old boy was only just clear of seven years' melancholia and less than a month from his death. But he is quite right in seeing that A.C.B. in a way 'kept him off'. Intimacy by correspondence, yes, but 'so far and no farther'. He never wanted worshippers or disciples, and always averred that social intercourse exhausted him. In fact his little quatrain on Percy Lubbock is something of a boomerang:

[1] Portraits of Irving, Bancroft and Hicks in the Garrick Club.

Come, I say, let us leave the rest,
I must be home for tea;
Not too much of the very, very best,
That is enough for me.

Arnold Bennett's rather Olympian patronage of H.W. has an ironical flavour now, for I suppose A.B's novels are, at least temporarily, every bit as dead as H.W's? And they were both anyhow at 4 a.m. perfectly clear-eyed about themselves. A.B. says somewhere: 'My work will never be better than third-rate, judged by the high standards, but I shall be cunning enough to make it impose on my contemporaries.' And so he was. Tell me what *you* think H.W's best. The punctual 'Pooter' episodes are delightful. But so is the whole book. That is of course what you ought to be doing, and I hope will now have time to do, as you 'feed on the arid bosom of Heinemann' (H.J., p. 74). Your days' activities make me feel positively faint. Do you ever have time to twiddle your thumbs—to ruminate? I expect your mind—in fact I know—moves very quickly. Mine moves like a hippo emerging from his wallow, with a good deal of mud clinging to him. And on Friday I address the Rotarians of Woodbridge. I think I shall tell them to fear God and keep His commandments, and then sit down. I am told they are not a very lively lot, but I suppose there could be no better instance of a contradiction in terms than 'a sprightly Rotarian'.

I notice, by the way, that you never write about politics. Acid references to Eden or Dulles, curses about the T.U.C. etc., are conspicuously absent from your bright and brimming page (in Henry James's not *very* taking phrase). Partly, I doubt not, for fear I might reply in kind. Have no fear. Old Maurice Headlam's long and barely legible letters are full of anger and lamentation about Asquith's handling of Ireland and the Liberal heresies of the early 1900's—it is like hearing the moaning of dinosaurs, so immensely long ago it all seems. But the old thing is much more amiable than Cuthbert whom, I gather, you avoided at your literary dinner, or perhaps it was a case of 'How is it I haven't seen you in church lately, Giles?' 'Cos I ain't bin.' I greatly like your attitude about bores, i.e. you steer and manage them and don't resent them, knowing full well (but I didn't discover it till much older than you are) what good folk many of them are. Which reminds me of a recent par in the *New Statesman* by A.J.P. Taylor who avers that the greatest bore *he* has ever heard of is Lord Acton. Has he ever heard anyone who knew Acton talk about him? Their admiration was limitless. Taylor then jeers at that famous aphorism of A's about power corrupting, as windy rot, adding that many an engine-driver is not corrupted. God in High Heaven, why do our clever historians, our learned scientists, our experienced public men say and print things which no house debating society would have tolerated in old days? Julian Huxley, Prof Hogben, A.L. Rowse all have these moments of adolescent dogmatism.

Back to politics for a moment. Dulles! My cousin Oliver two years ago told me he was, in international politics, simply *the* bull in a china-shop—being almost indistinguishable from that animal in face, figure, intelligence, impulsiveness, and capacity for destruction. Surely his dictum that diplomacy is the art of skirting the edge of the precipice without falling over is of breath-bereaving folly. And now he thinks that he may have over-simplified what he meant!

But enough of Mr D. I am getting much pleasure out of the correspondence about old Asquith and his bridge-game. Lady Violet wields a sharp pen. Her voice and B.B.C. manner are not to us attractive, but she generally talks better sense than many of her colleagues. Tuppy Headlam used to say that the brilliance of her talk was to some extent spoilt by the frequency and accuracy with which she spat in the eye of the one she was talking to. Not an uncommon failing among the voluble. Trollope did, and so did Browning, though I feel sure the aim of both was more haphazard. Who is Henry Fairlie who swaggers weekly in the *Spectator* and is *frightfully* proud of having coined the title 'the Establishment' for those who really pull governmental strings—the Cliveden set, Geoffrey Dawson, the higher clergy etc.? How venomous people get when things go wrong and the scapegoat hunt is on. G. Dawson was a very pleasant kindly fellow with honest and high-minded aims, but no-one would guess it from the Boothbys and Co who have reviewed the book. Do they all really persuade themselves that they would have seen the path so clear through the thirties and forties? They are not really very different from the 'Any Answers' critics who ascribe all our woes to poor little Eden—as they will the frost and snow which will be upon us next week. But I lay myself open to the snub Fitzgerald gave one of his correspondents: 'Don't write about politics; I agree with you beforehand'.

Sydney Cockerell and Henry James are there against the day when the Rotarians cease from troubling. I shall be impervious to anything January can do while they last. Oh yes, just one more thing. When H.W. lectured at Eton (superbly; the boys loved it) I reminded him at dinner that in a short story he had written of some man 'He was at Eton, and had therefore had no education'. He exclaimed 'Heavens, did I really say anything as cheap as that—exactly the type of remark I particularly hate in anybody else's book!' I liked him very much. You probably know who wrote that contemptible obituary in *The Times*—but probably won't say. Maugham's behaviour over *Cakes and Ale* would *not* have pleased Mr Gladstone—or Q. Victoria either for that matter. I suppose such words as 'cad' and 'lie' are just as *vieux* as 'gentleman'.

22 January 1956 *Bromsden Farm*

That was a whale of a letter I found waiting for me on Friday, and you can imagine how flattering-sweet I found all the splendid things you say about my book. That *you* should have read it twice, and chuckled the second time, is enough to turn my head—or indeed to set me writing again if I only had subject and time. You can see, can't you? that I couldn't possibly have allowed Hugh's life to be written by the wrong person: the least shift of emphasis would have wrecked it, and originally I took on the job *faute de mieux* and with the utmost diffidence, never having put more than 1500 words together before. Hugh's best books, I should say, are *The Dark Forest*, *Mr Perrin and Mr Traill*, *The Old Ladies*, the *Jeremy* books, and as a curiosity *The Killer and the Slain*. When I read them *all* again in 1946–51 I found most of them fairly easy reading—but then I was looking for this and that, and so perhaps prejudiced.

No, I seldom, alas, have time to ruminate or twiddle my thumbs, let alone stand and stare, and the lack of such amenity has a cumulatively crushing effect. My mind does in fact move very fast (on the surface, *bien entendu*, a sort of jet-skater), and that is its most effective quality, though it makes me intolerant of slowness and stupidity. I read about politics a bit, as we all must, but take little real interest, particularly since the disappearance of Winston, the last of the giants. Eden's toothy complacency, total lack of oratory, and record of indecision put him in the Atlee class (though I suspect *he* was much shrewder than he appeared). As for Dulles—God help us all! Do you remember his taking a revolver as a present to General Neguib?! The only hope I see for the so-called Free World is Adlai Stevenson, a man of wit, culture, and a breadth of outlook such as only Winston and F.D.R. have shown these last thirty years. Adlai, did I tell you? was married to my wife's first cousin (who left him directly he was elected Governor of Illinois), so he is one of the family. I have seen him only twice—once in New York, once in London—but was most impressed and charmed. I published his little book of lectures (*Call to Greatness*) last year, and now have in the press a bigger book called *What I Think*—mostly speeches and articles—which should have some importance in this Election year. If Ike runs they all think he'll get in. If he doesn't run, Adlai should romp home.

Henry Fairlie is just a journalist—a very clever one too, I should say, however much one may disagree with him. Incidentally, I see you don't give FitzGerald his capital G! The years that proof-correcting has eaten make me whip out my pencil at the smallest irregularity!

Oh yes, that filthy *Times* obituary of Hugh was written by a creature called Herbert GRIMSDITCH, a louse on the outer fringe of journalism. The obituary arrangements at *The Times* are haphazard and unsatisfactory. The smallest civil servant—Sewage Disposal Officer in Uppingham—automatically has at least a half-column about him in standing type in the office, but writers and artists are not provided for till they are eighty. At the death of Constance Garnett, who had translated the whole of Russian literature into English and was an old lady, they hadn't a line written or anyone capable of writing one. Eventually in despair I drove up to Hampstead and waited while old H.N. Brailsford very kindly wrote a short and quite inadequate piece (while his forty-years-younger foreign wife plied me with coffee and sweet biscuits. Poor girl, I think she must have gone home by now). The obituaries of House and Wade I had to write myself, after complaining to the editor (Haley), who promised to wake the department up. Ian Hay, by the way, got one-and-a-third columns because he held some high staff position in 1939. I didn't grudge it him, but as a writer he couldn't have 'rated' more than half a column. For many years Mrs Belloc Lowndes's husband was in charge of the 'morgue' at *The Times*. He was extremely deaf, and every day one of the sub-editors would fling open the door of his room and bellow: 'Any OBITS today, Lowndes?'

These last two days I have managed to get a little further with the new edition of Allan Wade's Yeats Bibliography, thus fractionally reducing the load of guilt which overwhelms me whenever I stop to consider all my literary-executor work that still waits to be done.

For Christmas an American publisher sent me an immense anthology of U.S. literature (mostly snippets) which would make a splendid bedside book if it weren't too heavy to hold. In it the other day I found a wisecrack of Dorothy Parker's. Some tiresome woman was being discussed, and it was said: 'Anyhow she's always very nice to her inferiors.' To which D.P. retorted: 'Where does she find them?' Which reminds me of D.P's better-known joke. When someone told her President Coolidge was dead, she said: 'How do they know?' I expect you knew both those already.

Last week I took my twelve-year-old to *Charley's Aunt*: it wasn't very good, but his agonised laughter made my evening. I also saw an excellent production of Ibsen's *Wild Duck*. To me he is one of the greatest dramatists, and this perhaps his best play. Are you interested in the theatre?

Tomorrow all the documents concerning the Heinemann merger have to be signed and sent out to my shareholders, who certainly won't understand them any better than I do. Most of the faithful creatures will certainly have mislaid their share-certificates—oh well!

Last night I re-read some of George Moore's *Memoirs of my Dead Life*, and found it just as gently and preposterously charming as of old. I'm sure this and the *Hail and Farewell* trilogy are his best books. What do you think of him? Or don't you?

Yes I did descry the beautifully assured skill of your tightrope achievement—surely *some* of the reviewers must have noticed it, though they have for once a goodish excuse, viz that after a score or two of pages the reader ceases, so to speak, to hold his breath, so entirely is the smallest *wobble* imperceptible. I remember once seeing Cinquevalli, and, after a bit, not wondering at all when he balanced a cue on his chin and *three* billiard balls on the end of the cue—so miserably evanescent is the sense of wonder. He would surely be knighted nowadays—and would deserve the honour much more than most others—having definitely done something which no-one could remotely regard as possible. In fact, sir, he has enlarged the scope of human potentiality.

Grimsditch as a reviewer's name is almost pure Dickens. What an outlandish choice to deal with one who after all had been a leading novelist in the minds of very many readers, and had been immensely more kind and generous to numerous fellow-men than Grimsditch, I suspect, ever was to his mother, still less his aunt. No doubt that obit-notice was his swan-song. *The Times* notices do seem very capricious. At one time Eton masters got much more space than they were intrinsically worth. Toddy Vaughan fans were with us for weeks, and there was really nothing to say about him except that he was literally the best of little men—*qua* character. But (as you know *ad nauseam*!) Mr Chips is always overpraised.

Your attitude to politics is very much the same as mine. Eden's 'toothy complacency' (thank you!) strikes a very thin chord after the melodious bayings of the old bulldog. Just imagine E as P.M. in 1940! I agree with you about Adlai S, but it was ludicrous and pathetic to see how bewildered and embarrassed the U.S.A. politicians were to find a candidate regarding politics as a matter of principles and ideals. He surely is of the Lincoln stamp (L a *superb* man. My father once had a gamekeeper *exactly* like him).

FitzGerald: *touché*. I've always rather prided myself on getting names right—never put a foot wrong with Ranjitsinhji or even Fetherstonhaugh. But I grow old, Master Shallow, though even *in articulo mortis* I believe I shall still remember that Attlee has two t's!

But perhaps you put one on purpose like one of Tennyson's Cambridge friends who always wrote oxford with a small o—mainly, as far as I recollect, because at Oxford they admired Byron more than Shelley. The modern Oxford don is not markedly full of 'sweetness and light', which M. Arnold (quite rightly) said was the *sine qua non* of all real civilisation. The Taylors, the Rowses, the Trevor-Ropers—they generally seem to be at someone's throat. Perhaps they always were. At Cambridge too they are pretty acid about each other. Not that dear Monty James ever was, and I fancy old Cockerell was never harsh to or about *him*. I found those letters—mainly *to* him—absorbingly interesting. There are some grand ones. Who on earth is or was T.H. White, of whom there is a quite mad picture? There is some lovely stuff from him, and I forgive him—as God will too in due season—for saying Bradman had an 'ugly' style. Palairet and Woolley were the Ciceros of batsmanship, Bradman was the Caesar—line, economy, precision, moving like *Euclid's* line, if you take my meaning. UGLY! My God! But never mind—any man may make a gaffe—in fact every man has—and there are worse than this. What a fine honest old fellow Sydney C is. That correspondence with Sister Laurentia goes straight to one's heart; the mutual understanding is a thing of beauty, or would be if that Keats expression hadn't been hopelessly hackneyed. And laughter came upon me 'like a sudden glory' at the schoolboy's most penetrating answer that Cosmo Cantuar was 'half-man and half-horse'. (William Temple would have liked that. He had a laugh like *all* the sons of God.)

And then the other book, the Henry James letters. As always H.J. half fascinates, half infuriates me. No one, surely, ever displayed the infinite resources of word and phrase as he does. No nuance of feeling or fancy, no undertone of even the faintest audibility, is beyond the reach of his pen. But when he goes on and on and on, unravelling every tiny strand in—often—some quite commonplace network—well now—again the illumination is splendid and satisfying (as on Pater, p. 178). But too often there is a great peacock's-tail of verbiage—no, what *is* the right metaphor? Shall we say a rich overture of melodious chords leading to no particular tune. Sometimes the not very uncommon event of his being late with a reply produces a positive flood of apology, self-reproach, explanation, that is very wearisome. One oughtn't to read too many of his letters on end. After all, each *is* a work of art. Old Gow[1] always said, no sensible man ever dreams of looking at more than a *very* few pictures when he visits a gallery. But I do put it to you that the letter to Hendrik Andersen on p. 228 touches the confines of what is bearable.

The two Dorothy Parker tales are first-rate—especially the one about Coolidge. Both were new to me. I know a few, some cruel enough, e.g. that on K. Hepburn's ranging the whole gamut of human emotions from A to B. K.H. must be a fine creature—fighting back with courage and success from being what the Yanks genially call 'box office poison'. Was it D. Parker who wrote that deadly little quatrain on some golf-course:

The golf-course lies so near the mill
That almost every day
The labouring children can look out
And see the men at play.

But if you quoted that at the bar in the club-house at Sunningdale, not a stockbroker would flinch. That, no doubt, is how they came to be stockbrokers and can afford to belong to Sunningdale G.C.

When are you going to have less on your plate, my dear Rupert? Whenever I have been behindhand with chores I found the resulting state of mind irksome and horrible—it was like being overdrawn at the bank. But I suspect you are too goodnatured, and there is no remedy for that. Yeats's bibliography must be enormous.

I envy you, going with the twelve-year-old to *Charley's Aunt*. I remember taking Humphrey to *Treasure Island*, in which his ecstatic enjoyment was only just not equalled by the horrid feeling that every scene brought the play's end nearer. I can remember my own delight at *C's Aunt* (also *aetat* 12). When the young man poured tea into the top hat, I felt that life had no more to offer. I used to love 'going to the play', but I don't hear well enough nowadays to make it worthwhile, and, you know, they *do* mumble more than they used to. Proof? I can still hear Edmund Gwenn and Marie Löhr, who learnt to speak when audibility was a virtue. But I still *read* plays with great pleasure,

[1] A.S.F. Gow, Eton master, later Fellow of Trinity, Cambridge.

though often mystified by the critics' enthusiasm over what seems to me tosh. But I don't say anything about it to anybody.

P.S. G.M's *Hail and Farewell* is one of my great favourites. Who was it described his smile as 'like sunshine on putty'?

29 January 1956 *Bromsden Farm*

Yes, Michael Sadleir noticed what you call my 'tightrope achievement', though he used another circus analogy: I (blushing, but only slightly) enclose a copy of his review: you might send it back sometime, and when I carry out my threat of driving you over here from Eton I shall inflict the whole glowing press-cutting book on you. My word, that will be a day!

If Hutton is knighted (sorry to jump about so—like a knight at chess perhaps—but I am re-reading your splendid letter and commenting as things come), if, I say, our Len receives the accolade, I shall rely on you to back my campaign to get Frank Woolley the O.M. Do you remember that willowy figure *leaning* on the ball and thus speeding it to the boundary? And was not Macdonald the most *beautiful* bowler ever? But you will probably bring up another candidate from an earlier day—and I have yet to see Tyson in action.

Times Obits. If you live to be old enough, you're sure to get columns: which perhaps partly explains Toddy V. How much space did Broadbent or Luxmoore get? W.S. Maugham, who satirised the benefits of longevity in literature so amusingly in *Cakes and Ale*, is now the most overpraised G.O.M. of letters since Bridges. A*tt*lee indeed! All square for the moment on spelling!

Scarcely had the Cockerell book been published when the poor old gentleman was taken off to hospital—I fear his last journey. Anyhow he got his copies of the book before Christmas, sent them all out, and received delighted letters from everyone. He has been bedridden and almost blind for years, and was very difficult to deal with. T.H. White is a madman of near-genius, used to be a master at Stowe, and rather shamefully dodged the last war by emigrating to Eire. Now he lives—and drinks—in the Channel Islands. He has written dozens of books. Yes, Dame Laurentia is the highspot of the Cockerell book—in fact I should say she *makes* it. The present Abbess is writing a biography of her, which John Murray is to publish, but I guess we've had the quintessence of her lovely nature here.

About my beloved Henry James I can understand but not share your feelings. You're right about his infinite verbal resources—never a word used accidentally—but you miss, it seems to me, a lot of the *humour* in what you condemn. Those trails of words covering nothing, or hiding his true opinion, spanning a vacuum, I find richly droll. Do you know this telegram of his, refusing an invitation:

IMPOSSIBLE IMPOSSIBLE IMPOSSIBLE IF YOU KNEW WHAT IT COST ME TO SAY SO YOU CAN COUNT HOWEVER AT THE REGULAR RATES ASK MISS ROBINS TO SHARE YOUR REGRET I MEAN MINE.

And did you ever read a lovelier letter of condolence than the one to Mrs Stevenson? You're probably right about not reading too many on end, though I can take any number.

I share your dislike of chores undone—'the unlit lamp and the ungirt loin'—but am now fatalistically accustomed to them, just as I am to the bank overdraft, which has been in existence ever since I can remember. Another letter from the bank manager yesterday—and in September my younger boy starts five years of Eton! How, a year later, the elder boy is to be kept at Oxford I can't for the moment imagine—but I have become adept at shutting the longer-term worries from my mind, and am prostrated only when they catch up with me in a rush, as the business worries did last year. Meanwhile literary chores loom up endlessly, and if I had leisure and quiet I should enjoy most of them. Last Monday I dined with Eric Linklater at the Savile Club; he is a dear fellow and most amusing. He promises this year to write a short novel for me to publish (I did one some years ago—*Mr Byculla*—and also a book of short stories). On Wednesday night I dined with two Jesuit fathers at Rule's in Maiden Lane (believe it or not). We began with a dozen oysters each and continued in similar style, talking a good deal about Gerard Manley Hopkins, whose copyrights belong to the Society. I was feeling gay, and in gratitude perhaps for being treated as fallible human beings, they blossomed handsomely. Otherwise there's little to report save the daily heap of correspondence and flurry of visitors in Soho Square. One lunch-time a friend and I took sandwiches to the new René Clair film, *Summer Manoeuvres*, which is wholly delightful. There's something rather attractively wicked about going to a movie at mid-day, particularly if you don't do it often. The sub-committee of the London Library, to which I afterwards hurried, seemed a trifle tame in comparison, and dear Harold Nicolson waffled more than usual. He had a slight stroke last year, but seems to have recovered completely.

Have just heard on the wireless that H.L. Mencken is dead: he could be very witty, as witness this remark from a letter to Hugh Walpole:

> Reviewing here [Baltimore in 1922] is a hazardous occupation. Once I spoke harshly of an eminent American novelist, and he retaliated by telling a very charming woman that I was non compos penis. In time she came to laugh at him as a liar.

Poor fellow, some eight years ago he had one of those strokes which leave you perfectly well but unable to read or write, and in that twilight world he has existed ever since. My friend Alistair Cooke, a great admirer of H.L.M., has been down regularly to see him.

1 February 1956 *Grundisburgh*

Now that is something like what I call a review. He has actually taken the trouble to see what the author was trying to do and get a clear notion of the nature and extent of the problem confronting him—and never once has he drawn attention to himself and how much cleverer he is than *hoi polloi*. The opposite end of the pole seems to me to be the sour young prig, anonymous, alas, who reviewed the S.C.C. volume in the *Listener* last week. He is *very* sniffy about most of the letters (not mentioning Sister Laurentia at all!). Thus G.B.S.'s letters in this vol. are 'of no permanent value', Max B. is sneered at *en passant* as a 'professional dilettante', no 'significant writers or painters of the period are represented', most of the letters merely prove that letter-writing is a lost art, and he ends with a pontifical dictum that nobody in the world has a right to make. All the other reviews that I have seen hit the appreciative nail on the head.

Wilfrid Blunt tells me that old Sydney is going rather rapidly downhill. W.B. likes the letters very much and *professes* to be delighted at being confused in the index with that majestic old libertine his great-uncle. G.B.S. of course never wrote a letter or p.c. that wasn't worth reading, and, as always, one piece of silliness or downright statement that is just not true, viz on p. 185 that people who get books for nothing never read them. Sheer bosh, anyway, as regards that shower of gifts from my fairy godmother imperfectly disguised as a leading London publisher. The Carlyle, a beautiful fat volume, has arrived and I have already browsed at large. As with all such compilations, I at once begin to pick holes about the omissions—like a peevish man before a magnificent banquet, 'Why are there no pigs' trotters or umbles?' But I miss some of the 'show pieces' in *The F.R.*, e.g. storming of Bastille and one or more of the death scenes and the splendid finale, the conflagration of all the gigs in the world. And shouldn't there be something from his noble essay on Johnson? In *Past and Present* the catechism entitled 'Pig Philosophy' can never lose its point as long as political economy holds the field. But perhaps Julian Symons deliberately chose less familiar passages. Not that any of T.C. is familiar to modern readers. They *will* think he is a philosopher or a historian, when, of course, he is a poet and dramatist of great power—and of course humorist.

I would not for a moment have you think I miss Henry James's *fun*, or at least a great deal of it. Two of my favourite letters are the one to Walter Berry about the suitcase, and that to John Bailey[1] refusing to join the English Association. But sometimes, no doubt, that iridescent cloud of words conceals from me, as it did from the recipients, the mischief that lurked in the affectionate smile. It is reassuring that Laski was even blinder than I. And George Moore too. To which your reply will be much the same as the Duke of Wellington's about the destination of Napoleon's bones, viz that you don't care one twopenny damn what either of them says. And my applause will not be half-hearted.

I entirely agree with you about Woolley. When he played a characteristic innings, anyone who saw it was temporarily unbalanced

[1] John Cann Bailey (1864–1931), literary critic, married George's aunt the Hon. Sarah Lyttelton.

and scorned the very notion of Trumper, Hobbs, Hammond, Macartney and Bradman. As I heard Charles Fry say, 'But for that hole in his defence, he would have been the greatest of all'. Macdonald, yes, was a lovely sight too, but you are talking to one who saw Tom Richardson, about whom N. Cardus wrote his very best article, though he seems to think—quite wrongly—that he has written better stuff since. What poor self-critics most writers are.

Did you know A.A. Milne? I met him twice at Cambridge half-a-century ago, but cannot remember his saying anything at all; he was extremely shy. I liked his *Punch* things, though of course the light-hearted 'Rabbits' belong to a long dead world, and all our John Wains and Amises would bury them deep in the lumber-room whose door bears the fatal damnation 'Escapist'. *The Times* says A.A.M. wrote two detective stories but I know only *The Red House Mystery*—a very good one, I thought, but I don't know that anyone else did. He must have made a packet out of 'Christopher Robin', though, according to Dorothy Parker, American children 'frowed up' when they read it—or perhaps only she did. Did the Yanks like your *Hugh Walpole*? Because Geoffrey Davson who wrote the life of his grandmother Elinor Glyn—with much skill and good feeling—was scolded by the American press for *not* guying her *à la* Lytton Strachey. Queer unpredictable people they are. Your Mencken tale is delicious—much better told by him than a similar situation is by Wycherley in *The Country Wife*. He was an entertaining writer, rather short in the temper I suppose. I once pointed out to old Agate M's fantastic adjective for Dr Johnson—'finicky'. What he meant no doubt was 'pedantic', i.e an 'outer' rather than a complete miss. I hope they will be meeting soon.

This letter is rather like human life as summed up by Hobbes, i.e. poor, brutish, and short. 'Solitary' too in a way, for we have no resident staff. All right in summer, but now taps and cisterns freeze away merrily with nobody to stop them. I bustle about rather futilely with paraffin and sacking, but no tap does anything but sigh in a forlorn little voice when I turn it on. It will be all quite different when you come in April even if the roof *has* fallen in, as it threatens to do.

The best news, my dear George, is that since last Monday morning I have, for the first time in many months, felt perfectly well. Tasks which have loomed impossibly for ages now seem nothing, and I have been pitching into the Yeats Bibliography like one o'clock. I don't know whether it was the cold weather (which in itself I detest) or simply the end of a particularly depressing trough of low pressure—anyhow it's an ill blizzard . . .

I can't say I knew A.A. Milne, though I met him sometimes at the house of his father-in-law, Martin de Selincourt, and saw him quite a lot at the Garrick. *Not* a likeable man, I should say. On top of great natural shyness he cultivated a deep grudge—against life, I suppose, though I can't imagine why. The combination rendered him pretty well unapproachable, at any rate by younger members. The son, Christopher Robin, a nice chap, now married and running a bookshop at Dartmouth, screams at the sight or sound of the famous children's books—feels, in fact, rather as Beachcomber did when he wrote:

> Crash! Bang! Nobody cares.
> Christopher Robin has fallen downstairs.

Whatever D. Parker says, the books were tremendous best-sellers in America. My *H.W.* had wonderful reviews over there, but sold scarcely at all. Reverting to Beachcomber, I daresay you never see the *Daily Express*, but twenty years ago when I used to see a lot of B in London (he is an Old Harrovian called J.B. Morton) he was immensely gay and amusing. One day when we were walking down an extremely crowded Fleet Street, he suddenly went up to a pillar-box and shouted into the slot: 'YOU CAN COME OUT NOW!' I liked very much his poem on Tolstoy, of which the refrain ran:

> He ran away from home when he was ninety,
> And his golden hair was hanging down his back.

And he summed up the jargon-bosh of art- and music-critics beautifully by announcing: 'Wagner is the Puccini of music'. He always told me that the readers of the *Daily Express* were (often understandably) unable to distinguish between his funny column and the rest of the paper. In proof he told how one day, short of a paragraph and late with his copy, he filled up the space with these words: '*Stop Press.* At 3.55 pm yesterday there was a heavy fall of green Chartreuse over South Croydon.' Next morning he received *six* letters from six people assuring him he was mistaken: they had all spent that afternoon in South Croydon and were positive that not so much as a drop of green Chartreuse had fallen! After that he gave up.

Thank heaven the thaw has arrived, leaks and all. I managed to keep the Soho Square flat tolerably warm, but the gas-pressure sank so low that I could get hot water only by boiling a reluctant kettle. Downstairs men with blowlamps battled vainly each day to thaw lavatories and washpots. I suppose your activities with sackcloth and paraffin are your excuse for not sending me your essays! Or was it sackcloth and *ashes*? I feel like a schoolmaster baiting the transmogrified Mr Bultitude.[1] 'Come on, show up your homework, Lyttelton, or I shan't send you any more of those lovely prizes!' Seriously, do send them along. And why not write a book of memories? You could beat old Jonah at his own game, bless him. That's exactly the sort of thing people love to read today. Please consider seriously.

My friend Janet Adam Smith (did I tell you about her?) has been asked by the Buchan family to write the 'official' life of John B. I think she'll make an excellent job of it, treating his life as a romantic success-story—from Manse to Vice-Regal Lodge. She knew and liked J.B. and has the necessary Scottish background. I've encouraged her to accept, and said I'd love to publish the book.

One joke last week. Someone (I don't know who), hearing that Randolph Churchill was on the *Queen Mary* with Eden, said: 'I suppose he's the camel to break the straw's back.' Otherwise too cold for witticisms, and a mercifully unsocial week. From tomorrow I have something every night, from which I shall hope to dredge you a few oysters, if no pearls.

[Here I was summoned to a new flood from thawed pipes in the kitchen. Water everywhere, and all the stopcocks labelled 'Key to the Gymnasium' or some such nonsense. All is now comparatively well, but it has grown late and I must creep to bed, leaving this letter short and dull.]

[1] In Anstey's *Vice Versa.*

Next week we will discuss the Sirens' song and the alias of Ulysses. Keep warm and cheerful, dear George, and write me another of your delicious letters. Goodnight.

9 February 1956 *Grundisburgh*

How *perfectly* splendid to hear that you are now really in health. It just makes *all* the difference, for when *that* fortress is secure the onset of practically any foe is seen to be, in the genial Rabelaisian lingo of the barrack-room, merely 'p—and wind'. (Is it ridiculously Victorian, un-Laurencian, un-Aldingtonian etc to be physically incapable of writing some words in full? I take heart from remembering that old Shaw said *his* pen simply would not write some of the words printed in *Ulysses*). Conybeare[1] always maintained that if you could sleep and eat, you had nothing really to complain of. I don't think that is wholly true, though he clearly believed it of himself. Often, when he played fives, his heart palpitated in a way that would have sent anyone else in a bee-line to the nearest specialist. He merely thumped his chest angrily, saying 'Go *on*, go *on*!' till his terrified heart didn't dare disobey. And, of course, even when he was still playing football, you could hear his ribs clattering like castanets as he pounded down the side-line. He cured a poisoned thumb by scrubbing it with a nail-brush till there was not only no poison left, but practically no thumb. A good man—would have been still better, if married. Not that that is true of everyone!

Of course, my dear Rupert, you must know very well that it is really *your* fault that my letters just go on and on like the drips through the ceiling from a burst pipe (how fresh and up-to-date our similes are!). *Your* letters are the cause of that, for as I told you, after reading one my head is a-bubble with comment, question, admiration, new things to think about etc etc. Would you have me burst like a cistern (again!)? No! Then I must cleanse the stuffed bosom at your expense.

John Raymond *not* very good on S.C.C's letters, in the *New Statesman*. Why is *charm* so suspect nowadays? Is the slum and water-

[1] A.E. Conybeare, Eton master.

closet side of life the only thing one can be sincere about? Or of course those dingy 'dark gods' of D.H.L. Raymond too praises Freya S. How delightful and reassuring I find your agreement with me! I agree that there are some odd little passages of commonplace and conventionality in Sassoon's letters, but nothing like enough to base an indictment on. And that strained, shrill sentence about T.H. White. Who, exactly, *is* J. Raymond? A novelist, a mandarin, what? He writes like one of those who in St Paul's (?) phrase 'consider themselves to be somebody'. Must I think the same of him?

What you say of Milne is very interesting. What grudge can he have had against life? I should have thought he was conspicuously a favourite of fortune's. But who can tell? The excellent Jonah, who has sent me his *Beyond Belief*, can't stomach the notion of original sin, which is one of the very few things that to me seem obvious, and the disbelief in which is surely at the bottom of much of our present discontents. Forgive this solemnity. It springs from my reading *Oxford Apostles* by Geoffrey Faber during the week-end, and not finished yet. *Quite fascinating*! I can't put it down, even, or perhaps especially, because my feelings about Newman steadily mount to a sort of nausea—or would if he were not so completely remote. All that passionate almost hysterical feeling about Mother Church, that unintelligible conviction that evangelicals who regard Christ's words as more important than those of Aquinas are 'deep in error and sin'. One cannot begin to agree or sympathise. I am in fact rapidly reaching the point which C.E. Montague did about Bourchier's Macbeth, that 'even murder cannot be as serious as all that,' substituting 'religion' for 'murder'. What *leagues* away we are from Newman's belief in eternal punishment, of which Jonah makes excellent, and wicked, and unanswerable fun. The really horrible, unworthy, and only-to-you-mentionable thought comes into my mind, that the right treatment of the young Newman was that coarsely advocated by a Guards colonel, as to what should be done with a new, rather namby-pamby subaltern: 'Put him to the stud!' and p. to the s. he was with, no doubt, the manliest results; he may even be a colonel himself by now. And then dear Dr Pusey, on whom the effect of Mrs P's death was that he would not lace (button) up his boots or shave regularly, and got steadily fatter! He was all for flagellation but reluctantly eschewed it because it gave him bronchitis. There is really no limit to the pathetic absurdity of these great men.

I don't see the *D. Express*, but Beachcomber nearly makes me. A darlin' man, as Joxer Daly would say. My son Humphrey's favourite writer. He will like the green Chartreuse story. I don't suppose South Croydon has much truck with irony—any more than an Ipswich policeman when the butcher from whom I got my sausages, hanged himself. I asked the policeman (who had told me the news) whether it was safe now to get sausages there, and he assured me quite gravely that all would go on as before! Rather gruesome, I grant you, but in Rome etc, and many parts of Ipswich are still medieval in atmosphere and sentiment.

That was a very ill-tempered little fling of winter last week. We had three bursts but were lucky as to place and time and avoided any flooding. There were some dreadful catastrophes in Woodbridge. One practically bed-ridden old lady with no staff except a daily (*not* on Sundays) was flooded at 3 am on Sunday, and had no idea at all what to do, except telephone wildly for the plumber who couldn't make head or tail of her incoherence (having American blood in her, she probably insisted on calling the stopcock the stoprooster). He eventually found her distracted and drenched, adding to the deluge with a ceaseless flow of tears. It really was a heart-rending tale. And now the thaw has come, we shall have the same story next year. The recently built houses are the worst, because lead-piping in 1956 is markedly inferior to that of 1856. Progress! Is there any mention of burst pipes in Newman's *Apologia*? There is not.

John Buchan I met once or twice and liked very much. His was really rather a wonderful life. Didn't he pay for every bit of his schooling and Oxford by scholarships and writing stories? What grit the Scots have! And with him there was none of their dourness and long upper lip. I knew a good Scot who putt the weight with me at Cambridge. He was a scholar, son of a blacksmith, who never would come to the C.U.A.C. dinners because he had no evening clothes. He was a friendlier chap than a fellow-countryman who made *no* friends. So some kindly souls thought to get him to join the Gaelic club. They called and he received them with silence (and a very bad cold). They were eloquent about the fun and friendship he would get from the club. He said no word till they had finished, then in a hoarse bronchitic croak, 'Is McTavish a member?' Ah, his one friend! 'Yes, yes, indeed he is, he—'. 'Then A'll no' join'.

12 February 1956 *Bromsden Farm*

If you studied your *Times* last week, you must have seen a number of references to the most devoted of your correspondents. At midnight on Tuesday they rang up to ask whether the news of the Heinemann merger was true: I said yes, and they printed a paragraph about it on the middle page on Wednesday morning. Later that morning Pat Ryan (the No. 2, who does most of the work and is a first-rate journalist) rang up to say that he and the Editor were most interested in the whole thing, and would I give them an interview! I said I'd never heard of an interview in *The Times*, but it was their paper and I was agreeable. So that afternoon, after a meeting of the committee of the Royal Literary Fund, I had a cup of tea with Ryan at the Garrick and talked about post-war publishing. Afterwards he scribbled down a few words and said he'd telephone at 6.30 and read me the result. This he faithfully did, and apart from a word or two there was nothing to alter. I complimented him on his accuracy, and the interview (only slightly cut) duly appeared on Thursday morning. To round off the week, the Third Leader yesterday morning, which was in fact about something else, began: 'This week an ineluctable process has been carried a step further: another young publishing house, high in reputation, has joined up with an older firm.' So you see I have, however dimly, been in the news!

Where else have I been? Spending an evening with the Linklaters on their way to Kenya, giving lunch to a wild Welsh clergyman-poet, having a drink with Nancy Cunard in Jimmy's Bar at the Café Royal, dining at Putney with the Arthur Ransomes, visiting Viola Meynell just recovered from pleurisy, attending the fiftieth birthday of my old Oxford friend Harman Grisewood (who was head of the Third Programme and is now Second in Command of the whole B.B.C.), interviewing an American publisher, driving through snow and ice to eat an excellent luncheon at Heinemann's printing works in Surrey, taking the chair yet again at the Society of Bookmen—just a routine week, you see, and from the look of my little engagement book next week will be worse. Yesterday I corrected the proofs of a whole novel—a good historical one translated from the French—and in the evening my wife and I battled our way to a cocktail party at the Osbert Lancasters', some four miles away. They were obviously 'working off' all the locals, and the room was soon hot, smoky and noisy. Of all so-called entertainment the cocktail party, it seems to me, has least to be said for it. Nasty sticky little drinks taken standing, no proper conversation, nothing worth while to eat. Anyone that one *does* want to speak to is immediately seized away by somebody else—I'd much rather stay at home and write to you!

My son has suddenly been made Brigade Transport Officer, and although he was presumably chosen on merit, the appointment neatly puts paid to his fortnight's winter sports and his week of home-leave at Easter. It is a Captain's job, and if they only give him the rank—and, more important, the *pay*—he may feel compensated. I don't know whether National Service officers can rise so high: I never heard of it happening before. He writes gaily and at great length about skating, goose-shooting and the opera in Düsseldorf. Youth is a splendid thing.

Now I shall read your splendid letter again. Who is John Raymond? you ask. A plump young man of thirty or so. The son of Iris Hoey and a light comedy actor called Cyril Raymond. He works on the literary side of the *New Statesman*, under my friend Janet Adam Smith, and is generally on the side of the angels. Very agreeable to meet and extremely intelligent.

I've long meant to read *Oxford Apostles*, and your words may well bring me to the sticking-point. G.F. has for many years been struggling with a book about Jowett, which should be interesting too. You so often touch on questions of religion that I should perhaps tell you that I believe in none of it. I hope you won't be distressed, as I fear Jonah was when I told him. Original Sin, yes, but the Resurrection of the Body, etc, no. Don't think that I wouldn't like to believe: of course I would, and of course I realise that the lack of belief is at the bottom of most of our troubles to-day. Clearly one can go only a certain distance by intellectual ways—the final step must surely be an act of faith. I seldom go to church, but I like it when I do—the hymns and the wonderful words and the general *Gemütlichkeit*—but I simply don't believe a word of it. Not an Atheist, you know, but an old-fashioned Agnostic. One could hardly fail to be interested in a subject at once so fundamental and so fantastic, but I am generally too busy to spend much time on it. You must write an even longer letter, please, and tell me your own views.

I was sad to read of Jelly's death yesterday. He was a darling old fellow, much beloved by all his old boys. I'd like to go to his funeral, but fear it may not be possible. Now I must read a manuscript about elephants in Burma. Did I tell you I have agreed to make (for love) a 300-page selection of Edmund Blunden's poems for Collins to publish? The first copy shall be yours. Do you know his poetry? *What* a lot we shall have to say in April!

15 February 1956 *Grundisburgh*

I missed your interview in *The Times*, and for the best of reasons—it wasn't in my copy! I have just searched it, keenly alert for anything relevant. 'New hope for the Leper' detained me for a moment (Carlyle might easily have called a publisher a leper!) but not for long. Then there was the news that after all you were not to be the new Bishop of Coventry, nor to represent Australia in the coming summer. Nothing else seemed remotely relevant, and I think they played their old game of omission or addition in their late issue, which is the one we get. I saw the Third Leader, and, not for the first time, vaguely wondered what exactly the word 'ineluctable' meant. It has no more a positive than e.g. 'disgruntled' though P.G. Wodehouse made happy play with 'gruntled'. I guessed the leader was about you. And I hope, now that you are happily launched on calm waters, that the result will shortly be visible in a stream of books on the *Hugh Walpole* level, written by a mind entirely at rest in a sturdy and eupeptic body.

I suspect that when your background is tranquil you really rather enjoy your pillar-to-post existence which would send me potty in a month—not that a surprising degree of pottiness cannot be achieved by a vegetable life in Suffolk. *Some* of those you meet must be good value, even at cocktail parties (what a delightful number of likes and dislikes we have in common!). My loathing of these silly gatherings, insipid beyond words for both mind and body, is, I am glad to say, a local scandal, so I rarely get asked. I think my hosts are rather grateful really—so much less liquor to provide. Is Harman Grisewood related to the mellifluous Freddie? The BBC is in rather rough water at the moment. I wonder how my old fag Sir Icicle Cadogan is facing it. Calmly, I am sure. After all he dealt for years with Vyshinsky and Molotoff without a hair of his impeccable head being either lost or ruffled—any more than he did when I found fault with his toast in 1899. He could write some very interesting F.O. reminiscences, but he won't. I asked him once and he said he never wanted to think of any Russian or many U.S.A. diplomatists again.

I wish I knew your son. He sounds a fine chap. Goose-shooting, then the opera, that is life worth living. How admiringly, wistfully, enviously, Marlovianly one could write about youth. Had, by the way, that ghost of Conrad's any prototype or was he another Jedediah Cleishbottom, or Housman's mysterious and absurd Terence?

I am glad to know about John Raymond, as I dimly remember thinking something of his well above the usual standard of *N.S.* young men. Raymond Mortimer once told me, when he was running the literary side, that he was always toning down their asperities. I remember Arthur Benson's comment after reading a derisive and ill-natured review of a book of his in the *Cambridge Review*. 'Yes,' he said meditatively, 'that is the ugly side of youth—pleasure in giving pain'.

Religion—yet another matter on which we agree. The notion that any views of yours could shock me is fantastic. (But let me anticipate your riposte that you think meanly of people who say they are *unshockable*; especially young women who usually mean that they have read the *Decameron*.) Let me try and shock *you*! Like P.G.W's Russian novelist on his colleagues, I spit me of the Virgin Birth, not merely as untrue, but as dehumanising Christ and making his life really pointless. Very crude and juvenile etc, I admit, and *think* of the great men of infinite wisdom and subtlety who have believed it! But I can't help that. As the Japanese student said 'A man must float on his own bladder', so there it is. I wonder at Jonah being shocked, as he doesn't believe in Christ's divine origin as different from that of all of us. He is particularly infuriated by the insistence on the Almighty's demand and liking for *praise*. George Herbert's 'But oh Eternity's too short to utter all Thy praise' throws a grim light on life after death—at any rate in heaven. And apropos of that I can't help thinking 'Oh ye ice and snow, praise ye the Lord' as absurd as any human utterance. My eccentric uncle Albert's substitution 'Oh ye strawberries and cream' (when the page was out of his prayer-book) was surely no more outlandish. Legend has added 'Oh ye bacon and eggs', but that is going rather too far, as Watts Dunton said about the story that Swinburne wanted to tell Max Beerbohm.

And 'believe' is much too big a word to use about life after death. I vaguely feel, I occasionally hope, but that is all. That great man Judge Holmes surely hit the nail when he said 'I see sufficient reasons for doing my damndest without demanding to know the strategy or even the tactics of the campaign.' Was anyone *ever* influenced in his conduct by thoughts of the next world? I don't believe it. And how right you are about the outstanding beauty of some of the liturgy. I still feel hot anger at the memory of Jackie Chute altering 'indifferently' to 'impartially' in that wonderful prayer of Cranmer's in the Communion service 'Almighty and ever-living God'. You may (no I don't think so) say it was a venial substitution, and the rhythm was not gashed as those coxcombs (as W.E.G. called them) the Revisers did when they altered 'charity' to 'love' in *Corinthians*. But, gosh, the sermons! or at least nine out of ten, though I have heard good ones (the best ever, I think, at Eton, from George Birmingham!)[1]. I expect you agree with Birrell who said that the glow of a good sermon always made him regret that religion was not true. Bad ones put me in such a rage that my wife says church, which I attend pretty regularly for much the same reasons as you, obviously does me more harm than good. But it doesn't when I read—as anyone can who takes any trouble—to an entirely attentive audience the story of Absalom's death, Elijah in the wilderness, *Job* chapter 28, the last chapter of *Ecclesiastes* and many, many others. But, Good God, what a troll. I might be in a divinity school 7.30 Monday morning. My excuse is that, in your words, anything so fantastic and so fundamental keeps on surging up in one's mind at the oddest times, and one of the points

[1] The name under which Canon J.O. Hannay wrote many popular novels.

(there are *scores*!) of this wholly delightful correspondence is that anything and everything which does that must be communicated. 'All occasions invite His mercies, and all times are His seasons', if any apology be needed!

Jelly's death was very peaceful and quite unexpected; though no doubt very fragile, he was entirely himself, and as you know, I saw him a few weeks ago and gave him your love, which clearly pleased him. He had been a little tired and not read his *Times*, but as he finished his beef-tea, he said 'I think now I will read a book' and as his man was helping him to sit up, he just died—like a bird dying. A very good way to do it. 'Many the ways, the little home is one'. And now presumably he could tell us all about it, though, dear Jelly, he would take his time about it! He was sound old oak throughout. To be immensely high and even rigid principled, inflexible, and kind-hearted ought not to be a rare combination, but somehow it is. No one was ever more respected and indeed loved.

19 February 1956 *Bromsden Farm*

What a magnificent letter! I got home tired and cold on Friday evening, changed into my old (perhaps I should say 'older', for my London ones are by no means *le dernier cri*) clothes, and sank into my chair by the library fire with a glass of whisky and hot water. And there, to complete my enjoyment, was your letter (which often dawdles till Saturday). I savoured it luxuriously with my whisky—what a treat!

You didn't miss much in that *Times* interview: indeed I can quite see that it was thought rather too exciting for the far-flung *abonnés*: everything to its own place. Do you remember (irrelevantly) how A.B. Walkley was sent tickets for a play at Richmond, and returned them to the Editor with a note saying: 'I was engaged as *The Times* dramatic critic for central London, not for Asia Minor'? (I expect it's in Agate somewhere.) The trouble about what you so rightly call my 'pillar-to-post' existence is that I *used* to enjoy it immensely, but now do so less and less. It's such an expense of spirit in a waste of gin-and-prattle—but it's certainly easier to endure when one's feeling well. Here are a few snap answers to your questions. Harman Grisewood is a distant cousin of the ineffable Freddie. Marlow, I fancy, had no prototype: I've always imagined (without any concrete reason) that perhaps, writing in a foreign language, Conrad found it a help to, as it were, push the narration one degree away from the first person. Perhaps Jonah wasn't really shocked, and in any case I mollified him by listening to an hour or two of spiritualism. I saw the old pet last week. He and Evy were at dinner with Robert Lutyens in his beautiful new studio off Victoria Street. Do you know him? He is a gifted man—has been musician and architect, and is now quite a good painter. His sister, Ursula Ridley, was there too: a lovely person. Jonah seemed in good heart: his next volume, *An Edwardian Youth*, is in proof, and he is now starting a third. Ursie told us that the reception after one of her sons' wedding was held at Lumley Castle (they live in Northumberland), and during a moment's pause an old friend of the family was heard loudly proclaiming (with rolled R's): 'This is the r-room in which years ago I pr-roved that it is impossible to be r-raped!' And while we're on funny stories, I can cap your delightful Japanese saying with another. E.S.P. Haynes once told me of a Japanese lawyer who sent him some man with a glowing letter of recommendation, extolling the fellow's gifts and versatility, and ending: 'In fact, as you would say, he has a finger in every tart.'

But we must return to religion. How splendid that we feel the same about it all. Anticipations of heaven (even Sydney Smith's 'eating *paté-de-foie-gras* to the sound of trumpets') always seem to me almost as forbidding as foretastes of Judgment. I'm all for a good sleep, than which few things are more consistently enjoyable. R.I.P. seems to me the nicest wish one can make for anyone. I much like Judge Holmes's remark. I must certainly read that correspondence), and have nothing to say in favour of the Revised Version of the Bible. The miraculous language of the Authorized is surely one of the luckiest things that ever happened in English Literature.

Jelly's funeral service was in every way suited to his spartan integrity (no comfortable chairs allowed in boys' rooms). Chapel was arctic, and the serried rows of beaks swaddled in scarves and overcoats looked scruffy but well-meaning. Some of the old guard (Dobbs, Young, Cattley) looked like shrunken and frozen replicas of their old selves. Quite a decent sprinkling of old boys, and the west end of

Chapel looked reasonably occupied. The service itself was utterly Jelly in its lack of concessions to the weaker spirits. The psalm was unsingable by the layman (one of those in which the caesura seems to shift disconcertingly), the hymn was unknown and very dull, the prayers inaudible. Only the Provost's clear, firm reading of the familiar words from *Corinthians* touched the imagination, but as the dear old fellow's coffin was carried out I thought sentimentally of the tens of thousands of times he must have attended Chapel, and was glad I had come down to bid him farewell.

Last week wasn't too bad, though I'd had enough of it by Friday. I entertained two of my many widows, one to lunch and one to dinner at the Garrick. I've been reading the *Life of George Moore* by Joseph Hone—a difficult job very well carried out. Charles Morgan was chosen by G.M. to be his biographer and sat at the old man's feet for years taking notes and asking questions. When G.M. died Lady Cunard refused to let Charles see her letters from G.M., and Charles, believing them to be essential documents, gave up the biography, which Hone took on (still without the letters). (Charles afterwards summed it all up in a first-class little book called *Epitaph on George Moore*.) It is these same letters to Lady C. that I have now got hold of, and want to publish (after I've brought out the short memoir by Lady C's daughter Nancy). There are 270 surviving letters, and I can see no reason why they should have been withheld—though I suspect she may have destroyed the vital letters of the first few years. I think Charles believed they would solve the riddle of G.M.'s impotence or otherwise. Those that remain do not, but they do show that Lady C. was in many ways the love of his life, and they present a much more sympathetic portrait of him than any I know. Lady C. was a vain society woman, who bothered about him less and less as he grew older. The whole situation reminds me of Landor's poem to Ianthe: you know, although she wouldn't bother about him,

> I have since written what no tide
> Shall ever wash away, what men
> Unborn shall read o'er ocean wide
> And find Ianthe's name again.

Do you admire Landor as much as I do? The Moore letters will need careful transcription (he could never spell or punctuate) and some annotation: just the job for me! But I still have Yeats and Hopkins on my plate, and the Oscar Wilde letters, and the 300-page selection of Blunden's poems—phew! I often think that if I had even one day with nothing else to do, I could write you a letter that might get within sight of your own splendid ones—what a hope!

23 February 1956 *Grundisburgh*

What, in the last resort, is there to be said for February? A positively whoreson month surely, and why did that admirable adjective ever drop out of the language? Or, for the matter of that, the superb Chaucerian verb to 'swink'.[1] It wouldn't do in the welfare state of course, though no doubt good men do swink in the fields and coalpits. The real idlers are to be found in the building world—as the excellent bricklayer who lives in our garden admits. He is a striking exception—loves doing his work well and quickly. He left his recent master because this wretch told him that a particular job must be 'made to last till Thursday'. My chap—an eccentric in 1956—held that, as it could easily be done by Tuesday, this order was dishonest. 'What laughable simplicity' was his mate's reaction. But he will come out on top on the Judgment Day—or would if there was one when 'the ungodly, filled with guilty fears, Behold His wrath prevailing'. Why so cross when He knew they would behave like that and in fact made them so that they were bound to?

As to Conrad's Marlow, I expect you are quite right; it is easier in many ways to put an invented character in place of yourself. One of the (to me) few remarks of Wilde's which is more than a bit of verbal fun was, 'Man is least himself when he talks in his own person. Give him a mask and he will tell the truth'. A mask is a hiding-place. Shakespeare could always say that Hamlet's notions were not his.

I am glad Jonah's book is well on the way. I presume it is all about Oxford. Are there any good university novels? *Sinister Street*? or Stephen McKenna's *Sonia? Tom Brown at Oxford* was a flop. But then fundamentally Hughes was an ass, which old Jonah certainly isn't. I

[1] To toil.

don't really know him at all well, and am always surprised to find how many people find him an old *bore*. Do you subscribe to that? His touch in print is not at all heavy.

I can't quite make out from your rape story how the lady proved its impossibility. Miss Tishy in *Jonathan Wild* was about to be ravished when, 'by a timely compliance, she prevented him.' Apropos, I remember a trial for rape at Ipswich before old Humphreys who died last week. It was a clear case, but the jury said 'not guilty' as in East Anglia the conviction is very strong—fortified by numberless events in the war years—that no girl can be raped if she doesn't want to be. Humphreys, to the scandal of a legal friend with me, asked the foreman how they had arrived at their verdict, and subsequently discharged the defendant with the words 'You're a very lucky young man'.

As to heaven, why has nobody ever faced the fact that immortality *per se* is intolerable whatever we shall be doing in it, unless we have minds and bodies and tastes and faculties so different from anything we can imagine that it isn't worth talking about. There will probably be something, because 'this pomp of worlds, this pain of birth' looks, by and large, so very futile if it is all there is. And Judge Holmes didn't think there wasn't any strategy, only that he couldn't begin to see what it was. I am glad you liked his remark; I knew you would. He strikes one almost at once as a first-rate man—using that adjective sparely and only when it is deserved. You will also like him on George Moore, 'that delightful blackguard G.M. He simplifies the steps to copulation as Raphael does the mountain in the Transfiguration.' I am delighted to hear about these letters. As 'dear Edward' Martyn said when asked about G.M's good qualities, 'He hadn't any'. Max was kinder, but then G.M. had not made an ass of him as he had of dear Edward. I expect E.M. was right and that G.M. lied, and backbit, and fornicated (in the spirit if not in the flesh!) whenever he had a mind to. But as a writer! I can't do *The Brook Kerith* and some others, but *Hail and Farewell* is a constant delight. A fatal book to open—you just go on and on, oblivious to all else. Do you remember how he proved to his brother the Colonel what a bad writer of English Newman was? A heavenly passage. I wonder how he got past Peter at the gate. C.M. Wells's chief objection to St Paul was his abominable Greek. Perhaps he has purified it now. In any case the lingo presumably is some celestial kind of Esperanto.

I like your vivid little picture of E.L.C's funeral. I wonder who chose the psalm and hymn. Musicians probably, who are mainly mad. I remember Elliott (H.M.) shewing me a list of hymns and asking me what I thought it was. I perused it and decided it was a list of the most popular hymns. No. It was the hymns the swell musicians wanted omitted from the new edition of A. and M. Practically all were retained. 'Scruffy but well-meaning' is *fine*. But it cuts deeper than for this occasion, being in fact a pretty accurate epitome of the whole tribe of us at all times. But of course the times are scruffier. Ainger never washed up; Luxmoore never wheeled a pram; Broadbent never shovelled snow from his roof. These things make for scruffiness. You won't, I hope and think, mind a certain amount here on your visit. The fatted calf shall be on the table, but the table will be in the kitchen, or if warm, the room next to it which has risen in life from servants' hall to staff hall to dining-room—much as a barber has to hairdresser, chirotonsor, and now I believe to 'appearance engineer'—in Noo York of course. You must look at our hospitality much as you do that tie or tea-cosy from your aunt at Christmas, i.e. not at the thing itself but at the feelings behind it.

To revert to the important topic of George Moore's impotence. Alexander Woollcott suffered from the same suspicion. Do you remember the rather repulsive letter of triumph he wrote to somebody over the proof the previous night had vouchsafed that the suspicion was false? James Agate told me that he had often been likened to A.W. but not I imagine in this particular disability. Woollcott records in one of his books his high appreciation when my colleague Booker was summoned one Sunday afternoon to his kitchen where his cook had been murdered, and on seeing the body, asked 'What dangerous clown has done this?' Somerville's cook too was murdered and the intrepid man went to the kitchen armed with a niblick. It is the Windsor barracks which provide these thrills; the hero of *The Ballad of Reading Gaol* had cut the throat of the Eton postmistress who had jilted him. Sixty years ago this summer. But I expect you knew all that.

Landor—yes immensely good in bits, but after a few pages my

attention wanders. That marmoreal perfection—something cold and hard—what is it that chills me? Whenever anything of his is quoted, one is tempted to read more, but then one soon stops. But you are in good company. Swinburne and John Bailey knew what was what, and you won't mind Coleridge saying L had 'never learnt to write simple and lucid English'—on a par with his announcenent that Tennyson knew nothing about metre. That Ianthe quatrain is lovely. I must ask old Gow what Housman thought of him.

A mad world. Today I get a box of assorted confectionery from Callard & Bowser (to G.W.L. and two others) because C & B are in some mysterious way connected with a company of which my brother-in-law is a director. I knew nothing of this company but am a trustee of his marriage settlement, and presumably ought to send packets of butter-scotch to my fellow-trustees. The accompanying letter is signed A.E. Allnutt. The letter s should clearly be added. You probably know all the ropes in such matters. What shall I do? If you ignore my question, I shall send you a square or two of naked toffee, and await your reactions with interest.

26 February 1956 *Bromsden Farm*

February is indeed a whoreson month, and I share your regret at the disappearance of that admirable epithet. Its current American counterpart, sonofabitch (often abbreviated to s.o.b.) is a poor substitute. Incidentally it is a word which the visiting fireman should use with circumspection, since by means of emphasis it can be used to express every shade of disapproval, from affectionate raillery to utter loathing. 'Swink' too is an excellent word, which we must revive. In your list of university novels you forgot *Zuleika Dobson*. No, I wouldn't class Jonah as a bore—far from it—though there are a few subjects from which it is advisable to head him off. But doesn't that apply to us all? History doesn't relate *how* the lady proved the impossibility of rape—forgive my skipping about so; I'm re-reading your excellent letter and commenting as I go. I agree that without some sort of after-life this one is futile, but why shouldn't it be? Many of the most agreeable things are. I notice that when people can think of no other reason for the existence of heaven and hell, they usually fall back on the futility of everything without them, but I can't accept that as an argument. It's agreeable to hope, with Judge Holmes, that there is a strategy beyond our comprehension, but I can't see it as more than a pious hope. Which reminds me: do you know Belloc's unpublished ballade about Mrs Willie James, one of Edward VII's ladies? The *envoi* runs:

Prince, Father Vaughan shall entertain the Pope,
And you shall entertain the Jews at Tring,
And I will entertain a pious hope,
But Mrs James shall entertain the King.

I can't tell you how much I'm enjoying the transcription of those George Moore letters: you'll enjoy reading them, I know. A great many are undated and one has to rely mostly on internal evidence to give them a year, and if possible a month. Luckily the old boy generally referred to the book he was writing, which is a great help. I lunched on Thursday with C.D. Medley (aged 85) who was G.M.'s friend and solicitor and was left all his copyrights. He is a charming old chap, completely on the spot and full of good stories. His account of the burial of G.M.'s ashes on the island in Lough Carra was uproarious. He is delighted at my suggested plans, so it looks as though I can go straight ahead. I feel rather guilty about Yeats and Blunden and all my other tasks—but they'll get done in time, and just now I'm so full of G.M. that I can do that faster than anything else. Let's hope no new project arrives too quickly! I didn't mean 'scruffy but well-meaning' to be as derogatory as all that: it well describes myself, if it comes to that, and I no longer feel at home anywhere where the phrase doesn't apply. So have no fears about my April visit—and I'm an ace washer-up! What magnificent sidelights you throw on literary and other history: I had no idea of the connection between Oscar Wilde and Eton. Were cooks everywhere likely murderees—or only at Eton? You're dead right about Landor: I meant to say in my last letter that he is tolerable only in bits. But what about *this* bit?

'Do you remember me? or are you proud?'
Lightly advancing thro' her star-trimmed crowd,

Ianthe said, and look'd into my eyes.
'A *yes*, a *yes* to both: for memory
Where you but once have been must ever be,
And at your voice Pride from his throne must rise.'

wouldn't you love to have written that? I would.

You must of course eat the butter-scotch (or pass it on to your grandchildren—didn't I notice the arrival of another last week? many congratulations) and write a fulsome letter of thanks, so that part of your Christmas present nuisance may be solved this year. What else can I tell you? The Lit. Soc. on Tuesday was agreeable. Tommy Lascelles sits at one end of a long table, I at the other. On this occasion Tommy thought it was his duty to take on Cuthbert Headlam, and I was happy between Sparrow and Jo Grimond, Liberal M.P. for Orkney and a most agreeable Etonian, more than ten years my junior. Next to him was Donald (now Lord) Somervell, who has literary interests and is most friendly. Across the table from him loomed the benignant but deadly form of Lord Dunsany, who will bore you to sleep on the subject of rock-salt if you give him a glimpse of an opening. Nugent and Fleming were there, charming as usual. I attended several other parties, none worthy of comment.

Next week looks mercifully clear, so perhaps I'll be able to get on with some of my literary work in my flat. On Wednesday I shall go to Christie's to watch the sale of Allan Wade's books, and to bid up any lots that look like going too cheap. I simply *love* book-auctions, but am so easily led astray at them that I don't generally even get the catalogues. If I ever become rich. . . . I can think of no circumstances in which I could ever have *enough* books about me, let alone too many. It's some sort of collector's mania, I suppose. This house is bulging with them, and still they come. I am getting on with the arrangement of E. Blunden's vast collection in Soho Square, with much enjoyment.

1 March 1956 *Grundisburgh*

My uncle Edward, with towering and characteristic exaggeration, used to say that a problem which had, since civilisation's dawn, baffled all the profoundest intellects of Christendom was—how to combine a full household attendance at family prayers with a hot breakfast. Well, without going quite so far as that, it is a constant puzzlement to me why the Russian leader should be always pronounced by our pedantic announcers as Krusch*o*v if spelt 'chev', or conversely, why spelt 'chev' if pronouced 'chov'? A small matter you will say—quite rightly—but so is a very small stone in one's shoe. Are the Russian vowels different from ours—like the Hebrew ones—with the fatal result that Luther and Co decided that where our A.V. puts *a*, the letter *i* is nearer the Hebrew, so Samson in the German bible becomes *Sim*son, and the Gates of Gaza were carried off by a bank-clerk in spats and a bowler hat. How careful we should be about letters. Tim Nugent must have told you how some good batsman, disliked by everybody, was reported as 'making another four past extra-cover—a perfect sh-t', and unluckily printed *i* for o in the last word. Well, once again the rather degraded little word 'thaw' has become the most beautiful in the language—greens and browns again outside the window in place of that leprous white. And of course our drive is of the constituency of a haggis. All the ways are very 'slabbery', as Swift says,—or 'stolchy 'which men of Suffolk say, going one better than the Dean.

Yes, of course, I grant you *Zuleika* (does it go on a *little* too long?) and of course there are others. I don't or didn't think E. F. Benson's *The Babe B.A.* was very bad, though no doubt it would read very absurdly now. And *Julian Home* by good Dean Farrar. How I did enjoy *St Winifred's* at the age of twelve. Also Talbot Baines Reed's *The Fifth Form at St Dominic's*—superb. They all drank like fishes and bullied like SS men, but were as pure-minded as the lilies of the field.

I grant you, also, that the futility of this life, and none after death, is not an *argument* at all, but surely the *feeling* is so strong and universal that only men like Professor Hogben and Julian Huxley think it should be ignored. And that immensely omniscient and fearfully silly Jack Haldane. I accept your expression 'a pious hope'. To so many of us that *is* pretty well all it amounts to, but it seems to me an unconquerable one which we must nurse, though to our dashing young intelligentsia that is mere 'wishful thinking', which for some reason has been elevated into the sin against the Holy Ghost. I never know quite why the drains are nearer the heart of truth than the dew, or facts than fancies. Both these last, of course, *can* be very dangerous.

I am delighted to hear the George Moore letters are well under way; they will be great fun. Yeats and the rest must wait. G.M. would, of course, have had 'an uproarious burial'. Is Hone's Life good? I have never read it, though I believe I met Hone years ago in Horace Cole's room at Cambridge. As so often when Irishmen are present, the evening ended with a free fight, the ammunition on that occasion being mainly the enormous stores of fruit—pineapples, melons, etc—which Cole always kept. Luckily somebody, earlier in the evening, had had the foresight to hide his shillelagh and his buttonless foil, the one with which he converted Leslie Stephen's son Adrian to Christianity—till he got back to his rooms, sported his oak and immediately apostatised.

Wasn't that an excellent review of your Carlyle book by Peter Quennell? One of the few who appear to realise the old crab-apple's purely literary magnificence; his portraiture is surely unsurpassable. I wonder if it would have been if he hadn't had all those gastric ulcers. It is or used to be the fashion to overpraise *her* letters, which to me have an overdose of ill-health and domestic servants. It was only recently that I came across a trenchant verdict by someone that she could be a relentless bore with her protracted Scottish stories. A formidable pair they must have been with their united dyspepsia and insomnia and nerves.

Yes, that is just what *I* like about Landor—a six-line jewel; it couldn't be better. It shall go into my book—which I ought to have begun to keep fifty years ago, but like a fool didn't. Of course it would have had a lot of rubbish in it, but what does that matter? Did *you* go through a stage when you thought 'We are the music-makers'[1] the finest poem in the language? I still think puppies must and ought to have a period when they roll in rich, soft mud, and at sixteen or so a boy should be enjoying lush, highly-coloured, 'vox-humana-with-tremolo' stuff. His literary muscles will be all the better for going through rather than round the exotic, scented jungle. To colleagues who said that florid writing in adolescent essays made them sick I used to say to be made sick was one of the things they were there for.

[1] By Arthur O'Shaughnessy.

Apropos of which please tell your friend John Raymond that to put in print 'paterfamiliae' as the plural of paterfamilias demands and deserves the verdict of the great Bentley on some scholar's emendation or translation—'it is enough to make a man spew'.

The butter-scotch mystery has not been solved but it is shortly going to be—as the Gordian knot was loosened—by my grandchildren eating it. You probably know Callard or at least Bowser—not to be confused with Hodder, Stoughton, Chatto, or Windus. Where do such names come from? I had a friend at Cambridge, a very good man, who, poor chap, blushed every time he introduced his fiancée—Miss Sadie Smucker. Do you remember how pleased *The Times* was when the chief figure in some stormlet in a naval tea-cup turned out to be Bandmaster Barnacle—and again later on, when a boxing referee, who came within an ace of being justly lynched, was called Lou Magnolia?

Jo Grimond I never really came across at Eton, but good men have always spoken well of him. Those literary dinners must be fun, though I suppose, like old-boy gatherings, the most regular attendants *are* the bores. I could have warned you against Dunsany forty years and more ago, even then a tremendous talker, on much less interesting topics than rock-salt. Is he otherwise a good chap? So many bores are. Dear old George Chitty, for instance, with his hollow, booming voice. Once in an evening here he suddenly said 'Have I ever told you the origin of parish boundaries?' I said no, and unwisely forbore to add that *not* to know about them was much the happiest state. He then began. In three minutes Pamela was asleep, in five I was, and soon after he was himself. So if *you* want to know the o. of p.b. when you come here, you will be disappointed.

4 March 1956 *Bromsden Farm*

How often, in things great and small, we seem to agree! I too am irritated every time the announcer says Krushchov. I've always understood that Russian words and names, like Arabic, can be transliterated only approximately, so that Turgenev and Tourgeneff, Mohammed and Mahommed are all equally wide of the mark. If so, in God's name why not, as you say, transliterate them phonetically? Irrelevantly this reminds me that William Nicholson, the painter, once said to me (apropos of his son Ben's militant Christian Science): 'If the doctors knew a little more about religion, and the clergy a little more about medicine, it wouldn't matter which you consulted, as long as you had a good nurse.'

Was today springlike in Suffolk? I walked to the village (for the papers) in bright sunshine. One yellow crocus is blooming in the garden, many snowdrops, and my wife reports seeing a goldfinch: perhaps spring is after all not so far behind. I so agree about 'wishful thinking', which, together with 'escapism', is one of the most agreeable, and indeed profitable, of pursuits. This is the first week-end for ages on which (largely owing to the printing dispute) I have not been burdened with proofs—or manuscripts. After dealing with a batch of George Moore letters I made a little progress with the Yeats bibliography. The dating and annotation of the G.M. letters is the greatest fun. Some fifty still remain undated: of them a few must always remain so, since they contain no clue, but most of the rest I hope to pin down. When I have time to discover in the London Library details of the programmes of the various Leeds Musical Festivals (luckily only triennial, dates in the new Grove, files of *The Times* in the basement), at least two more letters can be dated.

This sort of mild literary detection in a good cause suits me to perfection, and I'm still finding it hard to concentrate on less interesting themes. If you're really going to start up your commonplace book again, I must find you some items. Of course I revelled in 'The Music-Makers', and still rather suspect the taste of anyone who didn't. I thoroughly enjoyed the toffee, but can claim acquaintance neither with Callard nor with the delightfully named Bowser. The first firm of solicitors I ever consulted was called Smith, Rundell, Dodds and Bockett, and even then I appreciated the pedestrian opening into such Dickensian heavy weather—better than Dodson and Fogg, I should say. An Oxford friend of mine had (still has) as his full name George Cospatrick Duff Sutherland Dunbar. Isn't that a pentameter or something like it? I'm sure Dunsany has a heart of gold, but one seldom gets much further than the rock-salt, with which his waistcoat pockets are stuffed. Chitty always *looked* the most awful bore, but I never spoke to him, and so missed the soporific of parish boundaries. Talking of Eton, I am once again incensed at the way in which boys are entered, or not entered, for houses. I had a lot of trouble with Fred Coleridge over the elder boy, and now exactly the same thing is happening once again. To start with, if one puts the boy down the day he's born, the housemaster's list is already full: most people seem to enter gleams in their fiancée's eye! Then the child is provisionally accepted. A year or two before he's due to go, one asks for more definite confirmation, and each time I have been assured (verbally) that all was well. Then, six months before the boy is due to arrive, I have each time been told that he's twelfth man, or one place off the guaranteed list—by which time it's much too late to do anything else. I bullied Fred into taking the first boy (who did very well) and am now attempting to bully him again. I quite see that housemasters must insure against 'wastage' by entering more boys than they can ever take, but I think that all the time the parents should be told exactly how matters stand. Does this happen in all houses? In all schools? I somehow don't think it applied to G.W.L.'s.

Last week was delightfully uneventful. Only one wedding reception (Rosamond Lehmann's daughter's), where I found myself breast to breast with all literary London, shouting and sweating in a small room in Park Lane. I fled after half-an-hour, just as they were going to cut the cake. On Wednesday I sold the rump of Allan Wade's books at Christie's (on behalf of his widow). They did quite well: the total was just short of £300. Next day I received no fewer than four invitations: to respond for the Guests at the annual dinner of the Antiquarian Booksellers' Association in May (yes): to address some foreign booksellers on publishing for the British Council, 5 guinea fee (no): to speak on 'anything' to the Oxford (Undergraduate) English Club, 'just a short talk, about 55 minutes,' no fee (no): to write an article of 1200–1400 words on Post-War Publishing for the *Financial Times*, fee *20 guineas* (yes!). I accepted the first for love, the last for money. My father was much delighted at being introduced to the Lord Chief Justice at Pratt's the other day, and being asked by that worthy whether he was 'the publisher'! Notoriety may have its advantages, but I'd much rather remain anonymous—except of course to a few very *cognoscenti*.

Spring is still just round the corner here. Seen through a window, it seems to be in full career, but one step outside the door a disillusioning breath from Finland checks the staves which the first real day of spring sets me trolling. We can't match your goldfinch. I don't think in any case goldfinches think much of East Anglia. And of course as bricks and mortar spread like blight, the bulbul which used to swarm, 'hollerin away fit to bust' as the village publican put it, prefers to remain in Persia or Arabia—or perhaps has even migrated to Buckinghamshire, and floods 'those reverend vegetables', as Gray called the beeches of Burnham, with his tireless melody.

Hopkins, like Yeats, is another man in whom you must educate me. I retain in my memory (or half-retain) a rich little passage about Oxford a 'towery city . . . cuckoo-echoing, bell-swarmed, lark-charmed, rook-racked, river-rounded. The dapple-eared lily below thee'. That's the stuff. I hope Wystan Auden (an absurd Christian name?) will put that in his pipe. But I don't go all the way with dear Dr Leavis, who, I read, said somewhere that there was no English poetry between Shakespeare and Hopkins. How *can* a man be such an ass as that? Where did I read that there is an excellent cheap and perceptive commentary on Hopkins? Please tell me, if you know. I am at present in the senile stage of not understanding modern poetry. I have *not* descended to the next stage, viz saying it is all rot, and hope I never shall. I never *was* any good at French poetry—quite tone-deaf to it, though I could always see the lovely precision of French prose. Old John Bailey was very fond of both. Every Sunday throughout his life he learnt a passage of prose or poetry by heart, and declaimed it half aloud. French was often on his lips. My commonplace book is always being fed nowadays, when my memory weakens steadily, as of course it always does. Send me any first-rate stuff you come across. Your taste so often chimes with mine, and almost certainly is far better when it doesn't. How could it be otherwise when you are in continual contact with men like Cuthbert Headlam and Lord Dunsany? That was a lovely solicitors' firm; 'Dodds and Bockett' are perfect. Did you ever read Samuel Warren's *Ten Thousand a Year*? (I have never met anyone who had!) The solicitors in it were Messrs

'Quirk, Gammon, and Snap'. But that Peacock habit with names is often tiresome—though I rather like 'Mr Going Gone' for the name of an auctioneer. How good Conan Doyle was at names. Jephro Rucastle and Colonel Lysander Stark have a fine villainous ring about them. But, Gosh, how thin some of those stories are. Even in the best, e.g. 'The Speckled Band', the house alterations of Dr Grimesby Roylott (another superb name) could hardly have helped rousing suspicion. But his women are simple souls mostly, even though one outwitted Sherlock himself.

Is Angus Wilson a good man? I see he reduces *The Forsyte Saga* to dust and ashes in last week's *New Statesman.* How jealous they all were, and still are, of Galsworthy's immense vogue. And the line they take is always so lofty that they miss the main point—that so many of his characters do strike the ordinary reader as being live men and women, and one reads on wanting to know how they got out of their difficulties, and usually satisfied with the way they do it, and with G's comments, and elucidations, and undertones throughout. And I'll eat my hat if 'Indian Summer of a Forsyte' is not a beautiful and moving bit of writing. But what *frightful* contempt our highbrow critics pour on that view.

And I *will not* be bullied into reading Jane Austen over and over again, as the David Cecils and others say one ought to and they do. And I *will* say with my last breath that Miss Bates in *Emma* is a *shattering* bore, Mr Knightley only just not a tremendous prig, and Emma herself vain, conceited, and unamusing—and indeed crying aloud for smacks on that area of her person which no doubt she would rather have died than allude to.[1]

Are you coming across some resounding 'gaffes' in George Moore? D. MacCarthy somewhere hints that G.M. had really read very little and that mere deliberate mischief played a great part in his dicta which listeners were glad to have for their wit and sometimes were shrewd enough. 'What is Conrad but the wreck of Stevenson floating about on the slip-slop of Henry James?' is beastly good, though (of course) unfair. But how I do enjoy the old rascal; how attractive are

[1] cf. 'I may have confided to you that, bar Miss Bates, I was bored by *Emma.* I feel bound to test your friendship by this blasphemous admission.' Mr Justice Holmes to Sir Frederick Pollock, 27 September 1929.)

complete absence of principle and an unlimited love of mischief, both apparently quite unselfconscious!

I agree with you entirely about entering a boy at Eton. It is often quite maddening. You must be firm with Fred Coleridge; your lad, having had a brother in the house, *must* have a stronger claim than others on the list. Housemasters do get so spoilt when sought after as C. is. It is worth remembering that parents who really do make a fuss always get their sons in. There *are* difficulties, of course, and the Winchester alternative is not attractive, i.e. boys entered on one list and doled out to housemasters. Parents don't know what house a boy is going to and have no choice. Gaitskell, Cripps, Crossman and Douglas Jay obviously all went to the wrong one.

11 March 1956 *Bromsden Farm*

I don't know which commentary on Hopkins you have in mind, but I have most of them and will seek you out something suitable. The interesting thing is that his poetry (although not published till 1918 or much read before 1930, when it had an appalling influence) was in fact written in the Victorian heyday, 1860–80. He was a great original, but you're right in condemning Leavis's pronouncement as bosh. Why do you irritate yourself with Leavis at all? I don't. I enjoy the Sherlock Holmes stories enormously still—not for their plots but because of the delicious period atmosphere of hansom cabs, fog, gaslight, muffins and all the rest of it. And for some of the splendid dialogue—'Hand me my rattan, Watson.'

Angus Wilson is highly intelligent and a wonderfully good mimic. Until recently he was in charge of the Reading Room at the B.M., but has now retired to devote himself to literature. He's about forty. His new novel, I'm told, has been chosen by the Book Society, so his retiring gamble looks like coming off. I read *The Forsyte Saga* in 1929 when I was driving through France and Spain with Peter Fleming, and thought it very good indeed, though when I went on to read the sequel, *A Modern Comedy*, I thought that G's touch grew less sure with each succeeding generation. He knew his contemporaries and his immediate forebears, and he fell in love with his cousin's wife: that gave him the outline of the *F.S.* Later he had to rely on his creative imagination, which by itself wasn't powerful enough to mask his ignorance of his juniors: perhaps if he'd had children the later books would have rung truer.

My George Moore work goes busily on. In most senses of the word he was quite illiterate—couldn't spell, punctuate or form letters, shied at the simplest proper name, was ignorant of the most elementary facts and books, etc—but behind it all, without pause, he was, the 'dear addicted artist' (as your friend Auden said of Henry James) devoting his whole life to the production of literature, careless of all else. He re-wrote his books on every set of proofs and for every new edition: a great part of his income must have gone on printers' bills. His bibliography is one of the most complicated you can imagine. I'm sure you'll be much touched and interested by these letters when you read them.

Fred Coleridge seems to have been stunned by my last firm letter: at all events he hasn't attempted any sort of come-back, and I only hope he hasn't just mislaid the letter. Why does Winchester produce all these Socialist leaders? Though I suppose we can't speak, with Dalton, Strachey and his Lordship of Pakenham!

Last week I dined out twice, once with the Chairman of Thomas Tilling Ltd (used to be a bus company and now owns most of Heinemann). He is a most remarkable man called Lionel Fraser, aged sixty. His father was Selfridge's butler, though you'd never guess it, for Lionel has the classless distinction of many Scotchmen. He is chairman of several other huge companies and is very rich. His two boys have been to Eton. All this amalgamation is his doing. Anyhow he and his wife gave me an excellent dinner in their rich flat in Lowndes Square. I'm told Lionel was a gay dog in his day, but now he and his wife are teetotal, non-smoking Christian Scientists—perhaps it's his wife's influence. Nevertheless they plied me with first-class sherry, claret and brandy, which among glasses of water made me feel like an inordinately heavy drinker.

The other dinner was purely bibliographical—at the Garrick with John Carter (late K.S.), John Hayward, and Tim Munby (late of Sotheby's, now Librarian and Fellow of King's, Cambridge). All great bibliophiles, and the talk was of 'issues' and 'states', collations (not of the eating kind) and bindings—great fun. On Wednesday I had a nauseating lunch with an old traveller in Tibet (survivor of Younghusband's expedition of 1904) at the English Speaking Union. All the food seemed to have been drenched in vinegar, or indeed in the wine which tasted of vinegar—ugh! Next day I attended a solemn conclave at the Oxford University Press to discuss Hopkins's *Notebooks*, and eventually persuaded them that the only hope of getting the job done is for them to find a qualified student (perhaps an American living on a fellowship grant) to do it under my supervision. If that comes to pass it will be an enormous weight off my mind. I have sworn to polish off the Yeats bibliography by the end of April. That will leave only the George Moore (a brief and easy task) and the Oscar Wilde letters (a much bigger job). Then perhaps one day I'll start writing another book of my own: I think of it occasionally in my bath.—Now I must have a shot at that article for the *Financial Times*, and I've sent you nothing for your commonplace book, only a lot of commonplaces instead. Bear with me, dear George, and don't restrain your gay and witty pen, for I am in constant need of just such deliciously diverting commentary as you bring me at the end of each week.

14 March 1956 *Grundisburgh*

The man Leavis, and why do I bother about him. I have just been at Cambridge, and things are even worse than I thought. Most of the young men teaching Eng. Lit. in our schools are disciples of his, and *all* American students think he is the cat's whiskers—the main reason, they tell me, being because, according to him, there are so few books worth reading, which, of course, is good news for students. And, my dear R., the real sin against the H.G. is *teaching the young to sneer, not* in saying 'Thou fool'.

I enjoyed my week-end, as I always enjoy the converse of academic folk, its great merits (what John Morley said of Mark Pattison applies to several dons I know: 'the ineffable comfort, in his company, of being quite safe from an attack of platitude'), and its delightful and absurd occasional childishness. One night I stayed at King's where dear

George Rylands and the Provost, a charming man,[1] told me that in some dispute at the Fitzwilliam old Gow was really being very tiresome and obstinate—and indeed very rude, none of which I had any difficulty in believing. The next night I was at Trinity, where Gow told me that the Provost of Kings 'had behaved like a cad', which, *me judice*, he was clearly incapable of doing. That Housman blend of an impossibly lofty and unsympathetic standard with needlessly abusive words is really very regrettable and unhelpful. Though, no doubt, a little astringency is an essential ingredient in an intellectual society. Too much '*O Altitudo*' is horrible.

Old George Trevelyan was in hall. He is rather deaf, and sat for the most part eyeing his plate with a sort of aloof and brooding ferocity—a look as of thunder asleep but ready. And once or twice it flashed and rumbled finely, e.g. at the recollection of the way in which *The Times* treated Abraham Lincoln at the beginning of the Civil War. Isn't that grand—unappeasable wrath at injustice however ancient? I believe if someone had recalled how Ulysses outwitted Ajax over the armour of Achilles we should have had another cloudburst. (I asked George Rylands if he knew you; yes, but not well, I gather. But he did say, *sans phrase*, 'Easily the best publisher in London', so there!) Your Heinemann tale is fascinating; there can be very little in common between managing a bus company and managing a publishing business, or even butlering for Selfridge; it is as incongruous as a prominent boxer (Gully) becoming Speaker of the H. of C. Do you think, if the acute eye of Lionel Fraser had lit upon you years ago, he might have spotted you as cut out for a bus conductor—or still earlier as one with the perfect touch for mixing a salad or 'frapping' the champagne? I expect he might have. You all-round men can turn your hand to anything.

I agree about Galsworthy. Anyone ought to be able to see how good his picture is of late Victorian times, and indeed of Victorian figures; those Forsytes are *very* true to life—some of them hardly distinguishable from relatives of mine. And, though still, to me, immensely readable, his touch in the later books was insecure. Too stiff in mind and spirit I suppose. Nobody seems to have been tremendously fond of him. But you know, lit. criticism hasn't got beyond, or has reverted

[1] Stephen Glanville.

to, the old Jeffrey, Croker, Lockhart habit of using words, not of disagreement, but of abuse and contempt for those who like what the critic doesn't and *vice versa.* Angus Wilson says G. is admired now only by 'the more stuffy of academic critics' and 'of course' foreign professors, and 'conventional middle-class readers'. What is this but narrowness and conceit? It is emphatically the Leavis note (sorry!). Raymond Mortimer is a refreshing contrast and *can* estimate fairly what is not really to his taste (surely the hallmark of a good critic?). Oddly enough, Housman *could* do it. I remember some review of his of a book by old Saintsbury. H. had some legitimate laughs at that bubbling, caracoling style, but quite warmly praised his essentially sound judgment. Did you see R. Mortimer's review of Henry J's letters in the *Sunday Times*, and didn't you think it first-rate? I have cut out and pasted in the paragraph in which he deals with the common charge of wordiness—a very perceptive and convincing passage.

And of course that passion for 'getting the thing down in the right words' gives George Moore the dignity of which, apart from it, I imagine no human character ever had less. One's admiration for a hangman may be very small indeed, but Pierrepoint's indignation at the bungling of Ribbentrop's execution rather warms one's feelings towards him. I would in fact gladly have bought my beans and peas at the shop he ran between-whiles.

I will push the Wykehamist problem a little further past the question Why are they Labour-leaders to Why are most of them such *prigs*? Cripps, Crossman, Douglas Jay all share an indefinable smugness. We had several O.W.'s at Eton and many had the same taint—to the great impatience and contempt of others who hadn't, and in fact were very good men. It is, I fancy, and always has been too close a community with little fresh air from outside. I suppose too that to be in a minority and rather clever often makes the prig. Dalton, Strachey, Haldane? And only the last was a Colleger. John Carter I recollect as an excellent chap (English Extra Studies of course!), a contemporary of John Maud's, who to my simple mind was so nice that he has been widely suspected of insincerity by nearly everybody else. 'Charity suffereth long', said St Paul, and I fear she has succumbed to her torments and no longer exists. With which insufferably brilliant kick of verbal heels I take my leave of you, and you go back, shaken, but resolute, to your financial article—which Lionel Fraser will read and at once put you at the head of the financial department. Do you remember the man whom H.G. Wells smothers with scorn in some book because after his first in 'Greats', fellowship etc he didn't know the difference between 'deferred' and 'preferred' shares?

18 March 1956 *Bromsden Farm*

Your letters, unlike mine, get better and better. This last one, with its account of your Cambridge outing, is especially good. That glimpse of Trevelyan in Hall is a fine flashlight portrait. I agree with what you say of Raymond Mortimer's breadth of sympathy, or tolerance and lack of priggish superiority. I first met him on a raft in the Mediterranean off the Cap d'Antibes in 1926, and we have been friendly ever since. I see him at London Library committee meetings and he's always most agreeable. Your references to A.E. Housman are timely, for I've just had submitted to me (and am half-way through reading) the manuscript of a biography of him by an American called Watson. It's decently and painstakingly written, but so far I doubt whether it adds much to what Gow, Laurence Housman and others have already told us. Some day there will presumably have to be a final consideration of that grim and thwarted existence, but I'm not sure this is it. To help me make up my mind I have to keep referring to the other lives and studies (all of which I've luckily got), so it's taking up rather a lot of time.

What can I tell you of last week? On Monday Peggy Ashcroft came to the flat for a drink. She is rehearsing for Enid Bagnold's new play *The Chalk Garden* and was gay and friendly. I can never quite get over the oddity of seeing someone you were once married to and now seldom see. I can *remember* exactly what I used to feel about her, but I don't feel it any more—just a deep and tender affection surrounded with memories. All rather moving and agreeable.

On Wednesday I lunched agreeably (though the food is v. moderate) at the Athenaeum with John Lehmann, and on Thursday I was taken to a cocktail party given by the literary editor of the *Observer*, a jam-packed gallimaufry in which I spoke *inter alia* to Arthur Koestler, Lord Montagu of Beaulieu and Gilbert Harding. The latter told me a delightful story. During the recent visit of the *Hamlet* company to Moscow, old Ernest Thesiger was missing for several hours, and the other actors feared for his safety. When he eventually returned unharmed he explained that he had been trying to buy some chalk with which to write on the wall of the Kremlin: BURGESS LOVES MACLEAN. Now I really must have another shot at that ill-fated article, and if next week you receive no more than a postcard, you'll know that I've won through and been promoted to the headship of the financial department!

21 March 1956 *London*

I always rather hate London—so noisy, and crowded and inhuman. All those countless faces of the great army corps that streams out of Victoria at 9 every morning, practically indistinguishable from each other, being all the same colour, all expressionless, all knowing their day's work will be boring. Who was the young man in Kipling, who 'trod the ling like a buck in spring, And looked like a lance in rest'? Well, he was never in this crowd. My bedroom has a good view of the Sloane Square crowd. I am interested to see how many young women share the illusion that a woman goes any faster when she runs than she does walking. I shall take an early opportunity of telling old Gow that the best judges are agreed that the Provost of King's is a first-rate chap, and beseech him by the bowels of Christ to think it possible that he may be mistaken. He can be as vitriolic as Swinburne sometimes and I shouldn't be surprised if he has on occasion begun a letter in the style of S's to Emerson, as reported by himself: 'I reminded him that he was a toothless ape. . . .'

Talking of judges I spent this morning in the court of Mr Justice Hilbery. Not very interesting. A lot of talk about how far a stiff ankle reduces the agility of a foreman-plumber. Hilbery pooh-poohed a good many of the points of both counsel, which I suppose shewed his impartiality; he is one of the rather grumpy, mumbling judges, but I believe not a bad one. I heard him once holding forth to great purpose in dismissing a claim for compensation to a man who had fallen off a perfectly sound ladder. 'Nowadays if a man chokes over a biscuit he sues the confectioner; it is all rubbish'.

Did I ever tell you the howler I came across in E Trials? After the Israelites had crossed the Dead Sea they were to erect a memorial of stones and . . . when they ask 'What mean ye by these stones' . . . etc. Give the context etc of 'What m.y.b.t.s.' Answer—'These words were spoken by Agag when they were stoning him to death'. What a patient and good-tempered impression this gives of A.! Do you, by the way, know Housman's two great pieces of prose—the letters from the University to King George V on the death of his mother and at his jubilee. The second *is* I think in one of his brother's books about him, but the first is hard to come by and if you don't know it, I shall copy it out and send it.

C.M. Wells's[1] 85th birthday party was very pleasant, though of course the table has many ghosts round it. *He* looks a well-preserved 55. I sat next to him and again besought him, as I always do old Plum Warner, to string together the really rich reminiscences from behind the scenes of their cricket life. Plum W. *will* fill his books with stuff like 'I shall never forget the wonderful hospitality of the Governor of N.S.W. and his gracious lady', which one could write without going nearer to N.S.W. than the lavatory at Victoria, when what would be of lasting Pepysian interest is to hear what Darling said to Trumper when he had a devilled cold pork-chop for breakfast on the morning of the Test Match—like that yokel Tom Wass when to his lbw appeal the umpire said 'not out' on the grounds that the ball would not have hit the stumps, Wass said 'It would a' had all three b——rs out of the ground'. But half the journalists and indeed book-writers don't know the difference between what is interesting and what is not. I have just read two books of outstanding interest, viz *The Tudors* and *Queen V. and her P.M.'s* by a *really* crusted old Tory, Algernon Cecil, but obviously an immensely able man—now dead. My brother-in-law Leconfield convinced him that Lord Melbourne was the son of L's ancestor Lord Egremont (who was the father of almost everybody) and it was going to be in the revised edition of the book but A.C. died too soon.

[1] Former Eton master.

'Half the journalists', you say, 'and indeed book-writers don't know the difference between what is interesting and what is not'. Never in your long and valuable life, dear George, have you uttered words more profoundly true. Nor can they distinguish between the relevant and irrelevant, the amusing and the dull. But the gift of so distinguishing is surely just what we mean by 'taste', and ours is not, alas, an age of taste. William Nicholson, the painter, once told me he met an old man in the train who confessed sadly: 'My trouble has always been that I can't tell one thing from another': an extreme case, no doubt, of the current malady. Sometimes as a publisher one is able to tidy writers up a little, removing their worst excesses, but many stubbornly persist in their idiocy. Lord Egremont would be an admirable subject for biography, had not some pious descendant destroyed most of his papers.

On Wednesday I dined late with Rosamond Lehmann and took her on to a party given for Diana Cooper in the palatial house of Edward Hulton. Among pictures of incredible value and beauty we found some thirty or forty members of high society, drinking champagne and waiting for a conjurer, who turned out to be excellent and prevented one from having to talk too much. I eventually got home gratefully about one a.m. Next evening I had to preside at the annual Ladies Night of the Society of Bookmen—some 120 people in evening dress at the Café Royal. Elizabeth Bowen, the guest of honour, spoke admirably, beating down her stammer by will-power. I had to do quite a bit of speaking, and this too passed off well, though I had prepared nothing. More than ever am I convinced that after-dinner speaking, like so many other things, is a matter of practice, and the conquest of nerves which practice brings—particularly if one knows one's audience well. It's satisfying when one pulls it off, but I'd be delighted if I never had to do it again.

Now in the midst of George Moore, I'm grappling with the proofs of Peter Fleming's *Spectator* pieces, and also, most incongruously, with a typescript collection of unpublished letters by William Beckford. I published his Portuguese journal for the first time a few years ago, and I suppose I'll do these letters too, though I have never found B's personality even remotely attractive. That coy mixture of bric-à-brac, homosexuality and self-pity leaves me cold, though I must admit that he could write beautiful English. The standard life of him was written by my friend Guy Chapman: I brought it out when I was at Cape's and reissued it from RHD Ltd after the war, so, however unwillingly, I seem to be Beckford's modern publisher. Incidentally, his father's house still stands at the corner of Greek Street and Soho Square—a convent or some such. Have you, by the way, read Guy Chapman's excellent book on the Dreyfus Case? If not I'll send a copy straightway. There must be lots more books on the firm's list that you'd enjoy: I'll send the list and hope you'll speak up.

This letter is the dullest I have ever written—to you or anyone else. Once long ago at Duff's house, I asked Belloc what he was writing. Rolling his French R's he replied: 'I am wr-riting a book about the Cr-rusades so *dull* that I can scarcely wr-rite it.' Bless him, I know exactly how he felt. H.B. was a wonderful talker, but I thought Edgar Wallace even better. Did I tell you of my acquaintance with him? I've got to the stage when I can't remember what I *have* told you! Pray you, forgive and forget. Perhaps the four days of Easter will find me less tedious.

29 March 1956 *Grundisburgh*

This correspondence is the centre, the apex, the zenith of my week. If there were faint signs of scrimping towards the end of my last letter, I will now tell you the odd reason—I was having intermittent bouts of nose-bleeding, of all childish complaints. *Not* due to blood-pressure or apoplexy, though of course, like all who are rarely ill, I was convinced it must be, but merely a very normal weakness of veins in the nose which often attacks the elderly; one's handkerchief wildly exaggerates, and when I said to my doctor, 'Who would have thought the old man had so much blood in him,' he was rather shocked, and said blood had a way of seeming much more than it is—obviously the reply which Macbeth ought to have made to his lady. Not that I suppose a little cauterizing would have done much for Duncan.

Now, before anything else, your visit. Next week one platoon of grandchildren arrives; they go on the 24th, and in any case are in a caravan which almost doubles the capacity of the house. Another slightly smaller platoon will be here when you arrive on the 24th, and there will easily be a room for you, and as to meals, as my wife says quite truly, one more or less makes no difference, and she much wants to meet you. It is always possible, however, that your feeling about children is the same as that of a man I knew at Harlech who, when their happy cries reached his ears in the club-house bar, uttered his simple *cri de coeur*: 'I should like to break their bloody little necks'. He was a tireless and conscientious drinker, and Nature saw to it that, as such, he should have the thirstiest conceivable name—Saltmarsh ('Curse Nature' said Bat Masquerier; 'she gets ahead of you every time'. And if B.M. rings no bell I shall explain it in the same tone of voice as that in which Sidney Webb told D. MacCarthy what the initials L.G.B. stood for. A further clue. B.M. went on to say, 'To think that *I* forgot hymns and a harmonium'.) On the other hand, you may share the view of a greater man than Saltmarsh or even of B.M.'s creator, who 'dearly loved a knot of little misses'.[1] You must be quite frank. You and I will not really be harassed by them. We shall tire the sun with talking, but shall not be put off by a happy yell or two.

The Law. Yes, whenever I have a free morning in London I haunt the Queen's Bench. Why? Because at least four times in six there is good entertainment, as Max Beerbohm found. What is the theatre or county cricket in comparison? A good cross-exam or even more a summing-up gives me intense pleasure. But I hear less well than I did, or else the judges mumble more than they did, and I am often tempted to call out 'Speak up', thereby emulating the bravest man *I* ever heard of who, as Lord Russell of Killowen began his summing-up, said to him 'Make it snappy, old cock', and evoked a tornado of wrath which would have flattened a forest. Unluckily it was last week near the end of the term when they mostly have non-jury cases. The jury not only provide much of the fun, but as every single member, male and female, obviously comes straight out of a George Morrow drawing, judge and counsel have to speak clearly and simply. I never, now, go

[1] Dr Johnson.

to the criminal court, though I have in my time seen three murderers at close quarters, one being Brides-in-the-bath Smith, a very unattractive looking man, who from time to time hurled coarse and abusive words at counsel and witnesses. But as a man on trial for his life cannot, obviously, be committed for contempt, the judge merely reminded him mildly that he wasn't doing his case any good, and reduced him to mutterings, which, being close by, I understood were directed mainly to casting doubts on the legitimacy of the judge's birth, which even a layman like myself could see were irrelevant.

I enclose the Housman speech, having already copied it into my book. To me it seems very fine. The sentiments in such a speech must be conventional, and *every*thing depends on the phrasing, which, again, must not be either reach-me-down or far-fetched. Devilish difficult. And I suppose our young critics would call it by some such name as 'Mandarin' English. Among the many boundaries that are almost daily being submerged and levelled, that between dignity and pomposity is one—like that between sentiment and sentimentality. I read last week a rather deplorable book by Hesketh Pearson and M. Muggeridge called *About Kingsmill*, because I always liked K's writings (not novels) and noted scores of shrewd and witty remarks. And this wretched little book does him no sort of justice, but goes on tediously recording the loudness of his laugh, his sovereign scorn for politics, war, science, sport etc, his inability to suffer fools gladly (the most unlovable trait) and quotes too many of his sayings that are merely undergraduate wit.

And now I am embarked on D.H. Lawrence's unliterary criticisms, undeterred by noting on one page his stating that Shelley's poetry was 'a million thousand' (sic) times more beautiful than Milton's, and by pages of, quite literally, intolerable babblings about pornography. I ask you, is anything in life or literature, past or present, in earth, heaven, or hell, anything more devastatingly tedious than D.H.L.'s interest in the human genitalia? But presumably a great many not wholly unintelligent people are taking it seriously. On other topics too he can be—to me—almost unintelligible, but that may not be his fault! But I should like to test some of his intenser admirers thus—shew them a bit of poetry that he quotes and ask them 'Is he going to praise this to the skies or blast it with utter contempt?' I don't believe they would often be quite sure! But there ought to be a close time for talk about D.H.L. just as, more often than once, there ought to have been about Shaw, whose absurd will is now to be in the news. I don't understand why Jim Pitman, a very pleasant and sensible fellow, should be supporting that imbecile thrusting upon us of a new alphabet, or what *any*body supposes would be the great gain thereby. But I get cross about too many things and people! My God! your last week would have polished me off, and I should now be sipping beef-tea with the blinds down. But I should have enjoyed the conjuror, remembering how often I have seen them perform *sheer* miracles—no other word. The things they did were *not possible*.

A little sojourn for you among us Suffolk yokels should be a rest from what must be practically continuous cerebration. William Beckford is a new one, isn't he? I remember only one thing in *Vathek* but it has always pleased me—some monarch was a little queasy and 'of the x number of dishes placed before him he could taste of no more than thirty-two.' Like that other good trencherman (some old actor) whom J. Agate loved to quote, detailing what he regarded as a good dinner, with the parenthesis 'counting fish as nothing'. My *Vathek* has vanished—borrowed probably by a boy and not returned. Did B. write finely? I have forgotten. I haven't read Guy Chapman's *Dreyfus Case* and should love to. But, my beloved Rupert, how can you make the fortune that is your due if you give away books like this? If I was remotely like a really good man I should austerely refuse to profit so blatantly from your generosity, but, as I have told you, I just cannot pretend that they (and you) don't give me endless pleasure. I have just re-read with the greatest pleasure *The Next Million Years*[1] which comes from the great firm. I always enjoy books which make practically everything anyone does or says now of complete unimportance. I hope it sold well? I have some memory that several reviews shewed the same sort of reaction as they did some forty years ago when Inge derided democracy and was instantly dubbed 'the Gloomy Dean'. And *all* his misgivings have been underlined by events. But reviewers, like, in fact, almost everyone, want to hear 'smooth things' and throw stones at Micaiah the son of Imlah. Perhaps less so in '56 than in '06.

It shews you the state of my memory when I tell you I can't

[1] By Sir Charles Darwin.

remember if you were at Oxford. Because I am gently pointing out to Oxford friends that their great university has suffered the last humiliation, viz being universally hailed as heroes for losing the boat race by less than had been expected.

Easter Monday, 2 April 1956 *Bromsden Farm*

The moveable feast has shifted my letter on a day, but I hope to post it this afternoon. Your splendid one arrived punctually on Saturday morning. In the middle of last week my wife, whose blood-pressure is always like Ponsford's score at the end of the second day (200 not out), collapsed with strain and overwork. Four days in bed have put her right again, but they held up some of my work and play. A kind neighbour came and stayed here till I got home on Thursday evening, after which my twelve-year-old son and I coped as best we could, with the sporadic assistance of a daily woman. Unfortunately my daughter, to whom the task would have been child's play, is away till this evening. At one moment, in an attempt to distract the child, I began with him a new 800-piece jigsaw on the dining-room table. It proved more difficult than I expected, and apart from the need to finish it so that we can all eat there again, the infernal thing has a hideously compulsive attraction. No doubt the occupation has some therapeutic value, but it wastes a helluva lot of time. I do hope your nose has stopped bleeding: however harmless, it must be a disconcerting propensity. Bat Masquerier has me stumped: please elucidate.

I knew Kingsmill slightly—a fellow of infinite charm and humour, but without scruples of any kind. For many years he lived on advance royalties which he wheedled out of publishers on account of books he had no intention of writing. When I was at Cape's we published his most entertaining life of Frank Harris, but (like all K's books) it failed to sell. I remember his delight at a paragraph in the *Scotsman* concerning the publication of André Maurois's books by the Bodley Head, one of whose directors was called Boswell. The paragraph made much of 'the old alliance between France and Scotland' etc, but Kingsmill happened to know that Maurois's real name was Hertzog, and Boswell's Bussweiler: they were both in fact German Jews. Ever after H.K. referred to *Bussweiler's Life of Johnson*. Hesketh Pearson is indeed a delightful chap to meet. I agree that he is the arch book-maker, all the same his life of Oscar Wilde is the best so far: the only one that brings out the all-important point about Wilde, which was that he was irresistible in his charm, kindness and generosity. Also I shall certainly read H.P.'s forthcoming life of Beerbohm Tree, for there is no other. I agree that there should be a close season for D.H.L., but I am still interested in Shaw, not as a dramatist (one can scarcely sit through any of his plays today) but as a journalist; he was surely one of the best ever: have you read his volume called *Pen Portraits and Reviews*? If not I'll lend you my copy: it's splendid stuff. I'm also interested in G.B.S. as a phenomenon in the world of letters, in which he knew everyone for so long. I'm encouraging an American to compile a bibliography of his writings. Jim Pitman has surely a vested interest in that ridiculous alphabet, hoping to publish it along with all his shorthand books.

Beckford. I've never cared for *Vathek*, but in his travel books and elsewhere he wrote beautifully. I'll send you his Portuguese journal tomorrow: it chronicles a lot of extremely small beer, but some of the English is pure and lovely. Glad you like *The Next Million Years*. The trouble with it, to my mind, is that C.D.'s dullness and lack of humour come out in his style. If only I'd had the publishing of his sister (Gwen Raverat)'s book! I cursed Geoffrey Keynes for not bringing along *all* his in-laws!

I *was* at Oxford (Balliol: two terms: 1926-27: left of my own volition), but dissociate myself from the Boat Race and all its ramifications.

I have now finished the transcription of all the George Moore letters (270), but my secretary is ten years behind with the typing, and I still have forty letters to *date*: I'm still enjoying it hugely. The Yeats bibliography meanwhile lies heavy on my desk and my conscience.

April 24—*very* good. The fatted calf's friends have been told to warn him that he must put his affairs in order. The only fly in the amber is that it is *much* too short a visit. Even if we talk the entire time we shall do no more than touch the fringe of the numberless topics that need discussion. However, let us remember, as Carlyle used to say, 'Have we not all eternity to rest (talk) in?' Though, since we are assured that all things will then be made plain, what the heck will there be to talk about? I refuse, with Jonah, to believe that we shall be praising God *all* the time. After, say, King George IV, or Colonel Wigg M.P. or Mrs Aphra Behn have praised Him for two or three thousand years, won't the time *ever* come when, like Johnson with Hannah More, He says 'Pray consider what your flattery is worth before you are so lavish with it.'

I suspected darkly that Hesketh P. might be a very good chap, though his pen may be looseish. My dislikes are almost entirely paper ones and very easily dispersed—of people I have known, apart of course from Rayner Wood[1] and one or two mainly elderly women, I can't at the moment think of any. In fact, like, was it, Margaret Fuller, I accept the universe ('Gad, Madam, you'd better!').

As to Shaw, I mainly agree with you. His political, educational, philosophical theories, which always strike me as not more than emphatic half-truths, bore me a good deal, and of course that wearisome cocksureness; for surely in all who venture to explore man's predicaments in this world and the next, a certain basic *humility* is a *sine qua non* to win the sympathy and understanding of any except those who like short cuts and certainties. 'To be uncertain is to be uncomfortable, but to be certain is to be ridiculous', which I must have quoted to you before, but I do so again, partly to dispel *your* fear of repeating yourself, but mainly because it appeals to me strongly. (It is from Goethe, on whom Julian Symons *ought* to have quoted Carlyle, who exclaimed as he translated the unreadable *Wilhelm Meister*: 'G. is the greatest genius who has lived for a century, and the greatest ass who has lived for three!') But Shaw. His handling of the English language is a never-failing delight. Never was a verbal

[1] Eton master.

rapier wielded with such precision, swiftness and grace, nor was there ever a controversialist who met and blunted the rudest attacks with such perfect good temper (e.g. the row with Kingsmill). I was delighted to find that Max B. shared to the full my liking for his dramatic criticisms. And I have the *Pen Portraits and Reviews*, than the best of which he never wrote anything better. One or two, e.g. Poe and Vernon Lee, irritate me wildly. What great stuff he would have written if he had had a bigger *heart*. If I had to point to the best sentence he ever wrote, I should quote that little handful of words about Ellen Terry in old age[2] Did he ever write anything else that really moves one—except perhaps the last speech of Brother Martin in *St Joan*?

Bat Masquerier. Please read without a moment's delay Kipling's 'Village that voted the Earth was Flat' in *A Diversity of Creatures* and then tell me, hand on heart, if anything cleverer or more deliciously high spirited has ever been written. But I suspect you know it, and have merely forgotten B.M. It is only we pedants who have that poring and glutinous memory for names.

I love *Bussweiler's Life of Johnson.* (But is the author of *Col. Bramble* really a German Jew? He hides it well.) It is very odd that Kingsmill's books never sold. They are *full* of good stuff. I have just acquired and begun his *Frank Harris,* much attracted by the opening scene in which M. Murry burst into tears. I must read H. Pearson on Wilde. The Borough Library has books like *The History of Grocery* or *Your Poodle* but all their faces straighten when Wilde is mentioned. One is always reading that W's charm and wit were irresistible, but such eulogies don't get one very far—and out of some or even many of his recorded witticisms most of the flavour has evaporated. But when Shaw, M. Beerbohm, E.F. Benson, D. MacCarthy and many others *all* put him easily head of all talkers, there doesn't seem to be much doubt about it.

I wish the Raverat book had come your way. I imagine there is a formidable amount of sheer *luck* in your job—some small quirk of fate and you miss a best-seller. The only really bad luck I remember having at Eton is missing by ten minutes getting a first edition of

[2] 'She became a legend in her old age; but of that I have nothing to say; for we did not meet, and, except for a few broken letters, did not write; and she never was old to me.'

Paradise Lost for fourpence. Cyril Butterwick[3] got it and became a Collector from that moment. He is now a great authority on silver, which *he* says requires no brains or flair, but merely industry. I don't believe it.

I have to respond for Ipswich School to the Old Ipswichians next week. What on earth am I to say? The great name in their history is Cardinal Wolsey, who left it on record that he meant the school to be greater than Eton or Winchester. But how can that be mentioned without ironical thoughts intruding? A more profitable line is perhaps to draw a parallel between their early histories e.g. two headmasters, Nicholas Udall of Eton who was imprisoned for bagging the college plate (and possibly for vices which in Macaulay's words about Frederick 'history blushes to name') and an Ipswich H.M. who got into trouble for boxing a lady's ears. Udall afterwards became H.M. of Westminster, but the Ipswich man was never heard of again.

I look forward eagerly to the additions to the Hart-Davis bay of my library. Your list arrived this morning. My mouth watered but my lips are sealed—as too are the veins in my nose through the red-hot needles of Dr Mackenzie. Have you noticed how, sooner or later, all doctors are called Mackenzie? I don't know why, but it is so.

P.S. I have just re-opened this to add a word of *immense* thanks for the three lovely volumes. Your kindness really is unique—and I hope you know now that I never use adjectives carelessly. The hall this morning looked like Xmas Eve. What *can* I do in return? Nothing but thank—like the last words of *The Wrong Box*—'Can we do nothing for the man in the cart?' 'Nothing but sympathise', said Michael.

8 April 1956 *Bromsden Farm*

The worst has happened, and yesterday the postman brought no fine fat envelope from Suffolk: moreover I leave tomorrow before his advent, so shall just wait till next week-end and a double ration, trying meanwhile to make bricks without straw. Last week was short and uneventful. One night I was woken at 2.30 a.m. by a policeman ringing the wrong bell, couldn't get back to sleep, and solaced myself

[3] Eton master, later a Director of Sotheby's.

by reading Max's *Around Theatres.* (Have you got it? If not a copy shall fly to Grundisburgh. It's the greatest fun.) 'Here', I said to my wakeful self, 'is a sentence that George will like.' About Clement Scott's book of dramatic criticism Max says: 'He is generally in the wrong (as must be any man who regards Tom Robertson as a terminus), but he is never dully in the wrong. If a man is dull, rightness in him does not conciliate me. If he is not dull, wrongness in him is for me no drawback.' And so on . . . Oh how I long for *leisure*, in which to re-read this and a hundred other books! Every time I read a chapter for pure pleasure I have a guilty feeling about proofs and manuscripts. Lots of them are amusing, but reading for pleasure is reading *what* you fancy exactly *when* you fancy it. Don't you agree? Reverting to Max—until I republished this book it had been issued only in an expensive limited edition. He chose its contents from his contributions to the *Saturday Review* between 1898 and 1910—*but* there are as many other pieces just as good as these, and one day I hope to publish them also.[1] My dear Allan Wade spent years copying them all out in the B.M. and then typing fair copies, so I have all the material in my hands if the old gentleman can only be got to agree. He is very frail now, and loth to make decisions. My plan for a series of volumes of his uncollected drawings has been held up for months by his disinclination to sign a contract—and yet he always claims to be very hard up. I am in the middle of reading the first draft of Peter Fleming's book about Hitler's projected invasion of England in 1940, which is going to be excellent. I urged him to include every small detail of those days, since young people are ignorant and older ones enjoy being reminded. I always found when I was young that the most obscure period of time was that which was too old to be news and too young to be history—the day before yesterday, as it were.

Next Saturday we all have to attend the wedding in London of an orphan cousin of mine (daughter of the aunt who lived at Aldeburgh). This will entail hiring a complete outfit at Moss Bros, except for a beautiful grey topper of Duff Cooper's. When Diana was sadly giving his things away, she easily found recipients for everything except his hats, for he took a huge size. My head is even bigger, and one week-

[1] They eventually appeared as *More Theatres* (1969) and *Last Theatres* (1970).

end at Chantilly she discovered this. I in fact wear a hat about twice a year, but she was relentlessly generous, and I returned to England, much to the suspicion of the customs men, with twenty-seven hats—black and grey toppers, a bowler, a *grey* bowler, a panama, a yachting cap, three deerstalkers, an opera hat and any amount of trilbys and Anthony Edens. Luckily my elder son makes some use of them. I have promised to visit Chantilly (it's a lovely house) this year, perhaps in June. There's always wonderful food and a press of distinguished people, but I generally spend plenty of time in Duff's fine library.

To-day, despite cold grey skies and intermittent rain, I made a start on the year's mowing, and feel worn out by the unaccustomed exertion. Normally I take no exercise of any kind, except (whenever I can) swimming in the sea, which I adore. If you take exercise perpetually (as P. Fleming does) you can never stop, and it becomes a sort of religious ritual. Apart from disinclination, I haven't time. Have you read Leslie Hotson's fascinating piece on the back page of the current *T.L.S.*? Devilish ingenious, and almost certainly right.[2] Trust the scholars to remove a line's poetry by showing that it means something! I doubt somehow whether producers will pay any attention.

My work on the George Moore letters continues to be the greatest fun, and I think the result will be a most unusual and moving book—out early next year, I hope. One of the depressing things about publishing today is that it takes seven or eight months to get a book out (it used to be much less) and therefore one can look forward too far with sickening certainty. The period of gestation being so unduly delayed, one is heartily sick of most books before they see the light, and I know it's a mistake to take a book at all without *great* enthusiasm at the outset. But I mustn't bore you with this dreary shop. In just over a fortnight you'll be getting it all *viva voce*, heaven help you. I *am* looking forward to the occasion!

10–11 April 1956 *Grundisburgh*

This is a bad week—a constipation of committees, if the collective noun be allowed. I should greatly value your views on *direct grant*

[2] Giving a new interpretation of Falstaff's dying words.

schools and their future, with special consideration of their advantages or the reverse over *state-aided* schools. On practically all these committees I move about in worlds not realised, but whenever I suggest resigning on the grounds of uselessness, the chairman enfolds my hand in a warm wet one of his own, and stresses fervidly (but unconvincingly) how incomputably valuable the presence is of a stout, elderly, inattentive layman who never says a word, and mostly does not know, or care, what the rest are talking about.

Oh dear, my beloved Rupert, how *can* I, how can anyone, refuse an offer of Max's *Around Theatres*? And yet how can I for very shame say how much I should love it? You really must, when you come here, tell me the name of some *enormously* expensive book *you* want, or how on earth is my conscience *ever* to become less anaemic? Yes, I did read with vast admiration Leslie Hotson on 'green fields' in the *T.L.S.*—easily the most interesting thing in it. Old Johnson did I think accept 'babbled', but he would have approved of L.H. in general and in particular, 'The reading of the ancient books is probably true, and is not to be disturbed for the sake of elegance, perspicuity, or mere improvement of the sense'. The H-D annexe to my library contains three Leslie Hotsons. They are immensely enjoyable, but, my word, they do make one feel ignorant. Is there anything he doesn't know about Shakespeare? Similarly, is there anything of Max's which isn't sheer delight? I do profoundly sympathise with you about reading. There is one wrinkle in your brow which I spotted as being chiselled entirely by daily frustration in the matter of leisure for reading. But shan't you soon have more freedom through Heinemann? That is what we all hope for you. I thank whatever gods may be that at 73 my taste for reading is undiminished, and another blessing at that age is that you no longer read what you *ought* to read, but what you want to.

I have just finished Kingsmill on Frank Harris, about whom I read all I can find—as I do about Hitler and Co—from a sort of fascination—thirsting to discover how and why any human being became so frightful. No one—not even H.K.—ever succeeded in convincing one of F.H.'s reputed charm, any more than anyone ever did about the fascination of Adolf's eyes. Did you ever see F.H.'s autobiography? I suppose it is a collector's piece now. Has it any merits outside what George Forsyte called 'the nubbly bits'? I like the incident of F.H. getting someone to buy six O. E. ties for him. Ford Madox F. had the same peculiarity. *Pauvre humanité*! Max, I heard from Percy Lubbock, is getting very frail now. Many years ago someone described him as having 'the face of an angel-sheep turned into a kid's, and grey with its baby old age'. I wonder what he looks like now.

Peter Fleming's book should be good fun. He had an excellent article recently as 'Strix', about the absence of *giants* in modern times. He could have mentioned—but didn't—old Warre. He had no eloquence, when he entered a room there was no one else in it, however full it was. When he left a schoolroom at Eton and—mistaking the cleaners' cupboard for the door—crashed into a medley of pots and pans, not a single boy smiled. But when I, in D5, pecked while stepping up to my desk, and sat in the w.p.b. it made their day—and their Sunday letter home.

Hats! I take size 8. My head was always in the swede rather than the grapefruit class, and the humorous fates saw fit to inflict me with a form of osteo-arthritis of which a main effect is a slow and steady growth of the occipital bones. And whenever I look in the glass or see a snapshot of myself, I am reminded of Petrarch's simple statement 'Nothing is more hideous than an old schoolmaster'.

I have never actually dealt with Moss Bros, though I once made a jolly good joke about them when a daughter asked if my tail-coat at her wedding came from them. 'No.' I said (like a flash, as they say) 'It comes from Moth Bros'. The man of one joke, like the G.O.M. I have never had more than two hats—always envy those who have eight or ten, without somehow being able to emulate them. Perhaps because I cannot remember the day when I did not have to have them made for me—shoes too. Never off the peg. A great bore. And it is not as if the contents of a large head were any more valuable than those of a small. Arthur Balfour had a very small head—also Lord Roberts, Mr Dulles a large one.

East wind again today. Coming back from London yesterday I saw no spot of green on any tree—springs are not what they were. Rooks have started building much too near the house, and wake me, shouting like auctioneers, at 6 a.m. My wife was told by some village wiseacre that a bonfire under the tree at dusk frightened them away for good. She lit one last night. *This* morning I was roused at 5.30 by the hoarse and hearty cachinnations of every rook in Suffolk, as they delightedly surveyed the lawn covered with the calcined débris of last night's bonfire. But be of good cheer—your room will be on the other side of the house.

19 April 1956 *Grundisburgh*

I cannot wait for your letter before thanking you for the most delicious volume which has just arrived—and the fitting words in which to do so elude me with the same ease and distance as that with which the conversation of Mark Pattison avoided platitude. But if you see a queue of dromedaries entering Soho Square, loaded with jewels the size of pigeon's eggs, brocades, and all the spices and gums of Arabia, you will know that my gratitude is assuming a tangible form—as the parish magazine says when the departing vicar is presented with a pair of embroidered slippers.

Saturday 21 April 1956 *Bromsden Farm*

All this week I have vainly sought a quiet moment for writing to you, but only now has it come. It was a slight relief to my conscience that you sent only a postcard this week. I shall be with you soon after you get this, but your splendid letters must be answered first. To-day I drove some of my family to the Cotswolds to lunch with my wife's stepmother. Afterwards we sat at the foot of the Broadway Tower and gazed over what would have been the coloured counties if they hadn't been obscured by mist—most enjoyable. Now I shall read your letters again and comment . . . I must question you about Rayner Wood, who is clearly *sui generis* among the few people you have disliked. I know you'll enjoy *Around Theatres*. I fear Max is dying: he is in a clinic at Rapallo, surrounded by devoted friends and just fading away. A whole tone of voice will perish with him. He was the perfect *petit maitre* (in the literal sense), adorning all he touched. I can see that I shan't have time to re-read 'The Village that Voted . . .' before Tuesday: what nicer bedside book could I have at Finndale House? Unless you sternly forbid it, I shall arrive at Ipswich at 6.12 on Tuesday, and would like (if it's not too hideously inconvenient) to leave by the 8.45 train on Thursday morning. I hate to be so fleeting, but publishing nonsense hems me in.

That article of Peter's about 'Giants' arose from a discussion I had with Lord Dunsany at the Lit Soc. In the middle of it I suddenly realised that Lord D clearly considered *himself* a Giant—which made the discussion impossible. What else have I done? Been to a sherry party given by the Poetry Book Society, at which T.S. Eliot made a dry little speech: been to the dentist and the doctor and a London Library committee meeting: taken the chair *for the last time* at the Society of Bookmen: visited Stephen Potter in an attempt to wrest the manuscript of his new book from him: ushed at my cousin's wedding in the partially restored Chelsea Old Church—and afterwards drank champagne in the House of Lords (where my cousin's brother is a Clerk). Last week Joyce Grenfell and her husband took me to see my ex-wife in *The Chalk Garden*, an immensely entertaining play—full of faults no doubt, but witty and wonderfully unstereotyped, so that one never knows what any of the characters will say next (Tchekov has the same merit), whereas in most new plays one can see sentences ahead. Joyce told me she had sent one of her own long-playing records to a pansy American film star, whose boy-friend reported: 'My dear, he couldn't have been more pleased if you'd sent him a choirboy!' American and Canadian publishers are swarming in London—oh yes, that dreary article in the *Financial Times* upset Heinemann's and Lionel Fraser terribly, and I had to apologise for printing it without their knowledge. What nonsense! Who could possibly be influenced by it? Now I shall go to bed and finish this in the morning.

Sunday morning

The warmth and sunshine of yesterday have vanished with Winter Time. Nought, as perhaps Shelley said, shall endure but Mutability. Each time we have to alter the clocks my wife refuses to acknowledge the change for at least twenty-four hours—which leads to some confusion, particularly since she is no surer than the rest of us whether the clocks should have gone forward or back. These particular Sundays are always days of missed meals and argument.

29 April 1956 *Bromsden Farm*

I enjoyed every moment of my stay with you, and am already looking forward to the next. Every single thing about the house and garden is so *right*, so welcoming and so peaceful. Pamela is an angel, with her lovely smile, her splendid cooking, and her charming acceptance of being read aloud to. I hope perhaps next time there'll be a sale for me to go to with her, for that is one of my pleasures which I hadn't confessed to you before. I love being able to imagine you, thinly dressed, in your rotating summer-house, following the sun round as you write your splendid letters.

I can't wait to polish off all my chores and hasten to the beauty of the moors, 'the silence that is in the starry sky, the sleep that is among the lonely hills'. My address (which is divulged only to my wife and my secretary) is c/o G.P.O. Keld, Richmond, Yorks. Write there and I'll send you back screeds of Wordsworthian sublimity. The spring is always even more backward up there, and it's fun to have this lovely season twice over, with a second crop of primroses etc. All to-day I have been mowing much too-long grass with an old hand-machine, thinking enviously of your string of automatic engines. The cricket pitch in the meadow had to be cut too, and my twelve-year-old's cricket season opened on the same day as the Australians'. I have bowled at him till my arm aches, and as the meadow has six sheep in it, there are additional hazards to be avoided. I sent you the *Baldwin*: have you got G.M.Y.'s other books? You'd certainly love them and I have them all on my list (except his masterpiece, *Portrait of an Age*, which the Oxford Press wouldn't let go). Let me know if you'd like them. Did I tell you what G.M.Y. said of the O.U.P.? 'Being published by the Oxford University Press is rather like being married to a duchess: the honour is almost greater than the pleasure.' I could—and doubtless shall—write you a whole letter about G.M.Y.

I wrote most of my Walpole book on the Yorkshire moors, and there if anywhere I could one day write another book or two. How I wish you would do the same: an autobiographical and anecdotal book: it would be superb, for your mind is wonderfully stocked and mellow, and you have perfect taste and humour, the two essentials. Please think about it, and forgive this hurried scribble, which takes you endless gratitude and much affection.

2 May 1956 *Grundisburgh*

Well, things do *some*times come up to expectation, even in this wale, as Mrs Gamp put it. And your tiny visit did. (I speak from *our* point of view!) Do your ears ever tingle, or are those of publishers 'punch-drunk', so to speak, like those of pugilists? If not you must have wondered what was the matter with yours last Thursday and after. No guest has ever fitted in so quickly and beautifully—so there! I won't say any more, because your sharp eye must have seen how we were enjoying your being here. And by the way, there must just be a special word of thanks for that poetry-reading. We are both enormously fastidious about that—the rarest, surely, of all accomplishments—and we could have listened to you for hours. The Greek Ambassador in 1916, Dylan Thomas, and R.H-D have alone spoken the language exactly as it should be spoken. You might tell me sometime who, today, is worth listening to on the air. I can't bear those 'church' voices, or that instantly detectable note 'how well I am reading this'—these constitute the Scylla, and the Charybdis is almost as bad, the 'chatty' or 'no-high-falutin'-nonsense-about-*me*'. I have heard on Xmas Day in the First Lesson 'Wonderful, Counsellor, Prince of Peace' etc read as if they were the names of stations on the Underground. The truth, of course, is that the path between too little expression and too much is a very narrow one.

A million thanks for the Baldwin Life which I have just finished. Bloggs Baldwin[1] scores a point or two against Young, but they don't really amount to a great deal. G.M.Y.'s two chief points—the disastrous and lasting impression made by that notorious speech,

[1] Younger son of the Prime Minister.

which even intelligent people misunderstood, and B's great and admitted deficiency as a leader, summarised by some shrewd critic as 'S.B. always hits the nail on the head, but it doesn't go in any further'. The person Bloggs really has a grievance against is the compiler of G.M.Y.'s index, where several of Y's guesses or mere suggestions appear as facts, e.g. 'S.B. craves popularity' referring to a sentence beginning—'And it *seemed* to me——'. And I do think G.M.Y. is naughty sometimes in writing 'He would'——do so and so, i.e. reporting as habitual some action of S.B.'s of which the evidence was incidental. But it is an *immensely* interesting book. As to Bloggs's, I don't understand what the *Times* reviewer meant when regretting that his 'literary and political equipment' was hardly adequate. Political perhaps, but his book to me seems excellently written. What do you think? Baldwin's career, his superb speeches, his abiding vision of what the word 'England' meant and means, his ceaseless striving to take a long view and not a short—all give point to a sentence in the *T.L.S.* review of Winston's history 'The whole action of history seems to prove that it is more dangerous to be intelligent than to be warlike. Culture is not only futile but, when combined with kindness, almost always actively fatal.' He is talking of kings of course, but if you think how much *wiser* a man Asquith was than Ll.G., or how superb Winston was in war but how unreliable in peace politics, one finds oneself bleakly facing the question 'Is it not true that it is easily possible for a man at the top to be too *good* to be successful?' And of course there was Mr Gladstone. What a fog one is in! The Creator really did make things too difficult. However I read in the *Sunday Times* that the earth is only one among at least a hundred *trillion* planets, and end up agreeing with Bishop Creighton who reassured an anxious seeker after the truth that it is 'almost impossible to exaggerate the complete unimportance of everything'.

You never told me how you really liked 'The Village that Voted . . .' Not extravagantly, I have a suspicion. It appealed to the adolescent in me. But I find myself practically always liking the things you do. That couplet you quote from old Daddy W. has been a favourite of mine for decades. It is a nice happy picture I have in mind of you 'treading the ling like a buck in spring' day after day, so that when you return to Soho Square it will be said of you:

'There was a hardness in his cheek,
There was a hardness in his eye,
As if the man had fixed his face,
In many a solitary place,
Against the wind and open sky!'[2]

What fine *bone* there is in so many of old W's best things, so that they last like the beauty of some women, untarnished by the passing years. I wish you had known John Bailey. He could laugh at the solemn old egoist, but had boundless reverence for the central deep-rooted *core* of him, and often enlarged on his likeness to Milton—both so crabbed and unlikeable in ordinary externals, but inwardly of such majestic stature compared with the common run of great men. What has happened to that book of some months ago which set out to prove that the love of W. and Dorothy was incestuous? What lofty times we live in!

Yesterday I went to Ipswich and found the town packed with people intent to see the Duke of Edinburgh, and one had to butt one's way through them. They weren't particularly excited, and the only vivid impression I got was of the conspicuous ugliness of East Anglian women. When I commented on it to an old inhabitant, he said Ipswich was famous for this, and always had been. The N.E. wind I suppose, though one would expect this to give the features a fine austerity—not the bunlike, haphazard, expressionless lumpishness of imperfectly poached eggs that met the eye everywhere. But perhaps all English crowds are much the same. I had been summoned with the other school governors to see him lay a foundation-stone (of the School Hall for which there appears little prospect of our ever being able to pay) but I meant to be at Worcester to see the Australians. In the end the keen wind deterred me. However it now seems to be loosening its three-month-old grip and the summer-house is the place to be (if one can't get to Keld!), blossom and bird-song all round. The *one* snag of your visit was that the day you were here was the only one in in the last fortnight on which it offered no welcome.

P.S. I don't think it needed to be put in writing, but no harm in doing

[2] Wordsworth, 'Peter Bell'

so, viz that there is *always* a bed for you here and what Adie[3] used to call 'a little rough food', *and* a glass of sherry before it, whatever evidence you may think there was to the contrary.

P.S. 2. How right I was not to have been at Worcester yesterday. Cardus is quite right. Except in a few spots cricket is nothing like the game it was, and all the writing-up of it is like much modern art-criticism, i.e. the Andersen fairy tale 'The Emperor's New Clothes'. I see old Munnings is again protesting—on the right side, but I don't suppose the old ass helps much. I recall Henson's rage when *supported* by Bp Welldon on some controversy with clubfooted arguments—a rhinocerine gambolling wherever the ice was thinnest. As H. summed him up, he 'could neither speak with effect nor be silent with dignity'.

P.S. 3. When I was young it was wholly wrong for anyone except bowler, wicket-keeper and first slip to appeal for a catch at the wicket, still less for l.b.w. Now deep square-leg joins in. Bah!

7 May 1956 *Keld, Yorkshire*

Your huge and exquisitely addressed envelope must have caused quite a stir in the village post-office. The couple who run it (and the Youth Hostel, of which it is curiously part) are away on holiday, and the post-office is being looked after by two undergraduates from Leeds University, whose hobby (or perhaps job or mania) is to measure the depth of water in the local rivers. Since these are all mountain streams, full of deep pools, shallows and waterfalls, the lads have quite a job on hand. Were I a crow or a bee, I could reach the village in five minutes, but this cottage is perched on a green hill and is accessible only on foot, horse, tractor or jeep. The climb takes a good twenty minutes, including pauses for breath, but when one gets here the sight is magical—ranges of hills, one behind another, on every side, all green with pasture up to the brown-and-purple line of the heather-clad fells (there is no arable land in this dale—Swale-dale). The furthest mountain, about eight miles away, is just in

[3] Eton master.

Westmorland, and for all I know dear Roger and other friends live hard by. For this and other reasons I beg you to keep to yourself all knowledge of this place and my connection with it. Scarcely anyone knows about it, or where I am, and nobody here (all farmers, villagers etc) knows I'm a publisher or anything else about me. One can't have one's name on a million or so books without its getting known, and though such notoriety may have advantages on occasion, I flee from it joyfully to this beautiful and anonymous spot. The cottage is tiny and completely primitive—one room up, one down, a tiny kitchen, a coalshed and an outside E.C. Water has to be fetched in buckets from a spring a few yards away. It's like camping out without the discomfort of tents and the weather. There is a tiny shop in the village, and a delightful farmer supplies eggs and milk. For more advanced shopping the town of Hawes (in Wensleydale) is only eight miles away, beyond a precipitous pass called Buttertubs. Almost the most miraculous thing about this hill (which is called Kisdon) is the *silence.* The only sounds are those of sheep, curlew (surely the most mournfully romantic of all bird-cries), plover, skylarks and grouse. Otherwise *nothing*, save when the wind whistles round the cottage, as it did last night. Like all the other houses in the dale, it is built of the local grey stone which goes beautifully with the green of the fields. I fear this description is poor and scrappy—and I meant to do it so well—perhaps next week?

I brought a mass of books along—George Moore, Blunden's poems (to be selected) and the everlasting Yeats bibliography, but so far have done little except desultory background reading—and lying in the sun. On Saturday, tell Pamela, I went to a sale in a village called Patrick Brompton, near Bedale, and bought a mass of miscellaneous objects, including a fine Victorian card-table (one that swivels and folds up) for 12/-. There were no china figures for her, nor wall-clocks. Yesterday I read S.N. Behrman's book about Duveen, the picture dealer (I thought it might contain some reference to G. Moore and Lady Cunard, but it doesn't). I expect you read it when it came out: if not it's well worth getting from the library. What interests me so much is the sequence of events—the great Robber Barons of America, shrewd illiterates who made millions out of oil and railways and department stores and canned meat, easing their consciences by buying works of art, for which Duveen and Co charged them enormous prices. Then, to save death duties and at the same time win themselves immortality, they bequeathed all these masterpieces to the American nation, and now nobody cares how much Duveen rooked the old boys, since the results are so splendid.

I haven't yet read Bloggs's book, but shall do. I've instructed my secretary by postcard to send you the other G.M. Young books, and shall look forward to your (I'm sure delighted) reactions. The three collections of essays were put together by me, with the old boy's grudging consent. When you've read them all I'll write you a brief pen-portrait of their author. One of the joys of reading W.W. is the way those lines of thundering magnificence suddenly crop up amid a lot of bathos. 'And mighty poets in their misery dead,' with the three fine lines before it, is all mixed up with that dreary leech-gatherer. This country is tremendously Wordsworthian—much more so than the present-day Lakes, which are trodden down and exploited disgustingly.

Clearly we should have been at Worcester on the *second* day: Benaud's innings sounded grand. I have the newspapers sent up here, but they reach me a day or two late, and I linger over all the bits I am usually too busy to read—leading articles called 'Rumblings in Cuba' and suchlike fantasies. Now I must stop, and eat some lunch before walking down to meet the farmer who is obligingly going to bring up my card-table and other purchases in a trailer behind his tractor. I have marked down two other sales in the local paper (which I read from cover to cover).

I have just looked out of the window and noticed that the clouds have descended round the cottage, making it even more deliciously remote. Yesterday I heard a cuckoo down the dale, so in the nicest possible way, you see, I am in cloud-cuckoo land.

Please give my love to Pamela.

9 May 1956 *Grundisburgh*

The breakfast table this morning had that best of all objects—far better even than a dish of salmon kedgeree, or a headline in *The Times* saying the atom bomb had been abolished, or that the price of coal was down—viz a fat little parcel of books. And the contents of those books! *Exactly* the sort of literature I love—comments wide and deep on men and things and books by a wise man who knows how to write. Life has, at all events at 73, no greater pleasure than that.

Keld sounds entrancing, and exactly the right thing for you after your positively ghastly life in London—at least for three-quarters of your day. Hawes, and Buttertubs, and Wensleydale—how full of strength and melody the names are. You won't be so foolish as many are on a country holiday, i.e. fill the whole day with exhausting walks. A wise passiveness is your line. And on such a Wordsworthian basis I rather think a Wordsworthian sonnet or two is indicated. Keld and Kisdon and the curlew all cry out for it. I don't remember that he ever mentioned the grouse. The sounds surrounding me at this moment are more commonplace—blackbirds and thrushes, the mowing-machine, oh yes and the nightingale which is just as vocal here by day as by night, and the bird which 'shouts all day at nothing'. It was Mrs Warre who once asked 'What is that bird I hear every morning which seems to be saying Cuck-oo, Cuck-oo', and then like George Moore—'What is the joke? Please tell me if there is a joke. I do like a joke.'

Pamela is green with envy over your 12/- card-table. Mary hasn't answered yet about what I persist in calling *your* clock. The young *don't* answer letters much. Nor, for the matter of that, do many of the old, and some who do leave such long gaps that it isn't a correspondence at all. Literary folk are mostly bad, though they used not to be. I have just re-read Humphry House on the Dickens correspondence—and of course there are Byron, Lamb, Thackeray, Meredith, James, Shaw, all of whom were just as busy as e.g. Alan Dent and Cardus who are very costive, though their quality is good. I suppose Q. was the worst that ever was. At an English Association meeting the Secretary once revealed that two letters, two postcards, and a telegram had all failed to extract a word from him.

A day or two ago I judged the reading and declamation at Ipswich School. My Dear! The young beak had, *me judice*, *not* chosen the pieces well, in view of the fact that, as he admitted, the boys were a weak lot, and if you want to realise what bathos can be, I recommend the declamation of Louis MacNeice's 'Prayer Before Birth' by a bunch of adolescents, wholly lacking in imagination but over-supplied with adenoids and the accents of Stratford-atte-Bowe. In 'Kubla Khan' several pronounced 'Mt Abŏra' as 'Abōra'; Carlyle was said to have propounded a 'hypothēsis', and Cassius as being as 'life' not to be as 'live to be in awe' etc and, with Caesar, to have stemmed the torrent with hearts of 'contrōversy', which, I suppose, comes from America. I did what I could to cleanse their tongues of this—also of that B.B.C. way of stressing the second syllable in 'hospitable' and 'despicable' which have always been *bêtes noires* to me. But I felt it was trying to pluck the brands from a fire which had got too strong a hold. As you said recently, we who think reading and speech and accurate understanding and appreciation to be important are in a conspicuous minority.

I remember the Duveen book and the stimulating blend of the absurd and the pathetic in the spectacle of what you call the Great Robber Barons, illiterate to a man, overwhelmed by their gold as an Indian village is by the jungle, frenziedly spending it on pictures of which they knew nothing. Rockefeller emerges as a really enlightened man compared, say, with Andrew Mellon; and Nuffield as a positive saint. (A dear little plebeian, who expressed extravagant happiness after a day's golf with a team of Tuppy Headlam's—i.e. beaks and dons, because 'I have had a whole day with a lot of friendly and intelligent men, and not one mentioned money. If you had any idea how rare an experience that is . . .'). You must tell me all about G.M.Y. some day. His writing gives me enormous pleasure. What does he look like? That is very important. Carlyle always had pictures of those he was writing about all over that fantastic 'sound-proof' room. Do you know his pen-portrait of Daddy W. in the *Reminiscences*, with his green eye-shade which 'flirted out' from a little stand as he munched raisins at someone's dinner-table. Not that he was a good judge of poetry, for though he liked Tennyson's 'Ulysses' he also liked 'The May Queen' and 'Dora'.

I am aflame with rage about yesterday's cricket at Leicester. What an opportunity the Leicestershire captain missed! When it was clear that the Australians regarded the occasion not as a cricket-match but as net-practice, he should have put on two underarm bowlers, and if Johnson had protested, he could have answered, 'But if this is not a cricket-match, why shouldn't I use it to train a pair of lob-bowlers?' I hope, if the Australians take this line about the county matches, their gates will fall heavily. The situation is curiously like that of the atom bomb. Just as the universal conviction that this is deadly for all does nothing to stop its being made deadlier every year, so everybody's knowledge that cricket is much duller than it was doesn't prevent players continuing to prod and poke at thirty runs an hour, and, mysteriously, does not yet keep more than a few people away. Perhaps on the analogy of 'Who drives fat oxen must himself be fat' we can be sure that Who likes dull cricket must himself be dull. But I warn them. They won't get *me* to go and watch if they go on like this. That'll learn them! To all of which you (like God) will say 'Doest thou well to be angry?' and I (like Jonah) shall answer petulantly 'Yes I *do* well to be angry'.

15 May 1956 *Kisdon*

It isn't long walks that are likely to be my downfall here, but a deliciously monumental sloth, caused perhaps by the air and the altitude, which make everything a pleasure so long as it is done slowly and in one's own time. Yesterday I did in fact make a ¾ circumambulation of Kisdon (which is an island girt with rivers), about half-way up, scrambling over rocky outcrops and treading delightedly on thick mountain grass, studded with primroses, cowslips, anemones and dog-violets. The walk took about 2½ hours—all pure pleasure. I forgot last week to mention the dry-stone walls which take the place of hedges everywhere, winding inconsequently up the hillsides and dividing the green, green fields into every kind of shape. Made of the local stone, and matching the scattered farmhouses and byres, they blend perfectly with the natural scene, into which no trace of industrialism intrudes. An occasional tractor far away—otherwise this outlook cannot have changed for a century or two. The longer I stay here the less can I imagine why anyone chooses to live anywhere else.

I knew you'd enjoy G.M.Y. and am most happy to have been the means of bringing him to you. No more of gratitude: it's pure self-indulgence on my part, since I want you to share in all the good and interesting things I've published, without having to bother with all the failures and mistakes. G.M.Y. is tallish and thin, with a long thin pointed nose. Very little hair and that quite flat on his scalp, so that more than anything else he looks like a judge who has mislaid his wig and is feeling the cold. I think in fact he *does* feel the cold, probably has a bad circulation, and in winter wears an enormous astrakhan overcoat which he purchased in Tsarist Russia. He was educated at St Paul's and Balliol, and was then some sort of a Civil Servant (this part of his life is obscure and never mentioned) until he retired at about the age of fifty. Up to then he had not written a word, but had read (as you can see) enormously, and remembered everything in a Macaulay—Monty James way. Peter Davies published his *Gibbon* and *Charles I and Cromwell* in the early thirties, and then I wrote to him, suggesting a collection of essays etc. This produced *Daylight and Champaign* (which I brought out when I was at Cape's), and after the war, when I started up my own business, I reprinted these three books, and published the two further books of essays and *Baldwin*. What I hadn't realised until *Baldwin* was that all the other books came largely out of his head, where their subject-matter had been brewing up for many years. *Baldwin* demanded a lot of *work*—going through papers, writing to people etc—and that he wouldn't or couldn't do. On top of that he found that his personal affection for S.B. was gradually turning to some sort of contempt, if not actual dislike—so it's no wonder the book wasn't first-rate. He tried to abandon it ¾ of the way through, but I brutally compelled him to finish it.

His private life was unusual. Where or how he lived when he was a Civil Servant I don't know, but possibly with his father, who lived at Blackheath and died there at the age of 99. Anyhow sometime in the late twenties G.M.Y. corresponded on some literary topic with Mona Wilson (sister of Sir Arnold W. etc), and she asked him down for the week-end to an attractive, old, but very uncomfortable house she owned at Pewsey, near Marlborough. To cut a long story short, he stayed there for twenty-five years, until M.W. died a year or two ago. There was, so far as I know, no just cause or impediment why they shouldn't have married, but they just didn't. I'm sure their relationship was entirely intellectual and companionable, without any sexual feelings—indeed I wonder whether either of them ever had much sex-life of any kind. Miss Wilson (as he always referred to her) was ten years older than he—a little hunchbacked old lady when I knew her, rapidly going blind (her cooking was terrible: since she couldn't *see* what she ate, the food was either raw or cindery). She smoked a little pipe, which he lovingly filled for her. She wrote lives of Blake and Sir P. Sidney (both of which I reissued), and a number of other books, all learned but, let's face it, *dull*. The house was very dirty and untidy, full of books and papers, but they were charming together, and I loved visiting them. Once during the war I called unexpectedly about 3 p.m., and from the confusion following my knock it was clear that G.M. was still in bed. Eventually he arrived half-dressed and unshaven but very welcoming. Eventually Miss Wilson got so blind, old and ill that she had to be moved to a home where she mercifully died. She left him everything, but he couldn't bear the idea of living alone in the house—couldn't have managed it anyhow, for he is quite unpractical—so he sold it and moved into All Souls where, John Sparrow tells me, he complains all the time. He has become a great hypochondriac and never stops having himself overhauled by doctors. They all say he's perfectly well, and it must be nerves. This infuriates him and he tries another. He's a year or so younger than you, I fancy, but in his ways might be your father. He says he can't write any more, and that his memory's going, which, as I've told him, simply means that it's now rather better than most other people's. If he lives to his father's age the other Fellows are going to need all their patience! Oh yes, every year he and Miss Wilson used to take a holiday at Lechlade, where G.M. used to row them violently about on the stripling Thames. I visited them there once and drove them to Burford, where we spent some time vainly looking for the tomb of John Meade Falkner.[1]

When I re-issued G.M.'s old books I started, as is my compulsive habit, to verify his quotations, and found they were all slightly wrong—see his essay called 'The Imp'. Fancy having all that in one's head! On his seventieth birthday I gave a dinner for him in the private

[1] It was there all the time.

room at the Garrick, which I think pleased him. I forget exactly who was there—Sparrow and Jonah and Harold Nicolson and three or four others—look at *my* memory! G.M. always assumes that one is his intellectual equal and makes no concessions in his conversation. This, though flattering, often carried matters well over my head until I knew him well enough to ask for explanations of all the allusions I couldn't understand. As Geoffrey Madan said, he is not a polymath but a pantomath. I wish I could somehow stir his old age into cheerfulness and some sort of activity. There are lots of other things to answer in your letter, but they'll have to wait till next time. If I don't carry this down the hill now I shall miss the post. Have been to two more sales. One of the auctioneers was a great wag: 'How mooch for this Gandhi table—dark legs and no drawers?' It was a bamboo table.

18 May 1956 *Grundisburgh*

It is *all* to the good that you are having a good laze. Curiously few people are sensible about holidays; if not walking, they go sightseeing and to picture-gallery after p.g. of all fatiguing activities. Many play golf, and one odd effect of that pursuit is that they return to work *manifestly* stupider than they were. It is, I think, the company of other golfers. Among my fortuitous but immensely precious circumstances I count almost the luckiest that when they began monkeying about with the game of bridge I couldn't be bothered to learn all the new stuff, so dropped out. If I had not, what aeons I should have wasted, e.g. in January at Brancaster, and here with the Cranworths, he having ceased to read and *must* be entertained. And one is very vulnerable in the country; they know one has no excuse—except that one doesn't want to! You will be amused but not surprised to hear that a friend of mine was *angrily* told off by Cuthbert Headlam for joining a small shooting party in the North when he was not a bridge-player. And they tell me—or did a few years ago—that it is essential for a girl to play a decent game of tennis and also bridge. Two centuries ago in France she had to be able to talk, i.e. the level of civilisation was definitely higher.

Your locale does really sound positively Arcadian. Charles Fisher used to maintain that peace was not perfect till you could hear a sheep cough half a mile away, and Kisdon sounds as if it filled that bill. Thank you for the vivid picture of G.M. Young, who is my daily companion. 'My mind to me a Kingdom is' could be claimed by him more justly, I suspect, than it was by George Wither. Like old Samuel J. who wrote his *Lives of the Poets* without looking up anything but an occasional date. You say G.M.Y. is querulous, hypochondriacal, irritating (at All Souls), inaccurate, and work-shy, and so work up to the very natural conclusion that he 'might be your (my) father'!—even though my nose is not pointed, nor my hair flat, nor do I feel the cold, nor do I know one tenth as much of men and books as he does—so it must be in his other attributes that we meet!

I have just started on the *Gibbon* with great relish—only one really grave defect: on p 50 I note *Lyttleton.* A pity; it may seriously spoil its sale. And I have also got from the library the *Portrait of a Man with Red Hair* which I don't think I ever read—for my bed-time story. One of the real blessings of old age is that one does with very little sleep.

I shall have some fun in a fortnight's time when I address the Naval cadets at Greenwich roughly on the pleasures of reading, but on less Victorian lines than that suggests. Do you think I can fairly make the point that a man who quite obviously does not wash *cannot* be a good critic or indeed a good man? No, I think it won't quite do. Someone might call out 'What about Dr Johnson?' My friend at Greenwich hopes I shall quote some fine stuff. At the moment I have in mind Conrad's account of the return of the *Narcissus*, John Fortescue on the Death of the Black Prince, Masefield's description of the storm in *Dauber*, Carlyle's account of Robespierre's end, Johnson's letter to Chesterfield, Meg Merrilies' 'Ride your ways, Ellangowan'. What else? On the whole I am avoiding poetry except in snatches, but I have a feeling that there is some tremendous bit of invective or satire or humour that I have forgotten. If any idea strikes you, please let me know. I gather their literary knowledge is not great, and their tastes are not highbrow. They are young men of action. I shall certainly tell them of your auctioneer, also of another who in selling a gallows described it in his catalogue as 'picturesque hanging wood'.

At last the summer has come to these hills, and I am sitting behind the cottage, having just breakfasted there. The sun is truly *hot*, there is almost no wind (unusual up here) and larks are everywhere about me in the sky. I have fallen so deep into the gentle rhythms of this primitive life that a slice of lotus (or perhaps lot*o*s) does for my sustenance, and it's a miracle that you're getting a letter at all. NO one else is. Nor will it be a long one. Your splendid hour's worth of biro reached me yesterday, with the news of Surrey's victory. Will you be at Lord's on Saturday? I have promised to take a lady friend, so shall be in the Rover seats. I shall drive sadly to London on Thursday. The news that my secretary is in hospital with glandular fever does little to encourage me. I shall go home on Saturday evening, and write you a proper letter from there on Sunday. I fear I made G.M.Y. into a monster instead of a darling, which he is. When you've read all the books, why don't you send him a fan letter to All Souls? He'd be delighted. Point out the Lyttleton howler. Charles Fisher's definition of peace grows truer with every passing year. These last two Whitsun holidays I have not stirred from the height, but on the distant road below a stream of vehicles passed constantly, out of hearing, thank God.

If you go on reading the *Spectator* you will soon resemble Charles Whibley, of whom someone said he had so many *bêtes noires* that being with him was like living in Haiti—scarcely a white in sight. But I daresay it's good for you. E.S.P. Haynes always said that rage improved the flow of adrenalin and helped his asthma. Have you read his (E.S.P.H.'s) three *Lawyer's Notebooks*? If not I'll lend you my copies. He was a true eccentric, about whom I could (and doubtless will) write you pages. Your Greenwich list is fine: what about adding a paragraph or two of Bunyan, about the trumpets sounding for him on the other side? When I was nineteen and my beloved mother died I was saved from death and destruction by *Pilgrim's Progress* which I carried about in a bag and chanted aloud to myself most comfortingly on every possible occasion. The only other thing in the bag was a huge bottle of liquid sleeping-draught, which eventually lost its cork and saturated Bunyan—but he had done his saving work by then. Up here I have re-read G.M.'s *Avowals*, *Conversations in Ebury Street*,

Memoirs of my Dead Life and *A Storyteller's Holiday*—all with great pleasure. Now I must find some more amaranth and moly to prop myself on. Send me a p.c. to Soho Square with your movements.

25 May 1956 *Grundisburgh*

Biro again I am afraid. Don't take it to mean I don't hate the thing. It has almost every defect from the calligraphic point of view, but if one is writing in an armchair, and *if* the cover of the same is just back from the wash, and *if* one's wife has that strange feminine dislike of seeing black ink-spots on the aforesaid cover—well then the B. comes into its degraded own. Not that my fingers are not extensively smudged well before I have reached page 3. It makes one's youth seem very distant, when every boy in Trials found two quill pens in his place: and what a lovely crisp twittering, as of short-tempered but nice little birds, filled the room as we narrated *ventre-à-terre* the exploits of King Tiglath-Pileser, or listed the products of Asia Minor. There is a fine letter somewhere of Hensley Henson's lamenting the difficulty of finding good quills, and being forced by the steel nib into 'a revolting scribal scrupulosity'. When Wilfrid Blunt tried to interest a publisher in his book on the Italic Hand the man told him that this was the age of the typewriter, and no one but his (W.B's) aunts would read the book. But the good man was wrong, because the odd, largely excellent and partly priggish and precious, revival of the sweet Roman hand was just beginning, and is now in full swing. There is a society which meets and is lectured and magic-lanterned to from time to time. I attended one once and was at once reminded of a gathering of Baconians (of whom I was once one, though not in spirit) and, as then, felt very giggly. Why do the males of such societies run so much to Adam's apples, and wispy moustaches, and pince-nez, and the women to shiny noses and strangled contralto voices?

How sorry one is about M.B.[1] *The Times* was good on him, wasn't it? They nearly always are on such occasions. But I quite expect the *Spectator* and/or *New S.* to strike the wrong note and I shall go all Whibleyan again. I am permanently so about our Press.

[1] Max Beerbohm died on 18 May.

How good to find you have the right view of Bunyan. Such greatness of *character* in almost every page. How is it entirely uneducated men get to write like that? There is nothing better than the trumpet passage—and several others like that marvellous little message of Vanzetti's to his judge which I enclose. I had some copies printed for Extra Studies—after your day. I expect you know it, but perhaps have not it actually by you. I once sent Winston a copy after he had been to Eton to judge the Loder Prize, and at dinner was talking about literary style. I mentioned this. He expressed interest. I said I would send him a copy. I did so. He made no acknowledgement. *C'est la vie!*

27 May 1956 *Bromsden Farm*

Lord's made me think of Cardus, which made me wonder whether you have *The Essential Neville Cardus* (ghastly title), which I selected and introduced for Cape in 1949. Apart from selections from the earlier cricket books, it contained C's account of the Test Matches and Gents v. Players of 1938, which I had luckily preserved from the *Manchester Guardian*. The book is out of print, but if you haven't it I'll get you a copy. Let me know. I'd like you to have it.

I can hardly describe the reluctance with which I drove south on Thursday, exchanging all that peace and beauty for the petrol-fumes and racket of London. I found my desk a pyramid of letters awaiting my answering—and no secretary! A temporary one, God help her, arrives tomorrow. Fancy your having been a Baconian! Were you interested in the opening of that tomb the other day? As someone well said, the crackpot American must have 'wept like anything to see such quantities of sand'.[1] Which reminds me—where does this splendid phrase come from—'I see them at their work, these sapient trouble-tombs'? I feel sure it's Lamb, referring to some nonsense at Stratford, but can't run it to earth.

[1] Mr Calvin Hoffman had recently persuaded the authorities to open, at Chislehurst in Kent, the tomb of Sir Thomas Walsingham, brother of Elizabeth I's spymaster, in the belief that it contained proof that Shakespeare's plays were written by Christopher Marlowe. There was nothing in the tomb but sand.

Rutherford sounds one of those batsmen sent us for our good. How old *laudatores temporis acti* like myself hate them, forgetting men like Quaife and Albert Ward, the Mrs Humphry Wards of the cricket-field. Though to me Quaife was never really boring. Unlike my ancestor 'whose every limb was a blemish, every movement a disgrace', his handling of the bat was that of an eighteenth-century exquisite with his clouded cane and snuff-box, and gave one the same pleasure as Irene Vanbrugh arranging the flowers at the beginning of the second act of *The Truth about Blayds* (and *what* a good second act!). But he didn't prod and shuffle about like the Rutherfords. When you talk of left-handers you are thinking of Woolley and not of Philip Mead, Clem Hill, or William Scotton who had no graces, though horribly efficient. C.B. Fry always maintained that left-handers were fortune's favourites as they got more loose balls than right-handers. Someone countered this by pointing out that the normal bowler's off-break was to them a leg-break, i.e. much nastier. *Quis rem decernet?* Scotton committed suicide, probably to avoid being murdered. He made 91 in seven hours in a Test Match. You could make a very fine side of suicidal cricketers, beginning with Shrewsbury, Albert Trott, Stoddart, A.E. Relf, Richardson—just as a fine Eton XI could be built up of expellees!

I should *love The Essential Neville Cardus*. There is no writing on cricket to equal his early books. And how nauseating his too numerous imitators are (like biographers who aped Strachey and poets who wrote about sheep and cyder in Miltonic blank verse). Am I right in thinking that Charles Morgan's hailing N.C's cricket reports as 'Meredithian' a little went to his head? Tim Nugent once complained that an N.C. account of a day's play left him in a complete fog as to which side was in, let alone having the better of it. But, at his best, there is certainly a touch of something like genius about him.

I joined the Baconians from sheer curiosity. I left them because I thought they were so rude and silly and childish about all who continued to think S. was still S. And I still continue to think there is something very mysterious behind the whole story. And I incline to old Agate's theory that S. wrote the plays, but that Bacon had a persistent finger in them; he added—*more suo*—that S. was probably B's 'fancy-boy'! The Baconians are immensely boring about these cryptograms; I suspect any clever fellow can produce more or less convincing cryptograms out of anything. Do you remember Ronnie Knox's brilliant establishing of the real author of *In Memoriam*, i.e. Queen Victoria! I don't know where your excellent quotation comes from. 'Trouble-tombs' certainly sounds Lamb-like.

My excellent son-in-law, an Artillery man, has in the last ten days demolished the old decaying bridge over the stream, and after felling three trees, has built a new bridge. I have hammered in a few nails, but it was really a one-man achievement, and has saved me about £40 to £50. And while he has been doing that I have been looking up passages and verifying quotations and inventing mild jokes for naval consumption. And his bridge will be there next year, when my Greenwich utterances will have vanished from the face of the earth like morning mist. But I am used to that. Crace[1] once likened teaching to painting a portrait with a sheet between one's brush and the canvas. Stroke after stroke and you never see the results.

3 June 1956 — *Bromsden Farm*

To-day is my elder son's twentieth birthday, and the family has been briefly but happily reunited to drink his health in one of our last bottles of champagne. He is on leave from Germany till the 18th, my daughter came home for the week-end, and my younger boy for the day. They were all very young and gay and handsome and happy, and they unknowingly provided one of those rare occasions when one can see in one glance that all the hideous sacrifices entailed in their education have not so far been wasted. I don't mean that I'm feeling pleased with myself, just a trifle reassured. Also yesterday I saw a spotted woodpecker in the garden for the first time—there are many green ones about.

Last week was easier than I had expected, chiefly because the temporary secretary turns out to be a jewel—quick and accurate and nice. Considering that every name and address was new to her, she

[1] J.F. Crace, Eton master.

did wonders, and the arrears should be cleared off in a few days—of correspondence, that is, for the pile of MSS awaiting my attention before being sent to the printer is formidable. Also a splendid new one turned up—two hundred letters from Max Beerbohm to Reggie Turner, covering the years 1892–1938. They're delicious, and you'll love them, though (like the George Moore ones) they'll need some editorial notes. One quotation I can't resist copying out for your private eye (for it's copyright etc etc):

> Did I tell you about Oscar at the restaurant? During the rehearsal he went to a place with my brother to have some lunch. He ordered a watercress sandwich: which in due course was brought to him: not a thin, diaphanous green thing such as he had meant but a very stout satisfying article of food. This he ate with assumed disgust (but evident relish) and when he paid the waiter, he said: 'Tell the cook of this restaurant with the compliments of Mr Oscar Wilde that these are the very worst sandwiches in the whole world and that, when I ask for a watercress sandwich, I do not mean a loaf with a field in the middle of it.'

Isn't that charming! I knew you'd enjoy it. Max's ashes are to be buried in St Paul's (how wide his eyes would open at the news!) on, I think, July 2.

I think applause did to some extent go to N.C.'s head, but it's difficult to imagine how one could write about cricket year after year without getting bored with the ordinary and trying to introduce something a little different. He has often sworn he would write of the game no more, but always his love of it draws him back.

Some week-end I must go to Chantilly to stay with Diana Cooper, and Arthur Ransome will never speak to me again if I don't visit him and his wife in their new cottage near Ulverston, and on August 30 I have promised to take three of my family (and the car) to France for a fortnight.

Oh yes, in these letters Max reported that some author (can't remember who—a woman, I think) kept three card-indexes, one for the living, one for the dead, and one for publishers! That must be the one you so flatteringly showed me on your desk.

6 June 1956 *Grundisburgh*

You say you are 'not feeling pleased with yourself', only 'reassured', on a day when your family is all round you, 'gay and handsome and happy', and when you also saw a spotted woodpecker! My dear, it was a day to be marked '*meliore lapillo*' surely. After all, the late Duke of Devonshire so regarded the day on which his sow won a first prize. That old Philistine would probably have thought the spotted woodpecker was a sparrow with measles. Not that I must seem to pose even for a second as knowing about birds. Not only did I never have good enough sight, but the Lyttelton clan were always deplorably insensitive to Nature's sights and sounds when young. Later in life they are much less so, but then of course they spend their time, perforce, in vain regrets for lost chances. And even now Pamela says my thrills over the nightingale and kingfisher are mainly 'literary', and I have a sad suspicion it may be true. Apropos of which, please tell me who wrote the four lines:

> When were you chipped from the blue bowl of air
> To haunt our vernal valleys, kingfisher?
> Love moves through valleys even more enchanted,
> Where rivers of the heart are halcyon-haunted.

Because, as C.M. Wells used to say about, perhaps, a chorus in the *Agamemnon*, 'Of course it's pretty good'. I hope you agree? Your disagreements are always stimulating. I think one's distaste for 'over-writing' grows with age, though not, one may hope, to the morbid extent visible in old Maugham, M. Murry and even Desmond MacCarthy (who was curiously disappointing the only time I met him—in judgment, not in amiability).

I say! Two hundred Max B. letters! Did *that* happen on the same day as the woodpecker? If so, beware, for you must be one of those the gods love. That Oscar tale is lovely; I have been grinning all day over it, and the self-control I shewed in *not* telling it to two intelligent friends at the Club puts me in the St Anthony class. I wish I could be at the July 2 ceremony.

Another thing in which we don't see eye to eye is *listening* to the ball-by-ball progress of a Test Match. There are such lengthy periods when nothing seems to happen. Watching on a good TV set might be altogether another matter, but the only set nearby is the Cranworths', and they are not very good at the knobs. The only cricket I ever saw on their TV was merely ghosts folk-dancing in a snowstorm. It didn't even come up to the Giants' Causeway, which old Samuel said was worth seeing, but not worth going to see. A nice distinction. Australian cricket talent is much *thinner* than it was. So is ours; leave out four men on each side and it is Second Upper v Eton Mission. The modern cricketer's fragility is a great puzzle. Plum Warner's theory is that all that massage they get rubs all the juice and elasticity out of their bones and sinews! However that may be, in days when they had no masseurs, thirteen men were taken on an Australian tour and though *one* usually drank too much, the rest played match after match without an ache or pain. Very rum. Temperament plays a bigger part in all this modern publicity than it used to. You need as thick a skin as W.G.'s who couldn't see why anybody should be nervous as 'there's only the next ball (rhyming with "marl") to play'. But Bradman, who also had no nerves, told me (!) in 1948 that he was sick to death of the crowd outside his hotel and the forty letters a day. Is there anything, which has any popular appeal, which is not grossly overdone?

I was quite overwhelmed with the majesty of Greenwich, which I had never seen before. The first sight of it struck me more than any building I have seen, except perhaps the Acropolis, though for that my mental soil had of course been fully prepared. I know nothing of architecture, but surely Wren at his best is unsurpassable in the matter of proportion and dignity—without pomposity, like the best prose! The young naval officers were an excellent audience—deceptively quiet when I began, but like hounds on a scent when a joke or a good point appeared, and the reception of the good stuff (e.g. Johnson's Chesterfield letter, Fortescue's Death of Black Prince etc) was so exactly right that I felt encouraged to end with the story of Housman's paper at Eton when *he* ended by quoting *Paradise Lost*, Bk III, 'Thus with the year seasons return, but not to me . . .' They got it all right, and I felt to the full the happiness of realising that they, and I, and John Milton were all of the same race—so different from my feelings as I sneaked away from the Old Ipswichian dinner, rather in the manner in which I imagine a man emerges from a brothel—hoping that no one will see him! It was a very enjoyable experience. The young instructor who takes the same view of literature as Leavis, i.e. hates practically everything that everybody else likes, had been *ordered* to be present by my infuriated friend, the director of studies, to whom he had pooh-poohed Max Beerbohm. His expression was mainly glum but brightened slightly when I quoted Ivor Brown's version of the Lord's Prayer in officialese. He hoped it might somehow dim the prestige of religion. I imagine all Leavisites are virulent atheists. The whole trend of my discourse, viz that there was much enjoyment to be got out of reading, went plumb against his mentor's notions and teaching. I am glad to say these do not seem to be making much headway at Greenwich.

My days are disagreeably full of school governors' meetings this summer. The knell of independent schools really seems to have struck and—literally—six times as many parents are talking of last straws and camels' backs than ever have before. And as all state-paid schools are cram-full what is to happen? The grim ironical truth, too, is that a great deal of all this education is to a great extent wasted. How often per month do you think in the small hours that *all* our problems are insoluble—including who is to go in first for England?

P.S. By the way I always wanted to ask, why are there no letters to and from *you* in the Hugh Walpole book? Surely you had some. I have read it again. The human interest in it is endless. What a lot of sourness and jealousy there is among the literary set! Always was, I suppose. I like W.S. Maugham's bland unblushing admission that he lied when he assured H.W. that Alroy was not H.W. Ought I not to dislike W.S.M. as strongly as I do?

10 June 1956 *Bromsden Farm*

It was lucky that I seized the fleeting moment of last Sunday to write to you, for to-day, though one of my children is still here, and my reassurance holds, there is no spotted woodpecker, no gleam of sun, and all is submerged in a dank, dripping, Tennysonian greenness, with the cuckoo of a joyless June calling out of doors. At the end of our small lawn (as I hope you will soon see for yourself) there are five tall laburnums, whose lavish shower of gold lasts perhaps for two week-ends, and not once yet has it been warm or dry enough to sit outside and enjoy them—no summer-house, you see, and my library is on the other side of the house. I don't, alas, know who wrote those lovely lines about the kingfisher. My knowledge of birds is minimal, but my delight in them unbounded.

Over-writing is, or should be, a fault of the young (a healthy one, I maintain), and therefore less and less likely to please as one ages. At all events I'm always more excited by a new writer's manuscript that overflows like a cornucopia than by a spare and trimmed one—no, not always, but generally.——There I took time off to re-read the final pages of *Earlham*: exquisitely beautiful they are: I must read the whole book again: it will surely be read as long as anything's read. Oh, George, how many books there are to read and re-read and enjoy and talk about, and how little time I seem to have for this, my greatest pleasure! Max's funeral has now been fixed for June 29, the only day thereabouts that I simply can't manage. I promised my daughter to be at the prize-giving etc which marks the end of her year at the Institute of Agriculture near Northampton: my wife can't go because she is teaching at a little school in Henley, and I can't disappoint the child. So those exquisite ashes will have to be lowered to their lasting home without my adding the immediate tribute of a tear.

I was sure your talk at Greenwich would be the thundering success it clearly was, but if I had realised that you hadn't been there before I would have enlarged upon its magnificence. I first saw it from the river, whence indeed it was meant to be approached, and was overwhelmed. Then, between the wars, I went to the Maritime Museum with my friend Wyndham Ketton-Cremer, who had sold them a Van de Velde seascape to pay for a new roof for his house. The museum itself is full of lovely things, and I was overwhelmed all over again. Then, last year or the one before, I went with Diana Cooper to see the Queen Mother reopen the rebuilt chapel. Diana had presented a beautiful altar-prayer-book in memory of Duff's time as First Lord. Did you see the chapel? Of its kind it's the loveliest I've seen anywhere—such perfect proportions and full of light. My *bête noire* Cantuar officiated and it was all most impressive. What room or hall did you speak in?

There *are* a few extracts from Hugh's letters to me in the book, but I am everywhere disguised as 'a friend'. I realised that either I must appear a good deal, or not at all, and the second alternative was so obviously right that I studiously avoided the first person singular—or plural. For instance, as you may have guessed, I was the 'friend' who intruded on his last meeting with Virginia Woolf (pp 421–22)—an enchanted occasion. I have a boxful of Hugh's letters to me. I can't believe you've read the book *again*! Didn't you find any grammatical, syntactical or other solecisms? You are at perfect liberty to dislike Willie Maugham: his character is indeed detestable in most ways, though he has always been charming to me, and I once saw him do something extremely kind. He is the exact opposite of all he pretends to be, i.e. sentimental, a poor prose-writer, and (if it suits him) quite generous. His ambition, I believe, is to *leave* more money than any writer in history (Shaw's £300,000 is, I imagine, the present record). W.S.M.'s only child, Liza is now married to John Hope and lives about three miles from here, though we seldom see them. I am obliged to see so many too many people in London during the week that in the country at week-ends I cultivate the reputation of a boorish recluse.

13 June 1956 *Hagley Hall, Stourbridge*

I have dashed up to my ancestral home for two days as a brief *ventre-à-terre*, as someone called it, from which to attend a Governors' Meeting at the Abbey School, Malvern. My nephew lives here in a cheerful state of bankruptcy, and ancient aristocratic squalor. I am writing in my bedroom, as through all the state-rooms, library, sitting-rooms, pass sightseers from the Black Country and Birmingham; gazing, with less expression than one would think possible on the human face, on the good lord, the mad lord, the bad lord, a Van Dyck or two, 'The Misers' by (in my day) Quentin Matsys but now said to be someone else whose name eludes me. For a time they were mysteriously stationary outside the house, where there is nothing special to see except the broken corner of a stone under the window where my Uncle Bob all but shot Mary Drew, and the spot where I fell off my bicycle in 1895. The coins thus extorted keep the wolf a yard or two from the door, audibly growling and visibly impatient, as if anxious to get the job done and move off elsewhere.

There is an unfathomable sadness brooding over the place, for all the happy family in nursery and schoolroom, as the traditional English country-life of over two centuries moves steadily to its close—against which no doubt we may, indeed must, set the rounder cheeks and better clothes of the Hagley villagers, but no one ever suggested that the old order was in a particularly cheerful mood as it yielded place to the new. Even Beatrice Webb, when older (and wiser) than she had been, became increasingly dubious about what she had thought so obviously and undeniably good. I am reading her diary with great interest and a good deal of skipping. She is somehow *not* very easy to like—why? Her judgments are shrewd, incisive, well put, but to me there is too much hard cocksureness about them, difficult though it often is to pin it down. How witch-like she became, so bony and scraggy! And am I being absurdly stupid and fastidious and what-not in disliking rather strongly the picture of her 'curling up on her husband's knees in the twilight'—both of them well over 70? Probably. But at the same time I admit they lived a fine life and did a fine job etc etc. So long as I never have to meet her in Heaven above or the earth beneath or the waters under the earth.

I plan to go to Greenwich again quite soon—by water, in a barge festooned with garlands, large enough to contain a small but exquisite orchestra playing Handel's Water Music. That Chapel, yes, my spine tingled like Housman's cheek as he thought of that verse in a psalm. One of D.H. Lawrence's 'dark gods' no doubt.

No, I haven't definitely re-read *Hugh W.* but the book has been in the dining-room, frequently read in when Pamela is out for tea etc. No solecisms etc discovered and so many good touches e.g. Mr Pooter. There is a Mr P. in me too at times, who very nearly made me pass Hagley station asleep this afternoon, at the end of an absurdly short journey from Malvern. I must have some more talk with you about H.W. and several things I want to ask. How right you are about W.S.M. as a writer. *The Summing Up* is *stuffed* with clichés. And what a fatuous ambition to *leave* half-a-million. What fun he could have bestowing it in sizeable chunks on worthy objects, and now the Government will bag two-thirds of it and spend it on God knows what.

I must stop; the night is far gone. Nothing is audible but the cough of an asthmatic sheep, and the nocturnal rustle of the Hagley ghosts. The late Dr Rendall had battalions of them at Butley Priory, but they didn't bother him. 'I brush them aside', he replied when asked. At 84 he had no fire all the winter; a two-hours walk kept him warm until tea-time and then he went to bed. A tougher man than the English and Australian cricketers of 1956. They must take to noughts and crosses—and even then some will sprain their thumbs on the pencil.

17 June 1956 **Bromsden Farm**

I write to you from the depths of a most appalling task. I have an American authoress called Ruth McKenney, who normally writes funny books, of which I have published half-a-dozen with some success. About four years ago she and her husband (a delightful American of great wit and integrity) decided they must make some money by writing a long historical novel. They chose Napoleon's campaign in Egypt as background, and read a great deal of history. They wrote and rewrote the novel for months and months until, sometime last year, when it was 7/8 finished, Ruth cracked up under the strain and (not to put too fine a point upon it) went off her head. Her poor husband Richard asked me if I would read the manuscript, which was then 900 pages long, and encourage her to continue. Although I loathe historical novels I did this (it took weeks), correcting the grammar, punctuation and French as I went along, besides removing Americanisms, anachronisms and so on. As such things go it wasn't at all bad, and might well have been a winner, especially in America. However, my encouragement proved useless: Ruth got dottier and dottier, their money began to run out, Richard couldn't get a job here and she refused to go back to America (they were once Communists). Eventually, some months ago, Richard gave up and committed suicide (sleeping-draught) on her birthday—a classic psycho-analyst's pattern: her birth = his death. He was a darling man, and his death saddened and also infuriated me. It also brought Ruth more or less—and however temporarily—to her senses. She seized the manuscript and rewrote every word of it, putting back all the errors I had so carefully removed and doubling the length of it all, so that it now occupies 1800 pages of typescript (about 400,000 words). After Richard's death, as a gesture, I made an agreement to publish the bloody thing (though how that is economically possible I don't know) and now she is waiting expectantly for my opinion of it. Since I *may* after all publish it, I feel obliged to correct it all again—which does not make for speed. I began the fearful job yesterday and have only reached p. 177. Clearly it will take me weeks, and I have so many other things, more interesting and important, to do. I sit with it in my library, longing to read *any* of the books that surround me rather than this hideous work which has already killed one good man. Keep all this under your hat, please, and send me your sympathy.

Very many thanks for your letter from Hagley. I like to think of you among the tranquil ghosts of your ancestors, though the future of such splendid institutions is gloomy. Soon all will be rows of identical council-houses topped by television masts—'long live the weeds and the wilderness yet'. I haven't read Beatrice Webb's diary, and don't much want to. Do you remember Nicholson's wonderfully revealing portrait of them both sitting most hygienically by a hideous red-brick fire-place? Did you listen to Hesketh Pearson talking of Chesterton and Belloc this afternoon? That splendid telegram of G.K.C.'s to his wife ('Am in Wolverhampton. Where ought I to be?') reminded me of your almost passing Hagley station. The point about Willie Maugham's fortune is that the Government will get almost none of it, since he has been careful to live abroad these many years, and the bulk of his royalties has been earned in America.

During the week I attended committee meetings of the Royal Literary Fund and London Library. Also dined *chez* Veronica Wedgwood with Rose Macaulay, John Lehmann, Sir T. Kendrick (Director of the B.M.) and another girl—an agreeable evening with dressed crab and strawberries. My son's leave is passing in a whirl of theatres and dances: he flies back to Düsseldorf on Tuesday. The younger boy failed to get a scholarship, as I expected, and sits for his Common

Entrance tomorrow. On Saturday we must watch him play the king in *Henry IV Part I*—out of doors!

Pursuing material for a George Moore footnote, I have just read a book about the Druce-Portland case. Who could invent such fantasies? I enjoyed it very much. I love reading and writing, George, and literary editing and research, but the mechanics of *publishing* grow, I must confess, ever more wearisome. Just now I wish Napoleon had never lived, let alone ventured to Egypt—oh well! My dear Edmund Blunden is arriving in England on July 28 for a month or so, partly staying at Soho Square, so my weekly letters to Hong Kong will have a breather. I write him only as much as can be squeezed on to an airmail form—on Sunday, just after writing to my children and before writing to you. He answers most weeks: sometimes a letter takes only two days!

Midsummer Day 1956 *Lord's Pavilion*

(1) Cardus. A *delightful* present indeed. At his best—and he often is—there is no writer on any game to touch him. And I join issue with you—and him—as to his early work being inferior. You have cleverly left out his over-ripe period—the tour in Australia of '46–'47.

(2) This is just to cheer you with the news that I see no chance of writing a letter till Sunday. Here all day watching, and rest of day talking. I am at the moment surrounded with Forsytes—whiskered, jowly, Tory, querulous, magnificently fatuous and fundamentally imperishable, thank God.

(3) Later from ground. I have been asked to play. May has leprosy, Cowdrey swallowed a bit of egg-shell at breakfast and the surgeon will be here shortly, Richardson has been stung by a bumble-bee but will almost certainly be fit for the Oval match, Evans cut himself shaving, Graveney's mother has lumbago. So have I, but there is literally no one else.

(4) At 9.55 there was a queue outside the ground from Swiss Cottage, any number under thirty years of age.

(5) Roman society was ruined by '*panem et circenses*', i.e. Test Matches, Football pools, and high wages. *Verb sap.*

24 June 1956 *Bromsden Farm*

How infuriating that you should be compelled to sacrifice some part of your Midsummer Day at Lord's in writing to me, who cannot have been more than a hundred yards away from you. I was sitting with a beloved female friend in the Rover seats just beyond the Press Box, and came into the Pavilion for a moment during each interval, vainly hoping for a glimpse of you. The sunshine was lovely, but the cricket seemed to me pretty dull. Did you go yesterday too? I hope so, for it was clearly the best so far. All I could manage was an occasional eavesdropping at someone's car-radio, for I was obliged to witness *Henry IV, Part I* at my boy's prep. school. He was rather good as the King, but the comic scenes were less successful: no little boy of twelve can begin to tackle Falstaff, and as the round Elizabethan oaths piped out in treble tones, I longed to know how Trueman was doing, and whether the casualty wards were filling up.

The 'sapient trouble-tombs' do come from Elia (E. Blunden knew at once)—from 'Detached Thoughts on Books and Reading', which is clearly due to be re-read by both of us. De la Mare's death is a grief: did you know him? One of the rarest and sweetest men I ever met, and his finest poems as timeless as Shakespeare's songs—all earth and air and spirit.

Although this letter may be a few words longer than yours, it is sadly short, for I am manuscript-ridden and proof-haunted and behind-hand with everything—all this cricket and Shakespeare, you see. George Moore and Yeats and Henry James and many lesser men are all waiting for their works to be tidied up, and every day new horrors accumulate. Forgive my brevity, please George, and hope for more next Sunday.

North Foreland Lodge
Sherfield-on-Loddon
27 June 1956 *Nr. Basingstoke, Hants*

And if this isn't an impressive address I should like to know what is. I am in the head mistress's drawing-room; pianos are doing their duty relentlessly all round; floors squeak and rumble to the impact of toes, which, individually, may be light and fantastic, but collectively bear convincing witness to the school dietary. I had at lunch the largest helping of pressed beef, salad, and potatoes I have ever seen, followed by a kilderkin of custard. The Chairman of the Governors is to the attendant girls as Benjamin was to Joseph. Later on the girls have tea at 3.50 and high tea at 6.30. I find that unalluring. My tête-à-tête spam with the headmistress at 7.0 is better. But I am often reminded of Virginia Woolf's *A Room of One's Own.* However it is a lovely place and they all look happy. What else do you want? Moreover there are three bull-points here. They play no cricket, they play no hockey, and they don't have a speech-day.

I saw every minute of the Test up to lunch on Monday. It was a little humiliating. Never but after tea on Thursday did England attack. Too many of our batsmen make the bowling look better than it is. Hobbs, Hammond and Co were much more dangerous after being in for forty minutes. Not so Richardson, Graveney, Watson and even Cowdrey second innings. They never appeared set. Trueman is a slinger rather than a bowler; village cricket in excelsis, the blacksmith doing his utmost. His run and Statham's are absurd—thirty-five paces from crease to starting-place. In comparison Miller is as antelope to buffalo. And every ball of *his* has brains behind it. I hope you noted how one umpire signalled a leg-bye like a man testing himself for locomotor-ataxia? Evans's wicket keeping was *superb.* The catches of Benaud, Cowdrey, Bailey and Harvey were as good as any I have seen—and Evans's stumping—quick as a flash off a foully laid ball. How grand was May! And how many of our critics pointed out the supreme quality of batting which achieves 60 and 50 in a Test Match when eye and touch are out? One, I think. C.B. Fry once told us how Ranji, afflicted by 'biliousness, bronchitis and corns' (sic!) made 100 v Lancs. 'That's great batsmanship, you know.'

I was in luck at the match. Best seat on middle gallery, *plumb* behind the bowler, and next to Gerald Kelly—disliked by many, but I found him, as always, excellent company. He and you together must know practically everyone of any achievement in England. But I should say he is less charitable about them than you are. He was full of tales about G. Moore, S. Maugham, Max B., A. Bennett etc. Didn't like Hugh Walpole (mutual I suspect) or Lord Jowitt or a good many others. Can be and often is pretty rude, I am told. Like me, he only goes to Test Matches, and I shall continue to go because I like seeing a great many old friends. The cricket, frankly, is not as worth seeing as it used to be, because it stands to reason that in a five-day match risks must not be taken; in three days they must. That is why Trumper told my uncle Bob that he liked cricket in England much better than in Australia. And why both sides used to score 60 an hour and now 30.

I must stop. Have read nothing for a week but *South Wind* in bed. Amusing but—? I need hardly say Gerald Kelly's description of the author was positively horrifying.

I have just shaken hands with ninety-three girls and said good-night to each. I never realised how much one human hand could differ from another in texture, temperature, moisture, grip, size and general character.

P.S. K. Miller. What a man! A tiger in strength and swiftness of movement. Did you see him on his way out pass a vast valedictory arm over Trueman who had just bowled him? He alone knows it is a game—and plays it with every fibre.

1 July 1956 *Bromsden Farm*

You saw all the exciting bits of the Test Match and I all the dull ones. The last rites on Tuesday were graced by hot sunshine and all the lithe genius of Miller, proving how one may smile and smile and be a tiger, but the batting was pathetic—neither aggressive nor defensive. Cowdrey was like a great bumble-puppy and May fearfully unsure. Only Bailey showed any mastery. Clearly the Australians deserved to win, and I take faint encouragement from the fact that Benaud's innings, which probably settled the fate of the match, was the only truly forcing one. It had begun to look as though Test Matches can be won without *hitting* the ball at all. Oh yes—as the Australians trooped triumphantly into the Pavilion, they fell back to let Miller go in first, but he pulled Langley forward in a charmingly boyish way and they walked in together. It's sad to think we shan't see Miller in another Test Match at Lord's.

Your girls' school amused me very much: I should love to have seen you drain your kilderkin of custard. I hope you did it in one manly draught, no heeltaps, and called loudly for more. I have never fallen in love with custard, have you? A superfluous and taste-destroying mush, I should say. On Friday I spent four hours at my daughter's speech-day at the Northampton Institute of Agriculture. She, bless her, got a distinction and two prizes, besides giving a most capable microphone commentary on a parade of Guernsey cows. She is now clearly much better qualified to run the nation's Agriculture than the wretched Minister, who probably knows nothing about it, and has to cope with Fisheries to boot. My younger boy, having (I now suspect narrowly) failed to win a Scholarship, took Common Entrance and has been placed in *Upper* Remove! This is surely something new, like Sunday Games which I understand are now *de rigueur*? Anyhow this should reduce his fagging to a minimum and perhaps ensure his eventual arrival in Sixth Form. Fred still says he has no vacancy till January, so the boy is to spend his first half under the roof of B.J.W. Hill. Do you know him? My elder boy gives him a good report and I enjoyed his *Eton Medley*: anyhow I'm most grateful to him.

Next week-end, by the way, I shall be in France, staying with Diana Cooper at Chantilly. I'll write from there if I can, but I don't know when it will reach you. I was prevented from attending either de la Mare's or Max's funeral: on Thursday morning I addressed fifteen travellers for two hours on the beauties of the Autumn List, and Friday was the speech-day. I am longing to polish off the editing of those George Moore letters, but other things pile up to prevent me, and when I get back to them I shall probably have forgotten everything.

I was sorry to read of Michael Arlen's death. He was another friend of my youth, always very friendly and charming. He looked awful, knew it, and described himself as 'the last of the Armenian atrocities'. He was an Oriental storyteller, like the author of the *Arabian Nights*, and his approach to writing was utterly realistic: directly he had made enough money (chiefly in America) he stopped writing altogether—and it was just as well, for his slender topical gift was already exhausted. Last week I was at two long meetings with four Coleridge scholars, drafting a manifesto which we hope will induce an American Foundation to cough up a grant big enough to finance a Collected Edition of S.T.C.'s works in twenty volumes! I know it's crazy to embark on such arduous and unprofitable tasks, but that's the way my fancy leads me. Tonight I must write a review of six detective stories: your stubborn silence on this matter convinces me that you take the stern moral line of most who disapprove of this particular nonsense. Oh well, I suppose we can't agree about everything. Are you going away at all this summer—or coming to London? Heaven knows when I shall get to you.

4 July 1956 *Grundisburgh*

All that you say of *custard* is of course true, and all really good men avoid it. But—how can I frame the words?—I have always *rather liked* the stuff! Made with eggs of course, not Bird's. I shall try to convert you when you next come here. When will that be? Shades of the prison-house encompass me next week in the shape of exam-papers, till about the end of August. My one spell of work in the year coincides with the universal holiday. My spade and bucket spend August gently rusting (I never had any truck with a *wooden* spade after arriving at the age of discretion. I hope you didn't?).

Don't misunderstand me when I congratulate you on your second boy missing his scholarship. He will, by and large, prosper more, *mentally*, in a good Oppidan house. Whatever collegers may, and do, say, College does have a narrowing effect on many. Tuppy, himself an old K.S.[1], always said the old K.S's were, considering everything, an extremely undistinguished lot. No one can say that Geoffrey Dawson was a failure, but somehow with all his intelligence, good judgment, kindness, sense of duty, high-mindedness etc he never seems to rise out of Class 2. I am not familiar with his leading articles, but his diary and epistolary style is markedly undistinguished. I suppose, if you are immersed in day-to-day problems, it is only the

[1] King's Scholar (Colleger).

really great men—like Lincoln or Winston—who can produce the profound generalisation, or the phrase which illuminates once and for all. I have only reached the end of the first war and the break with Northcliffe, so perhaps there is better stuff to come. Wrench's editing strikes me as rather amateurish; his interwoven narrative is often, in some way, out of key with contemporary events. And don't you agree that biographies of public men ought always to have the relevant *year* at the top of each page. Many of G.D.'s entries and letters have no date at all.

By the way, your lad should do well for one half at Hill's. A good sound fellow and by no means a bad slow bowler. At one time the boys' nickname for him was 'Trafalgar Hill' as he was said to weigh 18 stone 5 (1805). But now I fancy Fred could give him half a hundred-weight. He is a nephew of M.D. Hill's.[2] I thought his *Eton Medley* was never enough praised; it was a remarkable achievement by a non-Etonian.

That is an interesting little sketch of Michael Arlen you give. How rarely does a man know when to stop. *The Green Hat* now seems as long ago as Anthony Hope, Seton Merriman and Co. How completely best-sellers vanish as fashion changes. Probably you have never heard of *Phroso* or *The Sowers*? We stood in queues for them in 1900. When did I give you the impression that my nose was in the air about detective stories? I always buy one for a journey, but I do like them to be well-written, lively, and to have real people. So I am often disappointed. I think I have read 70% of the Christies, *all* the Sayers, Allinghams, Ngaio Marshes and most of the Dickson Carrs and Carter D's, Gilberts and Berkeleys, and Fitts. Please tell me some really good ones available in Penguin or Pan. I am through with P. Cheyney—too many cigarettes, bourbons, and curves—Ellery Queens and Yanks generally. Is Chandler any good? I still put *Trent's Last Case* first, with of course several Father Browns.

Gosh! Twenty volumes of old Coleridge! Can he bear the weight of that? I know nothing of his philosophy. He always seems to me one of those who astonish by the point and splendour of their obiter dicta and disappoint when one reads further—the plums are so toothsome, the rest of the bun so heavy. I quite expect to hear you are

[2] Eton master.

embarking on a new edition of the works of Klopstock or Werner. When I went to Weimar in 1906, I arrived at the Hotel zum Elefanten at midnight and the very first thing I saw from my window in the morning was a dog copiously micturating against the statue of Werner. I read a few of his poems and my opinion of them went hand in hand with the dog's. But perhaps we were both wrong?

Château de St Firmin,
Sunday morning 8 July 1956 *Vineuil, Oise*

Here I sit in my Uncle Duff's lovely little library, looking out over lawns to lake and trees, on the most beautiful summer's day ever. Also in the house are Isaiah Berlin and his newly wedded wife; Auberon Herbert who fought with the Polish army in the war and is now forever canvassing on behalf of that martyred but oh so boring race (Auberon is a Catholic: his sister is married to Evelyn Waugh); Norah Fahie who was Duff's secretary; my cousin Artemis, aged three, Duff and Diana's grand-daughter, and her English Nanny. Many others—Air Vice-Marshals, Rothschilds, all sorts—arrive for meals, and at the moment *all* the work of the house is being done by a Polish woman and a Chinese boy! Excellent luncheons for twelve are served by the pair of them, as though many more waited outside: it's an extraordinary achievement, reminding me of *The Bride of Lammermoor* and the servant (was he Caleb Balderston?) who kept up such a bluff. (Duff's Scotts are mostly first editions in original boards, which one scarcely dares open for fear of splitting them.) Next week the Polish woman is emigrating to Australia, poor brute (I can't make her understand that the Test Matches are *here* this year), and the household will have to disband until further staff can be recruited. To-day we are all to drive over to lunch with some other Rothschilds—the neighbourhood swarms with them—and no doubt the fare will be terrific. I am already swollen with the amount I have eaten and drunk since Friday. I came over in great comfort by train and boat, and shall return the same way on Tuesday. Tomorrow I must spend in Paris, pursuing a partially paralysed old pansy who claims to have collected Oscar Wilde letters for fifty-six years. We can't make out from his correspondence whether he possesses, or has ever seen, the originals of what letters he has, or whether he has just got a mass of typed transcripts of doubtful origin and authenticity. Since he is in his late seventies, was recently knocked down by a bus, and speaks *no* English, I foresee a trying day, particularly if it's as hot as this. I must also try to find someone to put me up in Paris tomorrow night. I forgot last week to suggest that you should write to Soho Square: never mind, there may be *two* letters waiting for me at home next Friday.

Do you know Isaiah Berlin? He was born in Russia, is a Fellow of All Souls, a brilliantly amusing—and very rapid—talker. He swallows most of his words, just as Rose Macaulay does. His wife is rich and beautiful. She has a lovely house at Headington and a flat in Paris. (Auberon has just come in and is trying to telephone—vainly so far.) All this is so far removed from my usual round that it makes a wonderful change. Gossip with rich people in lovely surroundings on a heavenly day might well pall after a little, but for a week-end it's amusing and even restful. You'd love this library and I'd love to go over it with you. No one else perhaps appreciates it now, which is rather sad, for Duff took such trouble with it. I long ago locked up some of the more pocketable rarities, like the three Keats first editions. No Sunday papers. What happened in the University Match?

12 July 1956 *Grundisburgh*

I meant my last week's letter to catch you on the wing, but see Burns on mice and men—and over this one lowers the shade of exam-papers and school meetings, not to mention lumbago which has been, as Arthur Benson said of ailments after fifty, 'peeping and beckoning' a good deal lately. All school governors are on the twitter about Burnham Scale salaries and fee-raising etc, and there are signs that parents, peering through the heap of straw on their backs, see the last one on the way.

As to the G.C.E. I am finding out the answers to the questions—many of which I set myself nine months ago—e.g. what exactly happened in that forest in the *Midsummer N.D.*, one forgets it every year, however many answers on it one has read. It is an absurd play anyway to examine on; the books are chosen by our superiors, and they make at least as many bloomers as those pundits at St John's Wood.

Your château interlude sounds delicious. St Firmin, Vineuil, Oise—the bouquet of exquisite vintages breathes from each name. And then Uncle Duff's library, Isaiah Berlin, Auberon, Artemis—my dear Rupert, is this a book by Norman Douglas?—No, there is no faint sweet odour of decay about it; Henry James perhaps; wasn't there a lady called Casamassima in your party? It is clear your company must have been of the best; I often hear I. Berlin put at the very top of good talkers. And I long to hear more of your visit to that 'partially paralysed old pansy' who says he has Oscar W. letters. What exciting encounters you are always having. I never knew your Uncle Duff though I should like to have and always enjoyed his writing. I suspect he regarded beaks and ex-beaks with at least prima-facie aversion, and who shall blame him?

I am much interested at the moment in the early life of H. James (published by you!) by L. Edel, 1953. Is the rest on the way? I have never heard you mention it. H.J.'s is a difficult character to grasp—all those layers of sensitive reactions, that mysterious back-ailment, which always recurred whenever brother William turned up! J.B. Priestley writes somewhere of J's characters seeming 'to have no employment beyond an obscure and suffocating kind of self-torture'. Surely H.J. himself? Your old G. Moore despised him, didn't he?—and one has to be very fond of him before one can quite stomach those overflowing affectionate letters. I sometimes have the feeling that it is possible to be *too* civilised and courteous, even granted there is no suspicion of insincerity? I cannot help being amused by the chapter about his obscure injury, and the swift and facile assurance of many critics that castration and/or impotence was what it obviously was. What a lot of Sir Gerald Kelly there is in everyone—'stuffy little creatures, human beings', as Romain Rolland said.

How different our respective lots are—you go lunching with Rothschilds, talking to I. Berlin, delicately savouring the essence of an exquisite library, fighting with beasts at Ephesus in the shape of literary men—a life of overwork, strife, interest and variety. My afternoon will be spent in (1) buying a tin of putty (2) mending a wattle fence (3) discussing the lavatorial needs of the Woodbridge prep. school (4) pointing out to my banker that in the matter of legibility—the *first* duty of a bank-clerk—all his b-c's are at fault (5) writing a testimonial for an old pupil saying, roughly, that as he has failed to make good as a chartered accountant he is bound to be a good schoolmaster (6) passing the time of day with Mrs Pizzey (7) a little folding of the hands in sleep. And yet in a million or two years putty and I. Berlin will be of equal importance—Well, well!

15 July 1956 *Bromsden Farm*

Evelyn Wrench is an ass, and I say that *all* biographies should carry the relevant year (and if possible, the subject's age) at the top of each page. Incidently I can't resist copying out for you a sentence from a newly published symposium called *The Craft of Letters in England.* In the chapter on Biography by J.I.M. Stewart (a Christ Church don who writes most amusing thrillers under the name of Michael Innes) occurs the following: '... and Mr Rupert Hart-Davis's *Hugh Walpole.* The last-named has an assured claim to be among the half dozen best biographies of the century.' This, I must confess, is the sort of thing that cheers one up after a week or two of other people's proofs have kept me from George Moore etc.

I'm delighted to have drawn you at last into a declaration in favour of detective stories, and will send you the titles of any particularly good ones I come across. Once, long ago, reviewing a Peter Cheyney for *Time & Tide*, I wrote: 'It is difficult to understand why these lovelies, when, as constantly happens, they are crushed to the manly bosom of the spy-killers, are not incommoded by the blunt-nosed Lugers which these gentlemen invariably carry under the left armpit.' P.C., swollen by success and vanity, forbade his publishers ever to send a review copy of his books to *T & T* again!

My French week-end was delightful. After lunch on Monday Diana drove me into Paris (Chantilly is about as far as Windsor is from London) through forked lightning and tropical rain. High up in the Boulevard Beaumarchais, near the Bastille, I ran to earth the old Wilde fan. His flat was indeed murky as a fox's earth: every window, and most shutters, tightly fastened on a stifling Turkish-Bath afternoon. All the time I was there (about 1½ hours) sweat was trickling down inside my shirt. He is a short man of seventy-something, with a thick white beard, masses of white hair, and spectacles. He received me dressed in trousers, a very *décolleté* pyjama-jacket and a dressing gown. At great length he described how he had been knocked down crossing the road, was now permanently lame, and moreover sometimes lost his memory in the middle of the lectures by which I imagine he earns his living. You can imagine the law-suit he is conducting against all and sundry. He told me that since 1903 he had collected every book, cutting, photograph and anecdote of Oscar, and he has shelves and cupboards and shelves and cupboards to prove his assiduity. Telling me he had written or translated more than 200 plays, he showed me glass cases full of puppets that belonged to D'Annunzio, also signed photographs of Sarah Bernhardt and goodness knows who. When I steered him back to Oscar in my halting French, he read me, with much emphasis and emotion, long extracts from his translations of *The Ballad of Reading Gaol* and the other poems. Then he produced two enormous files, which contained the programme of *every* production of *Salome* all over the world, together with photographs of lightly clad but hideous actresses in the name-part. At last I got him on to the letters, and he fished out a thick folder stuffed with copies of letters, all in his illegible old-Frenchman's hand, and all in French. After some discussion I promised to send him a list of what we've got, and he promised to re-copy and send me any of his that we lack, though I very much doubt how many of them are authentic. Beyond touching hands a little more than was necessary when handing me books to look at, he made no advances, and was I think genuinely pleased to have someone to talk and show his treasures to. The whole flat was dark, stuffy, hung with oriental hangings, full of books, pictures and *bibelots*—very ninetyish. Eventually I escaped with relief.

On Friday afternoon my two authors (Vincent Cronin and R.S. Thomas) and my old friend Wyndham Ketton-Cremer were all given prizes at the R. Soc. of Lit. Afterwards I gave a dinner (eight strong) for them in a private room at the Garrick, so didn't come down here till yesterday morning. Oh yes—in a French novel, read in the train,

I came across this charming 'Italian saying'—'A priest is a man who is called Father by everyone except his own children who are obliged to call him Uncle.' Had you heard it before?

18 July 1956 *Grundisburgh*

J.I.M. Stewart knows what is what. I read a lot of biographies and —quite seriously—I agree with him as to *H. Walpole*. Shall you be bumped by old Ervine on Shaw? What more *is* there to say of that fascinating and infuriating man, who had every gift in the world except wisdom—or does that need qualifying and emending? Now Baldwin had it, though for the moment one mustn't say so out loud. Do you remember him on B.S.? 'Shaw was charming with one person, fidgety with two, and stood on his head with four'. But talk doesn't count. I bet Shakespeare shewed off a good deal when the Mermaid was full. Not Bacon certainly—and what an oppressive companion he must have been. A meeting between him and Ben Jonson must have resembled God's conversation with His son in *Paradise Lost*.

I look forward to your tips about detective stories, just as I do my daughter's about films. One can have such disasters in both, and those blasted reviewers don't help at all. I love your remark about P. Cheyney, both for itself, and for it having stung P.C. He had an evil face. I read several of his books but got tired of them—those invulnerable Callaghans and Lemmys, who, after half-an-hour's man-handling by thugs, had a bit of a headache but were as spry as sparrows in two days. And those *incessant* references to cigarettes and whisky; in one story I counted twenty in fourteen consecutive pages. How boring such tricks become. I used always to notice how an Agatha Christie character would, on being asked an awkward question, 'pause for a minute', when she obviously meant 'moment'. But I rather fancy someone has told her about it, as I have not noticed it lately. Michael Innes's detective stories are not easy to come by. None has yet appeared as a Penguin. Someone told me they are 'caviare to the general', i.e. too clever and complicated. I remember enjoying *Hamlet Revenge* very much. Public taste is a mystery. We are all now to lose our heads over a young man Colin Wilson. I am sure I shall have no difficulty in disliking him. Do you know anything about him and his 'outsiders'? And the editor of *Truth* too seems to have an obscure knife in anyone who is not disgruntled and 'agin the Government' in most ways. Uncomfortable young men. I wonder if they realise the iron certainty with which the mere passing of time will shew up whatever is not genuine in their diatribes and their whole point of view. Swift's mind was a-boil with '*saeva indignatio*', which is very different from what *sounds* like petulant and resentful egoism. But that is not an opinion. It is such a mistake to damn a book one hasn't read (as Sir G. Sitwell told Osbert it was to expose oneself to the Germans entrenched forty yards distant). But as W. Cory stated, one of the faculties a good education develops is 'to express assent or dissent in graduated terms', and so few who write do that. *You* do in that excellent review of Henry J's *Notebooks*, but, as you point out about H.J. himself, the times will not again allow the leisure or society essential for such artistry as his. Among the lights which Edward Grey saw going out one by one in 1914, this is surely one.

There was an excellent point made in last week's *Time & Tide* by Norman Angell. He commented on the curious blindness of the TV Brains Trust, all of whom praised our system of education but had much fault to find with the Press, without *one* noticing that an education which produces x million readers of the *Mirror*, *Reveille*, etc cannot really be all that good. We keep on coming back to Percy Lubbock's great dictum that civilisation, far from being established, has really only just begun.

Your visit to the old Wilde fan is a gem of description; you call him up to all one's five senses and his oppressive surroundings, costive with the accumulations of age-long, undiscriminating hero-worship. I should like to have watched your face while the old bore droned on and on. But I expect long practice has given you a wonderful command over your features.

What agonies old Henry J. must have suffered when his courtesy and friendship clashed with his artistic integrity, e.g. when Mrs Humphry Ward wanted to know what he thought of her book. Condemnation usually does emerge, but so swathed in affectionate and apologetic trappings as often to elude the author's partial and prejudiced eye. *His* eye which missed nothing must have often delighted in the spectacle of human vanity deceiving itself for the nth time. A final question. Was anyone—not a relative—ever completely at ease with H.J.? Men, I mean, not women? Percy L. rather hedged when I asked him. So did John Bailey, who practically said he was better to write to than to talk to. That habit you mention of stopping a story before the point was reached, because he had got all he wanted out of it, was rather daunting. I should have wilted. Did anyone ever *yawn* when he was ranging the jungle in search of *le mot juste*? Did H.G. Wells listen patiently?

Thank you for the definition of 'a priest'. Very good. It goes into my large notebook—with your initials appended (there shall be no 'You will, Oscar, you will' against me). Do you know my charming ex-pupil John Verney? There is a delightfully humorous thing by him in this month's *National Review*. Do read it. It was rejected by *Punch*—being neither dull nor pretentious. (Don't *you* find *Punch* of today ghastly—except Hollis on Parliament and P.G.W.? J. Verney reminded me of a crack of his I hadn't met, viz 'An apple a day, if aimed straight, keeps the doctor away', which *I* call delicious.) I can't understand 75% of *Punch*'s picture-jokes, and when explained, don't think 'em funny. So what next? Next week great coveys of exam-scripts darken my sky, but a lyrical cry or two shall reach you.

P.S. H.J. and names—'*Peter Quint*' is a beautiful distillation of sheer poison. At Hagley there is a dark eerie corner on one passage, which for years has been known as 'Quint's Corner'. My nephew admits he always passes by it rather quickly.

22 July 1956 *Bromsden Farm*

The first Michael Innes you must read is *The Journeying Boy*, and I shall be surprised if some of it doesn't make you laugh aloud. All his books are immensely literary, which I always enjoy. I know nothing of Colin Wilson, but am not attracted by the sound of him or his book: his article on Shaw in to-day's *Sunday Times* seemed to me clotted and pretentious—but may be we are both prejudiced.

I too wonder whether any man was ever completely at his ease with Henry James, though clearly he could turn on massive charm at will. Some day I'd like to edit and publish all his surviving letters to H.W. Did I tell you that the surviving correspondence between H.J. and H.G.W. is being edited, and I hope to publish it next year. Later perhaps also the surviving Shaw-Wells letters. I've been meaning to read John Verney's book ever since it came out: now I clearly must.

On Wednesday I looked in for a couple of hours at the Gents v. Players, but it was dismal play, finally washed out by rain which also drenched me on the way home. I hope to catch a glimpse of the Australians tomorrow. At Paddington on Friday I ran into Roger and Mrs Fulford, on their way to Reading to hear Harold Nicolson talk about Jane Austen. If I lived on the Westmorland fells it would take something more exciting to drag me south! I had never met Mrs Roger before and was delighted by her charm and beauty. Guy Chapman stayed with me at Soho Square last week, and next Thursday Edmund B. flies in from Hong Kong. I shall bring him down here next week-end. Yesterday was my swan-song on the cricket field— the Fathers Match at my son's prep. school. I wasn't called upon to bat, bowled my own boy (1 for 0 in one over) and caught an inescapable catch. I felt pleasantly melancholy as I left the field.

26 July 1956 *Grundisburgh*

I have all day been reading the literary judgments of third-rate beaks at fourth-rate schools. These judgments are dictated to their pupils, who learn them more or less by heart, without more than half understanding them. One lot of boys, answering the question which they thought the best and which the worst poem in the *Lyrical Ballads*, said 'The Idiot Boy' was the best and 'The Ancient Mariner' the worst. Another lot said that Dr Arnold was the only subject in *Eminent Victorians* which Strachey had treated with sympathy and admiration. And, my God, the flat, indiscriminate, insincere superlatives many of them effuse with diarrhoetic prodigality! The poor lambs were clearly bored with *The Antiquary*, but one and all babble of Scott's 'incomparable' mastery in 'describing scenery' of all tedious arts. I have not this time come across many good jokes, the best so far being the statement of a young lady at some convent that the most unEnglish trait in Lord Nelson was his 'dreadful behaviour' towards Emma Hamilton. Well, no more of that. But you will see why this letter will be a drab affair.

Your cricket swan-song was impressive—much more than mine years ago. I didn't bat or bowl; I bent to pick up a practically stationary ball at point, and a moment later was walking delicately, like Agag, back to the pavilion in the iron grip of lumbago.

Old Shaw isn't getting much of a Press.[1] A.J.P. Taylor contemptuous and not—I thought—very good in the *Observer*, K. Tynan a good deal better. I doubt if I shall tackle the Ervine book. H.G.W. and Henry J. a wonderful confluence—what *had* they got in common? More perhaps than H.G.W. realised, viz a power of phrase—one of H.G.W.'s best gifts (which he despised).

I have just listened to a cello solo by Casals—perfectly celestial. The cello is a lovely thing—the Rembrandt of the orchestra, don't you think? I must stop. It is late and very hot. The room is full of moths, June-bugs, bees and I think a bat or two.

1 August 1956 *36 Soho Square*

Oh George, George, how have I forsaken you! Since Edmund Blunden flew in from Hong Kong last Thursday I've been busy entertaining him—a delightful task but disrupting all my routine. So you must be patient and understanding. E.B. came down with me for the week-end, and on Saturday morning we took him over to Eton to call on Hill, whom we all liked very much indeed. My goodness, that house (Adie's to me) isn't half noisy! I ran into your Bourne son-in-law in the street. He seemed to approve of Hill. On Sunday I drove Edmund over to tea near Thame with his old publisher, Richard Cobden-Sanderson (son of the Doves Press printer and grandson of Richard Cobden). The poet Ruth Pitter was there, and we got through a lot of cake and literary gossip. On Monday night, up here, I gave a little party for E.B.—drinks followed by dinner in Soho—mostly Coleridge-experts and very agreeable ones. Edmund is

[1] On the centenary of his birth.

starved for such company in Hong Kong and enjoys it all immensely. Last night I abandoned him, for drinks with Max Beerbohm's widow (intelligent, sympathetic and on the spot), followed by a dinner-party (ten strong) at the Hamish Hamiltons'. The company included the editor of *The Times* and other notables. I sat between Cecil Woodham-Smith and Moira Shearer. The latter is exceedingly pretty and easy to talk to. Mrs W.S. is good-looking in a hatchety way, but talks incessantly about herself in tones just lower than one can catch.

The joy of last week was Compton's innings v. the Australians. It was every bit as good as his wonders of 1947, using every shot, known and unknown, attacking every ball and utterly disconcerting Benaud and co. He made one realise again how drab and strokeless most of the batting is to-day. He couldn't run very fast, but his footwork otherwise was nimble and adroit—an immense pleasure.

Last week I also dined (a) with Eric Linklater and his wife and (b) with Jonah, who gave me a slap-up meal at the Travellers and said he would like me to publish his next book! After my idiotic refusal of *A Victorian Boyhood*, I found this offer most touching, and gladly agreed —but say nothing of it, for Macmillan does not yet know. Tomorrow I am slipping away to my Yorkshire hide-out for a long week-end. I meant to tell you to send your letter here. Never mind, I'll get two next week, and will try to send you a line from the fells. Don't let the exam-papers get you down.

3 August 1956 *Grundisburgh*

You must have had an excellent time with Edmund B. I hope you saw Eton on a good day and that he was worthy of it; it *can* look all right—and sound too when the traffic lets up a little and no one sings the third verse of the Boating song, on which Hugh Kingsmill was justifiably trenchant. But perhaps you found your guest was one whose eyes fill at the merest echo of 'Forty Years On'. I am glad you liked Trafalgar Hill. Are those Coleridge letters any good? Or are they in the G. Eliot class, which some reviewer said recently and bluntly are of steady unending dullness? I suppose it is some Yank who has published volume after volume of them. Why do they do it?

What about Laker?[1] I doubt if it will ever be equalled; and yet you know, he isn't really as good as all that. But the Australians are very poor batsmen off a plumb wicket. I am delighted you saw Compton shewing up the present-day batsmen; except May there just is not anyone like that. The in-swing and those short legs have stiffened up and slowed down the game and, whatever they say (and they say far too much), it isn't the game it was. In fact outside Compton and Miller and a very few others it is hardly a game at all. I haven't read Jonah yet. I see the *T.L.S.* says he is rather too nice about everybody, and somewhere else I read a cheap little sneer at all that Balliol splendour. And talking of cheapness, I have just marked forty papers on five English books from Malvern. Not only were they dreadfully bad and idle, but the tone was that of Teddyboys, flippant, blasé, shallow, sneery. I never read more deplorable stuff, which left me with the conviction that it must be a very bad school. They didn't ask for a report, but they are jolly well going to get one. One bright boy did a very bad paper and then saw fit to write a poem about Cleopatra, the last stanza of which began 'Cleopatra/ was the Egypt answer to Montmartre/ a most respectable tartra'.[2] It is to accompany my report.

I must get back to them. The first batch is really finished. I am writing this in the summer-house. It is raining; I have lumbago; the kitchen-sink is blocked; the fridge has struck work—and P. summons me to tea.

5 August 1956 *Yorkshire*

This is just a pastoral note from high altitudes to prevent your getting no letter next week. The heavenly quietude of this hilltop ringed with mountains sank into me the moment I arrived on Friday afternoon, and I am blissfully recharging my exhausted batteries before driving back to London on Tuesday. The scene here has changed little since May, save that some fields (I can see hundreds from this window, of every shape, all bounded by stone walls) are darker where the grass has become hay, and others are lighter where

[1] J.C. Laker took 19 wickets in the Old Trafford test against Australia.
[2] From *Salad Days* by Julian Slade (1954).

the hay has just been cut. The weather has been so bad that much of it seems likely to spoil, and yesterday's hot sunshine brought out tractors and horses and women with hayrakes. There is no arable land in this dale, just pasture for sheep and cattle, and the hay to feed them during the winter. Every prospect pleases, and man is miles away down the valley. This hill itself is carpeted now with wild thyme and meadow-sweet and other flowers in profusion. The plovers have left, the larks are silent; the grouse, apprehensive perhaps of the Twelfth, give an occasional honk; curlew fly past, their great curving beak silhouetted against the blue sky. Except for an occasional low or bleat, there is *no sound*—and to appreciate fully the bliss of that condition you should have spent a month or two in Soho Square, where a large section of the road is now 'up' and the whole crazy car-park still further confused. On Aug 28th (my forty-ninth birthday) they are going to start tearing down the house *next door* (an eighteenth-century one) and replacing it with—what? No one knows how many months of dirt and din we shall have to endure. Last week Edmund B. stayed with me there, charming as ever with his quick perceptions and nervous sparrow-movements. He will be sixty in November, and when I asked him the other day whether he didn't sometimes forget how old he was (as I do) and momentarily imagine himself young again, he said 'Yes, and when I was young I hoped that one day I should be able to go into a post office to buy a stamp without feeling nervous and shy: now I realise that I never shall.' How lucky one is not to have been born with diffidence that must cause agony. E. is off to stay with Siegfried Sassoon, then back to me, then to his Conference at Cambridge.

My best news is that an angelic Canadian professor called George Whalley (who is working on Coleridge) has offered to help me with the donkey-work of the Yeats bibliography, which as you know has been hanging about for a year—with G.W.'s help it should be finished in a week or two. George Moore has accompanied me here. Oscar Wilde awaits me in London. Say but one prayer for me twixt thy closed lips.

Your northern spell sounds delicious, and I hope has not more than temporarily made the *fumum et opes, strepitumque* of Soho Square strike too nauseatingly on all your five senses. For a brief spell Suez may have seemed no more to you than a name in a Kipling poem, but no doubt it is a very different story now. The letters I get from old Maurice Headlam are full of the damned place, and as his line is frankly, even blatantly, 1897, there is no basis for rational discussion. Perhaps there isn't anyway; we seem bound to be in some kind of soup whatever we do. What a lot of people don't realise that imperial gestures are futile unless there is imperial strength and unity behind 'em. It is disagreeable to find oneself seeing a good deal of sense in what is said by Silverman, Ziliacus and Douglas Jay, for it is practically an article of faith with me to regard them as always wrong. Do you remember in *The Lanchester Tradition* the beautiful sentence 'No cause was ever finally lost until the Bishop of X had made it his own'. Have you any 'foolometers'—people whose advice you ask, knowing that exactly the opposite to it will be the right course?

That shyness of E.B.'s. I have met it occasionally. Lady Patricia Ramsay (i.e. Princess P.) once told us that to that day (twelve years ago) she had *never* opened a door behind which there were several people without her heart sinking. Very different from B. Shaw—or shall I be really original and declare, à la Colin Wilson, that all G.B.S.'s conceit and cocksureness were merely a façade for the violet-like shrinking of his innermost soul?

I believe the really most distinguished O.E. quite unknown to the public is Sir Wyndham Deedes, who did wonderful work of some kind which I am unable to specify, in a part of the globe which I am unable to remember. I expect you know all about him and probably published his book on those overwhelming problems in—where was it? This—according to Max B.—is the rarest kind of distinction, which he, if I remember right, ascribed to the President of the Swiss Republic, whose name was on the tip of everybody's tongue but never emerged any further. Deedes I believe hated Eton, but then he was in old Mike's house, where unless you were a dab at some game you cut no ice. The Sitwells were at Somerville's, Robert Byron at Robeson's, all houses of which Philistia was manifestly glad. They should have been at Luxmoore's, Macnaghten's or Arthur Benson's; then they would have had a pleasanter spring-time. Oh yes, and the Actons at McNeile's—the only man who ever took Greats as one might take shorthand or book-keeping, and got a first-class. Do you know anything of one Brian Howard, who was going to make a name in literature or journalism, and has completely disappeared?

I have finished my first batch of Cert papers. Pretty bad most of them. It is pretty clear that the men teaching English in most schools are the most lowest forms of pond life. Hardly any answers have the kick or the warmth which *some* members of a class would reveal, if, say, they had been taken through *Julius Caesar* as Mr King took his lot through the Regulus ode. Even his sworn foe Beetle couldn't help saying 'Interestin' beggar, King, when he's on tap'. Occasionally the cloven hoof of Leavis appears, e.g. in the instructor of one school, half the candidates of which had a callow sneer at 'Tintern Abbey'. One bright boy, asked why Wordsworth laughed himself to scorn at the end of 'Resolution and Independence', said it was because the leech-gatherer had told him leeches were much scarcer than they used to be. And yet there are those who say W.W. had no sense of humour!

I am getting a great deal of pleasure out of Frank Swinnerton's *Background with Chorus. Full* of amusing and interesting gossip, and I like him as he emerges from the page. I wonder why he disliked Walter Raleigh so much; nobody else did. The letters which F.S. finds 'repellant' are surely often among the best. I met W.R. at Eton—A.B.R's dinner-table, where he said he had never, till then, had as much whitebait—or perhaps sardines—as he had always wanted. He also said that he had only said one really witty thing in his life, when asked what he thought of some very poor claret, by a host who thought well if it. W.R.'s answer was 'Minds innocent and quiet take this for a *Hermitage*'. But I agree with F.S. it is irritating to find him referring so often to Shakespeare as 'Bill' when writing about him. The don, anxious to shew he doesn't take himself too seriously. I have always enjoyed F.S's novels, but does anybody else?

Next week I shall write to you from Oxford where I shall be cooking the Cert marks—and I hope seeing that my report on the Malvern candidates is not bowdlerised. Oxford is sheer Hell in August—

packed with Yanks in ridiculous clothes, and all the most earnest societies having their annual gathering. Two years ago all the coal-black clergymen were there the first two days. An even more depressing community succeeded them—the plainest women in West Europe. We used to be housed in the Randolph Hotel, a pretentious place, costive with rich tourists, but now we go to St Edmund Hall (where there is a well-stocked cellar). There are some forty or fifty awarders, divided very much as some wag once said the Cavalry Club members were—one half of them would give all they possessed to be able to make water, and the other as much to be able to stop. It is true that in colleges the lavatories can be a very long way off one's bedroom, but the case is better than it was only fifty years ago, when there was quite a walk under the open sky, and *either* university in February—!

I have just finished a frightful book about the Gestapo—and 'much it grieved my heart to think What man has made of man'. It is a very sickening story, but it gave me one thing of value, viz Himmler's reference to Heydrich who, I suppose, was about as foul a creature as the vermin world has ever spawned. 'This good and radiant man.' Can you beat that? And talking of gems, and in the probably vain hope that you haven't yet read the book, Swinnerton gets Lloyd George in *two* words, comparing Asquith's mind with L.G.'s 'soiled quicksilver', and Austin Dobson, who 'crept like a wren in the thicket of contemporary allusions'; and he ends a fine portrait of old Saintsbury with the breath-taking facts that G.S. 'read *The Earthly Paradise* twenty times, and wished *The Faerie Q* were longer'. I wonder (but pretty confidently) if these things give you as much pleasure as they do me. Old-fashioned is definitely a term of censure to our modern young pundits. Poor lambs, they little know how precarious are the pedestals they stand on or the altars they raise, and what a sour smell incense has in a few years. And what *they* call old-fashioned sentimentality I call in old Saintsbury's phrase 'the purged considerate mind of age'.

How all occasions do conspire against me! This week-end, which was to have been devoted to you and George Moore, has been rent asunder by family complications. My wife's half-brother Michael Spears is dying of cerebral haemorrhage in the Middlesex Hospital. He is only 35. I should explain that long ago my wife's parents were divorced and each remarried, so that I kicked off with two complete pairs of in-laws. Her mother's second husband is Gen. Spears, the greatest living sh—t. Some 2½ years ago he let me down with a bang and I have never seen or spoken to him since. He and my mother-in-law had this one child, a charming boy but always ill, unsuccessful and unhappy. It so happened that when he fell ill on Friday my wife's step-mother was staying here—a sweet old widow (her husband, my wife's father, died ten years ago). My wife had to rush to London to comfort her mother, and I was left to cope with the other old lady and my little boy of thirteen. This I have successfully done—but at the cost of all else. To-day we drove the old pet home to the Cotswolds through a jungle of caravans and other holiday traffic. We lunched (having no cook) at the Trout at Godstow, which I remembered as an idyllic country inn. We found it invaded by some kind of Anglers' Reunion, for which beer could scarcely be drawn quick enough. However we got some lunch. Later we fetched my wife from Reading: exhausted, poor lamb, after a night in the hospital 'rest-room'. The doctors say there is no hope for the poor fellow, but he may linger in a coma for days. Tomorrow we shall park our boy with friends, and my wife will come again to London. Sorry to inflict all this on you, but it may at least excuse this miserable letter.

I found two splendid ones from you awaiting me. (At that moment my elder son telephoned from Germany—God knows what it cost him! As we weren't expecting him to ring up, neither my wife nor I could think of anything interesting or important to say.) Back to your letters. The S.T.C. correspondence is in a different class from G. Eliot's. I bought the two vols but so far have only dipped into them. To my mind May can't touch Compton for genius—that particular kind of inspired improvisation. May is a superb player, but I have seldom seen him play a truly unorthodox stroke, whereas some of Compton's beggar description.

Your Oxford visit doesn't bode too well, but may be you'll extract something amusing from it. How do you like this? 'French verse evokes an image of a carriage drawn by two horses both stepping beautifully; English verse of horses that can escape from their harness, spread their wings and take the air.' It's in a letter from George Moore to Gosse. Goodnight, dear George. Perhaps *next* week you'll get a proper letter at last.

18 August 1956 *Oxford*

We are housed in St Edmund Hall, and extremely well found in the matter of food and wine. Today Marsden and I lunched with the Cowley fathers, of whom Beasley-Robinson[1] is one. Why are so many monks indistinguishable from convicts? The close hair-crop certainly sets out in that direction, but it is the facial expression that completes the picture. I sat next to the Father Superior and disgraced myself by starting to talk immediately after the grace, and had to be checked by a wave of the hand while a reformed burglar read what I think was a chapter of scripture. After that he was most affable till a bell rang and they moved off like a parliament of rooks to tea or some form of worship. What a strange world they must live in! I couldn't stomach it for half a day, but they look contented enough, though without that inner radiance we hear of. Perhaps time and old age are needed for that. Bishop King of Lincoln certainly had it when over eighty years old.

What a coil of family contretemps has been tying you hand and foot. Some day you must clarify your whole family tree to me. What ancestor of yours was it who is mentioned in the life of Harriette Wilson—an M.P. I believe? I hope your ancestors were no more models of respectability than mine. One of mine certainly was called the wicked Lord Lyttelton, but, except for not extravagantly numerous breaches of the Seventh Commandment, I don't know that his villainy amounted to much, and there is no doubt he was excellent

[1] Former Eton master.

company. He was a gambler, but not for a long time did our elders reveal to us that he was a shrewd and successful one, whose ventures filled Hagley with fine pictures etc. And a hundred years later, how did the Duke of Devonshire so majestically maintain a reputation for wisdom and rectitude etc in between and in spite of regular and repeated visits to Skittles?[2] These were not kept dark; everybody knew, and nobody minded—while the very able Sir C. Dilke sank to rise no more after *his* escapades came out. Virginia Cowles's book is immensely readable; but what a grim picture of Victoria and Albert forcing the egregious Stockmar's education on the wretched Bertie. My father never had the smallest respect for B. because when at Cambridge—living a mile or so away—B. was forced to play cricket, the leading players were sent out to bowl at him. They did so, literally, and he used to fall down to avoid the ball. So my father reported, he being one of them. It is rather sad that almost everything that has come out about Victoria since her death makes her less admirable—so stubborn, narrow, and *selfish*. But there were great things about her. Do you remember the description of her (Strachey) entering a room with the Empress Eugénie—the loveliest woman in Europe, with the little round German widow—but there was no doubt which was the Queen, so superior is natural dignity to assumed. I wonder *what* she would have become with Albert alive for another quarter-century.

You don't tell me about F. Swinnerton. His book is delicious reading, and I should be disappointed to hear he was not a good chap. I have always heard harsh things said of that excellent writer Spears and rather gather he is apt to let everybody down in some way or another. Similarly, though I found him very friendly, Liddell Hart rarely gets a good press. His boy was up to me, and I had said in school the pundits' view was that Marlborough was a superior general to Wellington, whose forte was defence. L.H. came and talked about this to me on a Sunday afternoon—also how he had never understood why Leslie made so bad a mistake as to leave his impregnable position at Dunbar, and so he went to D. on one Sept 2 to see—and found that it was far too much exposed to bad weather for his troops. Interesting, but what about the hardy Scots?

Jonah's book[3] is full of rich echoes, though, as one review said, I

[2] A famous courtesan. [3] *An Edwardian Youth.*

suppose the spectacles through which he looks back on that galaxy of friends *are* a little too rose-tinted. I didn't like George Fletcher much, or C.R.L.F. at all—a prejudiced, denigrating man. Shaw-Stewart was immensely clever and very sneery, and dear Bear Warre must always have been very stupid and full of odd little affectations—and of course the *handsomest* man of 75 that ever lived. He can still touch his toes without bending his knees. I could do that last in 1902.

Thank you for George Moore on French and English verse; it goes into my commonplace book. What pleasure I do get from such things! And now I must get back to my galley-oar. This is sad scrappy stuff; odds and ends of time are no good to me. I like to have the morning stretching out before me, and the pigeons' soft voices telling of the passing summer, not too sadly for pleasure, and the two friendly bumble-bees that know better than you did what a comfortable place the summer-house is. Then, though they may not get on to paper, I have beautiful thoughts.

P.S. Did you know there is an English family whose name is Hodbod?

19 August 1956 *Bromsden Farm*

No letter from you this week: the fleshpots of Teddy Hall must have been too much for you! Are you still there, I wonder? The Spears boy is still alive, after ten days of uninterrupted coma, and it begins to look as though he may recover. But to what? The doctors say his brain may be affected, and another attack may come on at any moment. My wife spent six gruelling days in London, between the Middlesex hospital and her mother's house. Apart from the worry and fatigue, my mother-in-law and Spears perpetually bicker and nag at each other in a deliberately wounding way—surely the most tiresome of all forms of human speech—and this my wife found very trying at such continuously close quarters. I have told her that we must start for our holiday on the 30th, come what may—the car-passage is booked and all arrangements made. I'll send you the address next week.

My best news is that the Yeats bibliography is at last completed—

after more than a year! So one of the millstones is off my neck, and I can attend to the others. My selection of Edmund Blunden's poems will go to the publishers before my holiday, but George Moore and Oscar Wilde will be with me for many a day, not to mention two or three posthumous works by Max Beerbohm. Last week was comparatively quiet—August in London is usually a time when one can catch up with things. On Monday E.B. had some friends in for drinks at my flat. He had asked everyone he'd seen, but couldn't remember who they were, so we waited anxiously, and presently welcomed a second-hand bookseller from Woking, an out-of-work journalist from Brighton, two Chinese lawyers, my daughter (who happened to be in London), an enormous girl who used to be in the B.B.C. repertory company, my secretary (to whom E. had taken a mild fancy), Arthur Crook (who does all the work on the *T.L.S.*), the female representative of some American publishers, etc. As soon as it was decently possible I took my daughter off to dinner and a movie. Next week Edmund is at Cambridge, then back with me for two days before he reluctantly flies back to Hong Kong.

Tomorrow is the long-promised occasion of my younger son's first visit to Lord's. I only pray it keeps fine. He has never seen a first-class match and is tremendously excited. If there *is* play, he may see wickets tumbling to his heart's content, though I have a nasty feeling that his particular hero, Laker, isn't playing. To-day he asked me what I'd like for my birthday next week, and when I said a bird-table outside my library window, so that I can watch birds while I'm writing to you, he manufactured a most professional one in half-an-hour—a feat I couldn't accomplish in a week. Somehow I always expect my children to resemble me—did you?

At that point my wife brought me a glass of Bourbon whisky and water, so I continue refreshed. Do you know why it's called Bourbon (pronounced Burrbon)? Because it comes from Bourbon (pronounced as above), Kentucky. I learned that interesting fact recently and hasten to pass it on. Why Bourbon, Kentucky, was so named for the moment escapes me. I wish I'd read some good books lately, so that I could dazzle you with quotations, but all my spare moments have been spent grubbing up material for George Moore footnotes, the erudition of which will astonish few. It took me ¾ of an hour in the basement of the London Library to find enough for a footnote about Cora, Lady Strafford, a thrice-married American. Before one of her marriages (perhaps the second—to Lord Strafford) she thought it would be a good thing to get a little sex-instruction, so she went over to Paris and took a few lessons from a leading cocotte. On her wedding night she was beginning to turn precept into practice when her bridegroom sternly quelled her by saying: 'Cora, *ladies don't move!*' I need hardly say that this delectable anecdote is *not* in my footnote. The Oscar Wilde letters are going to demand a mass of annotation—just the sort of job I like, but *when* is it to be done? Meanwhile I haven't decided what books to take to France—some George Moore inescapably, some detective stories, Ervine's life of Shaw if the friend who offered to give me his spare copy keeps his word. Perhaps I shall find a delicious bookshop in France, full of everything I've always meant to read. If the sun shines I shall just sit gratefully in it pretending to read. Have I ever disclosed to you my passion for sea-bathing? It's the only form of exercise I ever take, and it makes me feel well as nothing else does. The very thought of it keeps me going from summer to summer—and here we are at the end of August without my having had a single swim! Pools, baths and rivers I don't so much care for. The Flemings have a pool in which my children happily splash, but I never go near it. I have put on weight again, and once French meals are behind me I shall do some strict dieting: I feel much fitter when I'm thinner: fat men I know are jolly, but I hate the tight belt and the full belly.

26 August 1956 *Bromsden Farm*

I have just spent five solid hours correcting the proofs of Stephen Potter's new book, and my eyelids are more than a little weary. There seems a time-lag in the arrival of your letters just now: the Oxford one of Aug 18 was waiting for me on Friday, but none of this week. Never mind—I shall probably find it on Wednesday evening, when I come home for the holiday. We start at 5 a.m. (!!) on Thursday, drive to Newhaven and embark the car and ourselves for Dieppe. The drive through France will take a good two days: it's 530 miles.

Sheltering from the ceaseless rain I shall probably send you a letter or two from there. My fear is that the Spears boy (who has now lain unconscious for seventeen days) will die between now and Thursday. If he does I shall take the children on, and my wife will follow by air after the funeral. On the other hand, once we've got away I fancy my wife will stay there.

The Harriette Wilson H-D (who does not cut a very attractive figure in her pages) was my father's great-grandfather, M.P. for Colchester, then Bristol (roughly 1815–31), well-off, bought some old masters from Beckford. I must have shown you his portrait by Lawrence in my office. Frank Swinnerton is a pet: a small, ugly, bearded, ageless-looking man. He giggles and chuckles a lot in an infectious way, is a brilliant mimic, and is full of malicious anecdotes which he tells without any malice at all: indeed I don't think there is any in him. When I had finished my Walpole book I told F.S. that there were a number of faintly unflattering remarks about him in it, all made by Hugh, and asked whether he'd like to see proofs in case he objected. He said NO: he didn't mind what was said and would much prefer the *ipsissima verba* to any bowdlerized version. I see him at the committee meetings of the Royal Literary Fund, which I accuse him of not taking wholly seriously, since he occasionally introduces a laugh into that otherwise solemn assembly.

My little boy's first day at Lord's was warm and sunny; he saw seventeen wickets fall and secured the autographs of A. Bedser and Loader (when they were taking the hat round for Laker)—altogether a most successful beginnning. I have a hideous pile of work to polish off before Wednesday eve. Forgive this miserable note. Let's hope the shadow of the Pyrenees will speed my pen!

27 August 1956 *Grundisburgh*

I am just home from Oxford—from where I do hope you got my letter. 'Fleshpots of Teddy Hall'! *Le mot juste*, I am afraid. They do us almost absurdly well in the matter of food and drink—a *first*-rate hock or claret *and* port or madeira of equal quality every night at dinner, plus whatever sherries and whiskies any jaded palate may require between-times—and even so, the Certificate Secretary tells me the total bill for the week's board is markedly less than it was at the Randolph exclusive of drinks.

Awarding is tedious work—as tedious as Dr J found the history of Birmingham—essentially because there is really not much objective certainty about the right mark for a short essay on the character of Brutus if the writer avoids mistakes of fact or spelling and grammar, and the chap who gets 92/200 fails while 94/200 passes. However we pass more who probably ought to fail than *vice versa*, and fear reproaches on the Judgment Day less than e.g. the marble-hearted mathematicians ought to. The *names* at English schools become odder and odder—beyond the wildest fancies of Dickens or Peacock. I put it to you that Patakakis (I hope the third a is long) is on the same level as Pumblechook.

Why don't the doctors let one die for whom life must be intolerable? I suppose in their hearts of hearts they doubt their certainties more than we know. Conybeare's dame died a year or two ago—she was operated on for cancer in 1912, but when they opened her they did no more as the case was hopeless. I believe doctors are always unanimous against euthanasia, but that some unofficially wink at it in actual practice. You may not have heard of the old woman who when asked if she favoured euthanasia, answered that she didn't know much about that but she was sure she preferred old age in Europe. A foolish old woman!

What an amount of work you do get through. I suppose you are a very fast mover—millstone after millstone chucked off like soiled collars. It is good news that you will get Jonah's next, unless the reading public suddenly stops reading and relishing him. I delighted in this book. How beautifully he writes! But I gather that modern taste deprecates 'style' and uses the word 'elegant' only as a term of abuse. Who was the 'leading critic' who was dubious whether one 'wanted to spend three hours of life visiting Balliol in 1905'? And who or what is he leading except a drove of *asses*? He would be scandalised if anyone ran down *Ulysses* from a disbelief in the worthwhileness of spending a day in Dublin fifty years ago. I am, as you have surmised, often in a rage—with God, the weather, politicians and pundits of all sorts, the Press, the T.U.C., in short to put it Wordsworthily, with 'what man has made of man'; and I am at the moment in a condition of bewildered irritability after reading Compton Mackenzie's *Thin Ice* and finding it duller than semolina (such reviews as I have seen are respectful). Flawner Bannal was quite right (in *Fanny's First Play*): 'You don't expect me to know what to say about a play when I don't know who the author is, do you?'

I like your company at E. Blunden's party and my mental picture of you keeping your end up with the Chinese lawyers and two-ton Tessie from the B.B.C. And I hope you asked (or will) Arthur Crook why the devil the *T.L.S.* is filled nowadays with foreign writers who don't *appear* to be of first importance, and why it assumes that its readers all understand German, Italian and Spanish. I am told that Pryce-Jones has had many complaints but, under a benign and courteous exterior, is quite adamant. Maurice Headlam complains that his reviews of books on fishing are often not printed, but that is not necessarily a black mark v P.-J.!

Did you and your son get a fine day at Lord's? The rector here prays every Sunday for fine weather, so far without visible result. How often August is a detestable month, but we forget it every year. An old friend of mine on the village green remembers the days before machinery when sometimes the harvest went on until November. He is over ninety and recently I came across him borrowing an *axe* from the blacksmith. He is a philosopher: 'They say there's nothing in old Swithun; but I hain't often found him wrong'.

We were all rather sensible at Oxford and only one mathematician wanted to air and hear views about Suez and the T.U.C., the rest of us realising that there is nothing whatever new to say about either. Things will be as they will be, and though these world affairs are as loaded with dangers as the clouds with rain, it is all devilish interesting. Except in late Victorian times, up to about Jonah's time at Balliol perhaps, the world never has been comfortable since the French Revolution—and perhaps it was never meant to be. A rum affair altogether! I must go to lunch—with what is claimed to be the dreariest line in all verse ringing in my ears 'The rain dripped ceaselessly down from the hat which I stole from a scarecrow'.

P.S. Just to acknowledge yours just arrived—good. Now the heart of our correspondence resumes its systole and diastole as before. I shall be with you in spirit among the Pyrenees. Breathe deeply and do nothing at all that you don't like. I hope and expect you will have a grand time; the rain must stop some day and September's history is much better than August's.

Hôtel de Paris
Hendaye Plage
Basses-Pyrénées

10 September 1956

Your splendid post-Oxford letter of August 27 arrived neatly on the eve of our departure and has now covered a deal of ground—650 miles from Dieppe to here, with two nights on the way, and visits to Chartres Cathedral and the Château de Chenonçeaux, which is built right across the River Cher from bank to bank in a most agreeable way. Lunch on the banks of the Loire at Blois, a brief crossing of the Dordogne to visit Nancy Cunard, who lives in a little converted barn, miles from anywhere and full of her books and pictures, including an exquisite Manet that belonged to G. Moore. I must confess that most of the journey was through pitiless rain, but ever since we hit the Basque country just over a week ago the sun has burned down daily from a clear blue sky: it was 99° in the shade on Saturday! We spend all day on the beach, or eating this hotel's excellent food, or sleeping. 'Directly there's a wet day I'll write some letters,' I've said to myself, but unbelievably there hasn't been one! I should explain that the hotel whose address I gave you, where we had booked rooms, turned out to be *beastly—on* the main road, nasty food—so we left after one night (paying a tenner as compensation) and drove on till we came on this delightful place—a perfect family holiday place—entirely French —with a huge sandy beach and the Pyrenees on three sides. The Spanish frontier is a mile away and we have twice driven over to amuse the children, though Spain (except in its sunniest south) is grimly poverty-stricken and desolate. Photographs of Franco everywhere, and armed police every few miles. The mountains are beautiful, and on our first drive we picnicked high up in the Pass of Roncesvalles. All the family are enjoying it hugely: all burned brown, and my hair is bleached to what the children call greyish-white but I prefer to consider the last glimpses of the blondeness of what H.J. called 'my fermenting and passionate youth'. As you know, I adore sea-bathing, which makes me deliciously relaxed and lazy. I have half a dozen detective stories; Swinnerton (on your recommendation) which I couldn't put down—I must send him a fan-letter; an American study of George Moore, *Ave*, half *Salve*, a great deal of the *Penguin Book of E.V.* We plan to leave here on Friday morning, crossing with the car from Dieppe on Sunday morning and getting home that night. It would be lovely to be welcomed by a letter from you. I brought the G.M. letters with me but have tinkered only . . . perhaps if it rains . . . you may even get another letter. Many of the villas here have cosy Basque names like ITZASUA. I must join the others on the beach.

13 September 1956 *Grundisburgh*

Welcome home—not that climatically, politically, financially or professionally you will find England at the top of its form. The last adverb refers to the immense pile of MSS etc you will find waiting for you. From your letter of today your holiday looks to have been first-rate, though to me a temperature of 99° would be sheer purgatory. Wrap up well at Henley. At the moment it is not raining, but the air bites shrewdly. I suppose a philosopher would extract comfort from the thought that never again will he (if aged 73) know so foul a summer, so fierce a July gale, and so damaged a harvest. It is odd to recall that in my six years at Eton (1896–1901) there was not *one* solitary drop of rain at any of the matches v. Harrow, and only one interrupted v. Winchester.

Glad you enjoyed Swinnerton's book. I should like—as the jargon goes—to associate myself with your fan-letter to him; I have always liked his writing ever since *A London Bookman* in 1928, and read him religiously every week in *John o' London's Weekly* until the Philistine owners stopped it because though paying its way it wasn't paying enough. Any good detective stories lately? I have just got from the Library the last Carter Dickson, but I gather it centres—for the nth time—on a murder committed in a sealed room with no possible way in or out. And the last Roughhead volume which has several letters from Henry James who appears to have had a strong taste for crime—like most good men. And I *have* read Graham Greene's *The Quiet American* and enjoyed it greatly—full of flavour. How good he is at getting the *atmosphere* both of an episode and of a character. One feels *sure* that the war in Indo-China was just like that; and the Quiet American himself rings uncannily true.

P.S. I am again a grandfather; Mary Stewart Cox has a boy and it is to be called—three guesses!!—RUPERT!

23 September 1956 *Bromsden Farm*

The holiday was everything that such things are usually not—boiling sun every day at Hendaye and all the way back to Dieppe, delicious food, perfect bathing, no English people or need to make conversation. Another week or two and I might easily have gone native in a big way. We drove back through Bordeaux, Angoulême, Poitiers, Tours, Chartres and Rouen, spending the night at Chinon, an enchanted and enchanting place where Rabelais was born. The ruins of a gigantic château (two towers and many walls and battlements) stand against the skyline. Below, the little town, crumbling mediaeval-looking, clusters down to the wide slow-moving river, the Vienne, across which only fields and trees stretch as far as sight. At night the floodlit ruins were magically beautiful. In the morning we saw the spot where Joan of Arc recognised the Dauphin, where the Templars were imprisoned, etc. I should like to go back there. France is the country to drive in—wide empty straight roads, no buses and very few lorries. The journey here from Newhaven was by comparison congested and tortuous. Now my sunburn is quickly fading, and I am steadily being resubmerged under piles of paper. The brightest spot is my office, newly painted pale blue with a new red carpet. On Tuesday my youngest starts his one half with Hill. Am I dreaming, or did Hill tell me there was one other boy coming for one half, and his name was Lyttelton? If so they will surely mess together most suitably.

27 September 1956 *Grundisburgh*

I have never really been to France—merely through it. I often have a suspicion that it, or at least the south of it, is the best country to live in. Away, of course, from all damned politics. But I don't really know anything about it. Though I know, I think, what Flecker meant when vituperating a certain (not *very* uncommon) English type of man, he burst out 'Go to France, bloody baby, and get educated'.

Pale blue and red! The colours of the Eton Field XI? And as good an Eton colour as there is. You must train your secretary to use 'cornering' and 'sneaking' as code-words warning you what sort of visitor to expect. Apropos of Eton you are right. My great-nephew has just struggled in and is at Bud Hill's for a half. I don't really know much about him, except that he has very nice manners and has been relentlessly coached in cricket. Tell me what your lad's reactions are in due course.

Keats, rather oddly, said that one of the things that made life worth living was 'Hazlitt's depth of taste'. I can do better than that and substitute—and with much greater truth—'R.H-D's generosity of heart'. Quite seriously, your gifts bring me more pleasure than anything that has happened to me for years. Humphry H. on Aristotle, as you rightly surmise, would be a bit beyond me. I *loathed* A. at Cambridge, partly, no doubt, because we were lectured to about him by Dryasdust in person—not alas, the beloved and brilliant Verrall (he had a completely inexpressible sense of humour, and once broke into helpless cackles when reading out a list of names in which Shufflebotham was followed, very reasonably, by Sitwell). How in the world did you get the Cunard book finished so quickly? Sheer mental agility I am pretty sure is the only answer—one of the most enviable of gifts. Old Quickswood had it, and so no doubt did Dr Johnson.

I will write to Swinnerton, if I can summon up courage—heartened by your assurance that he would like it. I really have enjoyed his writing so much that I ought to thank *some*body. My uncle Edward would have said the Almighty was the right recipient of gratitude for anything, but I don't know. He would detect a sarcastic note in my homage, just as He will when the various Harvest Festivals are celebrated during the next week or two. There must be a good many farmers who might echo what Mr Cayenne said on his deathbed ('I told him that God chastened those he loveth'. 'The devil take such love, was his awful answer'). It was M.R.J. who introduced me to *Annals of the Parish*.[1] Have I been a bore about it to you before? It is immensely good value and not nearly well enough known. No doubt Leavis thinks nothing of it.

Your clock awaits you in the old dining-room. Your bedroom is always ready like the Prince Consort's decades after his death; the fatted calf trembles in his shoes; the Sauterne is on ice. *Any* day up to Xmas except Oct 30 to Nov 9 when we go to Barbon. Roger F. is shepherding wife and sister-in-law over the Brenner Pass in a car whose clutch slips at times, and whose horn now and again hoots without a pause for forty minutes. It did so recently in London and every driver he passed shook a fist at him, thinking he did it on purpose. How immensely stupid and hateful so many otherwise sensible and amiable men are when behind the steering-wheel!

29 September, 1956 *Bromsden Farm*

I have decided that the only way to make sure you get a decent letter is to write in two sections—one on Saturday—so here goes. This morning, after the long sleep which usually blesses me on Friday nights, I came down at 10.30 on a sunny morning and read your letter over my breakfast of ripe melon: it was a magnificent start to the day. If you'll come to the Johnson Club, I'll certainly be there. Let neither of us take a guest, so that we can sit together and gossip steadily, regardless of the others. Could we not meet earlier—say at 5.30 or 6—and prime ourselves with a glass of something? I'd dearly love you to see my flat over the office, so that you will gradually know all my haunts, but fear the three flights of stairs might tire you too much. Let me know if you think it possible: you could see the blue-and-red office on the way up.

No, you've never mentioned *Annals of the Parish* before. Someone else was constantly advising me to read it—perhaps George Gordon

[1] By John Galt.

of Magdalen—and many years ago I picked up a charming little first edition, which I must now read, if ever I can find the time. In the late thirties I also picked up another Galt first edition for 1/6—*Ringan Gilhaize or the Covenanters* (3 vols, 1823). I've never read that either, but took it down this morning and was delighted by its opening sentence: 'It is a thing past all contesting, that, in the Reformation, there was a spirit of far greater carnality among the champions of the cause, than among those who in later times so courageously, under the Lord, upheld the unspotted banners of the Covenant'. If only a few novels of our day opened with such punch!

Thank heaven I'm not being driven over the Brenner Pass by Roger: I can't imagine his having much mastery over machines. I have been gardening to-day, weeding and clipping and trying to beat back the encroaching jungle. Mercifully it began to rain before tea and I was happily driven in to the letters of Oscar Wilde, which I am beginning to tackle seriously. Now I must go to bed. More tomorrow.

Sunday evening 30 Sept

To-day has been more like summer than most we've had this year, and I have been out of doors almost all the time, gardening until fatigue overcame me, and then reading St John Ervine in the sun. It's a fine meaty book, full of fascinating information. On Tuesday morning P. Fleming rang up to say the *Sunday Times* were going to print a 'profile' of him to-day. I said 'Hurrah!' That evening, when I got back from Eton, I found an S.O.S. from the *Sunday Times* asking me to write it. I tried to refuse but was finally persuaded. The trouble was that they gave me only 350 words. As I told them, 30,000 would have been far easier. However, after a couple of hours sweating blood I produced the right number, and they appeared to-day. Do you see the *S.T.*? Peter has been very nice about it, and as long as he's pleased all is well. Don't read the serialisation of his book, from which all the jokes have been sedulously removed, but wait for the real thing next March.

We duly delivered our boy to Bud Hill on Tuesday, and sure enough your nephew Charles was there, though I had only a minute in which to commiserate with him about the Bradman tragedy at

Worcester. Altogether there were five new boys, mostly with two parents each, and we all sat down to a sumptuous tea for which nobody had much heart. Then we left with a lump in our throat, though the boy was smiling and cheerful. Next day he wrote us a 5½-page letter, giving his first impressions. 'I tied my tie after four goes' etc. Not only does he find tails rather disconcerting, but he had apparently never worn *braces* before. Sure enough he is to mess with Lyttelton. Having taken Upper Remove, our boy is up to Lambart (some beaks seem everlasting). He failed his singing test after four notes, which is three more than it took B.J.[1] to fail me. My elder boy is coming on leave from Germany on October 13, and since he is playing the field game on Old Boy Day, and maybe the wall game some other day, he'll be able to visit his brother with good advice. Isn't the football season depressing! I can't wait for the umpires to get out their white coats in South Africa. You do me wrong in insisting that I disdained your summer-house. I thought it a perfect place, but not on that very cold day I was with you. I wish I had one here, though a sheltered porch on the South side of the house is a good substitute. Now I must turn to George Moore, who, for all my boasting, is not yet *quite* tucked up in bed.

3 October 1956 *Grundisburgh*

Your letter—like all of them—brings me many feelings, the top one of which is always sheer enjoyment, with its numerous offspring of sturdy little satisfactions. And a permanent element is a blend of gratitude, wonder and compunction. I reassure myself—nearly—by remembering that you sternly forbade me to think this wholly delightful (to me) correspondence could ever be at all burdensome to you, but, dash it all, look at the facts. I picture you after a day and a half's work, largely taken up with struggling with beasts at Ephesus, prevented from sinking back onto cushions by the thought that a letter has *got* to be written.

Meanwhile another shower of blessings upon your head for Cunard and Moore. I have read only a little so far, as I have been finishing off

[1] Basil Johnson, Eton music-master.

some boring exam-papers against time, but enough to know that once again, through R.H.-D, I shall have some hours of sheer happiness in good company into which no thought of Nasser, Dulles, Bevan, Cousins or Eden will intrude.

The Johnson Club. Yes, my dear R, certainly. I had refused but I will eat my words. Your suggestions are admirable. May I come round to Soho Square soon after 5.30 and see your flat, and go, primed to the bicuspids, off to Gough Square, roaring the chorus of a comic song, and ready to brave whole battalions of Johnsonians. No guest of course.

You will enjoy *Annals of the P*; it is *full* of flavour from Miss Sabrina Hookey with her face 'all shirpit and sharp' and her eye 'like a blue bead', down to Mr Cayenne who was a cross between Weir of Hermiston and Uncle Pentstemon in *Mr Polly*. I introduced it to Jonah who expressed keen delight. I have been clearing out some books lately—a very lengthy business, as sooner or later I get immersed in one. But one that must go is a contemporary newspaper report of the trial of William Palmer. Do you know of any fan who would like it? B. Darwin should of course have it, but I am sure he has got a copy; I don't imagine it is a collector's piece; it originally cost 1/-.

I read the paragraphs on P. Fleming in the *S.T.* and remarked to Pamela: 'How good these weekly things in the *S.T.* often are; I wonder who does them'. So there you are. And after your letter I read it again and realised that I *ought* to have spotted the author. That is the difference between the common reader and the good critic, no doubt. And now this morning comes P.F.'s *Rhinoceros*, at which *one* glance convinces me I shall enjoy hugely. But how am I to sleep this next week or two with the G.M. book and P.F. by my bedside? To which Pamela answers (the *cynicism* of wives!) 'Well you can't need much more after your evening doze over Winston's history'.

I like your vignette of your boy's and your day at Eton—that dreadful tea with the housemaster (Humphrey at Eton was all right as he only had to go 150 yards from home; but on his first evening at his prep. school, he sobbed frankly throughout—and half-an-hour after we had left was in uproarious spirits, which his mother was not. After that we always sent him with the odd man, and there were no more tears—till the day he *left* the school!)

Lambart—Leggy to the boys, but commonly—and more aptly—called by his colleagues 'The Widow'—is amiable, scholarly, all that there is of the most worthy, but, unless he has altered, a dryish teacher, as was his idol A.B.R.—a little lacking in red corpuscles. As Bishop Tommy Strong once said of a similar man, 'I felt that, if I said "Ass" to him, he would not reply by saying "Pig" to me; now you know that is all wrong.' I agree with the implied censure, though I don't quite see how a bishop could square that with turning the other cheek.

I get this from Tom Cattley[1]. A firm ordered a ship of some kind and were so pleased when they got it that they ordered three more. It was called Ajax and the firm asked that the three should be called Bjax Cjax and Djax. And if *that* doesn't convince you that I should have stopped pages ago and that senility is only just round the corner, I don't know what will.

6 October 1956 *Bromsden Farm*

It's splendid about the Johnson Club, and on October 16 I shall be eagerly awaiting you at 36 Soho Square at 5.30—what fun! I fear, however, that the post-prandial paper may be a little too exciting for one of your years and choleric passions, since it is to deal exhaustively with Mrs Barbauld! Do you think I could ask leave to take you out before the sermon, as one removes children from church, on the grounds that your nerves won't stand the excitement?

I'm immensely gratified by your approval of those paragraphs on P. Fleming. You'll find a number of oblique references to me in the *Rhinoceros*, particularly in the piece about learning to smoke a pipe at Oxford. I have my death's-head original still, to remind me of the most appalling sickness—much worse than seasickness.

To-day the sun has shone once more. and I have been taking much unwonted exercise—scything half the orchard, wheeling barrows full of earth uphill, dismantling the runner-beans, stacking logs, organising a bonfire etc. As a result I am almost immobilised, but pleasantly and with an agreeable sense of achievement. Meanwhile I am wrest-

[1] Eton master.

ling with the first half of a biography of 'Elizabeth' (of the German Garden) written by her daughter who lives in California. This chunk, which I fear covers only half the life, consists of 300 pages typed with a horrible American machine on transparent paper, so that one has to lift each page before one can read it. The book's not badly done (long quotation from me on H.W.), but it's on much too large a scale for its subject—which I shall tactfully try to tell her. The best story about Elizabeth (which I haven't yet found in the book) is that above her writing-desk she had written up: 'Peace, perfect peace, with loved ones *far* away.'

Sunday evening 7 October

So stiff was I this morning that I thought the only remedy was more gardening, so I struggled on until I broke the scythe in two and honour was satisfied.

P. Fleming looked in this morning, as he does most days when I'm here, bringing new paragraphs and a map for his book. He was a trifle *affairé* since he was expecting the Dalai Lama's brother to lunch! Before coming here he had walked for miles, cut down eight trees and read the Lesson at the Harvest Festival.

Last week I attended my bibliographical dining club, sat next to Sparrow and enjoyed the evening, though I must confess that the number of evenings when in my heart I wouldn't have preferred to stay at home reading and writing steadily declines. The next Johnson Club will be a shining exception. Did you listen to S. Sassoon reading his poems on the air last night? Good, I thought, especially the poems about E. Grey and T. Hardy.

We've had only one more brief note from Eton: 'The work is fairly hard but the masters are very nice.' No mention of Lyttelton or messing. We plan to take him to lunch at Monkey Island next Sunday, and I will report after that.

I have finished that chunk of 'Elizabeth', thank God, and am now correcting the typescript of the translation of a French historical novel. Did you read *The Iron King*?[1] If not I'll send it, and its sequel, and so on. He threatens to write thirteen—all about the Valois Kings—and I have contracted to translate five for a start (this is the third). I

[1] By Maurice Druon.

usually hate historical novels, but these are excellent. Forgive me if this is all stale buns.

I can't tell you how much I look forward to your letters on Saturday mornings: we made the plan at Tim's, didn't we? Bless his heart. He's always ringing up and asking me to most attractive dinner-parties at the last minute, and I fear my constant refusals are beginning to look churlish. In fact I love them both and wish I saw more of them, but as you know my life is complicated.

10-11 October 1956 *Grundisburgh*

Very good! Oct 16, 5.30, Soho Square. And how kind you are to warn me about over-excitement—Mrs Barbauld—why, Rock and Roll won't be in it. What do I know of Mrs Barbauld except 'Life we've been long together'?

I am sorry about old Chapman.[1] Not a man one cottoned to at once, but a foot cut off at 72 is altogether too drastic. Blood-poisoning of some sort I suppose, or perhaps senile gangrene. 'Many the ways, the little home is one', and should we not take Stevenson's view, 'By the time a man gets well into the seventies his continued existence is a mere miracle'? Less true than it was in R.L.S.'s day. Now we septuagenarians are as spry as grasshoppers—and some—not all—of us very like them in appearance.

I say! What fun the P. Fleming book is (*My Aunt's R*) and I was delighted to come across one really good review, which spotted (as I did—ahem!) how unfailingly he hits the note, *and* what a devilish difficult note it is. Many can get there or thereabouts, but to be always humorous when he wants to be, and *never* too humorous, or for too long; to be incisive and never dogmatic; to steer so exact a course between the various Scyllas and Charybdises that Milne, A.P.H., Nicolson, Lynd, Beverley N. by no means always evaded, is a brilliant achievement. I get a great deal of pleasure from reading some page or paragraph very slowly and noting the unostentatious ease with which he makes his points. Surely all who care about the art of writing must recognise how good he is? I remember telling him that story of

[1] R.W. Chapman, editor of Johnson and Jane Austen.

George Hirst's last day at Eton, and here it is unforgettably presented—and how fatally easy it would have been to get the ingredients wrongly mixed.

I liked the story of his—and your—first pipe, and read it again when I knew who his friend was. There is a fine blend of comedy and pathos in the certainty with which all freshmen go through the same hoops, and all are convinced that no one has ever been quite so original before. Did you exercise the same anxious and conscientious care in colouring a meerschaum as I did—in 1902, a vintage year for gay dogs, I assure you.

About 'Elizabeth' I never feel quite sure. Perhaps when her life appears all will be clear. Does anyone read her books now, and if they were as good as we all thought, why not? How odd is fame. *Every* critic at one time extravagantly praised the novels of one Leonard Merrick—and I never met anyone who had read one of them, and for twelve years have never seen his name mentioned. Even Swinnerton ignores him. I have not yet felt brave enough to write to F.S. I have finished Nancy Cunard on G.M. and enjoyed it greatly. But how difficult it is to see the old boy steadily and see him whole. He had the complete unexpectedness of those whose characters have no principles, only moods. Did anyone ever know for certain what he would like or dislike? We might easily discover that he put Mrs Barbauld far above all other women-poets. What, incidentally, has Mrs B. to do with Johnson? Are not all papers supposed to be in some way connected with him? I want to hear all about Nancy C. when I meet you; I seem to know her name absurdly well and nothing at all about her. Did she ever satisfy G.M's curiosity as to what lesbians actually do? I suppose somebody knows; I don't.

And now I am in the middle of yet another H-D book—*Nanga Parbat* and the various attempts to climb it. I have just arrived at the almost daily holocaust in the 1934 expedition. I have always liked mountaineering books, being myself the worst imaginable climber with a head that begins dizzying half-way up a short ladder. The pictures always give me a thrill. I have many blind spots, and you will be horrified to hear I stuck in *The Towers of Trebizond* about which the reviews are unanimous in praise. But I found all the Aunt Dottery and comic parsons too much. I am quite ready to be told I am wrong.

How a' God's name did you *break* a scythe? All I have ever managed was to lose the wedge, and in very early days I did once reduce one to the likeness of a giant corkscrew. Now I refer with insufferable pedantry to the chine and the nebs and the tang etc, and make quite a good job of the actual operation, though I am still fairly ham-fisted at the honing, though slightly better than when the local expert, feeling my edge, said he wouldn't mind riding on it.

I missed Sassoon on the wireless, not knowing he was a good reader of poetry. Tell me any others. Most I find intolerable, especially the women. Dylan Thomas was the best I ever heard—and of prose, of course, the Greek ambassador. I am teaching a village boy of ten to read; he reads all the words separately, ignores commas *and* full stops, and always renders the indefinite article as 'hay'. However, they tell me he bids fair to become another Stanley Matthews, so what does literary progress matter?

You won't find Tim thinking you churlish—he is the most loyal and understanding of friends. Do you realise that the anniversary of our first exchange comes in less than a fortnight? Your first is dated Oct 23. There's glory for you—or rather for me. It has been the greatest fun, and always will be till my day 'ringeth to evensong'.

Saturday night 13 October 1956 *Bromsden Farm*

My scything is not the expert job you clearly envisage, but rather a brutal and clumsy attack on huge outcrops of intrusive growths. The scythe snapped off (it was very old) close to the handle when the point caught in a mandrake root—perhaps one got with child—or similar snag. A new blade has now been bought and fixed on, but I shall leave the rest of the scything to my soldier son, who comes on leave on Monday and is good at such things.

This week your splendid letter was waiting for me on Friday evening. I shall pass on some of your shrewd praise of the *Rhinoceros* to its author, who will certainly rejoice, for he values your opinion almost as highly as I do. I never had a meerschaum, so missed the colouring fun. Fancy your enjoying mountaineering books: I share your bad head for heights but not your vicarious climbing. Some months ago I published a book called *Abode of Snow*, a complete history of the climbing of the Himalayas by an old pet called Kenneth Mason, of the Survey of India and later Professor of Geography at Oxford. It's clearly destined to be the Standard Work on the subject, and I'll gladly send you a copy if you'd like one.

I'm devoted to Rose Macaulay, but gave up trying to read her books *years* ago. Thirty years ago she was light and witty—which reminds me of my dear William Plomer. He lives near Littlehampton, whose chief local author was Mrs Henry Dudeney. William tried one or two of her novels and described them as 'so light that you have to hold them down'. Where was I with Rose? No matter: you'll have caught my drift.

Last week's Lit. Soc. was rather a good one. Tommy Lascelles couldn't come, nor mercifully could Lord Dunsany, so I persuaded Cuthbert Headlam to preside, thus effectively putting the length of the table between us. Nobody was keen to sit next to him, but I eventually pushed Bernard Fergusson and Gerry Wellington into the only-too-obviously-avoided chairs. Before dinner Cuthbert managed to deliver several of those unfair and depressing remarks which should never be made anywhere, particularly not at convivial evenings. 'When you're eighty', he said to me, 'there's nothing to do but wait for death'. 'You dreary old brute', I thought. By contrast my neighbour at dinner, Bob Brand, who is 78, was as gay and interested in everything as could be—I like him immensely. On my other side was T.S. Eliot, very genial and forthcoming. He gave me a fine Havana cigar and we talked most amiably of publishing and poetry. The others present were Fleming, Wheeler-Bennett, Lockhart, Nugent, Sparrow, Betjeman, Somervell, Ivor Brown, Casey (ex-editor of *The Times*), and Leslie Hartley. On the way in I ran into A.P. Ryan (of *The Times*) who recently published a book about the Curragh—incident or mutiny. He was naturally anxious, for publicity's sake, to try and get Winston to comment on those parts of the story in which he was involved, but the old badger refused to be drawn. Eventually some friend of Ryan's tackled him face to face. 'Have you in fact read the book, Sir Winston?' 'Yes,' said Winston, 'yes, I've read it—in a general way.' A fine parliamentary reply.

Oh yes—another of William Plomer's jokes. This summer he spent a month in South Africa, which was his home in youth and which he hadn't visited for thirty years. Somewhere—perhaps in Johannesburg—he saw a huge multiple statue in honour of some heroes of old, the Voortrekkers no doubt, on which he commented: 'Patriotism is the last refuge of the sculptor.' Have you read any of W.P.'s books? Some of them are excellent. I'm *still* struggling with the introduction to the Moore-Cunard letters. One clear day would see it finished, but where is one to be found?

18 October 1956 *Grundisburgh*

Literally only two words. I have retired to bed! Just the same as years ago—what the leeches absurdly call 'a mild attack of acute bronchitis'—the direct effect of Mrs Barbauld.

The other word is just that Philip Magnus was excellent company, that Ketton-Cremer and Iolo Williams were good value, that the profile of old Powell[1] was well worth prolonged study—yes, all that, but the high light of the entire day was that 1½ hours with you in the dim religious light of your room. Don't reproach yourself with the (perfectly true) fact that but for you I should have stayed at home. The real charge lies against that inevitable decree from above (?) that a mild ailment is easily thrown off up to the age of 70, coupled with the truth that no septuagenarian believes it till it has happened to him—and often not after that. In any case those careful pursy men who take precautions are *not* to be imitated. Mr Woodhouses every one of them.

21 October 1956 *Bromsden Farm*

I can't help feeling a trifle guilty, though it's true to say that if I had known of your cold I should have urged you to stay at home. If it's any comfort in your suffering, your presence completely *made* my evening, fused lights and all. I do hope you are better by now, and shall nervously await your next letter. I often think how agreeable a

[1] L.F. Powell, Johnson scholar.

day in bed would be (I haven't had one for years), provided one was feeling only slightly ill and had plenty of books and good food. Don't try and write a long letter till you're completely recovered, but a brief bulletin would be much appeciated. For some reason (perhaps merely our own happy conjunction) the Johnson Club seemed more human than ever before—at any rate at our end of the table.

Since I saw you my life has been overwhelmed by the Box-and-Cox appearances of my elder children—the boy on leave from Germany, the girl up from Wales to see him. He lost the keys of the flat, ransacked all my drawers trying to find a black tie, borrowed my bag and brought it back full of mud and water after playing the Wall Game—but to such a patriarch as you these irritations are only too well known. In my theatrical youth I once told a dear old cockney actor that the night before I had had too much to drink and been sick. A fond, nostalgic look came over his face, and he said 'Sick after drinking; it sounds like primroses to me, boy.' I'm devoted to my errant son, and he is a very present help in the abundant apple-harvest which is on us, since like you I'm not much good on a ladder. The quince-tree, seven foot high, is more my mark!

On Friday night I appeared for 4½ minutes on Commercial Television. This involved spending 2½ hours in a studio in Aldwych, full of whisky and sandwiches and a strangely assorted company. The programme was a half-hour news one and included Tom Driberg showing a film of Burgess in Moscow, Arthur Askey, Tommy Trinder, a film about German industry—and myself arguing with the book-manager of the Army and Navy Stores about keyhole-memoirs of the Royal Family (Creepy-Crawfie and the rest), which I said should be prohibited by law! Apart from two brief rehearsals, it was impromptu and rather fun. I was given a heavy all-over make-up, which took me back to my student days at the Old Vic. And for this evening's amusement they are going to pay me twenty guineas!

Flushed with this easy money, I go tomorrow at 5.30 pm to King's College, London, where I have promised to read (for love), to whatever undergraduates turn up, my friend Guy Chapman's lecture on 'The French Army and Politics'. (He isn't well enough to face the music himself.) I haven't looked at it yet, but must—if only to practise saying all the French names etc.

The *Sunday Times* have infuriated Fleming by sending all his articles to the Censor (whoever he may be). This personage has suggested that, instead of saying that if the Germans came we planned to use gas if necessary to stop them (as Winston told Peter was the case), Peter should say exactly the opposite! Naturally P. refused, so the whole passage is to be removed from the serialisation, though I have no intention of removing it from the book. The *Sunday Times* say their circulation has gone up by 40,000 since the serial began! I wish I knew how many copies of the book to print. 10,000 is a safe minimum, but I've a feeling that 20,000 would be more like it.

I'm so looking forward to your and Pamela's visit here at Christmas time: we'll fix the exact day later on: I shall probably be at home for four or five days. I daresay my sister and her family will drive down for Christmas Day—otherwise there will only be ourselves.

Now I must have yet another shot at polishing off that George Moore introduction: if I don't hurry up I shall get hopelessly confused with Oscar Wilde! Take great care of yourself: I don't want to lose you.

Finndale House
Grundisburgh
Woodbridge
24 October 1956 *Suffolk*

My dear Rupert

It is very odd how completely unable so many men are to put themselves in the place of their own audience—so very unlike the old Duke of Devonshire, who yawned during his own maiden speech because, as he told somebody, 'it was so damned dull'. It isn't a matter of brains at all. Dr Sheppard, once Provost of King's, is bursting with brains, but the blend of gush and childishness in his speeches is one of the most embarrassing things I know.

You *must* try a spell in bed; it is tremendously restful, and you could, like Winston (and many others), get through a lot of dictating to secretaries etc. And if your bed is well organised *qua* bed-rest, 'donkey' (i.e. bolster tied across bed just below the b-tt-cks), *and* the service of meals is cheerful, punctual, and lavish, life soon takes on a paradisal, Nepenthean, lotus-eating atmosphere which is deliciously demoralising.

Your family doings fill me with joy—so exactly like mine when home was still their H.Q.—keys, clothes (especially father's), trains, money—all are lost with the utmost regularity and unconcern. O Youth! . . . (here a little eloquent apostrophe from Conrad's Marlow. What a good story! Do you remember the death of the ship 'Judea, London. Do or Die'?) I look forward to meeting them all some day. And Dec or Jan will certainly see us at Bromsden Farm; one should be able to see one's best correspondents' surroundings as well as their face and form.

I entirely agree with you about all that Crawfie literature. But, human nature being what it is, how are those who run the Press ever going to forgo what is profitable and legal? If they knew their classics, they would only answer as Vespasian did when his prim son protested against his (somehow, I forget the details) taxing sewage. The old vulgarian laughed coarsely and retorted '*Pecunia non olet*.'[1] What have ninety years of popular education done to weaken commercial criteria? Less than nothing.

You refer, *en passant*, to your 'student-days' at the Old Vic. Why have I heard nothing about them? They must have been full of rich experience. You are full of surprises, and I shouldn't be the least surprised some day to hear you referring unconcernedly to the time when you ran a hummum in Belgrade.

I am for the moment in London for a meeting, and writing this in my club—the Royal Empire Society. Its name is the only thing un-drab about it. I am surrounded by coal-black clergymen—some conference, I believe. Christianity is marking time in Dahomey, where it is apparently impossible to persuade the natives that to eat a missionary is not the shortest cut to heaven. The policy shortly to be adopted is to send only young parsons from Balliol Ox and Christ's Cam, as practically all cannibal chiefs hail from one or the other. The fact that they are all to be lank, stringy, sallow young men rather shows that the Church is not wholly relying on the old college tie.

Yours ever
G.W.L.

Bromsden Farm
Henley-on-Thames
27 October 1956 *Oxon*

My dear George

My delivery of Guy Chapman's lecture on 'The French Army and Politics' at King's College, London last Monday was, I think, a decided success.[2] I prefaced it with a bit of dialogue about what Silas Wegg should read to the Golden Dustman:

> 'Was you thinking at all of poetry?' Mr Wegg inquired, musing.
> 'Would it come dearer?' Mr Boffin asked.
> 'It would come dearer,' Mr Wegg returned. 'For when a person

[1] 'Money doesn't smell.'
[2] Guy was recovering from an operation.

comes to grind off poetry night after night, it is but right he should expect to be paid for its weakening effect on his mind.'

Then I launched into the lecture with as much *élan*, punch, and *brio* as my lack of acquaintance with the script allowed. Knowing nothing of the subject, I probably read it better than Guy himself would have done, and he knows *all* about it! The audience (some fifty bodies 'of repellent aspect, remotely connected with education', old and young, black and white, male and female) sat motionless—whether riveted or stunned I couldn't be sure. The many French names (particularly those whose spelling seemed peculiar) I enunciated with such confidence and in so French an accent that they added to the wretches' stupefaction—enough of that.

My son's leave ends on Wednesday, and we shall miss him, despite the cyclone which he creates around him. My children have one tiresome trait in common: directly they get home, they put several long-playing records of American musicals on the radiogram in the nursery, turn it up as loud as it will go, open every door and then leave the house. I hesitate to turn the machine off lest I break it. Just now, in preparation for long winter evenings in Düsseldorf, the boy is trying to teach himself to play the recorder from a book: this produces a sound at once dismal and alarming. However, he has also picked all the apples, and after wrapping up and putting away enough for us, he peddled the rest from door to door in the car (a station waggon) and succeeded in selling 350 lbs at fourpence a lb! Youth—*youth*—yes, that is my favourite of all Conrad's stories, and I plan to include it in a volume of C's sea-stories for publication on his centenary in November 1957. I have a Mariners Library into which it will fit neatly.

My student days at the Old Vic were indeed full of rich experience, and one day you shall hear more of it. Which reminds me—on Friday evening my wife and I, the boy and a friend drove over to Oxford to see my previous wife (Peggy Ashcroft) in a play called *The Good Woman of Setzuan* by Bertolt Brecht, which opens in London next week.

I thought both her and the play enchanting, and remembered that it was in that very theatre in 1929 (when we were both acting in Nigel Playfair's tour of *She Stoops to Conquer*) that P.A. and I plighted our troth.

Afterwards, to please the boy, I took them all round to P's dressing-room—an agreeable but disturbing occasion. One thing has not changed: the first time I saw her act (in the same halcyon year) I knew she was the greatest actress I had ever seen (she was quite unknown then), and now I am more than ever certain of it.

Meanwhile, in the intervals of Oscar Wilde, I am still tidying up George Moore, and tomorrow I am to be received in audience by Sir Thomas Beecham, Bart. Since he supplanted G.M. as Lady Cunard's lover, he could clearly spill a bibful—but will he? I doubt it. Full report next week. I'm thinking of calling the book:

DEAR LADY OF MY THOUGHTS

Letters from George Moore
to Lady Cunard
(1894–1933)

It's a bit cumbersome, but utterly apt. What is your frankest opinion? The quotation[1] is from the dedication of one of his books, which runs:

> Dear Lady of my thoughts, dear Lady Cunard,
> Time turns all things into analogues and symbols,
> and in the course of the years I have come to
> think of you as an evening fountain under embosoming
> trees. The fountain murmurs, sings, exults; it
> welcomes every coming minute; and when the dusk
> deepens in the garden and the gallants enfold their
> ladies in scarves and veils and the rout disperses,
> the fountain sings alone the sorrows of the water-
> lilies to the moon. G.M.

Isn't that beautiful? I shall of course quote it in full. *The Evening Fountain* won't do as a title, since it implies twilight, whereas the letters start when she is a girl. I shall greatly value your judgment.

I have just listened to the News and learned of the death of my beloved friend of thirty years, Viola Meynell. In some ways it is a mercy, for she was suffering from progressive muscular atrophy, and had just reached the point where she could no longer walk or write,

[1] By kind permission of Mr Christopher Medley.

but I shall miss her a lot. I last saw her in August, when I drove over to see her in Sussex. Oh dear, I do hate people dying, don't you? V.M. wrote some lovely poems: here is one called Dusting:[1]

> The dust comes secretly day after day,
> Lies on my ledge and dulls my shining things.
> But O this dust that I shall drive away
> Is flowers and kings,
> Is Solomon's temple, poets, Nineveh.

She was a lovely person—and so I go sadly to bed.

Yours ever
Rupert

Barbon Manor
1 November 1956 *Westmorland*

Your letter found me here yesterday—the home of Roger Fulford, all among the moors, and altogether very pleasant and comfortable. Roger was delighted when I told him you had said—roughly—that you would prefer almost any form of death to being driven by him over the Brenner Pass—and he sends you his love. He really seems to me a very serene and skilful driver, and these moorland roads must be good practice for the Brenner. The roads are blind and narrow and gradients of 1 in 5 are quite common. Today we had lunch by the roadside in a spot empty of all life except an obviously short-tempered and resentful bull in the field over the wall. We thought Roger's duffle coat—dyed reddish, which he says was the local Liberal colour—was annoying it, though I read somewhere lately that bulls are in fact colour-blind (another mare's tale gone west). So he took it off and in a 'monstrous little voice' tried to placate the bull with endearments—'Bullie, bullie, poor old bullie,' which so increased its rage and hatred that it bayed like the trombones in *Tannhäuser*, and pawed a great hole in the ground; so we retreated—a little too fast for dignity, but, we hoped, not fast enough to indicate fear.

The countryside is endlessly lovely—mile after mile of what Hous-

[1] By kind permission of Mr Jacob Dallyn.

man calls 'solitude of shepherds High in the folded hill,' and the sky produces different effects with extraordinary rapidity. I am sure you would love it, and R. would love to get you here. Of course it *is* far away—275 miles from Grundisburgh in one day. P. says she finds that less tiring than taking two bites, and I rather agree. Roger has a large and very readable library. The Squeers country was very near us today, and we passed the abode of the famous old geologist Adam Sedgwick, a Cambridge eccentric. His bedmaker once sent his favourite chair to be re-seated. This was done in cane, and he was furious. He was always expecting sudden death and apostrophised her 'Woman, do you expect me to go into the presence of my Maker with my backside imprinted with small hexagons?'

I was not at all surprised to hear that your reading of G. Chapman's lecture went down well. Really good reading will carry off anything, and if the stuff is good—*a fortiori*. Silas Wegg was a happy thought. Hindenburg in 1916 said 'No, I read no poetry now; it might soften me'. Curious parallel. N.B. The *quietness* of an audience—except in church—indicates attention not somnolence. Somnolence is *always* preceded by fidgeting. As to your boy learning the recorder from a book, would it encourage him to know that that is exactly the way Humphrey learnt the trumpet? He never had a lesson.

George Moore's dedication is *delicious*. I discussed (I hope you don't mind; he is a discreet man) the title with Roger. As you say, it is a *little* cumbersome, and hasn't it just a soupçon of preciousness? I don't object—after all there are many such, and R. thinks that for that section of the public who want to read about George M. it doesn't matter, but that the Philistine would blush to ask his bookseller: 'Have you the Lady of my Thoughts?' But he thinks it is as good a title as the circs permit. You know, however, much more about these things than either of us, and also how much a title matters.[1]

I am sorry about Viola Meynell; such spirits are ill-spared from the world of today. Why have I never seen 'Dusting' before? It is exquisite and is on the way into my book next to the last entry which is Austin Dobson's

All passes. Art alone
Enduring stays to us;

[1] The book eventually appeared as *George Moore: Letters to Lady Cunard.*

The Bust outlasts the throne—
The Coin, Tiberius.

They won't resent their company.

We go back on Sunday, and next week I go to tell the boys of Bromsgrove that education is not a mere passing of examinations; they must read for themselves and ruminate. The headmaster says he is going to insist on his masters being present, as they are the real Philistines of the community. I expect I shall tread on a good many toes, but that is what toes are for—academic toes anyway.

When I get to the Judgment Seat, I will see to it that all is in 'the Book where good deeds are entered'. But of course I may be knocking at a different door and seeing—rather ecstatically—through its bars Byron and Helen of Troy, and John Wilkes, and Oscar Wilde and other terribly attractive company. Do you remember that delightful passage of Samuel Butler's which pictures Heaven as immensely tedious—Jupiter with Ganymede sitting on his everlasting knee, while in the other place Prometheus was having his liver agreeably stimulated by the vulture, and the shades all gather 'about stone-time' to bet on the distance to which the stone of Sisyphus will roll. Though I don't really like Butler and his sneers and his rather dreadful young woman—Miss Savage was it? How few satirical folk keep their contempt for the contemptible and don't let it sour all or nearly all their judgments. I like that remark of T.S.E.'s that the critical attitude ends by preventing one *enjoying any book*—and that is the ultimate damnation of him who shall be nameless, whom you will soon call my King Charles's head.[1] Housman was at Bromsgrove and I shall put that in their pipes. If the science master is there I shall ask him if *his* backbone tingles and the flesh of his cheeks creeps if he thinks of a verse from the psalms as A.E.H.'s did.

I end with a little *trouvaille* from Roger's shelves—the last stanza of a hymn 'in use in a church near Cambridge' seventy years ago:

Milk of the breast that cannot cloy
He, like a nurse, will bring;
And when we see His promise nigh,
Oh how we'll suck and sing!

[1] F.R. Leavis.

Don't tell Jonah[1] that because I want to next week.

P.S. Silly of me to enthuse about the moors; of course you know them well. But they can take it.

4 November 1956 *Bromsden Farm*

Your raptures about the moors struck straight to my heart, especially since you had clearly forgotten my passion for the neighbouring ones just across the Yorkshire border. That Housman line is splendid —'solitude of shepherds'—I must look it up.

I love to think of you and dear Roger discussing my G.M. title. I agree with all your gentle strictures, but it looks like an occasion for *faute de mieux*. I have made the great (but not wholly avoidable) mistake of getting immersed in Oscar Wilde before old G.M. was finally tucked up in bed with his dear lady. So this week-end, distracted by the garden and the ghastly state of the world, I have been making a fierce effort to catch up. Extra footnotes have been peppered into the text, the last five stubbornly undateable letters inserted with arbitrary haste, and now it only remains for me to revise the introduction, have it and the footnotes re-typed, and submit the whole caboodle to Sachie Sitwell (the owner of the letters) and C.D. Medley (G.M.'s literary executor). How long, oh Lord, how long? Meanwhile the notes to, and dating of, Oscar's letters provide the greatest fun. Unlike G.M., Oscar has occasioned an enormous literature of comment, biography, criticism, bibliography etc—much of it written by chronic liars like Frank Harris and Lord Alfred Douglas. Last week, following a clue in another letter, I ran to earth an unknown letter which O.W. contributed anonymously to the *Daily Telegraph* of 2 Feb 91—on modern dress—a great find, though I must confess the clue wasn't all that difficult to follow.

Yes, I knew those fine lines by Austin Dobson. They are 'imitated' from a poem by Théophile Gautier: does that mean translated or cribbed? I haven't got G's poems here—one can *never* have enough

[1] L.E. (Sir Laurence) Jones.

books. That hymn-stanza is superb. Jonah will love it, and I promise not to tell him first.

Oh yes—my interview with Beecham was most civilised and agreeable, but produced little of value. He was courteously hospitable, giving me sherry and a good cigar. His flat in Weymouth Street is very grand, white-coated manservant and all. Lady B., a good thirty-five years younger than he and good-looking, was present all the time, so I could see there was no chance of any indiscretions about Lady Cunard. I fenced round the subject with incessant questions and found his memory excellent. He rolls well-chosen words off his tongue with relish and precision. He told me all he could remember of G.M., but since they never spoke to each other after 1911, it wasn't much. I was there just over an hour.

He told me that George V went to the opera once a year—always to *La Bohème*. Once Beecham asked him if it was his favourite. 'Yes', said the King. 'That's most interesting, Sir. I'd be most interested to know why.' 'Because it's much the shortest', said His Majesty. An excellent reason indeed!

On Friday I went down to Sussex for Viola Meynell's funeral, travelling with Shane Leslie, who was grotesquely and most unsuitably dressed in a saffron-coloured kilt, with a bright green scarf round his shoulders. A bald head and thick tufts of hair on his cheek-bones (like Gow only more so) completed a figure from comic opera. However he gossiped entertainingly, and when we were met at Pulborough by a sorrowing brother-in-law, Shane said: 'I was here at the opening of the First World War, and I look like being here for the opening of the Third.' Twenty or thirty of the family were gathered sadly in the house I have known and loved so long. The service was a harsh Catholic one (not, thank heaven, a full mass) mostly in gabbled Latin. It was all very damp and chilly and sad, and I felt it had little to do with my dear Viola.

8 November 1956 *Hagley*

Of course I knew that your spiritual home is the moors, but—what is it the Doctor says in his preface to the Dictionary? 'What is known is not always present' then some rolling polysyllables about casual inadvertence seducing attention. No great man ever admitted error with more serene humility—unlike so many modern scientists who think that to know all about the atom establishes their right to dogmatise about man and his destiny. The Housman phrase comes from his 'The Merry Guide' which is my favourite, and if any Connolly says it is not first-rate, I shall tell him to have his ears syringed and his brain washed, after which he can begin to learn the elements of his job. The other pictures in the poem struck home as we journeyed southward—the hanging woods and hamlets, and blowing realms of woodland with sunstruck vanes afield, and cloud-led shadows, and valley-guarded granges and silver waters wide. Yes, yes, I know I needn't have quoted them all, but the writing of them gives me physical and mental pleasure (and of course you know that perfectly well, and will forgive).

I like your blunt label 'chronic liars' for Frank H. and Lord A.D. The former must have been immensely repellent always, but A.D. wrote some good poetry, and one must say that, even if put considerably off by his bland declaration that no one ever wrote better. A tragic life—and the physical alterations in him between the ages of twenty and sixty-five are simply those of Dorian Gray. I suppose one cannot have so loathsome a father without paying for it. I like the little interchange between old Agate and Douglas. J.A. wrote 'Milton's poetry flames in the forehead of the morning sky. Housman's twinkles in the Shropshire gloaming; yours, my dear A., glitters like Cartier's window at lunch-time.' To which A.D. replied 'Are you not aware that seventeen of my best sonnets were written in Wormwood Scrubbs?'

Jonah was in good form—he still has the figure he had at Oxford, and that was as good as any Greek's. He spoke of you with great affection, and the rest of his discourse was equally on the spot.

Roger and I teaed at Dotheboys Hall last Friday (at Bowes). They told us there was no doubt it *is* the building where Squeers's prototype Shaw had his school. Dickens of course said S wasn't founded on S but nobody believed him and Shaw was ruined. What an odd artist Dickens was (if one at all). Squeers was first a sadist, then a figure of comedy ('Natur' she's a rum 'un' etc), then a criminal. And D did much the same with Pecksniff. The truth no doubt is that—like Shakespeare—he didn't bother about probability or consistency, but just let his fancy fly—and, by gum, what wings each one's fancy had!

I must finish this to-morrow. I am not at Hagley yet but go there in a few minutes. To talk to the boys and masters of Bromsgrove. I shall quote that inimitable page of W. Cory's on the object of education, containing *inter alia* that you go to learn 'the art of indicating assent or dissent in graduated terms', and I shall not be able to resist pointing out how few of our newspapers and politicians do that.

I am once again writing in my club—and rather slowly, as I *must* hear why a stoutish man is urging a still stouter one to have a local and not general anaesthetic. I itch to tell the speaker to be more lucid and set my mind at rest on the precise nature and geography of the contemplated operation. I only think, and cannot be absolutely certain, that the trouble calling for the knife is a boil on the gluteus maximus, but it *may* be that distressing and almost universal complaint. ('Poor Alfred, he's got 'em again,' as Tennyson's doctor said when he read *Maud.*)

A beautiful smooth motor-drive in the dark landed my nephew and me here at 10 p.m. and I am now about to warm up my Bromsgrove discourse and try to persuade myself that it is less dull than I suspect it is. What a lot depends on the audience, and how they vary—from the nadir of the Ipswich Old Boys to the zenith of the Greenwich cadets.

11 November 1956 *Bromsden Farm*

Prepare for a short and scrappy letter. Long Leave has broken into my week-end brutally, and there are piles of proofs urgently awaiting correction. Before I forget it, have you seen the current number of the *New Statesman*? In it Priestley trounces Leavis splendidly. If you haven't got the paper, send me a postcard to Soho Square and I'll get you another copy. Pass hurriedly over the pernicious b-lls at the beginning of the paper if you have any regard for your blood-pressure.

I completely agree about Alfred Douglas's poetry—and with what you say of Dickens. Perhaps part of the inconsistency of many of his characters was due to the extraordinary way he wrote the novels—a monthly instalment at a time, and sometimes two going at once! Where does that sentence of Cory's come from? I couldn't, as my children say, agree with it more. Long Leave began with a bumper day, on which huge meals were fitted into visits to an Agatha Christie play and the film of *Moby Dick*, which is first-rate. Do see it if you have an opportunity: I'm sure you'd like it. Eric Linklater's boy is here too (he's at Marsden's), and yesterday E.L. himself came down to lunch. He's a sterling fellow and I loved seeing him, but he was here for five hours, and you, dear George, are the loser.

Little else to report from last week. George Moore has almost given way to Oscar. My enjoyment of literary detective work is unbounded: how happily would I settle down to six solid months of it! As it is, goodness knows how long this job will take me, done at odd moments.

15 November 1956 *Grundisburgh*

This too is a scraplet, as I am just back from Hagley and find a mass of little jobs that, I grant you, do not materially affect the progress of civilisation, but do take up time—and a meeting or two of course. November is the month for them. When I write to R.H-D I like to contemplate a gracious reach of time like smooth-sliding Mincius before me, unruffled by any little duties irrupting like tributaries. How *you* with no such quiet times ever manage to send me more than a p.c. is one of the world's mysteries.

Yes, I saw the Priestley article and greatly liked it. There seems to be a good deal of 'gunning' for Leavis, and the more the merrier. That contempt for practically all the stuff that has ever been praised and liked borders, to my mind, on the insane, like other forms of conceit.

There is no reason, my dear Rupert, why you should fetch us from Eton; give fool-proof directions and over we nip in our motor. We go to Eton on the 22nd, Saturday, and we can and will with pleasure lunch on whichever day after that suits you. I look forward to meeting your family—though under no illusion about what adolescents think of their father's old friends.

When I get a moment I will copy and send that page of William Cory's. It is one of the supreme utterances.

Once again you're out of luck, for it's eleven p.m. and I am too sleepy for a decent letter. To make up a little, here is a delicious letter from Sydney Smith:[1] I only hope you don't know it already. It was copied out for me by William Plomer, and before transferring it to my book, I thought you might like to put it in yours. Send it back sometime—no hurry. You speak of 'a gracious reach of time', a conception which I am rapidly coming to equate with Paradise, so crammed is every unforgiving minute—but one gets used to most things in time.

So glad you saw and enjoyed the Priestley article. I heard last week that Helen Gardner (a very intelligent English don at Oxford) was recently viva-ing a pupil or ex-pupil of Leavis's and asked her: 'Do you *enjoy* Jane Austen (or whoever)?' To which the girl answered: 'It isn't a question of enjoyment: it's a question of evaluation.' Ugh!

Cuthbert Headlam shirked last week's Lit. Soc. (praise be), as well as his brother's funeral. It was a good evening. I sat between Roger (to whom I talked most of the time) and Bruce Lockhart, who is an

[1] Dear Lady Georgiana [Morpeth]

. . . Nobody has suffered more from low spirits than I have done—so I feel for you. 1st. Live as well as you dare. 2nd. Go into the shower-bath with a small quantity of water at a temperature low enough to give you a slight sensation of cold, 75° or 80°. 3rd. Amusing books. 4th. Short views of human life—not further than dinner or tea. 5th. Be as busy as you can. 6th. See as much as you can of those friends who respect and like you. 7th. And of those acquaintances who amuse you. 8th. Make no secret of low spirits to your friends, but talk of them freely—they are always worse for dignified concealment. 9th. Attend to the effects tea and coffee produce upon you. 10th. Compare your lot with that of other people. 11th. Don't expect too much from human life—a sorry business at the best. 12th. Avoid poetry, dramatic representations (except comedy), music, serious novels, melancholy sentimental people, and everything likely to excite feeling or emotion not ending in active benevolence. 13th. *Do good*, and endeavour to please everybody of every degree. 14th. Be much as you can in the open air without fatigue. 15th. Make the room where you commonly sit, gay and pleasant. 16th. Struggle by little and little against idleness. 17th. Don't be too severe upon yourself, or underrate yourself, but do yourself justice. 18th. Keep good blazing fires. 19th. Be firm and constant in the exercise of rational religion. 20th. Believe me, dear Lady Georgiana, very truly yours, SYDNEY SMITH

egotistical bore. Martin Charteris told me that the script of my five minutes on commercial T.V. had been shown to the Queen!

On Thursday I dined with the Hamish Hamiltons. Earlier that evening I attended another meeting of the A.P. Herbert Committee on the reform of the law concerning obscene books. Yesterday my wife and I drove over to the Gollanczes near Newbury and took 9/- off them at bridge—quite amusing, but it cut six hours out of my week-end working time, which partly explains this wretched note. 'The bloom is gone, and with the bloom go I.' Next week, as I keep reiterating, you'll get something a little better.

22 November 1956 *Grundisburgh*

There is something odd and comic and reassuring in the way both of us are being harried and constricted by encroachments from the external world. Mine are nothing to yours, but to the superannuated man of leisure a prospective committee is a headache, an old boy dinner a heavy and a weary weight. This last is due this evening. The absurd thing is that I always quite enjoy it when it is once started, but that makes it no less of a hang-over. Anyway a speech is always that, and I am expected to be funny. On the way up, the train is about at Colchester when the conviction settles on me that not only can I not think of anything remotely funny, but that there isn't anything funny left for anyone to say and do. By Chelmsford a ray of light dawns, viz that the audience will be mellow enough to regard almost anything as funny, even if none have reached the stage described by Sir Thomas More 'with his belly standing astrote like a taber, and his noll totty with drink'. I am no clearer as to what astrote means than Mr Micawber was about gowans, but the whole sentence has a rich vigour and vulgarity which is surely very attractive. I suspect Sir Thomas More was of the same vintage as Sir T. Beecham, which I had not dreamt of before. *Utopia* is not beside my bed. That S. Smith is *fine* and I have transferred it and return it with many thanks. A rum thing is that S.S. was like old Johnson in many ways, but the latter in a letter to Boswell expressly commands him to be entirely silent about his mental and physical ailments, and then he will think about them less and 'then they will molest you rarely'. *S.S*'s advice to talk freely about them postulates a long-suffering audience. Of course the best bit of advice would have been 'come and sit in a corner when I am in good form'. And what boisterous fun he would have had with Leavis!

My mouth always waters when I hear of your company at the Lit. Society. Did you ask Roger about that bull? I imagine the conversation round the table to be of the finest vintage. I suppose like the Junior Ganymede, of which Jeeves was a member, the club rules forbid you to retail any of the *bon mots* lavishly begotten.

There is something very incongruous in A.P.H's being on an anti-obscene committee, or perhaps he is all for abolishing the present checks. As on many other questions (e.g. hanging) I find myself continually dashed by the opinions and personalities and (often) appearance of those on the same side. I shout 'down with hanging' confidently till I read the speeches of Silverman and Co. I want lots of freedom for books until I find myself marching in step with a cargazon of arch, self-consciously broad-minded swaggering females—shall we say like the daughter of a certain professor who was passionately keen about the right pronunciation of Latin and devoted half one lecture to showing the different sounds of 'qui' and 'cui'. But for each he gave a coot-like whistle which left them indistinguishable. He was a dreary little pedant, hirsute, bloodless, dusty, and was bumped by Housman for the Latin chair to his lasting chagrin. I believe no one knew more about those points in the Latin language which have the least imaginable interest. He couldn't have written and wouldn't have read 'Once in the wind of morning . . .'[1]

25 November 1956 *Bromsden Farm*

All occasions do inform against us. Sunday December 23 would be the perfect day for you and Pamela to come to lunch, but now you won't have your car, I suppose, and our petrol will be too tight for a double journey—damn! Or have you a solution?[2]

[1] By A. E. Housman.

[2] Petrol was now rationed as a result of the disastrous Suez expedition and the closing of the Canal.

I read of your Old Boy dinner in *The Times*, but they did not mention the witty brilliance of the Guest of Honour: taken for granted no doubt. Our dinners will not, I fear, survive Jelly[1], and although they were pretty dull I grieve at the breaking of yet another tradition. My uncle Duff used to make excellent speeches at the old dinners. Anthony Eden never once turned up.

The conversation at the Lit. Soc. is mostly confined to groups of two or three: the table is a long narrow one: later in the evening people circulate a little and change seats. Roger, who lunched with me last week in excellent form, says he always deliberately sits next to Cuthbert H., because he finds the awfulness so exaggerated as almost to be enjoyable. Also Roger much prefers him to Dunsany!

Tonight I must somehow write a review of six detective stories for *Time and Tide*: it should be eight, but I haven't had time to read the others, even in bed.

Yesterday I drove to Oxford and spent four hours in Magdalen library, checking and copying the Wilde letters there. Tom Boase, the President, gave me an excellent lunch in the middle. At the end I had twenty minutes in Blackwell's before they shut, and picked up a few scraps of Wildeana—that job is the greatest fun, if only I had time to do it properly. 'We work in the dark—we do what we can—we give what we have. Our doubt is our passion and our passion is our task. The rest is the madness of art.' I expect you know where that comes from.[2] Like you, I copy out for the pleasure of doing it.

Last week was much occupied by Harold Nicolson's seventieth birthday present. John Sparrow started it, but very soon the whole of the organisation devolved (as they say) on me. Getting from his secretary a copy of his address-book, we circularised more than 350 of his friends. Eventually 253 of them contributed £1370! Getting the cheque to him on the right day, with an alphabetical list of donors was a great nuisance. I also circularised them all again, telling them the result. On the evening of the birthday (Wednesday) Sparrow gave a small dinner for H.N. in the little private room at the Garrick. (I had to order food and wine—what next?) Apart from H.N., J.S. and myself, the party consisted of Raymond Mortimer, Jonah, Alan Pryce-Jones,

[1] Nickname of my Eton housemaster E.L. Churchill.

[2] From Henry James's short story 'The Middle Years'.

Jim Lees-Milne (contemporary of mine at Eton) and a young friend of Harold's called Colin Fenton. It was an agreeable evening, and H.N. was moved almost to tears by the whole day: he wrote me a charming letter afterwards.

Hardly had the fumes dispersed when the Duff Cooper Memorial Prize cropped up again in a big way. Constant telephone calls to Diana at Chantilly about getting Winston as prize-giver (which she did), a drive across London to look at Enid (Bagnold) Jones's drawing-room where the ceremony is to take place, much more telephoning to devoted ladies and champagne-providers, drafting and sending out a press release, etc, making sure the cheque (£200) is ready—phew! Enid Jones lives next door to Winston, which is a help, since they say he's not good for much more than twenty minutes now. Her drawing-room was built by Lutyens out of some old stables and is like an attractive stage set—at that moment another devoted lady rang me up here to say that Winston was going to speak only of Duff and would I get one of the judges who awarded the prize to say a few words about the *book*. Also, who is to marshal the press photographers? Unfortunately Hamish Hamilton (the publisher of the prize-winning book, Alan Moorehead's *Gallipoli*) is not on speaking terms with Randoph Churchill, who is now interfering actively—phew again! Oh for an ivory tower stuffed with books! All this takes place at 6 p.m. on Wednesday in Hyde Park Gate. At 7.45 I am supposed to be dining with the Priestleys in Albany in a dinner-jacket. No taxis, no petrol, no time.

29 November 1956 *Grundisburgh*

All is not entirely lost. We *mean* to go to Eton by car and, when there, may find the twenty-odd miles to Henley quite possible. Let us wait and see—as indeed one does every mortal day in more or less of a dither. How utterly repellent our days are, compared with those, say, of 1897, when nothing of the smallest importance happened the other side of the Channel, still less across the Atlantic. Still it cannot be denied that it is all beastly interesting. I shall continue to maintain that, even in the workhouse. And I shall have R.H-D's letters with me, which no one else will have, and what do all the little debits count against that? Do you remember Morris Finsbury's balance-sheet *à la* Crusoe beginning '(Bad) I have lost my uncle's body' '(Good) But then Pitman has found it,' and then realised that the spirit of antithesis was running away with him? I would bet on your loving *The Wrong Box* but may be wrong. Some very good men cannot stomach that corpse being bandied about, e.g. old Scott Holland who was about as good a man as you could find.

'Old Boys' are rather hang-overs, and one can have some very blush-making moments at them. Luckily this year John Verney was in the chair, and did the job perfectly. I caught a dreadful glimpse of myself now and then behaving exactly like that emetic Mr Chips, but the opposite number to him would I suppose be someone like Cyril Connolly or Jack Haldane, so what will you? Have you, by the way, read Hollis's *George Orwell* and if so, or even if not, can you tell me why he is so important? It is not fair to answer *1984* or *Animal Farm*, because he is regarded as very fine outside them and I can't quite see why. I like a good deal of his thinking aloud, but is it very profound or illuminating? I am rather on the fence about him, as about many things and people.

The slogan in literary London is obviously 'Who shall we get to do this? Oh of course R.H-D.' The dinner to Harold N. on the top of everything else. I really think somebody else might have ordered the menu—which I bet you did with great care. You don't tell me what it was—I always like to know that. J.M. Barrie, recorded by Tuppy, once said that the great merit of Phillips Oppenheim's books was the excellent eating in all of them. Another comment was that P.O. always tired of his book soon after the middle and then 'merely kicked it along to its end'. Tuppy had a complete set of P.O., which must have been as hard to collect as the whole of Trollope, of whom one has *never* read all.

Your account of the D.C. Memorial Prize preparations is delicious. Do tell me in full how it went off—all those non-speaks. The literary world sounds as full of envy, hatred, and malice as the academic. Winston, I heard last week, refused to speak to his constituents, not, as was said, because he had a cough, but because he is so sunk in gloom that he just cannot speak to anyone. I wonder how you found him. I suspect that his vision of England's future goes near to breaking his heart. What *little* men are governing us and everybody else at this time!

I am in labour with a speech at the King's Founder's Feast on Dec. 6—answering the toast of *Floreat Etona amicabilis concordia.* You see the difficulty at once. No Oppidan within living memory has been remotely conscious of any special affection for King's. And if I say much about Eton, well, there are very many non-Etonians at King's now, so that note must not be stressed. In fact I shall be skating on a pond full of patches of cats'-ice. But how can one refuse these flattering invitations some six months in advance? I have not the nerve to refuse, as a Trinity don did, an invitation in September to a dinner on Jan 31 on the grounds that it was always in that week that he caught one of his worst colds. Claude Elliott reassures me by saying that the audience is pleasantly tight, so it doesn't much matter what one says, but that is rather a dangerous line. Tightness may leave their critical faculties unblunted but remove the barriers to freedom of comment. Then home to a batch of exam-papers and silence—a good moment. Marking papers soon becomes as mechanical as knitting, and I *believe* each script brings in two shillings (it used to be one and ninepence). But of course the world *may* have come to an end by then.

P.S. Here is W. Cory on public school education—the last word, *me judice.*

[WILLIAM JOHNSON CORY ON EDUCATION]

At school you are engaged not so much in acquiring knowledge as in making mental efforts under criticism. A certain amount of knowledge you can indeed with average faculties acquire so as to retain; nor need you regret the hours you spent on much that is forgotten, for the shadow of lost knowledge at least protects you from many illusions. But you go to a great school not so much for knowledge as for arts and habits; for the habit of attention, for the art of expression, for the art of assuming at a moment's notice a new intellectual position, for the art of entering quickly into another person's thoughts, for the habit of submitting to censure and refutation, for the art of indicating assent or dissent in graduated terms, for the habit of regarding minute points of accuracy, for the art of working out what is possible in a given time, for taste, for discrimination, for mental courage, and for mental soberness.

2 December 1956 *Bromsden Farm*

I applaud your courage and persistence in the matter of driving to Eton for Christmas, and live in hopes of your both lunching here on the Sunday. Detailed instructions will follow shortly. On Friday (St Andrew's Day) I played truant from the office and spent most of the day driving people about—my wife to and from the school where she teaches, my boy and the Linklater child back here to lunch (their tutors having sensibly agreed), back to Eton for tea in my boy's room—altogether more than a hundred miles. And I was promptly rewarded for my altruism, since the Henley petrol-supply, which till then had been flowing normally, abruptly gave out yesterday morning, with the announcement 'No more till the 17th'. We have two gallons in our tank and are five miles from anywhere. How my wife is going to get to this infernal school of hers I simply don't know. I'm sure there is already a black market in coupons, but what use are they when the pumps are empty? A fortnight of the sort of hardship that this is going to mean, exactly coinciding with the P.M.'s last fortnight at Goldeneye (shade temperature 86), is not calculated to strengthen his popularity.[1]

Naturally I love *The Wrong Box*: how could you be wrong? Almost the nicest thing about it is that the details of the plot escape my memory fairly promptly each time, leaving only the Health Boots, and William Bent Pitman, and 'The *Athaeneum*—golly, what a paper!' and the Maestro Jimson—so that after a year or so I can read it again with fresh delight. I wish I could *now*, but if I ever have a moment (which seems unlikely) *Annals of the Parish* is first in the queue.

That passage of Cory is magnificent: exactly where does it come from? All this editing has produced a passion for exactitude in references. Copying it into my book I came on these two extracts, which I

[1] Anthony Eden was recuperating at Ian Fleming's house in Jamaica.

copied out many years ago. What do you think of them? And do you know who wrote them? I fancy they matched some feelings of mine at the time of copying. Here they are:

(a) I am a willow of the wilderness,
Loving the wind that bent me.

(b) As the bird trims her to the gale,
I trim myself to the storm of time,
I man the rudder, reef the sail,
Obey the voice at eve obeyed at prime:
'Lowly faithful, banish fear,
Right onward drive unarmed;
The port, well worth the cruise, is near,
And every wave is charmed.'

Write only on one side of the paper, and give your reasons for your verdict. The examiner examined!

I have *not* read Hollis's *George Orwell,* and I don't propose to, unless it is my only book on a desert island. Orwell is of no importance from the literary point of view, but for some I daresay he has the fascination of litmus paper or a chameleon: he was (slightly to change the metaphor) a sort of barometer of the Thirties and early Forties, going through and writing about *all* the experience of young left-wing intellectuals during those troubled years. If you and I cannot read him with pleasure, my dear George, let us be certain, even if ridiculous to boot.

I too always like to know what people had to eat: wasn't Galsworthy good at it? Do you remember *Old English*? At Harold N's birthday dinner I ordered hot lobster with rice, roast pheasant and *soufflé surprise,* with sherry, meursault, claret and port or brandy. When I was a boy I too had an almost complete set of Phillips Oppenheim (over ninety vols),[1] but at some moment I grew ashamed of them and gave them away. Nico Davies has a superb collection (he must have inherited the taste from J.M.B. or from Tuppy), to which I have occasionally added something. I chiefly remember a proliferation of cocktails, usually described as 'amber-coloured fluid'. I met the old

[1] I now (1979) have 153.

boy once on the Riviera and sat goggling at his feet. He was old, with a young and pretty 'secretary'.

The Duff Cooper Prize was duly awarded on Wednesday, in the presence of what the *Manchester Guardian* rightly called 'a small but glittering assembly'—all Duff's friends, so much so that it almost seemed as though he was there himself. My calling in Harold Nicolson to open the proceedings and mention Moorehead's book was immensely successful: he did it beautifully and briefly. Winston was terribly frail and tottery. Although his little speech was all written out, one couldn't feel sure he'd get through it without losing the thread. However, he did. (Beforehand he rather sweetly showed his script to Moorehead, to make sure he'd got his name right.) Moorehead replied in a few, very good, words, and then Winston, like an old hunter wanting more than a sniff of the chase, got up and said another sentence or two. It was all very moving and exactly right. Champagne flowed freely, and the old warrior drank some as he beamed round at his friends. Even in the grip of withering age he makes all our present rulers look like feeble pigmies. I couldn't stay as long as I'd have liked, since I had to rush home and change before dining with the Priestleys (scampi, partridge and delicious vanilla ice with lumps of ginger in it). A funny little party—two architects (Lord Mottistone, Jack Seely's son, and Paul Paget, who is a cousin of mine) and a lady from B.B.C. television—all very nice but the party seemed curiously pointless. After the others had gone I stayed on for an hour's cosy gossip with the Priestleys. I like him very much (a very old friend) and she is beautiful, as well as very intelligent. Now I must get on with my proofs.

5 December 1956 *Grundisburgh*

Does anything pleasant *ever* happen? Really this combination of humiliation, impoverishment, hideous inconvenience and insecurity in the near, middle, and distant future is very hard to bear. It is a very inadequate silver lining that Ike should be improving his putting, and Eden his tennis, breast-stroke and complexion. Surely he will be out in the twinkling of an eye, and his Government. No Govt can survive such hideous results, whether the action that produced them seemed at the time to be right or wrong. And the alternative is Gaitskell and Co. Assuredly 'we are for the dark'—except that nothing turns out quite as dreadful as one expected. I fear and suspect there may be exceptions. But, as a tiresome and sensible friend of mine says, 'There is nothing we can do about it, so why talk about it?' Like all such statements, it doesn't hold quite so much water as the speaker thought.

That is good about *The Wrong Box*. I wonder how true it is that Lloyd Osbourne wrote practically all of it, also that the *Athenaeum* never forgave R.L.S. for 'Golly, what a paper' and always gave him snooty reviews. *Pauvre humanité!* Some—many—good men have enjoyed *The W.B.*, Stanley Baldwin among them. Alington knew it really by heart, and M.R. James too, I believe. *His* memory was simply uncanny.

I do not know where that Cory passage comes from—I *think* from some 'Notes on Education'. John Carter would know, if you ever come across him. Cory was something of a genius, but he was very dogmatic in his opinions and often obviously wrong, e.g. when he said Tennyson's *Queen Mary* was 'altogether nobler' than *Hamlet*, that *Christie Johnstone*[1] was immensely superior to *Vanity Fair*, that Campbell would outlive Shelley, that Jane Austen's novels, except *Persuasion*, were in 1884 mere 'worsted-stockings'. Do you think that in seventy years someone will record as one of the aberrations of great critics that R.H-D thought nothing of Orwell? I don't think so; in fact what you say chimes in with my own doubts and suspicions. How a small and persistent clique can bolster up a writer's reputation. Landor's remark hits the nail firmly: 'We admire by tradition (or fashion) and criticise by caprice.'

I like your two passages; I suppose our moderns would condemn them as romantic? subjective? smooth? what? I wish I could place them.

Old English!! or rather 'A Stoic', i.e. story, not play. Just like *The Wrong B.* with you! It has always been one of my favourites—Germane soup; filly de sole; sweetbread; cutlet soubees; rum souffly, according to Meller, and old Heythorp added hors d'oeuvres (oysters as it turned out) and a savoury (cheese remmykin), and you remember

[1] By Charles Reade (1853).

'cook's done a little spinach in cream with the soubees'. This from memory; I don't *think* it is inaccurate. Your Nicolson menu pleases me; was it a really *fat* pheasant? There is *nothing* so good. By the way Meller told old H. he had 'frapped' the champagne a little. What exactly does that mean? I have never dared to ask anyone, because obviously one ought to know. I am no man of the world. I remember being quite ignorant what 'bortsch' was long after everyone else knew; I am not quite sure how to spell it now.

Your account of Winston fits in with what others have said. One would not be surprised at his going any day. He is the only man in public life with the undeniable insignia of greatness about him.

To-morrow I go to the King's Founder's Feast ('Doctors will wear scarlet; orders and decorations, medals or ribbons, will be worn'). Well that all sounds rather tremendous, but when I told them my tail coat had long been one with Nineveh and Tyre, they came down to earth and said half the company would be in tuxedos and quite a number in corduroys and jumpers. My speech is assembled, morticed, dovetailed, planed, polished and dried. Sometimes I think it will prosper, at others a swift and easy death is my only wish. Do *your* feelings on such occasions behave in so volatile a fashion? I take comfort from Roger's (I think) telling me that a Lord Mayor of London told him a few years ago that he had no nerves before a speech, and that he never prepared but said what came into his head, implying that his head could transmute anything into gold. He then, an hour later, made the worst speech R. had ever heard. You saw, no doubt, of Roger's windfall from the *Evening Standard* for his Suffragette book.[1] Very heartening news, and I suppose his sales will swell for all his future writings—just as Gerald Kelly's fees soared after he had painted the Queen Mother or one of them. Does the Chancellor pinch half of it? I shall be sitting next to Provost Annan at the Feast. Do you know him? They tell me he is very amiable.

Your Priestley party sounds poorly chosen. I expect he is good fun. I like his writing. I think I must re-read *The Good Companions*. Has it weathered the years well? And what a very good play *Dangerous Corner* was. Do you think a house-party at Hawarden eighty years ago would have shown much the same sort of imbroglio if the lid had been

[1] *Votes for Women* (1957) had been given a £5000 prize by the paper.

removed—Lord Acton a pansy, Mary Drew a mere Rahab, the G.O.M. himself a successful embezzler, etc? No, but I suppose quite a number of house-parties would have. One of the oddest things was the immense respect for old Devonshire, though everyone knew of Skittles and the Duchess, etc. And yet Dilke, who was immensely able, never lived down *his* amatory scandal. Was it merely that one mustn't be found out?

I am reading Basil Willey's *More Nineteenth Century Studies*, and enjoying it. Do you agree with me in always faintly but persistently disliking Cardinal Newman? That air of saintliness wears rather thin, when his (very sharp) temper was roused, and he had no width of sympathy. In disliking him I am in the dubious company of George Moore. You remember that delightful passage, in *Vale* I think, where he proves to his brother the colonel how badly Newman often wrote. Maurice Headlam, who was not at all like G.M. in all other ways, went so far as to say that Kingsley had the better of the argument which led up to N's *Apologia*, but I can't really believe that. Cuthbert H. asked me to write a little appreciation of Maurice in *The Times*, but I refused; although we corresponded pretty regularly, I didn't really know him well, and there wasn't in truth much to say about him. His letters were illegible and, though interesting in bits, had too many dull patches, when he would describe at length a house I had never heard of, belonging to some man I didn't know, with particular mention of how his elderly wife had kept her figure and looks, neither of which I had ever seen. He was latterly much depressed with the way of the world, and (like Tuppy) as really '*felix opportunitate mortis*'.

9 December 1956 *Bromsden Farm*

This morning I unaccountably woke up with a splitting headache, and despite repeated doses of aspirin it is still with me: so you must forgive a short and dreary letter. Several hours at work on the proofs of the Henry James bibliography have perhaps not helped, though it's the sort of work I usually enjoy. Jonah has sent me the first four chapters of his new book, which are delightful, especially one on stalking.[1] He has abandoned a strictly chronological and consecutive narrative, in favour of set pieces, scenes, incidents or character-sketches, with a chapter devoted to each, and so far it's working out very well. I've also got the first fifty typewritten pages (all she's written) of Diana Cooper's memoirs: they are enchanting, and if only she can keep it up, her book will be unique and altogether *her*. She's coming to London tomorrow and I must encourage and stimulate her to continue.

Those two passages I sent you last week are both by Emerson: surprising, don't you think? I have been reading Hardy. I love the old boy's poetry more every year—it's not primarily youth's cup of tea, I should say, but one of the consolations of middle age. I'm sure you know his 'On an Invitation to the United States', but nevertheless I copy out the first stanza for pleasure:

> My ardours for surprize nigh lost
> Since Life has bared its bones to me,
> I shrink to seek a modern coast
> Whose riper times have yet to be;
> Where the new regions claim them free
> From that long drip of human tears
> Which peoples old in tragedy
> Have left upon the centuried years.

I had exactly that feeling when I first visited New York, built on a rock without roots of any kind. How splendid that you are such a *Stoic* fan: 'frapped' simply means 'iced', from the French '*frappé*', which means the same.

I'm sure your King's speech was a huge success: pray describe the scene in full detail, with ample quotation from what you said. I do know Noel Annan and like him very much. He's well under forty, for all his baldness—very quick and intelligent. His wife (née Ullstein) is pretty, clever and amusing. I'm sure he'll be a successful Provost, and only hope he doesn't stop writing. His book on Leslie Stephen (his only one so far) is badly constructed, but has excellent things in it. I wrote to congratulate Roger—tax-free, I trust?

[1] *Georgian Afternoon.*

Fancy, Emerson! He is one of those men whom it is somehow difficult to read, but are devilish good whenever quoted. I read most if not all of the *Essays* at Cambridge and have his correspondence with Carlyle, but the thrawn old Scot was a better letter-writer—in fact one of the best there are, though I am almost alone in knowing that. There *is* another, much better man, who has said so in print, but I cannot remember who it is. Leavis, perhaps? Good God, how dreadful if it was. I am *quite* sure it wasn't.

The King's feast was immense fun. They were very welcoming. The Provost seemed to me entirely charming; he is on the way to being an outstanding success, which, in the most censorious community in the world, i.e. dons, is a remarkable start. The Vice-Provost, I fancy, was responsible for all the arrangements—an affable little man with whiskers of the *exact* shape, colour, size, and I suspect consistency, of mutton-chops, name of Saltmarsh. There was an old drunk of that name at Harlech (and if you come to think of it, it is hard to imagine a *thirstier* name) but I didn't quite dare ask him if he was a relative. I sat between George Rylands and John Carter, and nothing could have been more enjoyable. And only last week I asked you if you knew him (J.C.)! Really the lapses of the septuagenarian brain, because I had already noted that you had published his last book, and had rejoiced—because there is always satisfaction at seeing two good men come together. He was up to me about thirty-odd years ago; I had seen him very little since, but he is one of those rare and refreshing souls with whom one goes on from the exact place where one left off. He was interesting about the old villain Wise—shocked at the tales of his sordid thefts from the British Museum, because, as he very aptly put it, there was a certain loftiness of style about his forgeries which the other crimes altogether lack. Do you know George Rylands too? I expect so; in fact I shall give up asking you that otiose question. G.R. has what they call oodles of charm—and excellent wits too. And he is also very kind to me, which Tuppy used to say was all that mattered.

I agree T.H's poetry is immensely satisfying to the mature. Why did old Moore so dislike him? Not perhaps that old Moore's caprices matter. Didn't he also put Landor above Shakespeare and say that *Agnes Grey* was the most perfect prose narrative in existence? I suppose he often just made up his mind to play the *enfant terrible*.

I have just finished the Strachey-Woolf letters. Not fearfully good are they? Good things here and there of course, but Strachey is often trivial and V.W. often shows off, and on the whole one sees why many people spit at the name of Bloomsbury. And I suspect they would spit even more if all the names were given. Neither had any *humility*, and I am more and more blowed if that isn't the *sine qua non* of all goodness and greatness. The trouble is that if you are very clever and don't believe in God, there is nobody and nothing in the presence of whom or which you can be humble. For instance, Milton and Carlyle, for all their arrogance, were fundamentally humble, don't you think? Here endeth the epistle of George the Apostle.

I think we shall manage the motor-trip to Bromsden F. Your itinerary is fool-proof. 'Keep Left' seems the slogan. How does one avoid going round in a circle? There isn't a right-turn anywhere. But I must warn you that there is no way I cannot miss. I claim to be the only man who after going many miles on the Great North Road, and meaning to keep on it, suddenly found himself off it. Can you beat that?

I am temporarily swamped in exam-papers. What *is* the point of examining on the *Midsummer N.D.*? The candidates have all been told by their palsied beaks that the plot and the character-drawing are masterly—the plot being absurd and the c-d perfunctory. Not *one* of those flatulent impostors has told his candidates that nothing in the play is of the smallest importance or merit except a great deal of celestial poetry—oh yes and of course Bottom. One young woman—not in my lot—wrote that the two best characters were Pluck and Button. She passed all right. The exam was run by the Welsh Board.

Don't stand any rot from that headache. Bed for all ailments however small; that is how Lord Quickswood lived to eighty-seven, though always delicate.

My wife (her name, by the way, is Comfort—a New England name, which I believe she alone possesses in this country) is preparing an enormous joint of *spiced beef* for your and Pamela's visit. Apparently it has to be massaged with a different herb every day for a week—we'll hope for the best, and fall back on the Christmas ham if need be. You will also find here my two sons—Duff (20), who is flying home from Düsseldorf at hideous cost, and Adam (13), your great-nephew's messmate. My daughter Bridget (21) may not be home by Sunday. I rehearse all these names and facts so that you know what to expect. Wear old clothes, for nothing here is smart in any degree. We shall expect you between 12.30 and 1. What fun!

I saw Tim Munby last week at my bibliographical dining club, and he reported enthusiastically on your speech at King's. I wish I'd been there. Lord Quickswood seemed to receive a disproportionate amount of space in *The Times*—all about dim Church squabbles of long ago. Was he any good as Provost? I too have just read the Strachey-Woolf letters—very disappointing, I thought. Full of arrogance, and all the spice removed with the people's names. This scrappy book cannot enhance the reputation of either of them. I'm not sure I agree that it's impossible to be humble in spirit unless you believe in God—in fact I'm sure I disagree, and if I weren't so proof-weary would quote examples to prove my point.

The Lit. Soc. on Tuesday was good fun. We ate fillets of sole, roast turkey and roes on toast, with potable wines. I again (God help me) sat (or rather *was* sat) next to Bruce Lockhart, but on the other side of me was Laurence Irving, a wholly delightful chap whom I hadn't seen for ages. (Did you ever read his huge life of his grandfather? So far I've only read *in* it, finding it good and hoping for leisure enough to encompass the whole. Now it's so relevant to my Oscar Wilde investigations that I'm thinking of devoting the Christmas recess to it.) Anyhow Laurence and I talked for most of the evening about O.W., H.I. and kindred subjects.

My sister and her husband were dining next door in the big coffee-room, and I went in and sat with them afterwards. One day I spent an amusing hour in the National Portrait Gallery—seeing much that was new to me. I can stand museums and galleries for a short time only—do you find it the same? Soon one becomes overwhelmed by fatigue, air-conditioning and general surfeit. One of the merits of the N.P.G. is that the pictures are not, as in many galleries, hung so close together that one can't look at one without catching more than glimpses of its neighbours.

Most of to-day, except for garden duties and picking high branches of holly in pouring rain, I have spent wrestling with Fleming's proofs, partly alone and partly with their author. This is the *fourth* time I have read the book and I'm heartily sick of it, as I so often am of even the best books before they're finally printed. If only Peter had taken more notice of my remarks when I read the first typescript, we should have been spared many hours of irritating work. Now he has made so many major corrections on the page-proofs that I shall have to call for yet another revise before the indexes can go smoothly ahead. Years of contributing to *The Times* have introduced into P.F.'s prose woolly constructions like 'It would seem'—which to me is unacceptable in any context, and which I have now removed at least twenty-five times from this book. I daresay that all this trouble is quite unnecessary, since few realise or notice what has been done, but I hate to publish sloppy writing if it can be improved. And all the time I'm longing to get on with Oscar Wilde, and all the detective work it involves. Recently, for example, I got hold of an undated letter (most of them are) to Clement Scott, the dramatic critic of the *Daily Telegraph*. The only clue was a phrase saying, roughly: 'I liked your Ode very much, and thought it much better than Lord T's.' No verse by C.S. in the London Library, but luckily I have two devoted friends who are often in the Reading Room of the British Museum, and I asked one of them to get out all books of verse by Clement Scott (he published several) and see how many odes he wrote, and when. There turned out to be one only—a valedictory ode on the retirement of the Bancrofts, which was recited by Irving from the stage of the Haymarket Theatre on 20 July 1885. As soon as I got down here I rushed to the big life of Tennyson, and found that his lines on the marriage of Princess Beatrice were published in *The Times* on 23 July 1885—which means that I can date that letter within a week or so. See what fun it is!

But now I must turn aside to write a pithy footnote on the French novelist Huysmans for my George Moore book—not a dull minute!

Meanwhile the demolition of the next-door house in Soho Square is crashing on, with hellish noise and dirt. God knows how long it will take, or whether my house will stand up alone. Anyhow I hope to be here to welcome you on Sunday.

20 December 1956 *Grundisburgh*

'Counting fish as nothing': you remember the actor Elliston's parenthesis in his inventory of a good dinner. That is how this letter is to be regarded in our correspondence, for in four days we shall meet. I say, *spiced beef*! Are we in *The Arabian Nights*, or *Vathek*? How many dishes were there at the Caliph's feast, when the poor man was rather seedy, and could taste no more than thirty-two? But where is the spiced beef in that delectable banquet on your Christmas card which arrived yesterday afternoon? There is turkey, and duck, and ham and much else; and what a brave, new, *Old English* note the card altogether strikes. I shouldn't wonder if one of the dishes contained cheese remmykin.

'Comfort'! What a lovely name to have. Is it common overseas? I suppose the Puritans knew it. Milton would have liked it surely.

Old Quickswood was not a good Provost—so arbitrary and capricious, and quite sure that he was right. He loved argument, but Provosts aren't there to be argued with. But he was good with the boys and they flocked to the lectures merely to hear him introduce and thank the lecturer. He made very clear indeed the gap between the born speaker and the rest who after much sweat produce something that passes muster. He was about the readiest and wittiest I have ever heard. But he had nothing like the delightful friendliness of Monty James which put everyone at their ease, and never made one feel that one was unsound about the Holy Ghost.

I have followed up the Strachey-Woolf letters by reading Clive Bell on his friends. He questions the existence of 'Bloomsbury' as a one-time centre of culture, but, however hard to define, it was surely recognisable all right—like Housman's terrier and rat.[1] Does anyone deny that V.W. and L.S. and Co were exclusive, and fastidious, and highbrow, and contemptuous of past greatness, and mutual admirers, and if that isn't Bloomsbury, what is?

We shan't be able to talk about humility over the spiced beef, but it *is* exciting to find you disagreeing about it. You will I am sure produce some cogent evidence, but I warn you that an 18-pounder I sooner or later shall bring into action is to maintain blandly, infuriatingly, irrefutably, that a great number of people think they don't believe in God, who, in fact, *do*!

P.S. Unless the petrol situation is entirely *bouleversé* we shall arrive on Sunday at about 12.40—a little giddy from so much left-turning, but *all agog* for you and yours and SPICED BEEF!

30 December 1956 *Bromsden Farm*

Your and Pamela's visit was an *immense* success with all ranks, and we're already looking forward to your next. I only hope you didn't use too much of your precious petrol. Our festivities passed off smoothly, and the rationing-enforced isolation, added to the fact that I unbelievably had five consecutive days here without other publishing work, got me so engrossed in the dating, arrangement and annotation of the Oscar Wilde letters that I now look on all else as a gross and deplorable intrusion.

I was at the office only two days last week, and spent most of one of them looking up things like the Oxford Sports of 1877 in the London Library. *The Times* index for those years, while omitting all mention of music in any form, is full of sport and bankruptcies and suicides. Our rude forefathers liked their game well hung, I can see. Tomorrow I suppose I shall have to buckle on my full publishing harness: the Spring List (which will soon reach you) isn't too bad, but one always feels that the next list will be barren and impotent. The great thing is

[1] Housman said that he could no more define poetry than a terrier could define a rat, but he thought they both recognised the object by the symptoms which it provoked in them.

to work up a string of willing horses, each producing a saleable book a year, and so doing most of the work for one: most of my winners have been by one-book men, with all to do again. I lunched at the Beefsteak on Friday, with John Hugh Smith, who is utterly deaf, and three other dullards whose names I didn't know. That shows what comes of trying to be sociable! Next week, dear George, you shall have a longer letter. Meanwhile a happy new year and all blessings.

3 January 1957 *Eton*

I thought of writing a 'thank-you' letter after that Sunday, but then the fear that *you* might think it a trifle gushing prevailed and I didn't—probably wrongly, as it was disobeying both Arthur Benson and Dr Johnson, who said such impulses should always be followed. We did enjoy every moment of our visit enormously, and shall certainly pay another on a less grim day when the sunshine is external as well as internal. And I want to fix in my mind that study of yours where—*inter alia*—you write your letters to me. If you follow your usual practice you will next be writing on my birthday, Jan 6. Had I been a girl I should have been called Stella. The nurse of that day rose to still more rarefied heights and said to my mother 'You could have called her Etwol' (*Etoile*). But alas 'shades of the prison-house' etc, and when I got to school the star in the east had disastrously fallen from these and other such gracious associations, for it was a synonym for a visible fly-button. (Is that still so and was it in your day?) Attlee was born in the same week as I was, but any inferences to be drawn from that are, so far, jejune.

I had four days at Cambridge last week. Every day we walked through Downing College ('the first college you come to and the last you go to', as some wag put it) and I resisted the temptation to heave half a brick through the window of Dr L--v-s. One of my colleagues is Colin Eccleshare, who says you and he have met but no more. A good man. You probably know his chief at the Press, David. I may tell you that I gather from Colin E. that the general opinion in Press circles is that R.H-D is 'a very able fellow'. The Cambridge University Press column in *The Times* always seems to me to consist of books selected for their unreadability, but I suppose they are exempt from the normal vicissitudes of publishing. I have been reading with great pleasure in the Newman selections. So far my favourite is his masterly trouncing of Sir R. Peel and Brougham in *The Tamworth Reading Room.* It is superb in its ease and force—which come out particularly well when one reads it aloud, as I do when all have gone to bed.

John Hugh Smith I have known since 1892. He was at the same prep. school and house at Eton, and college at Cambridge, but we were never particular friends, though when we have subsequently met we have had an amicable crack. As a boy and young man he made rather a point of saying the wrong thing, and came in for a good many snubs—by which he was entirely unaffected. An able fellow and I suppose, like all Hugh Smiths, possessed of a sixth sense where money is concerned. A nice thing to have, but few nice people have it (epigram!).

We have had a very pleasant time here and seen a good many old friends; hardly any family men go away in the Xmas holidays and it is a good place and time for the children. When I was a boy only about six masters were married and their wives knew their place. Now practically all are, and some of the wives—well this is the season of goodwill and charity, so let us leave it at that. I am occupying the Dame's room. Her bedside literature is *all* the books about the Queen and a novel by Vicki Baum of quite startling indecency—all about an American faith-healer. He is said to be a saint and marvellous healer, but I don't know. His chief job (or 'assignment') was to cure a schizo, and one is led to suppose he has done so when the schizo strangles his sister (whom some time before he had raped). A very odd book. Queen Victoria would have hated it.

5 January 1957 *Bromsden Farm*

Many happy returns of the day. I have no suitable birthday present ready, so you will have to have it serially, as the books arrive from the binders. Did I ever send you the John Carter? I know I said I would, but perhaps Christmas fatally intervened: you must forgive my dotty incompetence.

It's fine to know that you and Pamela enjoyed your visit here and will come again—if we ever get petrol. Your reference to A.C.B. and Doctor Johnson reminds me of the stage-door-keeper at the Lyric Hammersmith in 1928–29. He was clearly a failed actor and looked like an aged pocket-Irving, small with long grey hair and a wonderfully histrionic face. I forget his name. Anyhow, he was always very nice to me, and at Christmas I gave him a present (I forget what). He wrote me the most charming letter, which I hope I've still got somewhere, in which he said: 'Always follow such generous impulses, dear lad'. He must be long dead. Now that you remind me, I remember hearing 'star in the east' applied to a fly-button. I expect you know the story of Winston in later years in the House of Commons. When a colleague tactfully told him that several of his fly-buttons were undone, he said: 'No matter. The dead bird does not leave the nest.'

Last week I miraculously found in Foyle's an almost complete set of bound volumes of a monthly periodical called *The Theatre* which Clement Scott edited from 1876 to 1896 (just the years I need). It includes lengthy reviews of all new plays and revivals in London, with the exact dates and full casts, as well as articles and theatrical gossip and excellent photographs of the leading performers of the day. It will be invaluable for my notes, particularly since I can refer to it in the office: I simply haven't time to spend hours in libraries, alas.

Now I must go to bed, and you are having your last read of the Dame's Crawfie and Vicki Baum—more tomorrow.

Sunday evening, 6 January.

Today has been soft and sunny, and I spent some hours agreeably extending the new brick path. I trust you had the same weather for your drive home.

I have just been struggling with a 200-word 'blurb' for the large selection of Edmund Blunden's poems which I did for Collins—a hideous task, which I have botched up unsatisfactorily. Tomorrow I'll have it typed out and then try to improve it. Generally I find that things read better in typescript, and best in print: which is encouraging while it holds good. Meanwhile the notes to Oscar absorb me. The trouble with footnotes (and this book will contain several hundred) is that they tend either to be bald, dull and severely factual, or (when one tires of that) to be full of fascinating but almost wholly irrelevant matter. For instance, I must have a note about the Roman Catholic church of St Aloysius in Oxford, which O.W. frequented as an undergraduate with R.C. leanings, and when I find that its architect was Joseph Aloysius Hansom, who also invented the Hansom cab, I can't resist putting that in. Anyhow, in the later stages it's easier to cut than to amplify, so I continue to indulge my fancy now and then. When this job is done, I shall know every kind of marginal detail of the history of the last quarter of the nineteenth century.

Now I must rewrite my Will—a largely worthless document, but it might as well be up to date—and prepare a manifesto about the Collected Edition, in twenty vols, of the works of S.T. Coleridge, for which I hope an American foundation will pay. If they don't, the whole thing is off. Tomorrow, God help me, I have to take the chair for a very intelligent female don called Kathleen Tillotson (her husband, also a Prof, edited my *Newman*). She is going to address the Dickens Fellowship—at least I think so, but I've lost the letter about it. Goodness knows what it's all about, or what I shall say. Perhaps luckily, I can't prepare anything without knowing what she's going to speak on. They asked me about eight months ago, damn them.

What splendid news about your nephew Charles.[1] 'Go out and govern New South Wales' no longer means what it did in Belloc's early days. I imagine this will at any rate postpone a final decision about Hagley? My elder boy used to mess with Norrie, son of the retiring Governor of N.Z., and spoke lyrically of the food-parcels from the Antipodes: too bad that Adam won't benefit likewise.

Oh yes—I had occasion yesterday to look at Henry James's biography of William Wetmore Story, the American artist (Oscar wrote to him), and was charmed by the beginning of the book's final sentence: 'Death came to him, as with a single soundless step, early on the October morning . . .' What more could one ask? But I have lots to do first: the teeming brain must be gleaned a little more thoroughly—just for the fun of it.

[1] Viscount Cobham, who had just been appointed Governor General of New Zealand.

It would be tedious and otiose—my favourite adjective, as 'sombre' and 'squalid' are Winston's—to tell you in every letter what immense pleasure yours give me, but I think perhaps it should be done each recurrent season. This is the winter declaration.

You say you 'have no birthday present'. Gosh! As that great man Humpty D. said, it is those who get non-birthday presents who are the fortunate ones, and who gets more of them than G.W.L.? And, my dear Rupert, the Prince of Darkness should go to you for lessons in temptation. Your catalogue makes St Anthony's ladies look like nuns ('blots upon the landscape' as Mrs Cornish said, but, suddenly realising they were R.C's as she was, added 'But what *dear* blots'!). I look forward eagerly to John Carter's book, especially after meeting him again at King's after many years. After a long spell in Suffolk my relish for good talk is positively morbid. Cyril Butterwick tells me J.C. is now at Sotheby's, and a major influence in increasing the prestige of the firm. J.C.B. is himself glossy with prosperity—Brigg umbrella, Poole trousering, Thomas footwear, etc. But he is one of those who are not spoilt by prosperity and was particularly pleasant and easy. I urged him to put on paper his experiences in the book-china-silver market, but he hates the pen, I fancy, and the world will never hear how he failed to notice something unique in a Byron volume he had bought, or how some dealer asked £5 for something he *knew* was worth £200.

That is a fine Winston you send. New to me. I do hope all these gems are noted down somewhere, otherwise half of them will be ascribed to Bevan. Not to Eden, I think, who has (as Winston feared) fallen to myxomatosis. It reads genuine enough, though no doubt the *Mirror* and *New Statesman* etc will be ready with their innuendoes and sneers. Did you read that enormous *T.L.S.* leader, which—I thought admirably—dealt with the fundamental fallacies of Socialism? I read it aloud to Pamela. It took one and a half hours—and how the leisure implied by that must make *your* mouth water. I don't believe you ever let up, and the columns and reviews in the Press leave me with the impression that you deal with a book a day. And yet you write long and lovely letters to decaying old jossers in the back-woods of Suffolk.

Your acquisition of Clement Scott sounds very good news. Old Agate would have revelled in it. And if your Oscar W. isn't a best-seller—but I don't know. What about that adolescent pretentiousness of Colin Wilson's going through, is it *nine* editions in a few months? If Tennyson were writing now, he would surely, if honest, revise his famous line to 'We needs must love the lowest when we see it': certainly, if referring to public taste. Of course you must not leave out such notes as the Aloysius one. All good men will like it. Have you in your O.W. and 1890 researches come across this poem of R. Le Gallienne, two stanzas of which I enclose?[1] It is presumably not a joke. Those were undoubtedly the days.

Thank you for your Belloc line apropos of Charles. Very happy. It will go to him forthwith; I am not sure that he doesn't think the appointment *is* like Godolphin Horne's (was it? I need hardly say my copy of those poems was lent to a boy and never returned), but he thinks, and I am sure, he is right to go. Anyway it is better that than settling down at Budleigh Salterton. The main crux has not been mentioned in the Press, viz that Charles is already sixteen to seventeen stone, and the standard of N.Z. meals is much higher than in England. He goes for five years, and I must prepare for the shock of seeing a nephew of twenty stone in my eightieth year. I don't know what the Hagley plans are; in any case it won't survive another Labour Government, like a lot of other things.

I have just embarked on Ervine's *Shaw* and expect a good deal of fun from it. I met E. once at the H.M.'s table at Eton, and he was good value, so robust and vivacious and full of flavour—and refreshingly and unrepentantly *wrong* in many of his judgments. He laughed us all to scorn for not pronouncing the letter R in words like 'four' and he was

[1] BEAUTY ACCURSED

I am so fair that whereso'er I wend
Men yearn with strange desire to kiss my face,
Stretch out their hands to touch me as I pass,
And women follow me from place to place.

The sleepy kine move round me in desire
And press their oozy lips upon my hair,
Toads kiss my feet, and creatures of the mire,
The snails will leave their shells to watch me there.

genially insulting—as in his book—about the trifling difference that there is between Eton and Borstal. But why, in his book, does he say that Flora Finching is in *Great Expectations*, and why does he insist on the spelling 'humourous'? I suspect that that springs from Shaw's spelling of 'humor' and 'color', which I always found irritating, especially as he claimed that it would save millions of man-hours.

I hope your speech at the Dickens fellowship lecture went well. Remembering your little impromptu oration about some pretty dim guests at a Johnson Club meeting, I feel sure it did. You were perhaps less pithy than old Powell, who myopically read out the names, *sans phrase*, and omitted that of his own guest.

P.S. I say, Rupert, *dare* I tell you? Yes I will; you said I was to. An odd but very strong taste of mine is books about large wild animals, and in your list I see Muldoon's *Leopards in the Night* and my mouth waters. To which your *right* answer should be. 'Your mouth can go to hell and you with it.' But you won't. What you *can* do is to look away and be silent as if I had said something unforgivably indecent —which I have!

12 January 1957 *Bromsden Farm*

I don't think of you as a 'josser', though I love the word: one degree less opprobrious than 'buffer', do you think? The long-delayed Carter volume will positively go off to you next week—also *Leopards in the Night*, if it isn't out of print. If it is, its successor, *The Trumpeting Herd*, will follow in due course. Fancy your being such an ardent carnivorophil—at last a taste we don't share!

The new Prime Minister[1] I greet with unqualified approval. Eton, Balliol, the Brigade of Guards *and* a Publisher! What more could one desire? Between the wars I served on various publishing committees with him and always admired his courage and common sense. In 1945 I very diffidently suggested to him that *faute de mieux* I should write the life of Hugh Walpole for him to publish (he was back in the firm

[1] Harold Macmillan.

then, being in Opposition) and he immediately and forcefully said: 'An excellent idea. I can't think of a better person to do it.' So my contract was signed by the future P.M., and my morale enormously enhanced. I first met him in 1927, when my sister and I stayed with the Richard Cavendishes at Holker. The only other members of the house-party I can remember were Lord Robert Cecil and old C.P. Scott of the *Manchester Guardian.* How I wish I had kept a diary—then and elsewhen.

I don't remember meeting the Le Gallienne poem before: the whole work must be sought out. It was not Godolphin Horne, but Lord Lundy:

> We had intended you to be
> The next Prime Minister but three:
> The stocks were sold; the Press was squared;
> The Middle Class was quite prepared.
> But as it is! . . . My language fails!
> Go out and govern New South Wales!

I did a lot of work on the Nonesuch Press collected volume of H.B.'s verse, and will look out for a copy for you, though it's hard to find, being a limited edition.

If you start listing the errors and misprints in Ervine's *Shaw,* you will wear your pencil down to a stub, but I enjoyed the book thoroughly—even as I was enjoying Laurence Irving's great tome until everything else broke in. Now goodness knows when I shall find time to finish it. The proofs of the Blunden poems came in last week, and I airmailed a set to the poet in Hong Kong, beseeching him to do the correcting. The indexes still have to be checked. It should be a lovely book: I'll send you a copy in June or so.

Today I cut down some large hazels with an axe, and the unwonted exercise has half-paralysed my arm. On the other hand I can begin to see why Mr Gladstone cut down trees whenever he had time: the action fulfils some primal instinct: do you agree? Now I must go to bed. More tree-felling, George Moore and letter-writing tomorrow.

Sunday evening, 13 January

I've felled some more trees, corrected some more George Moore, spent some time going through P. Fleming's proofs with him for the fourth time, read part of a manuscript (a biography of the Burnaby who rode to Khiva), slept for an hour by the fire (most enjoyable), and here I am again. The lecture at the Dickens Fellowship last Monday was a curious occasion. The Swedenborg Hall is a depressing *venue*—a grim room surrounded by long-dead, unknown and vilely painted Swedenborgians. Some sixty or so Dickensians turned up, mostly elderly and hard to rouse from apathy. The only person I knew was Angela Thirkell, whom I questioned about her Burne-Jones relations and Oscar Wilde. She was all smiling helpfulness. My introductory remarks made up in booming clarity for what they lacked in sense and preparation, and then Kathleen Tillotson spoke for well over an hour. Dickens's revisions in the various editions of *Sketches by Boz* were her theme, and very ably she handled it, quoting many amusing passages previously known only to the readers of *Bell's Life in London* in the early 1830s. But my chair was hard, and being cruelly exposed on the rostrum I was compelled to sit up and appear to be listening intently. 'Any Questions' produced the usual pin-drop silence, which I ended by asking a few myself. All was mercifully over by 9.30 (we got there at 6.45) and since Mrs T. refused all offers of refreshment I walked gratefully home to Oscar.

At the Lit. Soc. on Tuesday I sat between Donald Somervell and Harold Nicolson. The latter talked entertainingly about Swinburne's love of being beaten (if possible by muscular ladies), which he had learned from Gosse. Donald Somervell reminded me of Sydney Smith's saying: 'I had a wonderful dream last night. I dreamed there were thirty-nine Muses and only nine Articles.'

On Wednesday I went to a party in Robert Lutyens's studio for the unveiling of his recently painted portrait of my sister, which is a wonderful likeness. I spent most of the time talking to darling old Lady Emily. She is getting very old and frail, and I pray that her third and last book (now at the printers) will be published in time for her to enjoy it. Jonah and Evy were there, also my ex-wife Peggy and many other old friends. The news of Eden's resignation increased the jollity still further.

Two parcels on the breakfast table this morning, viz my new suit of clothes and John Carter's book—the latter obviously promising a great deal of pleasure, the former very little, because the only time *my* suits ever look nice and new is before I have worn them even once, and to open *this* parcel is on all fours with the sad little experience of a kindly butcher as he contemplates the happy piglet whose throat he is about to cut. That ironed and spotless tweediness in the box is full of reproach. You, I suspect, if not exactly dressy in your garden, somehow manage to give your shabbiness an aristocratic air. I shall never live down the Southwold vet telling my daughter that he had given a message for her to 'your man', who in fact was her father sawing wood. Did the chap expect me to saw in spats? J.C's book will on a rough reckoning give me about the 400th hour of enjoyment I have had from the firm of H-D. More really, because I often look again at books like the Cockerell letters, and the Moore, and the Newman—and of course *Hugh Walpole*, not from the firm. My brother Richard knows the P.M. quite well and thinks highly of him. But can *anyone* succeed as P.M. nowadays—times that are entirely revolutionary except (here) in the mere matter of bloodshed? But at least H.M. is sound in wind and limb. Grundisburgh has a firm belief that Eden has cancer, but like many other communities, it revels in what Mr Gladstone used to call the 'grubous'—a good blend of grim, gruesome, and gloom. I suppose that in history he will be relegated to that dim stratum where Perceval, Addington, Lord North and Co lie in dusty oblivion. And no doubt the archtwerp in Egypt finds no difficulty in convincing the simple-witted Arabs that it is *he* who brought Eden down.

Do you really tell me, Rupert, that you are not thrilled by lions and tigers and leopards and gorillas, or is it a relic of infantilism that I am? Jim Corbett's books are often looked into, and the page describing the appalling fury of the 'Bachelor of Powlgarh' tearing a tree to pieces about four yards away from J.C. flat on his face behind a prone trunk and eventually dragging himself away by his *toes*, still lying on his face, till he was out of earshot, and finding next day that the tiger, though silent for half-an-hour before J.C. dared to stir, *had* been there all the time—well that gives me more delicious shudders than any ghost story, or even Madame de la Rougierre in *Uncle Silas*.[1] A lion who carries in his mouth for four miles a dead buffalo, a gorilla who with *one* hand can pull seventeen men over in a tug-of-war, or, when vexed, grips a rifle-butt so tightly that it is *dented* by his finger-prints—well, as Faustus said, these things feed my soul. But I expect you, who face authors and Nancy Spains and such without blenching, do no doubt find lions and tigers very small beer.

Newman's writing is continuing to give me the deepest of all satisfactions—great thoughts, beautifully expressed, and springing from a manifestly great mind and character. What I *always* miss in B. Shaw is this feeling of *depth*. Churchill's speeches had it—echoes of great waters in the mainstream of English history and tradition—more than that, of *man's* history as he 'rolls darkling down the torrent of his fate'. I wish I could write. These metaphors roll and wallow about like cattle, but you see what I mean. I have just finished Ervine's great book, crammed, as you say, with misprints but vastly interesting. It leaves me with a greatly enhanced admiration for G.B.S's character and much less for his intellect. His toughness and patience and cheerfulness all the first half of his life were surely quite outstanding, as were his generosity and good temper. But I do find his pontifications maddening; so many even of the better ones are no more than emphatic and well-phrased half-truths. One of the oddest of St J.E's amusing kinks is his apparent belief that all Shaw's ladies were of outstanding beauty—a belief completely *bouleversé* by a page of pictures of the big four—*not* of course the enchanting Ellen Terry, and presumably Mrs Pat had plenty of allure. Curious, by the way, that both Mrs Shaw and Mrs Chesterton were allergic to conjugal intercourse. Not Mrs H.G. Wells apparently, but then, as one of his extra-mural women said, his body smelt like honey—which I find faintly repellent.

Fancy your meeting old C.P. Scott—did he strike you as formidable as many found him? I wonder what he would have said if N. Cardus, on the mat for writing 'from whence' instead of 'whence', had closed the interview by saying 'I will lift up mine eyes unto the hills from whence cometh my help'. It would have finished him no doubt.

[1] By Sheridan Le Fanu (1864).

Richard Cavendish. Was Lady Moyra there? Half a century ago she was the most attractive creature in mind and body and soul that I ever saw.

Thank you for your Lord Lundy correction: one should be accurate about these things. I had a pupil once who knew all B's cautionary tales by heart. Did they collect *every*thing of his, e.g. those tiny things about Lady Meyer etc and his inscriptions, some perhaps hardly printable, but I like:

> I am a sundial, and I make a botch
> Of what is done much better by a watch.

But the men of letters in the coming age will have no time for engaging trifles. More's the pity.

Tree-felling. Did I never tell you that it has always been a favourite exercise of mine, since the age of about fourteen, and even now I will on the smallest provocation fill my discourse with words like 'kelf', and 'spurning' and 'helve'. There is no exercise like it, though for the ageing the scythe is less exacting, the only trouble there being that unless you start young, you never get that razor-edge which makes the actual cutting ludicrously easy—just as there is nothing in carving but a really sharp knife—like your lady's ham-knife on that Sunday. My father was an expert with the axe, and indeed about trees altogether, and never could really forgive W.E.G. for being such a philistine about them; he only liked felling them and didn't do it very well. My father said you couldn't regard yourself as a really good axeman if you could not 'throw' a tree to within a foot of where you wanted, without a rope. As to the scythe, a Cumberland mower cuts a swathe ten feet wide. The normal mower is perfectly pleased with one of six feet. I do about five (when in form). The oldest mower in Grundisburgh is ninety-six.

Where the devil is Swedenborg Hall? Those societies—Dickensians, Baconians, *Johnsonians* etc—are always dreary affairs. Do you remember how Henry James shuddered—in about a thousand words—when John Bailey asked him to address the English Association? The notion that creative literature, or indeed literature of any kind, could be in any way helped or profited by an association clearly seemed to him sheer indecency. Your Dickens evening sounds pretty grim. Have you ever known anything but a 'pin-drop' silence when questions are asked for? At the Ascham Society meetings at Eton the same sequence was always in evidence. After a minute or two, Broadbent would utter a complicated sound composed in equal proportions of a snore, a belch, and a groan. Toddy Vaughan then gallantly saved the tottering situation with a question which proved, instantly and without a peradventure, that he had been unconscious throughout the paper. But what did it matter? In those spacious days the refreshment afterwards was toothsome, various, and unstinted.

I really must stop. Thank you for the Sydney Smith dream. Arthur Benson used to have marvellous dreams, full of wild fun and monstrous and irrational cruelties, e.g. himself about to be beheaded or one of his colleagues actually being hanged, inside a sort of cupboard, whence came a horrid noise of bumping and kicking.

19 January 1957 *Bromsden Farm*

So glad you've got Carter at last. I'm hoping to send you the *Leopards* next week, though I still can't share your enthusiasm for those great beasts.

Eden's cancer is widely discussed in London too: poor man, I wish him no ill, though I doubt whether he'll be as clearly remembered as Perceval (murdered in the House) or Lord North (lost us America). Addington is nearer the mark. And how many people could instantly say who was P.M. at the time of the Battle of Waterloo?

Reverting to your passion for wild animals, have you ever read *Elephant Bill* and *Bandoola*? If not, I will unwillingly encourage your aberration by sending them along.

C.P. Scott, as I remember, struck me as an object of compassion rather than awe. He was old, and his great qualities, unknown to me, were not immediately apparent in that huge rich house. Lady Moyra was a brisk and managing hostess, Lord Richard a dear old round-faced sheepdog.

Yes, the Nonesuch volume included all Belloc's printable verses, including many never printed before. I have often longed to assemble his unprintable ones, which are now available only in the memory of his friends. Did I tell you (I fear I did) of the time at luncheon at Duff's when he quoted his parody of A.E. Housman? It began:

When I was one-and-fifty
I found him at it still.
His eye was just as shifty,
He made me just as ill.

But how did it go on?

Yesterday I scrambled the George Moore letters off to the printer, but I fear the proofs will need some attention. Old Sydney Cockerell (he's dead but he won't lie down) has sent me a large bundle of letters between himself and my beloved Viola Meynell, who died the other day. They are naturally most moving and interesting to me—but to others? I simply don't know. And all the time Oscar is waiting for his annotation. For one short footnote one may easily write several letters and spend hours (albeit enjoyable ones) looking things up. P. Fleming left for Canada to-day after giving me a parting pheasant. If you read his piece in the current *Spectator*[1] you will learn of *some* of my difficulties with his proofs. My military son has sent us a letter of twenty-three quarto pages, describing goose-shooting on the Baltic. After standing waist-deep in liquid and icy mud for four days he brought down *nine* geese and drove back to Düsseldorf exulting. I've never much cared for goose anyhow.

Sunday, 20 January

I can't remember whether you take both Sunday papers. If so you will have been amused by the two reviews of *Newman*: Raymond all for N but against this book, Toynbee all for this book but against N. Oh well, reviews almost always cancel each other out neatly, but since we also got Harold Nicolson on *Margaret the First* (would you like her?) I can't complain of the amount of space, which at advertising rates would have cost the best part of £500.

The tree-felling is over, and two big bonfires have consumed all but the log-worthy stems. My brick path, which should be finished next week, has lately developed a strange curve, but I tell them they're

[1] 'A Goldfish's Farewell to his Bowl', reprinted in P.F.'s *The Gower Street Poltergeist* (1958).

lucky to get any path at all. Adam is preparing for his first half at Coleridge's and seems quite unperturbed. Next Thursday I have to preside over a 'Literary Brains Trust' at Rossall, whose exact locality I failed to look up before idiotically accepting the invitation. Hours in the train, a sherry-party in the Headmaster's study, a dinner in Blackpool, a sleepless night, more hours in the train—you shall have all the grizzly details next week. By contrast, last Monday–Tuesday I spent a delightful twenty-four hours at Brighton, visiting a friend who was recuperating there. I have always loved the place and felt well there: also its air contains a delicious feeling of truancy, for when I was a boy I was constantly ill and my mother always took me to Brighton to recover. As I forced my pennies into the slot-machines on the pier I rejoiced at not being at school. Even to-day that feeling persists, lending an extra zest to what is agreeable enough in itself. We sniffed the icy ozone, ate excellent meals, saw a rattling good film (*The Battle of the River Plate*) and made an exhaustive tour of the secondhand bookshops, of which there are a delightful number. I bought a dozen books and returned reluctantly to Soho Square, where the air is loud and dusty with the adjacent demolitions. I dined out on Tuesday, Wednesday and Thursday, all quite enjoyable, but when am I to do my Wilde editing? Sometime in February I shall go on a fruit diet for a week (my weight is steadily mounting), which means that I *have* to stay in all the time, since the sight of others eating is unbearable. *Then*, perhaps, I shall get some work done. What am I reading, you ask? Proofs and manuscripts and detective stories and Lily Langtry's memoirs (of great Wilde interest). The great Irving tome is still unfinished, chiefly because it's too large to carry about or read comfortably in bed.

24 January 1957 *Grundisburgh*

The *Leopards* have arrived—what is the collective noun, a 'slink', or perhaps a 'cruelty', though I think that is bagged for cormorants or something—bless them and you. They will accompany me to bed to-night and I shall dream of one coming at me 'like a torpedo', though covered with blood. You clearly regard my taste for them with tolerant derision, as if I still retained a taste for scooters or tin soldiers; but I stoutly counter-attack, and say that your indifference to the 'fearful symmetry' of a tiger and its 'deadly terror' is to me so odd as to be classified among the anfractuosities of the human mind, and if that doesn't abash you, nothing will. I am sure Peter Fleming will be with me, but alas he is far away on the billow. But I may be wrong. I remember a passage in one of his books in which he derided the crocodile's formidability and left the reader with the impression that there is little to choose between it and a tortoise, or some other beast which is usually asleep and very slow to anger or action when woken up. I have got *Elephant Bill*, a delightful book, but *Bandoola* is new to me.

Thank you for the Belloc quatrain. I wonder if Housman knew that parody of him by your uncle; he rather enjoyed them, and always said that the best was Hugh Kingsmill's 'What still alive at twenty-two, A fine upstanding lad like you?'

The Ascham Society often entertained a visitor, but one might easily have found himself in for a grim evening, e.g. Broadbent on Beddoes, or old Chitty on Anselm, or Toddy Vaughan on Poggio which extended over two sittings. Arthur Benson was secretary then and there is a pencilled word 'closure?' in the minute-book when he consulted Luxmoore as to what was to be done. L., who had early school the next morning, sternly nodded. Ram told me that the paper began with so long a passage in Greek that the members, convinced that the whole paper was to be in Greek, fell into helpless laughter. However, after six minutes or so Toddy stopped, looked severely round and said 'So wrote Plato'.

Your tale of your son among the geese is good, ending with your delightful anticlimactic-paternal comment 'I never much cared for goose anyhow', but you cannot conceal your pride in a son who spends four days up to the waist in mud and then writes twenty-three pages on it. Have all H-D's this unresting energy?

I only see the *Sunday Times* and of course read R. Mortimer on Newman. Like many of us, he clearly feels, when reading a vol of selections, that he could have chosen better. But I am not well enough up in Newman to agree or dis- in this matter. I found some of *The Idea of a University* rather hard going, but at such times I remember

Carlyle's contemptuous comparison of some man who decried Goethe to him, who 'complained of the sun because it would not light his cigar'. But one can always skip. Were N's letters so good? I have never heard or read of anyone else saying so, but perhaps they have. Why does Toynbee dislike N.? He had an unchristian temper, and I suppose a good deal of the Socratic capacity for making the worse appear the better cause, but somehow he is one of those who are outside the reach of our superficial, *prima facie* judgments, and he often said things which hit one, if I may coarsely say so, plumb in the wind. And it is worth remembering, but I hesitate to say with what feelings, that D.H. Lawrence called 'Lead Kindly Light' and 'Abide with Me' 'sentimental messes' as compared with what he called 'healthy hymns', viz 'Fight the Good Fight', which is to put *Marmion* above the Nightingale ode. Why must our geniuses so often be patently and infuriatingly *asinine?* Old Shaw and his alphabet for instance. Anyway it looks as if the sum of money at issue will all be wasted (or, as the solicitor corrected it, 'absorbed') in the costs.

I have just had a bit of luck—turned off a lot of muck from English stations and tried a foreign one and *at once* they began to play Bach's Air for the G. string, than which—to use the favourite ecstatic aposiopesis invented by Mrs Gladstone or her sister. And another bit of luck yesterday (this letter is ending like the majestic river Oxus, and is now 'shorn and parcell'd') I picked up a book by Margaret Mead—not at all a favourite author of Mrs Boffin's—and found among the bibliography 'A Study of the Pelvic Type' by *Ruth Christian Twaddle.*

Saturday night, 26 January 1957 *Bromsden Farm*

To-day I write triumphantly, for my brick path is at last completed! My daughter (who is home for the week-end) says it looks like a switchback railway, but Comfort, delighted and astonished that I should have accomplished anything so useful, is full of praise. Oscar Wilde has suffered of course: I must push on with him tomorrow.

The Housman parody was by Belloc, not Duff. My syntax must be at fault. Not that Duff couldn't turn a pretty set of verses when the mood was on him. One of the weeklies set as a competition a sonnet to be called 'On first hearing that Wordsworth had had an illegitimate child', the first line to be 'Byron! thou should'st be living at this hour.' Duff won it with this spirited entry:

Byron! thou should'st be living at this hour,
  We need thy verse, thy venom and thy wit
  To castigate the ancient hypocrite.
We need thy pith, thy passion and thy power—
How often did that prim old face turn sour
  Even at the mention of thy honoured name,
  How oft those prudish lips have muttered 'shame'
In jealous envy of thy golden lyre.
In words worth reading hadst thou told the tale
  Of what the lakeland bard was really at
When on those long excursions he set sail.
  For now there echoes through his tedious chat
Another voice, the third, a phantom wail
  Or peevish prattle of a bastard brat.

Not bad for an amateur, I should say.

Oh yes, another of my books has just been chosen by the Book Society—Vincent Cronin's new book, which comes out in April.[1] You shall have it when it's ready—a lovely book. We should now sell 30,000 copies instead of 6000—a great help to the firm, and to the author, who is an altogether admirable and charming person. How satisfactory it is—and how rare—when the prizes go to the right people! Since P. Fleming's book is also due in April, we shall have our hands full just then.

Sunday night, 27 January

Last week was exhausting. On Monday I dined with the Selwyn Jepsons in Bayswater and worked till 11.30 on Max Beerbohm's letters to Reggie Turner, which they own and I am to publish. On Tuesday I lunched most agreeably with Peggy, my ex-wife, at Wheeler's excellent fish restaurant in Old Compton Street: do you know it? That night I attended a disastrous dinner of my bibliographical dining club at the

[1] *The Last Migration.*

Garrick. Carter, who pretty well runs it, had run into Roger F. and asked him to come as a guest. The general rule is that there are no guests, except on occasional Guest Nights or by general agreement. Roger was, I think, unaware of this, and the slight *gêne* caused by Carter's solecism would soon have evaporated, had not *two* members, quite separately, *arrived* heavily inebriated. Michael Sadleir, poor lamb, is I fear in constant pain from cancer or some such and drinks to dull the pain: most pardonable but not conducive to good conversation. The other, a bookseller you wouldn't know, was sullenly aggressive and in his studied but only partially coherent rudeness to one after another of his fellows a seething mass of Non-U inferiority was quickly apparent. I managed to insulate Roger between Carter and Sparrow, but the rest of the round table was hideous. If Carter hadn't made the mistake of putting us in the big coffee-room instead of our usual private room, we might have been able to cope better with the situation; as it was the dinner dragged interminably, and I slipped away as quickly as possible, swearing 'never again'.

On Thursday morning, as I was boarding the train for Preston I saw Roger, and after lunch walked along and talked to him and Sybil, whom before I had seen only for a moment at Paddington. I liked her so much, and we had a delightful gossip. I was travelling First at W.H. Smith's expense, in company with their two publicity managers and my fellow-Brainstrusters, Dilys Powell, John Connell, and Hugh Ross Williamson—all very friendly and easy. At Blackpool, where we were lodged in an excellent hotel, we were joined by Frank Singleton, an old friend who edits the *Bolton Evening News*. Rossall is three miles along the front: luckily the H.M. was out of action with a slipped disc and it was raining so hard that we were let off a full tour of the school. After tea and drinks we faced 650 boys in Big School. They had prepared the best set of questions I've met and seemed to enjoy it all. The B.B.C. were everywhere recording, and half an hour of the programme is to be broadcast: I'll let you know when if they tell me. Then a six-course dinner, with appropriate wines, at the hotel. I sat between the School Chaplain and the Second Master's wife, both very nice. To bed exhausted at 1 am, and up in time to catch the 8 am train back. Dilys typed her *Sunday Times* film article all the way back while Hugh R.W. and I gossiped. I really must stop wasting time so frivolously. They pay fifteen guineas and all expenses, but the wear-and-tear alone comes to more than that. Goodbye till next week.

31 January 1957 *Grundisburgh*

I enjoyed the *Leopards*, as I knew I would. Muldoon doesn't, I imagine, know quite as much about them as Jim Corbett did, and his were mostly not so much man-eaters as cattle-eaters. Both had very narrow shaves, as no doubt anyone doing that job must have. The great Selous's advice to elephant-hunters was 'get *one* and be content, for elephant-hunting, if continued, must end in the hunter's death.' Two days ago I found myself at a film, *The Slave Girl*, a tale of ancient Babylon. Superb pictures (technicolor) of buildings and Assyrian dresses, armour, etc and a magnificently impossible story. The hero was shot a good many times through the heart, and tortured, and surrounded by scores of men thirsting for his blood; he leapt into a pool full of the largest crocodiles, wrestled successfully with two of them, and slit their throats. The heroine (whom everybody would call Semi-Rammis) was burnt at the stake but rescued just in time. The villain of course, after hitting the hero's sword, and having his own hit (no one but Lewis Waller ever made a stage-fight look convincing) was pushed into the crocodile-pool and they took—in every sense—tea with him. It was glorious rubbish but I enjoyed it.

I like your uncle's poem 'Byron! thou should'st' etc. As do so many, he strongly disliked the man Wordsworth, who must have been uniquely dried-up, stiff, dull, self-satisfied, arrogant, but at his poetic best—Who was it said 'He stumps along by your side, an old bore in a brown coat, and suddenly he goes up and you find that your companion is an angel', i.e. is at home in a region where Byron saw only George III and Southey having their legs pulled. I see the latest Byron book puts everything down to B having been a homosexual. But haven't we always known he was, remembering his own description of his feelings at school about Lord Clare? He must have been grand fun in company when not showing off, or on the defensive. Poor B., we must always remember he was a Harrovian.

I say, your bibliographical dinner! Is dear John Carter a bit arbitrary sometimes? I suspect he might be, like many another good man of strong character who has been strikingly successful. An odd coincidence that when your letter arrived, one of my bedside books was M. Sadleir's *Fanny by Gaslight* which I greatly enjoyed. I suppose *Esther Waters* started that genre?

I am glad you met Sibell Fulford, Pamela's favourite sister, but her large heart holds all of them. I expect you know S's last husband was my brother Caryl who died in 1931. Their boy—particularly promising—was killed at Anzio, not many yards away from Humphrey.

3 February 1957 *Bromsden Farm*

I fear you won't get your double letter to-day. Last Thursday I was walking briskly down Frith Street, on my way to the Beefsteak Club to lunch with the head of Scotland Yard (R.L. Jackson—perhaps you remember him—a huge boxer at Piggy Hill's—incidentally he never turned up for lunch, but that is beside what little point there is). The pavement was wet, I slipped on a thin film of dog's mess, and fell heavily forward, grazing and bruising one leg nastily. I don't need to tell you how heavily large men can fall: I was momentarily stunned, and had to be helped up by passers-by. Apart from a sore and stiff leg I suffered no ill-effects until yesterday (Saturday) morning, when (*post*, but I can scarcely think *propter, hoc*) I woke with a temperature of 101.4. Struggling up I spent the day muzzily by the library fire, and after a good sweat last night achieved subnormality this morning. Tonight I am feverish again: no other symptoms: it's all very mysterious: but you will understand why my usual plan of correspondence has gone awry, together with most of the work I brought down with me. I shall go up to London tomorrow, come what may. Not having had a temperature for *years*, I feel outraged.

Yes, Carter is a bit arbitrary at times, though I'm very fond of him. How delicately you corrected my misspelling of Sibell, bless you. Now I shall know!

Don't get up till your temperature is what it should be. My nephew Charles was tempted by a fine day to go and play golf too soon. Result six or eight months in South Africa to save his lungs. It is true that it was pneumonia that he was convalescing from, but the moral is the same. You are right about big men falling. Old Gladstone of course had a theory—rather like his thirty-two chewings of every mouthful—that to avert shock after a fall, one should remain some time *in situ*. So more than once passers-by were rewarded by the sight of a venerable statesman prone in the gutter, and returned home more than ever convinced that the G.O.M. was insane. But how dull it would be if great men had no foibles, like Barham writing *The Ingoldsby Legends* with a cat on each shoulder, or Dumas putting on woollen socks whenever he had a love-scene to write, or Johnson touching every lamp-post he passed.

By the way I have just been re-reading the *Lives of the Poets*. How full they are of good things! Anything approaching the nonsensical always evoked some delightfully weighty irony. When someone timorously suggested that *The Beggars' Opera* would encourage crime they were put in their place with: 'Highwaymen and housebreakers seldom frequent the playhouse, or mingle in any elegant diversion; nor is it possible for anyone to imagine that he may rob with safety because he sees Macheath reprieved upon the stage.' That should do much to restore your temperature.

My daughter Diana, let me tell you—though it won't interest you at all—is engaged to be married—to one Alexander Hood who moves in high circles among government officials and is a very good fellow. He is forty-two and she is thirty-seven next week and all seems just as it should be. The news is being broken to the Queen[1] at just about this moment and will appear in *The Times* on Saturday, being till then one of those secrets that about 150 people are well aware of. She will have a good life, travelling from time to time all over the world. He is a descendant of the great admiral, and Pamela was pleased to find in the *D.N.B.* that *he* owed his initial rise in the Navy to 'his friendship with the Lytteltons and Grenvilles'. She read no further, being daunted by

[1] Diana was working as Press Secretary in Buckingham Palace.

the extreme dryness of the author's English. Old Leslie Stephen's motto for contributors, 'No flowers', was often interpreted by them to mean 'Nothing but potatoes and cabbages'. They are less austere now I fancy.

10 February 1957 *Bromsden Farm*

I'm happy to say that my fever of last week-end vanished as suddenly and mysteriously as it came—some sort of safety-valve to make me rest a little, perhaps.

Yes, the *Lives of the Poets* are superb, and once again your words make me long for the leisure to re-read such splendid stuff. 'By the common sense of readers uncorrupted with literary prejudices, after all the refinements of subtlety and the dogmatism of learning, must be finally decided all claim to poetical honours.' Them's my sentiments, and yours too, I know. My beloved Edmund B. knows chunks of this book (as of most others) by heart, and is fond of quoting, as though it applied to himself (I copy for the pleasure of it):

> His morals were pure, and his opinions pious: in a long continuance of poverty, and long habits of dissipation, it cannot be expected that any character should be exactly uniform. There is a degree of want by which the freedom of agency is almost destroyed; and long association with fortuitous companions will at last relax the strictures of truth, and abate the fervour of sincerity. That this man, wise and virtuous as he was, passed always unentangled through the snares of life, it would be prejudice and temerity to affirm; but it may be said that at least he preserved the source of action unpolluted, that his principles were never shaken, that his distinctions of right and wrong were never confounded, and that his faults had nothing of malignity or design, but proceeded from some unexpected pressure, or casual temptation.

That's the stuff! What an epitaph! And how cunningly I pretend to write you long letters which are mostly copied out of books!

I read admiringly yesterday of Diana's engagement: your quiver of grandchildren will soon overflow. When is the wedding?

My soldier son returns to civilian life in about a week's time, and I'm hoping he'll feel in the mood for some active gardening. Oh yes—I read a nice remark the other day, a boy's apology for not returning a book to the School Library: 'Awfully sorry, sir, but I was waiting for it to dry off.' Last week I went to a small party given by a young author of mine called Michael Alexander, at which were gathered four of the most beautiful girls I've ever seen. Mostly 'models', it transpired, and aggressively illiterate.

I spent one afternoon in the London Library, happily compiling footnotes for Oscar Wilde. I met Rose Macaulay in the stacks, gropingly seeking the Theology section. 'You'll find yourself alone there,' I said. 'Yes', she answered; 'I always do.' And yet once I dare say that section was besieged by bearded scholars and earnest doubters. I am supposed to hand in a review of eight detective stories by tomorrow, but I've read only six and a half, so they'll have to wait a day or two. This afternoon I read in manuscript a new novel by another of my young hopefuls. It's no good at all, but I felt bound to read it all before telling him what's wrong with it—which is pretty well everything. That's how my time is spent, you see.

It's ten years this month since my firm published its first book (*Fourteen Stories* by Henry James) and the occasion gives me pause. Altogether I've published 310 books, including quite a few that I regret. Was it worth all that sweat? I suppose so, though if I could afford to, I'd pack up publishing tomorrow and just be a freelance literary bloke. As it is . . .?

When I at last met my friend Jackson, head of the C.I.D., last week he told me he'd recently met his old tutor Piggy Hill, who greeted him with the words: 'Hullo, Jackson, I understood you were dead.' Characteristic, I should say. There can't be so many eccentrics among Eton beaks in this egalitarian day. My second-half Adam has been asked to play chess for the School! Fred rightly forbade it, since the match was scheduled to last four hours.

Very glad to hear you are well again. I expect, as you say, that it was a sort of safety-valve. I was interested to read that old Shaw had severe periodical headaches all his ninety-four years. Let us charitably assume that they were responsible for some of his pronouncements.

I am pleased to hear of this further feather in E. Blunden's cap, viz that he knows Johnson's *Lives* so well; and thank *you* for your quotation 'His morals were pure' etc. *Who* is being so majestically dealt with? It must be someone I have not yet re-read; I am mainly browsing among the Sprats and Garths and Blackmores, not, so to speak, tackling the whales—Milton, Dryden, Pope. Do you, or does E.B., know the place in the 'Milton' where the Doctor splits an infinitive? The passage you quote would be a very good example to show the difference between the pompous and the powerful and precise—'long associations with fortuitous companions will at last relax the strictness of truth and abate the fervour of sincerity'. Every single word pulls its weight—which makes it all the more surprising that he wrote that Blackmore's prose was 'languid, sluggish, and lifeless' and that Shenstone's landscape gardening might seem absurd to 'a surly and sullen' spectator. But perhaps the adjectives have shed some of their associations over the years.

I say, Rupert! The Literary Society![1] And your *wicked* cutting away of *all* my just misgivings! Won't all Cuthbert H's acidities ('What's *he* ever done to be a member?') be abundantly justified? Though I grant you I feel the honour as much, every bit, as the misgivings. Let me be flanked by you and Bernard F. and dear Tim N. at any rate at first. Though I am bound to tell you, all my letters recently from Sir Cuthbert about his brother Maurice have been particularly gracious.

Pamela and I met on Monday all or nearly all Diana's in-laws-to-be, and very pleasant they all seemed. It really does seem to be one of those arrangements in which it is hard to find a flaw—a remark to which I can hear the Doctor's ghost countering 'Depend upon it, Sir, the history of man shows that no such flawless felicity. . .'

You among the mannequins! What *do* you talk to such lovelies with their empty heads about? Themselves I suppose. Do they enjoy their

[1] George had been elected a member.

lives? Are their 'morals pure, their opinions pious'? And do they pass 'unentangled through the snares of life'? What is Rose Macaulay doing in the theological department? There are so many things to talk to you about. You must have begun publishing roughly when we came here, i.e. your life's work began as mine ended. I remember getting James's *Fourteen Stories* and enjoying them. And in the ten years you have made a big name of R.H-D in the publishing and literary world. I too wish you had time to write.

In the train yesterday I was *thrilled* by *Moonraker* by Ian Fleming. Is he any relation to Peter F? It is very well written, so perhaps he is. Are his other books good? The book I read on the going-up journey was *Paradise Lost*—the creation of the animals, Book VII. It is immense —'the river-horse and scaly crocodile,' 'the parsimonious emmet' etc. How right the Russian Moujik was who told Maurice Baring that he liked *P.L.* because 'it makes me laugh and cry'.

Yes, that is Piggy Hill all over. Grizel Hartley and a friend once called on him at Ledbury, and finding him out, left a note in which they apologised for pinching a 'pair of Worcester Pearmain' apples. Two days later she got a p.c. 'They weren't W.P's., they were James Grieves,' and nothing more. There are no more Piggy Hills at Eton. But let me tell you, in your day there were nothing like the great eccentrics of my day. So the smoothing and flattening-out goes on, and soon Eton beaks will be as indistinguishable from each other as ants.

17 February 1957 *Bromsden Farm*

Yesterday morning I began a week's thinning cure. This consists of drinking nothing, and eating only fresh fruit three times a day. One feels alternately blown out and hollow, also feeble and ratty, but it worked when I did it before, and I hope to lose a stone. The one thing that becomes intolerable is to see others eat, so I have thankfully refused all invitations for the week, and hope to do a lot of work. Inevitably one becomes, for the time, obsessed by weights and measures, but at least I am not paying fourteen guineas a week, as at Tring for orange-juice. I'll report results next week.

I'm so happy at your joining the Lit. Soc. It wasn't even necessary to rig the voting. I don't say I would have done so, but I very easily could have. As it was, you romped home top of the poll. The others elected were Alan Moorehead and John Piper. There were six candidates for the three vacancies. As you will see, the electoral system is more complicated than the Papal one, and takes far longer. I fear that at your first appearance you will be bidden to sit next to the President, but thereafter I shall shanghai you to my end of the table. Last week's dinner brought Cuthbert to my side, with Ivor Brown on my other. After a few introductory prophecies of six weeks' hard frost Cuthbert mellowed considerably, and with a mixture of flattery and teasing I managed to keep him jolly until, when it was time for him to leave, he discovered we were thirteen, and refused to move until everybody rose together. Since half the members were out in the lavatory, this took some time to arrange, and in the meanwhile Cuthbert (looking himself like death slightly warmed up) told me of all the people he knew who had died through defying the superstition.

I rejoice in having found a scrap of Johnson which pleased you anew. It refers to William Collins, of whose works E.B. edited the best edition. Did I tell you that he (E.B.) is coming home in May for a six-months holiday with all his family? Goodness knows where they'll find to stay.

How splendid that you enjoyed *Moonraker*. Ian is Peter's younger brother—one year younger—and a most engaging character, though quite different from Peter. His other books are good too, though the bridge-game in *Moonraker* is his high spot so far. Originally he was in Reuter's, then a stockbroker, then in Naval Intelligence, now Foreign News Editor of the Kemsley Press. He writes a good bit of the Atticus column in the *Sunday Times*.

Last Wednesday I attended a luncheon-party at the Ritz, given by the A.P. Herbert (Obscenity) Committee for Tony Lambton and Roy Jenkins, who are going to try and get a second reading for our Bill on March 29. Six of us are going to watch from the Strangers' Gallery. After lunch I went on to the Royal Literary Fund, where, during the interminable reading of the minutes, I gossiped with Frank Swinnerton by writing notes on the back of the order paper, like boys in school. That evening I went to *At the Drop of a Hat*, an entertainment given by two men, one of them in a wheel-chair. I can't remember when I laughed so much. During one turn, an imitation of a tennis-umpire at Wimbledon, I became almost hysterical. Do go to it if you have a chance: I know you'd love it.

Tomorrow my elder son returns to civilian life, with two years' accumulation of kit, and I fear an overdraft at the bank. He has just spent a week-end in Berlin and reports that in the East Zone a gramophone record which here costs 37/6 can be bought for 4/6. My daughter reports from Wales that the latest trade-name (among Evans the Hearse, Dai the Pub, etc) is the Hire Purchase agent, who is known as Trevor the Never. More hot news next week.

21 February 1957 *Grundisburgh*

The last man I knew who took a thinning cure had a curious experience. He weighed 19 stone 10 lbs and for one exact year he ate and drank nothing *at all* that had a particle of fat in it. He kept up what he admitted was an intolerably severe régime, and on the 365th day he weighed himself again. The answer was 19 stone 11 lbs. So he went angrily and thankfully back to porridge and ham and 'cheese remmykin', and was quite happy for a year or two before passing out very much in the same way as old Heythorp did. On the other hand I used to find taking off a stone or so in the summer holidays quite easy. In doctors' jargon I have, or had, a very rapid metabolism—which cuts both ways. The sylph who faced a new division in Sept was the Boniface of December. What was unbearable (as you say) was to see Marsden breakfasting on porridge, sausages, cold ham, buttered toast *ad lib*, and continue positively stylitic.

The Lit. Soc. prospect fills me with pleasure, mingled with diffidence on realising the intellectual distinction of my fellow-members. I am interested to see A.P.H.'s name *crossed out*. Is there a tale behind that? Did he assume that the Lit. Soc. shared the tastes of Sir Gerald Kelly? Tommy Lascelles, whether deliberately or not, achieved a master-stroke of tact in telling me that among the original members was poet-laureate Pye, of whom all I know is that he put into rhyme several episodes in my ancestor ('the good Lord')'s *History of Henry II*, and of course Byron's 'Better to err with Pope than shine with Pye'. T.L's mention of him had the effect on me that, according to Miss Reynolds, Goldsmith's bow had on everyone in the room—it put them at their ease, because at least they knew they couldn't possibly make a worse bow than *that*. My excellent ex-pupil Bernard Fergusson has asked me to drink with him at White's and proceed thence and, thus fortified, to face Sir Cuthbert and Sir Malcolm and (I hope) Sir Terence. Any chance of *you* being there too—I mean at White's? Then I could face even his lordship of Dunsany with a cheer, as Browning did the unseen. I love your vignette of Sir Cuthbert refusing to rise till all the rest had, and retailing the fatal results he had known following thirteen at table. Why, in any case, should he mind, if he had been the first to rise? *Joie de vivre* is not a conspicuous element in his make-up. The picture of e.g. Roger hurriedly emerging from nether regions, hitching and buttoning, in order to restore Sir Cuthbert's peace of mind, is one I shall long treasure.

Confession is, they say, good for the soul. I *had* re-read the Life of Collins and—doltishly—not specially noticed the passage you quoted. I feel as foolish as I did last week when, standing at the bus-stop cross-roads, I signalled all clear to a van coming from Burgh into the Woodbridge-Tuddenham road at right-angles. A moment later there was a crash of ironmongery as a retired admiral in his Morris came down the W-T. road like a driven grouse. Do you know the feeling of not having the smallest vestige of leg to stand on? It is most unpleasant. The only ray of comfort I got was the sight of both of them reduced, if not to equanimity, at least to almost complete silence by my admission that the whole thing was entirely my *fault*. I too, like Hugh Walpole, have a strain of Mr Pooter in me.

Well, the Collins passage I did notice with particular pleasure was: 'A man doubtful of his dinner, or trembling at a creditor, is not much disposed to abstract meditation or remote enquiries.' Good but not as good as yours.

How right you are about that bridge game in *Moonraker*. Few know less about the game than I do, but it thrilled me. I.F. must be a devilishly clever fellow. All the scientific stuff in the book is at the very least immensely plausible. I must get hold of his other novels. I wonder why I never came across him at Eton.

I shall remember about *At the Drop of a Hat*. But the trouble is that I don't now *hear* in a theatre, unless I am very close. Usually humorous plays are the hardest to hear, as apparently all back-chat must go at the speed of a machine-gun, and it is too fast for me. Though, as the curate said, no one likes a bit of fun more than I do. (Do your family ever puncture you as mine do when they talk of some play or film and end by saying to me: 'It's frightfully good: you'd hate it, Father'?) And that can be said to me with perfect truth by practically all our leading critics, as you will realise when I tell you that I am very largely allergic to Jane Austen. I have been reading *Persuasion* on the last three evenings and often exclaiming how bad it is. Pamela, with that feminine commonsense which sees, and misses, so much, says 'Why do you read it if you hate it so much?' and is not at all convinced by my reply that it is because humility is almost the leading trait in a character of which thirty-eight years' experience should have shown her the beauty. Anyway, if your riposte is as indignant and contemptuous as I fully expect, my next letter will have plenty to say. At the moment all the 'demurrer' (legal) I can put in is to say *à la* Byron and Pye 'Better to err with Charlotte Brontë than shine with A.B.Walkley, Maugham, Cecil, and all those women who can't leave their idol alone'.

24 February 1957 *Bromsden Farm*

All is well. I am nine-and-a-half lbs lighter and have just consumed with relish a poached egg on spinach—my first hot food (or drink) for more than a week. I had hoped to achieve prodigies of work, but in fact felt too empty, feeble and *cold* to do very much except browse and sleep after a day in the office. My soldier son arrived back from Germany on Monday, went out to a party without the keys of the flat, and woke me in the small hours to let him in. To cheer me up, E.B. reports from Hong Kong: 'Sad to relate, on the menu tonight at Sea View I observed "Fried Prawns' Balls with vegetables $3.50" I could not explain my laugh to our Assistant Lecturer Miss M. Yee.' Don't you particularly like that 'Sad to relate'? I have written back saying I thought Nightingales' Tongues were the *ne plus ultra*, but clearly the East knows better.

A.P.H. only once attended a Lit. Soc. dinner. He sat next to Roger and never came again, or paid any subscription. How tiresome of Bernard to nobble you first. Never mind: I'll see you for a moment at the Garrick over our pre-prandial sherry, before Tommy nobbles you for dinner. I'll most certainly attend the Johnson Club on March 26 if you're going to be there. I shall probably bring a charming Canadian called George Whalley (a Professor, as they all are), who is an expert on Coleridge. You will certainly like him. What about a drink at Soho Square first? I'll try not to fuse the lights. Or perhaps the Garrick would be more convenient? As for your suggested Johnsonian recruits, Frank Swinnerton can seldom be coaxed from Cranleigh after dark; G.M. Young is, alas, gaga. He was a member for many years, and (goodness knows why) put me up for membership before he withdrew. Tillotson is already a member, D.B. Wyndham Lewis wouldn't get enough to drink, Charles Morgan is not frightfully clubbable. Jonah perhaps: is he an admirer of the Doctor? I must arrange for you to meet E.B. again when he's in England this summer.

You ask whether we disagree about anything. I think not, though I can't share your liking for books about large wild animals. Certainly I'm with you about Jane Austen, who has never been a great favourite of mine. But it's so long since I read her (except for one, of which more in a minute) that I'd like to try again with the cold eye of middle age before finally jumping down on your side of the fence. I see what so many other people see in her, but myself (tell it not in Bloomsbury) if I want to refresh myself in that period I prefer Scott. My uncle Duff adored her novels, and in the last week of his life, when he knew (consciously or subconsciously) that he hadn't long to live, he came to Soho Square on Christmas Eve, and, saying 'I've brought you a Christmas present: I hope you haven't got it already,' he pulled two slim volumes out of each pocket of his greatcoat. They were a first edition of *Northanger Abbey* and *Persuasion* (4 vols), in which he had written 'Old men forget but they are grateful when they remember'. I was much touched at the time, and when he died suddenly at sea on New Year's Day, the books became doubly precious, as his farewell gift. Later that year (1954), still moved by the same emotion, I re-read *Persuasion* in this copy, and persuaded myself (almost) that I shared Duff's admiration for it. But in truth I don't think I did. When, oh when, shall I have the leisure to try the others again and report fully to you?

Last week I had a brush with the Cabinet Office, who suddenly demanded changes in Fleming's introduction to *Invasion 1940*. Since Peter was (and still is) inaccessible in America, I rang up Sir Norman Brook, the head of the place and a very nice man with whom I had tricky dealings over both G.M. Young's *Baldwin* and Duff's *Old Men Forget*. To him I made a strong *ad misericordiam* appeal, explaining (truthfully) that 30,000 copies of the book were already printed, the author couldn't be reached, and his suggested alterations would involve me in hideous expense and untold delay. Audibly shaken, he said he would reconsider the question, and on Friday evening I got a note withdrawing all his demands. Phew! In fact I don't think he had a leg to stand on, but he's not the sort of person one particularly wants to make an enemy of.

All this week-end it has rained pitilessly, and I have gratefully stayed by the library fire, reading manuscripts. I'm in the middle of (a) Speaight's Life of Belloc, which is much better than I expected, (b) the new Michael Innes detective story, which is good uproarious fun. Charles Morgan's novel I have bought but not yet begun. On March 1st my George Moore proofs are due to begin arriving, and I shall have to shelve Oscar while I deal with them. What with those two, and Max B's letters to Reggie Turner, I shall be composing footnotes from now to Kingdom Come. Luckily I enjoy it, but time is always lacking. I envy you your leisure and your summer-house.

28 February 1957 *(Grundisburgh)*

At the moment
I am in Sloane Square
about to attend a meeting.

Your metabolism is in the championship class. Nine and a half pounds in, what is it, two weeks? I never managed speed of that kind. But doesn't that *cold* feeling mean that you are getting it off *too* quick? And I suspect February, even a mild one, is not the right month to start in. But I don't really know anything about it. The faculty itself is pretty feeble about diet—*quot medici tot sententiae.* Some years ago some ass started a campaign against spinach—full of oxalic acid, I think he said it was. Rubbish! It is almost my favourite vegetable, but a lot depends on the cooking. Swithin Forsyte, on his deathbed, was fretful about his cook not producing spinach equal to what he got at his club. How it pleases me to read that you relished a poached egg and spinach because I love it in spite of the sneers of so-called gourmets at the poached egg. Did I ever tell you that in the Hagley nursery each of us chose the dish for luncheon on his or her birthday. My choice was always mince and poached egg—and I like it just as much now. And if possible it should be followed by rice-pudding and rhubarb. I doubt if you will see eye to eye with me there. Of course if in the early Nineties we had known of fried prawns' balls I should have had to think again. I look forward to meeting E. Blunden again. Am I right in thinking he has some tie with Suffolk?

Yes, I too was hoping to drink with you before making my début, but Bernard F. was v. quick—and is such a good chap that I didn't see how I could refuse. And I *will* turn up at Soho Square on the 26th with great pleasure—or the Garrick, whichever you decide.

Your summary of the possible Johnsonian candidates I suggested is full of pathos—and humour too, alas—rather like Crabbe's Suffolk community, 'the moping idiot and the drunkard gay'.

Since my last, I have re-read *Mansfield Park.* It is much better than the insipid *Persuasion.* The Crawfords are interesting, and it is refreshing to find one of her snobbish dolls quite frankly committing adultery; but here again all the characters converse with exactly the same rounded amplitude which demands to be turned into Latin Prose. But some of the scenes and pictures are good. One sails along on smooth and shallow water under a mild blue sky. But I doubt whether I shall feel strong enough for *Emma.* It is very long. I shall have to keep all this *very* dark at the Lit. Soc. I am sure Ivor B., and Harold N. and many others are Janeites of the deepest dye. A sentence I treasure is one of Raymond Mortimer's: 'I am a great admirer of J.A. and therefore a little mad.'

I have with me—and am half through—*Lord Byron's Marriage.*[1] Immensely interesting. The highlight of it is of course the brilliant

[1]By G. Wilson Knight.

Don Leon poem of Colman's—very shocking and all that but as good as Pope *qua* skill. I imagine Lady B. was fairly bloody, and her family and advisers worse. Odd that B. should never for a moment have suspected that she and they might destroy his account of the whole affair, and so did not keep or safeguard a copy. Still, I suppose B. and marriage simply could not combine, whoever might have been his partner. The set-up reminds me of Henry James saying, when he heard Arthur Benson was to write the life of Rossetti for the English Men of Letters series. 'No, no, no, it won't do. *Dear* Arthur, we know just what he can, so beautifully, do, but no, oh no, this is to have the story of a purple man written by a white, or at the most, a pale green man.' I think I have it right; it came thirty or forty years ago from Percy Lubbock.

This will arrive on the same day as the G. Moore proofs and you will not find it so interesting, and you will be right, for I have just re-read it. Remember in mercy that yesterday afternoon I was at a meeting where the main topic was the operation of a sinking fund—which I always associate with sinking spirits. As a topic it is inferior even to *runts* (see Boswell).[1] I finish this at my club. The chairs round me are full of bodies. Some are alive, some not. We shan't know for certain till the rattle of tea-cups is heard.

P.S. I rather think Crabbe wrote 'The moping idiot and the *madman* gay'. Drunkard is better!

3 March 1957 *Bromsden Farm*

The English winter is worth living through if it ends with two such days as yesterday and to-day have been. I imagined you basking in your summer-house and pitying everyone else, though our front

[1] JOHNSON. 'Mrs. Thrale's mother said of me what flattered me much. A clergyman was complaining of want of society in the country where he lived; and said, "They talk of *runts*;" (that is, young cows). "Sir, (said Mrs. Salusbury,) Mr. Johnson would learn to talk of runts:" meaning that I was a man who would make the most of my situation, whatever it was.' He added, 'I think myself a very polite man.'

lawn was a delicious sun-trap and we happily lunched out there. The nine and a half lbs were lost in *one week*, and it *was* much too quick, and February is *not* the best month for such drastic treatment, but all is safely over, another one and a half lbs lost last week, and I am slowly getting into training for next Saturday, when I am to attend a Feast at King's as the guest of Leslie Hotson. I shall stay Friday and Saturday nights with Madeline House (Humphry's widow) in Cambridge, and return to London on Sunday, in time (I hope) to write to you.

Like you, I always go for minced chicken and poached egg if it's on the menu: never lets you down, does it? I'm crazy about rhubarb too—and rice pudding.

E.B. has indeed a most sentimental tie with Suffolk. He lived there for some years when he was first married, in 1919 or thereabouts. It was during those years that he found all the John Clare manuscripts in Peterborough.

The Byron book sounds extremely interesting. Wilson Knight is a crackpot, but at times I daresay inspired, as so many crackpots are. Does he attempt to *prove* (1) that Colman wrote *Don Leon*: (2) that C. ever saw the famous memoirs? I must read it.

Henry James's remark about A.C.B. on Rossetti is superb, and new to me. If only Percy Lubbock would write his memoirs! A lot will be lost if he doesn't, but I fear he is too old and lazy. I always send him any H.J. books I publish, and he always writes most appreciative letters of thanks. It's more than twenty years since I saw him. Shall I write and suggest a book of recollections? I think I will.

I'm just finishing the Belloc biography. It's a most capable and painstaking work, though I could have done with a few more personal touches (gossip, if you like) at the expense of many pages about Distributism, Politics and the R.C. Church.

The George Moore proofs began to come in on Friday, and I have been through all I've received, delighted with the letters themselves but horrified to find how much still remains to be looked up, checked, cross-referenced and shuffled into shape. My list of notes looks like this:

(1) When exactly did Lady C's mother die?
(2) Did Consols drop to 80 in August 1907?

(3) Who was Harry Lynch?
(4) Is the place in Ireland New Grange or Newgrange?
(5) What and where was the Diploma Gallery (1922)?

And so on. I already (on perhaps a quarter of the book) have enough to keep me in the London Library for an afternoon, and Oscar will have to hang fire while I'm at it. Between interruptions that major work rumbles on. I am now annotating Part IV (of nine), which covers 1883–1890. I keep getting new letters (mostly from America) which have to be interpolated, and often entail a rearrangement of the notes, since each person, book, event or whatnot must be annotated on its *first* appearance. I'm sure when you read the finished book you'll agree that all this detailed work is worthwhile—at least I hope so.

Fleming is back from America, exhausted and with a heavy cold. He reports that Harold Caccia is doing splendidly in Washington, but is increasingly fed up with Dulles, and indeed with Eisenhower, who sees no-one except caddies and reads nothing but brief 'digests' of world news. He is, Peter says, now almost completely insulated from the world and its doings—which is pretty terrifying.

One of my few rules in life is never to refuse the offer of a bookcase, since I never can have enough, and next Friday a *huge* one is being delivered at Soho Square, where there isn't a square foot for it: all would be well if I wasn't guarding E.B.'s 7000 books there for him. They'll be with me at least till 1961.

6 March 1957 — *Grundisburgh*

Again from the summer-house, but 'basking' is perhaps hardly *le mot juste*. The sky is the colour of a dead fish's belly, a deadly little breath from the East ('somebody's not using Amplex') is shedding that thin sad sort of rain that looks as if it was never going to stop. But a sweater, a muffler, and a rug enable me to despise its rather toothless moroseness, and a Haydn symphony puts the finishing touch to my equanimity—which in any case is at its height while I am writing to R.H-D.

I have finished the Byron book. Wilson Knight puts up a strong case, though apparently Lady B. still has her defenders, and like so many defenders they fly easily into temper. W.K. refers the reader to his article in the *Twentieth Century*, June 1956, for all the stuff about *Don Leon*. He thinks there is no doubt Colman wrote it; also that 'in all probability' C. had seen Byron's Memoirs (burnt). How prejudice does blind the critical judgment! Ethel Colburn Mayne dismisses *Don Leon* as 'little filthy brochures' telling of 'things unspeakable in villainous Alexandrines'. Well 'filthy' etc is a moral judgment, but as to villainous Alexandrines, (a) they are not Alexandrines and (b) they are frightfully skilful.

Do write to Percy Lubbock, insisting that he must write his memoirs. Of course he ought to. He knows more about Henry James than anyone, I should say. But he feels his years—though his eyes are much better; he writes with his own hand now—and never, I imagine, wrote easily. But he needn't write another *Earlham*; memoirs need not, should not, be so beautifully jewelled, or move with such grace (one really wants so many words to do it justice. Do you remember Keats's line 'Mid hush'd, cool rooted flowers, fragrant-eyed'? As some good man pointed out, he gets four out of the five senses into the line).

I am immensely interested in your remark about Desmond MacCarthy taking such trouble over his writing, because old Gow who had been pro-M. complained that his later reviews were 'shamefully idle'. The censure was mainly based on what he said was excessive quotation from the work reviewed. Gow can be hypercritical, but he is not as bad as Housman—his idol and indeed model, who used to say things like that about E.V. Lucas, who had at one time attended H's lectures in London and so, said H., 'I am responsible for his education—in so far as he can be said to be educated.' I have heard G. describe someone as 'not a serious scholar,' because though the man could read Plato and Lucretius with feet on the fender he spent no time on emending some text which, when emended, no one could possibly want to read.

I have just got from the Library the Holmes-Pollock letters, as I greatly enjoyed the Holmes-Laski ones. But Sir John P. (whom I suspect to be an ass), who edited them, has left in far too many letters about legal cases which are simply caviare etc. I also suspect that his father (Second Classic and Seventeenth Wrangler, if you please) had a good deal of Dryasdust about him. *All* the good things I have noted so far come from old Holmes. I like: 'Whenever I read Shakespeare I am struck by the reflection how a few golden sentences will float a lot of quibble and drool for centuries, e.g. Beatrice and Benedick.' Not new of course but profoundly true, and crisply put. I am a poor Shakespearean, i.e. I am, like most, overwhelmed by the poetry, but so often bored by the absurd action of the play and the characters, and *always* by the wit. And if to be luke-warm about S. and J. Austen doesn't put one beyond the pale in the Lit. Soc. what will? Probably I ought to have made these confessions to you before you proposed me. Holmes quotes with approval a Frenchman's answer when he was asked if a gentleman must know Greek and Latin: 'No, but he must have forgotten them'. That was in 1892. In 1962 the answer will be 'I don't know what you mean by gentleman; as to G. and L. nobody should know them; to do so would argue that much time has been lost which should have been spent on liquid hydrogen or metal-stresses.'

I am delighted to hear about Harold Caccia—a very good man. What a sinister picture of Eisenhower—at the head of the greatest power in the world. Do you know Winston's latest—about U.S.A. bungling: 'It wouldn't have happened if Eisenhower had been alive'? I have to choose my audience for this; it wouldn't do at the Ipswich Club. The answer might so easily be on the lines of my daughters aged between seven and thirteen say, on about Jan. 4 when I said 'Brrrr! It might be midwinter.' 'But father, it *is* midwinter.' They fell into the trap all right but only once apiece.

17 March 1957 *Bromsden Farm*

No letter from you yesterday—but then you had nothing to answer, and perhaps the Lit. Soc. flattened you out. It was undoubtedly the best evening since I've been a member, and this I can attribute only to your presence. I'm glad you had Donald Somervell next to you: he's most friendly, amusing and agreeable. We were lucky to be spared both Cuthbert and Dunsany. My end of the table was very gay. Eric Linklater told me he recently bought in an Edinburgh junk-shop a fine painting on wood of an allegedly 48 lb salmon. Underneath was inscribed 'Caught by Colonel MacGregor in the Tay, 3 June 1880'. Eric had this removed, and substituted 'Caught by Private Angelo in the Po, 1 April 1943'. Thus adorned, the trophy now hangs in Eric's Scottish home.

My visit to Cambridge was most enjoyable. Saturday morning I spent 'doing' the secondhand bookshops, and in the evening I accompanied Leslie Hotson to the Feast at King's. First-class food and drink, and agreeable company. I had a few words with Arthur Waley and E.M. Forster. Afterwards the whole party, several hundred strong and well primed, was let loose in the Provost's Lodging, where Mrs Annan and five other ladies were dining. What lovely rooms they all are, and beautifully furnished. I got away soon after eleven, and woke unharmed next morning. Moreover, my weight yesterday morning was exactly the same as it had been a fortnight before!

I did write to Percy Lubbock, but so far he hasn't answered.

I am in the middle of reading the galley proofs of the George Moore letters; it is essential I should finish them tonight, the hour is almost eleven, and you must forgive a miserable half-measure this week.

My son's departure for West Africa has been advanced to next Wednesday. When he gets back (in June) he immediately starts for Canada. 'Youth and the sea! Glamour and the sea!'

Last Thursday I paid my second visit to the French actors. Edwige Feuillère is a dream. *La Dame aux Camélias* was great fun, and I enjoyed the comedies too, though the language was harder to follow. Next week she assaults the Everest of *Phèdre*, and I shall be there to cheer her on.

The destruction in Soho Square continues brutally, but there are flowers in the garden, and occasionally spring in the air. My youngest was eventually allowed to play chess for the School, but was defeated by an elderly lady in a basement off High Street Kensington! What next?

20 March 1957 *Grundisburgh*

No, I didn't write because up to the end of the week I was rather up to the neck after the meeting of a G.B. of which I am Chairman, at which the Headmistress could not be present, and I had to write a detailed and careful letter about the meeting, and the numerous questions her absence left unanswered. The carefulness was necessary as the gist of much of the letter was that she was in some matters behaving fat-headedly, and—*inter alia*—that a teacher of biology aged seventy-two, *all* of whose eight candidates failed in the G.C.E., might perhaps not be a wholly adequate teacher of biology. Another letter I had to write which did *not* take long was to congratulate an Old Girl on winning the fencing championship in the Olympic Games—one of the five—was it?—English gold medals.

Never have I enjoyed an evening more than that with the Lit. Soc. That blend of friendliness and intelligence which seemed to me the pervading atmosphere is very heartening. Yes, Donald Somervell is one of those who puts one quickly and completely at ease. Tommy Lascelles too was in 'merry pin,' if one may borrow from John Gilpin. I had a good crack—up to 11.45—with Ivor Brown. I liked him.

That is a good tale of Linklater and the fish. Had you no *serious* fisherman at your end of the table? Usually they are rather stiff about such tales. The one I like best (pity you can't stop me if you know it!) is Chauncey Depew's attempt to deflate the story of a gigantic fish described to him. 'Was it a whale, perhaps?' and got a cold look and a calm reply 'We wos baitin' with whales.' Once I charged the beloved Monty James with laughing heartily at a story which I knew he knew, and got the—for him—brusque reply: 'Why not? It is an excellent story, and I was delighted to be reminded of it.' I didn't dare counter with 'Remind, indeed! As if you ever needed reminding of anything you had ever heard or read!' Like the dog Rab, he had a look sometimes of 'thunder asleep but ready'—when e.g. he suspected meanness of any kind or lack of charity.

I am glad Cambridge and King's shewed a gracious face to you. I too thought the college had some very pleasant people in it. Percy Lubbock always (though he is very fond of him) says E.M. Forster is a disappointing conversationalist. Odd, because some of *Abinger Harvest* and *Two Cheers for Democracy* is first-rate talk. I wonder how you found him. Percy, by the way, took *weeks* to answer my Xmas letter, and said that for some time his disinclination to put pen to paper, or indeed do anything, had grown into positive nausea. I think he begins to feel really old sometimes. The way I think it will take *me* is that described by H.G.W. to Frank Swinnerton 'Perhaps that's what old age is, Swinny; a little slower, a little slower, and at last feeling triumphant at getting across a room. It's horrible.' And although old age, like death, has been described a million times, every man finds both full of surprises, nearly all unpleasant.

I am interested to read that Belloc put *Rasselas* at the top of English prose. I have just finished Speaight's Life. How badly, somehow, B. managed his life, mainly through not realising the truth of St Paul's statement that it is not always *convenient* to utter all the truth. I suppose he struck the Oxford pundits as a very brash young man, and sometimes, e.g. the Dreyfus affair, deliberately wrong-headed. Still, why call it *All* Souls if so much brilliance and character is inadmissible. But I don't really know the ins and outs. I took a volume of B's essays in the train and found most of them, alas, very thin—no hint of the rich fun and quality of Godolphin Horne and Co. But, as by now you must know, my literary taste is capricious, imperceptive, antiquated, ossified, you may well disagree. I remember, years ago, setting *The Eye-witness* for Private Business—Hastings, Armada, Waterloo, etc as told by one who took part, thinking they must be exactly what was wanted to stimulate interest. It was a flat failure; the boys thought the accounts were very insipid—and so did I! That last picture of B. with a beard gives a profoundly sad impression.

P.S. Your description of the French play is very appetising. Do you agree with J. Agate that by and large French acting is in a different class from English? One thing I always approve heartily is that any French player who is not heard in pit or gallery is greeted with shouts of '*Parlez*'. They insist on getting their money's worth.

Sorry your son lost his chess-match. Old Ram's uncle never lost a chess match, because, when defeat loomed, he accidentally knocked the table over, pleading a sudden attack of cramp. *Verb sap.* I believe the school chess cup is the largest at Eton, presented by some fanatic. Ram was a chess blue at Cambridge but his Oxford opponent beat him. 'He was better with his pawns than I was' was Ram's verdict in 1950. I always regarded pawns as encumbrances to my dashing sorties.

Once again it's past eleven p.m. and having just spent four and a half solid hours on the George Moore proofs I feel drained of all sense and sensibility. I keep thinking I've finished with that infernal book, but even now I'm short of one illustration and shall have to compile an index as soon as the page-proofs are ready. Poor old Oscar hasn't moved an inch for ages. By the way, do the words 'The forest is like a harp' ring any bell in your well-stocked memory? George Moore puts them in quotation-marks as though they came from somewhere. Shelley? or where?

I got a charming answer from Percy Lubbock: 'I am afraid it isn't likely that I shall ever be younger or brighter than I am—but if such a miracle *should* happen, I will remember your pleasant suggestion.' I fear that's the last we shall hear of the matter.

You're quite right about that fishing story of Linklater's. I told it to Arthur Ransome, a great fisherman, and I could see he was a little shocked.

Yes, I agree with Agate about French acting. *Phèdre* last week was most beautiful and impressive, though I wished I'd had time to re-read and absorb the play beforehand. Like Greek Tragedy, Racine should be known almost by heart, so that the subtleties of acting and phrasing can be relished.

My elder son is now on the high seas bound for Dakar. In a note from Liverpool he reported a comfortable cabin to himself and added: 'The officers hardly speak at all, and eat incredibly slowly, but they are all very well-meaning. The Captain is broad Scottish and awfully nice.'

Yesterday, in lovely hot sunshine, Comfort and I had our first trial of strength with the new motor-mower. Neither of us had ever operated one before, but we found it most satisfying and enjoyable, though we did more than we realised and are stiff and blistered today. Last night we dined gaily with the Osbert Lancasters, who live in Henley. Osbert and I went up to Oxford the same term in 1926, and he hasn't changed *at all*.

Don't you rather like this footnote: 'The remainder of this paragraph, which Coleridge wrote with his gout medicine instead of ink, has faded and is all but illegible'.

I must say our end of the table [at the Johnson Club], under the—I am sure—approving eye of the Doctor, was very good fun. I was delighted to find that Christopher Hollis really enjoyed himself and expressed gratitude to me for getting him into the Club! Of course he produced a good guest in Muggeridge. What riddles human beings are! That kindly, civilised, understanding man under the same hat as the spiky, unbalanced wrong-headed reviewer of Francis Williams's history of the Press and pretending(?) that he prefers the *Mirror* and *Sketch* to *The Times*, the *Observer*, the *M. Guardian*, and that the taste for a nude bathing beauty and that for a *Times* Fourth Leader are on the same level. First thought on meeting him 'What an excellent chap!' First thought on reading his review 'What a Philistine!' But I suspect he enjoys trailing his coat. I liked him very much.

That paper I believe really to have been a definitely good one. But wasn't it dreadfully badly delivered? An intelligent Frenchman doesn't read *his* language like that—any more than a French orator would. Is it our native modesty? I sympathise with Arnold Bennett's exasperation when an Englishman sat like a graven image through Pavlova's swan dance till, near the end, a feather fell from her wing, on which the Englishman said 'Moulting'. No other word passed his lips.

What a nice young man your Canadian is; he got on swimmingly with Roberts. I had a feeling that if in that delightful hour *chez vous* the conversation had turned on modern poetry, my status as a country bumpkin with hair full of hay-seed would have been even more firmly established. I should not wonder to find that *Finnegans Wake* is an open book to him. Meanwhile I fight a stout rearguard battle.

Yesterday my main contribution to the G.B. deliberations about Woodbridge School was to have the word 'finalise' deleted from the minutes and 'complete' put in its stead. I was supported by the local archdeacon. The rest of them—sanitary inspectors, small builders, shopkeepers, auctioneers—were apathetic, till I said it was 'bastard American', when a prim shudder ran through the room and I realised, too late, that the lady-secretary was present and her face was scarlet. However 'finalise' *was* deleted.

I am in the summer-house surrounded by daffodils and my heart dances with them, and across the lawn is a cherry-tree in blossom, about which all I can say is what the historian of Solomon's reign said about the almug-tree, i.e. 'No such almug-trees were seen in the land' (which Monty James said was crossly interpolated by the scribe who was bored by the raptures being dictated to him). But of course every spring the earth's beauty is something new, never before seen. But how ludicrously brief it all is. Four or five days and the cherry-blossom one morning is merely white compared with its first days, for which there is no word. Daffodils do last longer, though not so long as I want them to. Few things do.

Dr Adams had a poorish day yesterday.[1] I don't see what his counsel can make of that Harley St Dr's evidence. I gathered in London that the conviction that he is guilty is widespread. Still *vox populi* is not always *vox Dei*, though it may some day be so regarded.

I am almost certain that line you ask about, 'The forest is like a harp', is in Shelley, but cannot place it. I shall have an exploration this evening; in fact I *have* just re-read *Prometheus*, and if anyone says it isn't tremendous, I shall have the greatest of pleasure in recommending their instant relegation to the nearest asylum. There was, by the way, one bright spot in Muggeridge's *New Statesman* article, where he indicated hatred and contempt for the man L--v-s.

31 March 1957 *Bromsden Farm*

Let us get one thing straightened out once and for all. I have been to far more dinners of the Johnson Club and the Lit. Soc. than you have, and I know, beyond, as they say, a peradventure, that it is *your* presence that makes these occasions *go*. So let us have no more pretence of its being to my credit—except in so far as I am stimulated to greater enjoyment by your being there. Incidentally, you had a tremendous success with George Whalley, who when I saw him again on Friday could talk of nothing but your wit and charm. No mention

[1] Dr Bodkin Adams was accused, and later acquitted, of hastening the death of some of his elderly female patients.

of S.C.R.'s conversation, or the speaker's dim delivery—just praise of G.W.L. So you see, I am not alone in my judgment!

I spent most of Friday in the Strangers' Gallery of the House of Commons, and though our Bill got its second reading, and we were given a good lunch at half-time, I was *appalled* at the abysmal level of speaking. Admittedly the big shots were absent, but we must have listened to twelve or fifteen speakers, on both sides of the House, and most were lamentable by any Eton House Debate standard. Goodness knows what made some of them choose politics as a profession. I can think of no more appalling punishment than to be compelled to listen to every so-called debate in the Chamber.

I adored your story of the Englishman watching Pavlova. I expect you saw her, but to me she is only a mythical bird, just as Nijinsky is a legendary faun. Actors—and even more dancers—can survive their last admirer only if they have been written about by a genius. Gordon Craig I consider a very phony genius, but his move-by-move description of Irving playing a scene from *The Bells* is immortal: do you know it?

I forgot to tell you that on Tuesday I had a most agreeable lunch with Jock Dent. We talked hard of Max and Agate, and books and the theatre. He is a charming fellow, but now I fear rather disappointed. Dramatic critic to the *News Chronicle* isn't much of a job in the public estimation, and his fortnightly cinema page in the *Illustrated London News* can be read only by people waiting to have their teeth out. Jock recently read through (or at any rate turned every page of) the first hundred years of the *Manchester Guardian* and he has kindly sent me a few references to Oscar which he had noted down. He can be extremely scholarly and assiduous when he's interested, and it seems a great pity he can't be harnessed to some solid literary or theatrical task.

Yes, most people seem to think Dr Adams guilty, but many believe he will get off: his counsel certainly seems very adroit. What else? On Thursday I went to see the Dean of St Paul's about putting up a memorial tablet to Duff Cooper in the Crypt. The Deanery is an exquisite house—red brick, 1690, Grinling Gibbons carving round the front door, full of pictures of old Deans—including one of the only two authentic portraits of John Donne. But of course it's much too big and cold for to-day, and I found the Dean very understandably recovering from a feverish chill. Previously I had met him only on committees, where he never speaks. At home he shyly talked about poetry and literature, in which he is obviously interested. He spoke at length of St John Ervine's Life of General Booth, and I must confess made me want to read it. Have you?

On Thursday night I dined with Reggie and Joyce Grenfell in their new flat in Elm Park Gardens—a gay and cosy evening. Have you ever seen or heard Joyce perform? She has just written another whole one-woman show which she is to give in the autumn.

My daughter has been home for the week-end, and luckily she is fascinated by the new motor-mower, so I was spared that this week, or rather liberated for other gardening activities, which have left me stiff and ready for bed. An old and dear writer-friend of mine has sent me the typescript of a 350-page novel about a juvenile delinquent in an Italian quarter of New York. I have struggled past page 100 and must somehow finish. But what *am* I to say to him? This sort of thing is the most painful of publishing hazards. You couldn't say the book was *bad*: it's just *dull*, and who on earth wants to read such stuff? By contrast, Ian Fleming's new thriller, *From Russia, with Love*, I got through in a flash. Put it down on your library list. Also the new Michael Innes, *Appleby Plays Chicken*. Or do you only get 'serious' books from the library?

4 April 1957 *Grundisburgh S.H.*
(summer-house)

I am not going to pretend that the first sentences in your letter did not give me great pleasure—nor would you believe me if I did. All I would say, as what I believe the lawyers call a 'demurrer', is that I can easily be as dull as Dulles in many companies. I read your opening sentence to Pamela; she was undoubtedly pleased, but I am not sure I did not detect in her attitude some tinge of resemblance to Hugh Walpole's vis-à-vis Wodehouse apropos of Belloc's eulogy.[1] But

[1] See *Hugh Walpole* by Rupert Hart-Davis, p. 403.

what wife of thirty-eight years' standing could ever see her husband as other than the humdrum old bore and egoist that he is? I always think Chesterton's crack one of his best: 'Every good wife will support her husband through thick and thin, though she is perfectly aware of the thickness of his head and the thinness of his excuses.'

I observe that the modern note is to be rather sniffy and patronising about G.K.C. Let them! He wrote much that was wise and much that was witty. I wonder if the anthology of him just come out is any good. I have again been reading in G. Tillotson's *Newman*—with a good deal of satisfaction, but with a growing feeling that he could have made it much better. Surely it is the sword-play of the *Apologia* and what led to it which is *now* the most interesting thing about it. It is all very well for Newman to deprecate the literary aspect of his own writing, but that is what appeals in 1957, not wire-drawn theological problems. What I like about *The Tamworth Reading Room* bit is the skill with which the argument and the language are handled. But as we saw ten days ago, these university professors don't think enough about their *audience*. We at Trinity in 1904 were lectured to by a very great philosopher who spoke throughout with his face turned to the wall. On the other hand Verrall was the last word in brilliance and fun—though what I chiefly remember is his crow of laughter when calling over the list of his pupils and finding that 'Shufflebotham' was followed at once by 'Sitwell'. Or probably I only remember being told that. He was what Joxer Daly would have called 'a lovely man'.

Percy Lubbock is not at all well—bronchial, cardiac, etc, can do nothing, even walk upstairs, sees no one, writes no letters. And I suspect he is rather a rebellious patient, especially as his wish to live is not very strong. I have known him for sixty-two years, i.e. longer than any non-relative. Who was the good man I met recently who shared my opinion of *Earlham*, i.e. as a book of almost unique beauty? It is about the only thing of importance I am quite sure of—much surer, that is, than I am of the existence of God or that a point has position but no magnitude. Though I quite see what Desmond MacCarthy meant when he said it would have been even better if now and then Percy had just let his narrative scamper along in any old words. I said—it was at the H.M's at dinner—'You mean one doesn't want all one's water filtered,' and D.M. looked at me as if thinking

'This chap isn't such a fool as hitherto I thought him' and said 'Yes; exactly.'

I am glad all goes well with Joyce and Reggie Grenfell (my old pupil). I have only met her once, and, like everybody else, liked her immensely. I particularly appreciated the cleverness with which she prevented dear Reggie from feeling and looking as does Mr Summerskill in the presence of Edith. Joyce must be almost of the calibre of Ruth Draper.

I note what you say of books to read. Do not think 'a God's name that I only read 'serious' books. I am fastidious about novels and thrillers, but love good ones, e.g. M. Innes. I ask weekly at the library for another Ian Fleming, but they are always out. There is some very succulent tasting in your Spring List; surely a winner or two among them. Does G.L. Watson come into the open on Housman, i.e. (need I say it?) as a homo? The emphasis on that side of humanity is really becoming alarming. This month's *Contemporary Review* has a review of a book on the negro problem in U.S.A. It contains the sentence 'Mr Furnas misses what is perhaps the deepest psychological reason for the tension in the South, the white man's fantasy that the negro has a bigger penis than the European male.' The author of the review is 'the grand-daughter of a slave now studying psychology at Bedford College'. I find the mental picture of her hurrying round the dormitories with a tape-measure faintly nauseating. On the other hand it is refreshing to picture Queen Victoria reading the *Contemporary Review* in Elysium.

6 April 1957 *Bromsden Farm*

I can see that these Lit. Soc. Tuesdays are going to interfere with our letter-writing if I don't look out. It would be absurd if you got this letter *after* our meeting, so I shall post it here tomorrow, and hope it will reach you in time.

I agree that Chesterton is greatly undervalued just now, though I am told that his first editions are much sought by collectors. Certainly time will winnow away a good deal of his minor work, but much will surely remain. I can't help pointing out that Joxer's phrase was 'a *darlin'* man', *not* 'a *lovely* man'. *What* a good play that was, and what a pity that O'Casey left Ireland and so cut himself off from his true source of material. But perhaps he'd already said all he had to say. Now he's just an ould grouch, doubtless the literary bully of the Totnes area, with a chip on his shoulder the size of the Nelson Column.

Gordon Craig's description of *The Bells* is in his book on Irving: I'll bring it up to lend you on Tuesday. Also the new Ian Fleming, if I get it back in time from another friend.

I am repeatedly amused by the Eton habit of writing all reports, except the Housemaster's, before the results of Trials are known. Both my boys are natural examinees and somewhat idle in class—which makes the reports on them amusing. For instance, Adam, after ending up *bottom* of D.2. got a Distinction in Trials, *and* the Trials Prize *and* Science Prize (ugh!) for Lower D—all this in his second half at Eton! Secretly I hope he will keep it up and be made O.S. as his brother was.[1]

Yesterday he came to London and I took him to a film called *Doctor at Large* (simple fun but no pain to sit through), followed by dinner at the Garrick, at which he knocked off a glass and a half of claret. To-day he has been delightedly working the motor-mower. Mercifully all three children love using it, but I foresee many summer week-ends when none of them is here, and there's the best part of a day's work in the job. I have worked so much in the garden to-day that I have practically seized up in all limbs. Goodnight, more in the morning.

Sunday morning, 7 April

The skies this morning, my dear George, are ashen and sober, the air bites shrewdly, and I fancy that Oscar Wilde will get more of my attention than will the garden. Adam, after striking a few lugubrious and tuneless notes on a large guitar which Leslie Hotson left here, has bicycled off to play with a friend.

Last week was wonderfully restful, since I managed to dodge all engagements, and so got through a pile of manuscripts and other work. I twice saw Elisabeth Beerbohm, Max's widow, who is a charmingly warm-hearted and intelligent person of great integrity. She is much

[1] In due course he was made Oppidan Scholar.

pleased that Merton have agreed to institute and maintain a Max Room, containing his books, drawings, letters, etc. I have promised to do all I can to get it going. Next Thursday I am going to the London first night of *Zuleika*—which Max insisted should be pronounced *Zuleeka*, though for singing reasons they call it Zulĭka in the play. You know, I expect, that Hardy said Dy̌nasts like that.

I shall soon have to spend an afternoon in the B.M. Reading Room, having collected a list of O.W. queries which I cannot answer elsewhere. Oh yes—about the 24th of this month I shall have the final (page) proofs of the George Moore letters. Would it amuse you (or rather, perhaps, could you bear) to read a set of them for me, looking for errors of fact, taste and syntax? It's not a long book, but I have spent so much time on it that I feel I may at this stage miss almost anything through over-familiarity with the text. So your help would be a great blessing.

11 April 1957 *Grundisburgh*

Anyone who thinks the Lit. Soc. is going to interfere with our correspondence must think again. Who was it who said 'the good is the enemy of the best'?[1] I am not *absolutely* sure what it means but I think the man meant something like e.g. your not writing because a Lit. Soc. meeting was approaching. How good and timely therefore was your letter last week arriving Monday *vice* Tuesday just to show. That was a very good evening again. The Duke and he whom the irreverent Roger always calls the holy fox[2] were most affable, and Tim and I had a good crack with H. Nicolson, who, *inter alia*, told us that Tennyson in his last years drank far too much and was often muzzy. Do you know at all who the 'small nervous Eton master' was who tried to talk to Tennyson in a high wind and came, no doubt, to a dead end, when T's first response was 'I don't know who you are, and I can't hear what you say'? It must have been before Toddy Vaughan's day. Pecker Rouse and Hoppy Daman were both mathematicians, and would have had nothing to say to him—or anyone else

[1] Voltaire said *Le mieux est l'ennemi du bien.*

[2] Lord Halifax.

—outside sine and co-sine. Arthur Benson once told me that small collegers hated being fagged to Rouse's because, though you could avoid some, you couldn't avoid *all* the empty bottles that were thrown at anyone who came into the house—i.e. the level of Rouse civilisation was that of the mining districts 150 years ago. A bad beak does *a lot* of harm. I never really lied without a twinge until I was up to Rouse, when I learnt nothing about x and y but all about how to lie. Perhaps some might say this is a very valuable lesson—essential for Etonians, of whom so many go into politics—but I doubt if we shall find it approved on the Judgment Day.

Were you up to me when the task was to describe the Judgment Day in the style of O. Henry or some Yank like that, and one colleger, remembering the sheep and goats of scripture, called it 'that day when the all-wool babas put the half-Nelson on the bearded Williams'? Not a bad try? I occasionally got a gem or two, and ought to have collected them. Do you recollect the Alington poodle—exactly like a typhoid-germ magnified? The boys had to suggest what Dr Johnson would have said about it: 'Sir, it is evident that the microscope has no monopoly of horror' seems to me an inner if not a bull's-eye.

How right you are not to allow my miscue on Joxer Daly to pass. Never, please, be tolerant to any such blunders I make. How curiously apt Ivor Brown is to misquote—so, equally oddly, was C.E. Montague. As to 'darlin', I feel almost inclined to say, like that conceited ass Clement Shorter, 'Fancy my forgetting that!' when he was taxed with some blunder about the Brontës.

I have enjoyed Roger's *Votes for Women* immensely. Tommy Lascelles once complained that R. could not resist making irrelevant and slightly indecorous jokes, and ditto smacks at Tories and aristocrats, but I see no sign of that in this book, though it is often extremely funny. It seems to me very well done, though it has one odd defect, viz extraordinarily sloppy punctuation. He seems to be very vague about the functions of the comma. Ought not the publishers to have pointed this out? You will know. He says calmly that he expects sour reviews, as the book has been a good deal boosted. We shall see.

The Lit. Soc. certainly hasn't spoilt your epistolary charm. I loved the remark about Alington's poodle. There is nothing whatever to be said for Clement Shorter, a snuffling, go-getting louse in the locks of literature. His grabbing of the Brontë papers was typical: did you read Margaret Lane's admirable book *The Brontë Story*?

Do you know a long, pedestrian, unique poem called *The Setting Sun* by James Hurnard? It was published in 1870. I have never seen the original edition, though I believe it's in the London Library, but in 1946 the Cambridge Press brought out a volume of selections from it, made by G. Rostrevor Hamilton. It's largely autobiographical and descriptive, flat and heavy-going, with occasional flashes of deliciousness. Here is one:

> Davenant was born upon the third of March,
> Waller was born upon the third of March,
> Otway was born upon the third of March,
> And I was born upon the third of March;
> But that affords no proof I am a poet.
> Thousands of blockheads in the lapse of time
> Were also born upon the third of March.
> Milton was born in Sixteen hundred and eight,
> And I was born in Eighteen hundred and eight;
> But what a mighty interval divides us
> Besides the simple interval of time!

Isn't that fun? I'll send you the book of selections if you'd like to see it. Also Gordon Craig and Ian Fleming.

Today I have gardened in the sun—'sweated in the eye of Phoebus'—and only hope that all night I shall sleep in Elysium. Also I opened the cricket season by bowling my youngest a few creaking overs in the meadow. Alas, at thirteen and three-quarters he already makes hay of my googly, which used to baffle him regularly.

On Wednesday I was one of sixteen at a stag dinner in the Garrick, given by Hamish Hamilton for the head of Harper's (American publishers). I was well placed between Fleming and Priestley, who was at his nicest and most amusing. Remind me, when we next meet, to tell you of the dentist in Didsbury: it's a story that needs to be told rather than written. J.B.P. also said, of the Adams trial, that the most sinister words in the whole business were those used by the Doctor when he was set free: 'Now I must get back to work'. Others at the dinner included Julian Huxley, Quennell, Pritchett, Connolly (ugh!), Brogan (on the wagon these two years and much the better for it), John Hayward, Rattigan the playwright, and some smaller fry. It didn't last too long, the food was good, the speeches brief and amusing, and I enjoyed it more than I had expected to.

On Thursday evening I went with Elisabeth Beerbohm and two other friends to the first night of *Zuleika*, which is delightfully gay and tuneful, although the leading lady is quite without looks, charm or talent. With someone looking like your friend Marilyn Monroe it would run for ever. Most of Max's subtleties have been 'ironed out', but here and there a genuine line pops up:

'The owls have hooted, Miss Dobson; it's too late for love.'

I must read the book again. We were in a box, and Elisabeth spent most of the time singing and dancing the relevant 'numbers' in the shadows at the back. She is the sweetest person, and we are firm friends. When I got home on Friday I slept for eleven and a half hours.

The demolitions in Soho Square have now reached a Wagnerian crescendo with the introduction of *three* electric drills working at once. Several times last week I was driven to dictate letters in the flat, and on Friday afternoon I took refuge in the Reading Room of the British Museum, where, among the rustle of black clergymen and wild-eyed researchers badly in need of a bath, I spent three hours looking up this and that scrap of peripheral Wilde information. Thank goodness the London Library and my own shelves save me from most of such drudgery. I adore literary research in fact, but I find the atmosphere of the B.M. both enervating and distracting.

In bed I am reading the new detective story by Nicholas Blake (Cecil Day Lewis). The scene is laid in a publisher's office (C.D.L. is a partner in Chatto & Windus) and I'm enjoying it greatly. Have you read his earlier ones? *The Beast Must Die* is the best. You must forgive so much of my letters for being literary—that's the way I am. What *should* I do without books? Turn jobbing gardener, perhaps, and rush home (as the Yorkshire Dales farmers do) to catch the latest instalment of The Archers?

Now I must write a footnote about Lionel Johnson (who introduced Oscar to Lord Alfred Douglas) and the terrible poem he later wrote to O.W., beginning: 'I hate you with a necessary hate'. How interesting and infinitely complex everything is!

17 April 1957 *Grundisburgh*

Peter Fleming's book[1] is enthralling! I know literally nothing of the public taste, but if it doesn't sell many thousands, then I shall mutter *à la* Carlyle 'The public is an old woman. Let her maunder and mumble!' I do hope the pleasant mental picture I have of shekels *pouring* into 36 Soho Square is according to the facts. Surely P.F's book is immensely good—so close-knit without ever being stodgy, and all his comments so full of wit and wisdom. Of course it was *his* luck to have such a story to tell, but *ours* that he had the telling of it. My *pulse* kept on changing its tempo as I read—not only at the hair-raising, touch-and-go happenings but also at his unfailing felicity of language. This last I put, with your letters, and the talk at the Lit. Soc.—and what else? not much—as the chief pleasures of my old age.

The Setting Sun has not come my way, but your quotation from it at least shows that James Hurnard must have been a good man—just as any ten lines from anything autobiographical from Mr—? would show him to be a man of four letters.

You are having the humbling experience of all fathers. Your googly is treated as poor Mr Pope's underhand service was by his daughter Marjorie.* He retired, feigning a sprained ankle, but the irreverent offspring of 1957 would see through that. But let me tell you when Pamela was teaching Humphrey divinity, and was emphasizing the incredible goodness of Christ, H., finding the wings of his imagination tiring in the void, asked 'Was he as good as Father?' When P., as is

[1] *Invasion 1940.*

* Cryptic allusion is the besetting and infuriating failing of beaks. Mr Pope *et fille* come from H.G. Wells's *Marriage*. I love Wells's novels when he isn't bullying, or girding, or putting us all in our places. G.W.L.

supposed, answered that he was even better, H. gave up and has been an agnostic ever since. (Do you remember how Birrell hearing someone decry George Eliot, prayed that God would smite him, and when God failed to do so, B. from that moment ceased to believe in Him?)

I say, Rupert, what company you do keep! That 'stag' dinner at the Garrick among all the wits. How you can put up with, and even show signs of welcoming, the senile droolings of an old usher is passing strange. Does V.S. Pritchett talk as well as he writes—or perhaps you agree with those who think his cleverness is a bit too thick? I suppose nearly everyone is convinced of Dr Adams's guilt, and that if those nurses' evidence had carried weight, he'd have been for it. I cannot help thinking his practice at Eastbourne will have shrunk a good deal these last weeks. Wherever he 'gets back to work' he had better manage that none of his patients dies, or heads will wag. He has not got a conspicuously attractive face.

How pointless, surely, that Zuleika should not be extremely lovely. Whoever cast a plain and charmless young woman for the part cannot have been in his right mind. I must read the book again. I remember delighting in it, but thinking—no doubt blasphemously—that it went on just a little too long. I expect you have got a lot of interesting stuff from Elisabeth B.

This is a lamentably disjointed letter, and the main reason is that I started doing my income-tax return this morning, and my mind, till that is off it, is the mind of a Suffolk yokel, threatened with melancholia. Why do all the shares I sell—at a small loss—start booming next day? Among the sayings which the late Geoffrey Madan claimed to have culled from Chinese literature and which some thought he composed himself there are three pleasing but grim items under 'The Three Illusions'.

(1) To think investments secure.
(2) To imagine that the rich regard you as their equal.
(3) To suppose your virtues common to all and your vices peculiar to yourself.

But I probably put his *Livres sans nom* by your bedside.

Fancy your saying that I must 'forgive' so much of your letters being literary. That is what I particularly enjoy, because there is no better topic for the pleasantest gossip—especially when it is interspersed with so much else of shrewd comment on men and things. Why does one's wife, when one says x is very dull, *always* assume that one's judgement is based on x not being at all *literary*. In vain I say I merely want him to be intelligent. I don't believe even the best wives understand more than a fraction of their husbands. Not that it matters that we are all 'in the sea of life enisled'. I shall look out for N. Blakes, having had *no idea* that he is Day Lewis.

Easter Day, 21 April 1957 *Bromsden Farm*

I was sure you'd enjoy Peter's book: he took infinite trouble with it, and (as you may remember) I read it in manuscript and two sets of proofs, correcting and commenting mercilessly. Alan Bullock's review in to-day's *Observer* is the first one that has seen the point, and The Critics were sensible this evening. Do write Peter a line—he'd be so pleased. His address is *Merrimoles House, Nettlebed, Oxon.*

You don't have to read all the Gordon Craig book unless you want to. The best thing by far, as I remember, is the detailed account of that scene in *The Bells*.

Tomorrow Elisabeth Beerbohm and two other friends are driving down for the day, and since Friday all ranks have been mowing, clipping, sweeping, uprooting and setting to rights. I am again stiff and aching, but pleasurably.

As well as Roger and a detective story, I am reading (for Oscariana) Whistler's *Gentle Art of Making Enemies*. Have you read it? A hotchpotch of paragraphs and angry letters to newspapers, from which the Butterfly emerges as most dislikeable.

Now I must limp up to bed. I fear this won't get posted till Tuesday, so I'll add a page or two tomorrow. I hope to goodness this wonderful weather holds for another day. I heard my first cuckoo yesterday, and lots to-day. How I love it! I imagine you surrounded by grandchildren, dispensing Easter eggs and seeking refuge in your summer-house.

Monday night, 22 April

Edmund B. announces that he will arrive in London on June 1st with his wife, four small children, and two Chinese nursemaids, and will I see whether I can get them accommodation for a few days. Having lived most of my life in London, I am totally ignorant of its hotels (I last stayed in one in 1917) and scarcely know where to begin.

I also learn that the aged American poet Robert Frost is to visit England this year. Did you hear him reading some of his poems on the wireless the other day? I think very highly of them, and more than twenty years ago I prevailed upon him by letter to allow them to be published by Jonathan Cape, for whom I then worked (they still publish the poems, curse them). After much correspondence the affair was settled by a telegram reading:

THE POEMS ARE YOURS AND SO AM I FROST

I have never seen him, and had given up hope, for he is over eighty, but now perhaps I shall have my wish.

Have you looked at that book of poems called *Union Street*?[1] I did send it to you, didn't I? I think it has the real stuff in it, and I'm delighted to see that two critics have already said so—*Times* and *Sunday Times*. The poet is a Cornish *schoolmaster*, and funnily enough a delightful chap.

25 April 1957 *Grundisburgh*

I *will* write to Peter F., and if he thinks my letter is otiose, supererogatory, ambivalent and many other adjectives whose meaning I am never *quite* sure of, well no irreparable harm will have been done.

Whistler always seemed to me the prize sh-t, though he wrote and said some good things. Was he ever nice to or about anybody? There is a big book to be written about sh-ts, there being such an infinite variety. It should be done by Hart-Davis and no other.

Your two books will be returning as soon as I get back. I read Ian Fleming's till far into the small hours. What an extraordinarily vivid touch he has whatever he touches—people or things. One is always holding one's breath or shuddering or agog in some way or another

[1] By Charles Causley.

about what is going to happen. I put it to you that, on thinking it over, the main flaw is that Bond never really does anything to show *why* the Russians rated him so high. Are not both he and M. *rather* easily bamboozled? I enjoyed it greatly, but was always expecting some brilliant coup by B., and didn't mind as much as I should have when he was bumped off. All his cleverness seems to consist—rather illegitimately—in his capacity to gather from people's faces what they are thinking. In cold fact jolly few people do that.

Craig's book *is* a curate's egg! The *Bells* chapter immensely acute and convincing, but I found much of the style so restless and high-pitched. Of course Irving was a genius; old Agate makes that clear enough again and again, but I thought it was generally agreed that—like Edmund Kean—it was *in spite* of his defects and mannerisms, whereas Craig sees them all as virtues, viz that '*God*', pronounced as you and I do, is 'deadly and hard', and 'Gud' is in the ripe old English tradition. Bilge, my dear Rupert! And Irving's walk was a dance, and preserved 'the last tingle of the mighty Greek tradition'. Will that really do? Finally it is surely silly to sum up *any* play of Shaw's as 'an accursed sermon in jam'? Shaw's not *very* harsh hint that one evening H.I. had drunk too much (which hint his son Harry approved of) is dubbed a lie, somehow proved by Craig saying that he once saw H.I. 'apparently intoxicated after eating a small steak and drinking nothing'. What a rum world these great actors live in—never seeing, hearing, reading anything except as providing an idea for the theatre. Thank you very much for the loan. Also for that little book of *first-rate* poetry. Who is Causley? and why have I never heard of him? He really *has* something to say and his own way of saying it. Pamela made me read *Under Milk Wood* recently, but I couldn't do much with it. Perhaps it demands to be heard. I gather many people love it. Do *you* read it with your pulses bounding? Is it well thought of in the Lit. Soc.? Does Sir Cuthbert know it by heart?

We have just bowed off the last of eleven grandchildren with attendant parents and nurses, and I revert from the role of Abraham to that of St Simeon, the summer-house being my pillar. I love them twittering and hopping and scampering and rolling about the place, daily missing homicide or suicide by a hair's-breadth, but there *is* a certain compensatory relief in finding the soap in its dish and not in the bath, and the ink in its pot and not on my cushion. I made the mistake of trying to read *Justine*[1] while the family played Racing Demon and uttered the screams and curses that appear to be part of the game—and I found that after twenty pages of *Justine* I had not the faintest idea what it, or he, or she was really at. And I have tried it again. No result! And they say it is superb. In ten years' time I shall be left high and dry by modern literature, and in writing to me you will feel you have joined the spiritualists and are communicating with a ghost.

By the way, I was told recently that poor old Percy Lubbock is in a bad way—physically better than a month ago, but very gloomy, and short in the temper, and self-absorbed—and immensely tiresome about politics, if you please, rather airing communistic views and contemptuous and angry when opposed. That does happen, I know; something hardens or softens in the brain, and the character changes. Nature is so far from being a lady that she is not even a gentleman. This is no way to treat the man who wrote *Earlham*.

Remember you said you might fix up a meeting with E. Blunden. Perhaps just before he goes back to China. Then he will go happily, feeling that whatever nostalgia may come over him, at any rate he doesn't meet retired pedagogues in China, lacking in hair, teeth, hearing, sight and understanding. You know all about it, adding, after saying Causley is a schoolmaster, 'funnily enough, a delightful chap'.

28 April 1957 — *Bromsden Farm*

I fear you won't get much of a letter to-day, for at any moment we are to be invaded by three supper-guests, and there's no knowing how long they will stay. Meanwhile here is a photograph of Duff Cooper's tomb, which may interest you. With a magnifying glass you should be able to read the words. It cost £600 and a lot of to-and-froing, including a journey to Belvoir to inspect the site. Have you ever been there? The Castle is spectacular—a towering Victorian-Gothic building, castellated to infinity, on a hill in the middle of a huge flat plain. Next time we meet, remind me to describe Duff's funeral: it was most dramatic. Now I hear our guests arriving—

[1] By Lawrence Durrell.

So *I* am the man to write a history of sh-ts! A backhanded compliment, if ever there was one. Frank Harris and Lord Alfred Douglas would bat high up the list.

Which reminds me—tomorrow is the last day of Adam's holidays and I have promised to take him to Lord's to see M.C.C. v Yorkshire. Snow is bound to fall.

Last week a friend told me (and I believe it) that when Ian Fleming mentions any particular food, clothing or cigarettes in his books, the makers reward him with presents in kind: 'in fact', said my friend, 'Ian's are the only modern thrillers with built-in commercials.' I too thought the behaviour of Bond and M. in this book puerile, but that Turkish chap was good, and like you I couldn't put the book down. I asked Ian if Bond was dead, and he said NO—after a long sojourn in the School of Tropical Medicine he will be fit for Opus VI, which in fact is already written.

You're right about Gordon Craig: he is one of the great frauds of our time, a poor actor, an impractical designer, hideous wood-engraver, and amateurish writer—but just occasionally he pulls it off, as with *The Bells*.

So glad you like Causley's poems. Up to last week I had sold 140 copies—and then, after two good reviews, I sold 200 in one week and may have to reprint. (I printed only 1000). No one has heard of him before, and you are assisting, midwifely, at the birth of a poet. Wasn't that a splendid review of Peter's book in the *T.L.S.* Peter says that, on internal evidence, it must have been written by someone in M.I.14—and who am I to contradict him?

2 May 1957 *Grundisburgh*

I put it to you that one of the main defects of continental education—so much more *efficient* than English—is that so many are educated above their ability. They all learn at school to talk about levels of awareness and integrity and where to 'place' x and y, and the rest of the horrid jargon. It is odd how that sarcasm of eighty years ago of some German professor, who said he approved of English education because it was so good for the mind to be 'fallow till the age of nineteen' is much nearer to the truth than was supposed. Or it was till these scientists began laying down the law about their intolerable lore. I see too that some important ass has been saying that three years' training is essential for every teacher—when nobody really knows what education should be aiming at. When old Q.[1] came to Eton he told us how refreshing it was to find a staff which didn't profess to know exactly how English should be taught. Years ago I was a member of the English Association Committee, on which Professor Edith J. Morley held forth interminably, her face radiant and moist, on the theory and practice of English teaching, and old Bradley, walking away with John Bailey, murmured 'It is a pity, besides being rather strange, that poor Miss Morley herself cannot write a paragraph of tolerable English.' Her *magnum opus* was an edition of Crabb Robinson's diary, which, after much enquiry, I am quite sure the libraries have joined into a conspiracy *never* to buy.

We are now at peace after Diana's wedding, and contemplate remaining so for some weeks. The wedding and the two previous cocktail parties produced great armies of London's brightest and best, and I had a number of fortissimo, amusing, but of course much too brief conversations with intelligent people, and much unsuccessful flight from bores. I gave Diana away—rather an irrelevant bit of ceremonial in 1957 surely—in the wedding finery I wore at my own ceremony in Babraham Church in 1919, and seam and gusset and band all stood the strain bravely. To-day's *Daily Sketch* mildly sneers at the number of 'cops' on duty outside the Royal Chapel and puts it down to the bride's 'hush-hush' policy throughout her engagement. They clearly resent anyone having a quiet wedding. 'Such a fuss about jazz-man's sister's wedding' (headline). Of course the police were nothing to do with her, merely routine for anything in that chapel. Does the Press *ever* get its facts quite right?

Thank you very much for the Duff Cooper photographs. I am glad you got Reynolds Stone to do the design. Did you compose that excellent inscription, the only word I don't feel quite sure about is 'trammels'. But I expect I am wrong—'which happens too often,' as Linky[2] said to and of Edward Halifax.

[1] Sir Arthur Quiller-Couch.

[2] Nickname of Lord Hugh Cecil, later Lord Quickswood and Provost of Eton.

Byrne ('Fuggy') once modestly disclaimed omniscience, but said he thought he knew pretty well where he could find anything he wanted. How delighted Alington was when I told him of Gow's saying that he had noticed that whenever we had in chapel the anthem: 'Where shall wisdom be found,' Byrne always looked self-conscious. A vain old peacock!

Yes A. Douglas and F. Harris certainly—and of course Baron Corvo,—and A.W. Carr, captain of Notts, and Colonel Repington, and old Rogers the poet. There will be 'fine confused feeding' in the book. You really must think about it when you have finally polished off Wilde and Moore.

That is amusing about Ian Fleming living via his books on Fortnum and Carreras and Moss Bros. I am glad Bond has recovered, but he must do more than a little easy fornication to get my vote. I.F. is too good a man to risk reminding one of Peter Cheyney.

I wonder who *did* write that *T.L.S.* review of Peter's book. Do good reviews sell books? I have heard that reviews make little or no difference, but I don't know whether it is true. I wrote to P.F. but forbade him to answer. At least three members of the Ipswich Country Club are about to read it on my urging. I can't promise they will buy it, but I think one will. Causley is by my bedside—with Shakespeare, *Earlham, Irish R.M.,* Ivor Brown's word-books and Humphry House, who very easily bears re-reading. I love re-reading. Each night from 10.30 to 12 I read Gibbon *out loud.* I read slowly, richly, not to say juicily; and like Prospero's isle the room is full of noises—little, dry, gentle noises. Some matter-of-fact man of blunt or gross perceptions might say it was the ashes cooling in the grate, but I know better. It is the little creatures of the night, moths and crickets and spiderlings, a mouse or two perhaps and small gnats in a wailful choir, come out to listen to the Gibbonian music—'Twenty-two acknowledged concubines and a library of 62,000 volumes attested the variety of his inclinations'—what sentient being, however humble, could resist that?

Did you say you'd read a set of proofs of the George Moore letters? Or didn't I ask you? Anyhow, will you be so angelic? They should be ready tomorrow, and I'll hopefully send them along. I'm deep in them myself already, preparing to compile an index (poor Oscar is shelved again). The whole caboodle should go to press in ten days or so. Meanwhile new manuscripts pour in, including a volume containing all the remaining correspondence between Henry James and H.G. Wells. This I shall certainly publish, but it must be *read*.

To-day, with no children at home, all the mowing fell to me, and I got it done in two and a half hours. Is your garden parched and cracking like ours?

G.L. Watson (whom I have never seen) is an American of (I imagine) independent means. The *Housman* is his first book, and he is now working on a biography of Mrs Jack Gardner the great Boston hostess and literary Mrs Leo Hunter of the late nineteenth century.

The words on Duff's tomb were composed by Diana and slightly revised by me. 'Trammels' was hers, but it seemed to me all right.

You ask whether reviews sell books. Single ones don't, but a concatenation of good ones at about the same time certainly does. Assuming that all literary-minded people read at least one daily, one weekly and one Sunday paper, a good review in all these within a week will probably stir them. 'I have said it once, I have said it twice, what I say three times is true.' Pinero always said that the only way to get anything across to an English audience was first to say 'I'm going to hit this man on the head', then 'I'm hitting this man on the head', and finally 'I *have* hit this man on the head'. This technique in a slightly subtler form he used in many of his plays.

I'd love to watch the creatures of the night listening to you reading Gibbon. Where exactly does that superb sentence about the concubines come? Of whom was he speaking? On the 14th I have to speak at the annual dinner of the Antiquarian Booksellers Association, and I could surely quote Gibbon to them. I haven't thought what to say yet, but perhaps I'll begin by saying that when I was a child I thought 'antiquarian' meant 'very old', and it wasn't until I became a book-buyer that I realised it really means 'very expensive'.

We didn't see the finish of the Lord's match, for we were there only on the Monday, but the sun shone incessantly, we saw Graveney bat, Trueman bowl, and Adam loved it all. To my horror I found that my favourite stand, the low white one between the Press Box and the Grandstand, has been removed, the Green Mound behind it levelled, and the whole space given over to concrete and a huge hideous two-tier cantilever stand, which clearly won't be ready this year. As is now usual in London, the only work on it was being done by West Indians, for whom the cricket naturally took first place. Of the Lord's of my boyhood only the Pavilion, the Tavern and the Mound Stand remain. What I particularly dislike about the new stand is that it entirely obscures those lovely trees. An old wiseacre I encountered told me he was sure it would affect the wicket by impeding the advent of drying winds from that quarter.

I have begun to read that new life of Sargent, and find it most interesting. He impinges on H. James, G. Moore and others of my favourites. The author is an American painter,[1] who writes decently and has taken great pains: there is an admirable catalogue of S.'s pictures.

Did I tell you Causley's book has been selling like hot cakes and is *reprinting,* which few volumes do these or any days. On the 15th I am to attend a lecture by Edith Sitwell, at which she is to read one of C's poems. Afterwards there is to be a dinner-party in her honour, given by the P.E.N. Club. See what lofty jinks you are happily missing!

9 May 1957 *Grundisburgh*

The G.M. book has arrived and I will begin my scrutiny at once with great pleasure and interest. You had mentioned it at the Lit. Soc. and I was delighted to do you a tiny service in return for the numerous blessings you have showered on me. Though I must tell you that a book I once went through, merely to discover the misprints, proved on publication, to have, I think twenty-nine left. But I will do what I can. (By the way for Causley's second ed. 'E*c*kermann' on p. 8, and 'star s*o*wn' on p. 27, though I am quite prepared to hear that the

[1] Charles Merrill Mount.

author *meant* sewn. He often moves in worlds unrealised by me, but that is because I am seventy-four, and anyway I found myself enjoying again and again what I didn't wholly understand. But as my kindly and intelligent old pupil John Bayley used to say, that doesn't at all matter, poetry not being merely for the brain.) You shall have the G.M. book back this week-end.

I expect you are right about 'trammels', and that I have allowed its associations to apply to too lowly a set of things. How on earth *is* one to get *exactly* right, either in use or comprehension, the tone and essence and value of a word? I remember once reading to my division an essay of D. MacCarthy in which he described the gait of an antelope and used the word 'elegant', just the word wanted in the context, but to the boys it obviously was wholly absurd. One in fact said it called up the sight of his aunt's appearance when dressed for church, and I don't suppose that his or anyone else's aunt ever bore much resemblance to an antelope, even in church.

That Gibbon sentence describes the emperor Gordian whose 'manners were less pure, but his character was equally amiable with that of his father'. Then comes the sentence I quoted, which ends: 'and from the productions which he left behind him, it appears that the former as well as the latter were designed for use rather than for ostentation.' I once used it at an M.C.C. dinner, referring to our cricketing ancestors' catholic tastes as evidenced in the almanac in each of the early Wisdens, when material was very scanty. There was easy fun to be got out of such entries as 'Oct 14: Death of Prince Leboo,' and 'May 7: Hippopotamus born at the zoo,' and 'July 21: Sir Moses Montefiore lands at Tangier on his way to S. Africa'. All genuine entries though I have not verified the dates. Now of course every year in May a solid little *cube* in brown paper arrives and turns out to be Wisden. There is no mention of Sir Moses in it. But most of the letterpress is very poor stuff compared with that in the Wisdens of cricket's golden age (1892–1912). It is disillusioning to one with my youthful loyalties to realise that the majestic MacLaren, with his 'superb crease-side manner', was an extremely stupid, prejudiced and pig-headed man, even in cricket matters. Plum always says he had the worst fault of a captain, viz pessimism about his team, expressed in their presence: 'Just look what they've given me—half of them creaking with old age, George Hirst fat as butter' etc etc. But let us remember that when Wainwright gave him a long-hop to leg to get his century off in a Gents and Players, he kicked it away and sternly ordered him to bowl his best.

But Good God, when I get onto cricket I drool like any old fathead in an M.C.C. tie (but just one more. A boy running h. for l. at Winchester cannoned head-down into E.R. Wilson on his way to school, looked up, and in horror gasped 'Good God,' to which E.R.W. gently replied 'But strictly incognito').

Will you please *swear* to tell me when I am a bore—not just when I strike a boring note, which all human beings do—but when the disease shews signs of taking hold. One's wife ought to, and sometimes does, but probably realises that after a certain age the poor man's alternative will be total silence. (Who was it, by the way, who, seeing outside a fried-fish shop 'Cleanliness, economy, and civility, always hot and always ready', remarked 'The motto of the perfect wife'? Gibbon would have liked that.)

I saw the beginnings of that stand at Lord's months ago, and augured the worst. It should impress you to know that *my* Lord's memories go back to *before* the Mound Stand. But I think you omit the Grandstand which hasn't altered except for Father Time at the top. The first Eton v Harrow I saw was from a box above the Grandstand in 1895; a waiter had an apoplectic fit just outside. We—my brother and I—felt we were seeing life.

Last week began with a daughter's wedding and just missed ending with a son's death. Humphrey with wife and son travelling about sixty on a one-way (i.e. double) road had a lorry right-turning just in front of him to get into the other lane. He has two black eyes, four stitches in forehead and three in hand, deep cut in knee. His wife bruised all over, child of one and a half unhurt, though its chair with tray in front was smashed. But somehow nothing affecting the trumpet is affected and he is playing it to-morrow night in Lancashire or Staffordshire. The police intend to sue the lorry-driver. He seems to have made what Belloc used to say was a very common mistake of army commanders, viz thinking your communications are safe because you hope they are. Humphrey was patched up at a hospital in Colchester, where they seem to have done everything fairly perfunctorily, didn't offer him any tea, though he had shed a good deal of blood, but two nurses, hearing who he was, begged for his autograph.

P.S. Do work in that Gibbon sentence in your speech. I assure you it is always a winner. Even antiquarian blood quickens and vents itself in hoarse salacious chuckles.

11 May 1957 *Grundisburgh*

Herewith my poor little gleaning.[1] But I don't really feel at all ashamed, because I never have come across a book more thoroughly and intelligently edited. It puts such old codgers as Aldis Wright and Colvin, who edited the letters respectively of FitzGerald and Keats, in the corner, faces to the wall. The amount of work you get into your day is positively staggering.

I find it a fascinating book, with some delightfully humorous episodes and touches (e.g. the 'Maud Emerald' pages) and very moving in places. What a pity he didn't keep *her* letters, and it seems odd that he didn't—though perhaps not odder than many things about him.

Of course, I rub my Victorian eyes at the frank revelation—approved, apparently, by relatives and friends—that for some years the bed played an important part in the relationship, but in connection with all that there is a gap between the generations.

I have a feeling that G.M's bedwork, and what he ever said about it, is regarded by most who read and love his books as mainly comic, but (a) I may be wrong and (b) it may not matter, though some reviewers have a clumsy touch. What a lot of luck there is about whose hands a book may fall into!

Many thanks for letting me do this tiny job. I thoroughly enjoyed it. And now some 'capable Scot' will come along and find another score of misprints.

This is *not* a reply to your week-end letter.

[1] Of misprints in proofs of the George Moore letters.

I hate to think what a nuisance the G.M. letters are being to you, but I shall await your strictures eagerly. Yesterday in six hours I compiled a rather sketchy index for the book which I think will serve. Goodness knows how long the Wilde index will take me when it turns up.[1]

Today produced thunder, hail and torrents of rain. Mowing was impossible, and next week-end I shall stand breast-high in tears amid the alien weeds. A bullfinch and P. Fleming have been the only visitors: thank goodness few 'drop in' unexpectedly here.

The trouble about the exact meaning of words ('trammel', 'elegant' etc) is not only that they mean subtly different things to different people, but also that their meaning and undertones actually change with the passage of time and alteration in manners. I daresay that Gibbon's broad blade carved out his meaning with more force and exactitude than did the bending rapiers of latter-day swordsmen. And what are you to do about America, where the *sound* of words is differently interpreted? I remember a rather good Galsworthian play about the iniquity of cutting down the copse in front of some country house. It pleased in London, but on Broadway they thought cutting down the copse meant a reduction in the size of the police force, and were baffled.

I shall certainly use that fine sentence in my speech, which I don't mind telling you I am dreading, together with the dinner that precedes and the dance (ugh!) that follows it. Can you imagine dancing with a female antiquarian bookseller? Nor can I. Nor shall I attempt the feat. Were you taught never to begin a sentence with the word NOR? I was, and I think wrongly; sparingly and judiciously used, the construction can be most effective. In *The Cruise of the 'Nona'* Belloc wrote: 'God sent me a pilot. Nor was he a pilot, as the events shall show.' Don't you rather like that?

I'll certainly tell you if I see any signs of your becoming a bore, but it does not seem to me a very likely contingency. I think that excellent remark about the motto of the perfect wife was made by Edward

[1] It took six months.

Thomas and reported by E.S.P. Haynes in his *Lawyer's Notebook*, though I suspect that you have improved the wording a trifle. If it wasn't so late I'd find the book and look it up.

I hate to question anything you say, but I could have sworn that the Grandstand at Lord's had been entirely rebuilt since I was a boy: how can the point be settled? Or are you unshakeably certain that you are right?

Adam writes from Eton: 'I find that if you are a "student" you can get *The Times* for twopence, and I am now doing this.' I doubt whether he penetrates further than the cricket news and the crossword puzzle, but it seems to me quite good for thirteen.

My elder boy, Duff, seems to have been engulfed in some Conradian heart of African darkness: we have had no word for weeks. His twenty-first birthday is looming (June 3), and I have neither money nor ideas with which to celebrate it.

Next Saturday I am to lunch at Merton College, to discuss the Max Beerbohm Room which they are planning: altogether the week is hideously full and I should have some fine confused impressions to pass on to you next Sunday. Now it is midnight and you have had enough, I'm sure.

15 May 1957 *Grundisburgh*

Can you tell me if it is true as I read somewhere that Lloyd Osborne wrote practically all *The Wrong Box*? He must have been good fun, if that is so. But did he write anything on his own—or was he devitalised by what one suspects the husky, dusky Mrs S. to have been—the terror that walks by day? A sort of Frieda Lawrence—though I never quite remember whether she was at the receiving or the discharging end of that plate-throwing.

That 'copse' story is lovely. It is all wrong, I know, but I *cannot* ever take Americans quite seriously—I mean their tastes and judgments and values, though now and then one strikes an absolutely Class I man, e.g. the late Judge Wendell Holmes. But either I always have bad luck with their novelists, or I just don't know my way about. I remember liking Steinbeck's first best-seller, but last week, seeing his name, I wasted half-a-crown on his *The Wayward Bus* to read in the train. Not a single character who was not either loathsome or silly. The blurb calls it a ruthless picture, showing what people are really like, i.e. all in need of an ounce of civet. Is the whole of U.S.A. thinking of nothing but the female bosom? We too shall be soon, judging by the cheap Press. It is all very rum. (By the way, how endlessly and overwhelmingly delicious is the last scene between George Moore and Mrs Craigie, when he dismissed her with a terrific kick on the behind —'or at least on the bustle'.) He would have relished the thought of you treading a measure with 'a female antiquarian bookseller'.

I hate all those rules like 'never begin a sentence with "nor", or end one with a preposition.' Once at Eton I was aware that the young prigs in College had a tremendous down on the split infinitive, so I showed them the list of great writers who sometimes used it—including Dr Johnson. They were shaken—which is all one can ever do with a young K.S. But I approve of a dictum of Judge Holmes mentioned above, viz 'All right to end a sentence with a preposition, but not a paragraph. That should end with the blow of an axe.'

Yes, of course that perfect wife story is in E.S.P. Haynes. I have found it this morning. When in doubt about a word or saying, look it up in Hart-Davis. I read the book when it came out, and was rather disappointed. Several good things but fewer than one expected. I think his palate was rather a coarse one; he did not know vintage from wood.

There are signs of cricket coming to life again—a twitch here and there, a faint clouding of the glass held over the mouth. But there are very few who can bat on a turning wicket. I will find out about the Grandstand. I may be wrong. I am not quite like E.V. Slater (rather an inferior man) who said that while his facts were often wrong, his opinions never were, but I have learnt that, at seventy-four, something one could swear was white, turns out on investigation to have been black as the night from pole to pole.

I can't resist sending you Charles Morgan's letter about the G.M. letters: you might send it back. An American friend also writes enthusiastically, saying: 'A law should be passed compelling you and you alone to be the biographer of all bitches and bastards and all flawed celebrities.' Which, as you will quickly realise, chimes in with your own suggestion!

I've no idea how much of *The Wrong Box* was written by Lloyd Osbourne, but judging by the dreary novels he afterwards wrote on his own, I should say jolly little. I remember him as a lugubrious and rather forbidding old boy in the Garrick Club. I wish now I had scraped acquaintance with him and heard something first hand about the great man. By the way, Oscar particularly disliked *Vailima Letters*, and made fun of the book in several letters. Frieda Lawrence I just met, and remember as a jolly, stout, overflowing woman.

Meanwhile my programme last week was endlessly exhausting. The Antiquarian Booksellers' 'do' lasted from 7.15 till 11.30. Mercifully I was next to an extravagantly good-looking film-star called Phyllis Calvert, whose husband was in the chair. She was charming and gave me strength to cope with the honest bookseller's wife on my other side. The first speaker was W.S. (Lefty) Lewis, the American millionaire who has cornered Horace Walpole and is producing (with a team of editors) an endless edition of his letters. He told one or two anecdotes of book-buying. Then came the President (the film-star's husband), who was fluent and quite amusing. By the time it came to my turn the company (about 180) was desperate with boredom and ready to laugh at anything. I started off with a brisk joke: they roared approval: and thereafter I had them captive. The Gibbon quotation stopped the show long enough for me to consult my scrappy notes, so really I owe it all to you!

On Wednesday I put on my dinner-jacket at 5.30 and attended Edith Sitwell's lecture on Poetry in the Church Hall, Westminster, which was *packed* to the ceiling. She is a poor lecturer, and the poems she read were largely inaudible, despite a loud-speaker in front of every seat. It lasted an hour, and then I repaired to the I.M.A., a musicians' club in South Audley Street, which has just about the best food in

London. Our hosts were the secretary of the P.E.N. Club and his wife. I was happily placed between two beloved old friends, Rosamond Lehmann and Veronica Wedgwood. Opposite us were Dame Edith and John Lehmann. Charles Morgan was on Veronica's other side. The old Dame was most affable, not to say amusing, so the whole thing was highly enjoyable.

On Thursday I was Donald Somervell's guest at a dinner in the rebuilt Inner Temple—very like dining in an Oxford or Cambridge college, though lawyers in the mass are not exhilarating. Donald himself is good company and very nice. When I got down here on Friday evening I slept for eleven hours.

Yesterday I drove to Oxford and lunched in the Common Room at Merton. The Warden (a philosopher called Mure) was most friendly, as was the young librarian. Basil Blackwell was at lunch, which, though exiguous after my three banquets, was sufficient. Then I was shown the room which is to be devoted to the permanent Max exhibition and discussed the arrangements. Then to New College, where I had a long talk with David Cecil, also about Max. Then a delicious hour's browse in Blackwell's, and so home. To-day has been devoted to mowing, clipping, uprooting and all the rest of it. Osbert Lancaster drove over this evening, bringing a jacket (five weeks overdue) for Peter F.'s new volume of reprinted pieces.

21 May 1957 *Grundisburgh*

Of course I *knew* I was right about your editing of those letters; anyone could see it was masterly, but it is always pleasing to be corroborated by one of the real pundits like Charles M. It so happened that the next day I embarked on a huge book which cried out for editing, and—but not only for that reason—bored me a good deal. Henry James's life or picture or what not of Mr Wetmore Story. It is full of letters containing sentences like 'Tell Gilbert not to bother about that commission, and certainly to pay no attention to whatever the wretched — says about the reasons for it, which no longer apply.' Not a ray of light on Gilbert, the commission and its reasons, or who or what 'the wretched —' was. A very mealy-mouthed anonymity, surely, after a gap of nearly a hundred years? I suppose the really faithful Henry James fans love the slow wheelings of his mind behind the scenes of Mr Story's doings, but I felt like wading through treacle. And how solidly uninteresting Browning could be in his letters! Of course every man is two men or more, but the poet and the diner-out ('Who was that too exuberant financier?' as a lady said) reached the limits of incongruity, surely. And is any great man so hard to get a clear notion of as Browning? I cannot imagine him walking, or talking, or smiling—and least of all in love with that bony little spaniel-wife, or father of that futile little bounder his son.

I send you (*not* to be returned) Gow's letter about Watson's A.E.H. book, and add to it two riders (1) that I doubt if G. is any judge of the intensity of Housman's emotional life in youth. However reticent H. was to other friends, to G. he would have been still more so. And after all some of H's lines and stanzas surely could not have been written by a man who did not feel deeply. 'Hectic' rather begs the question. And (2) Why *should* W. be in sympathy with H's kind of scholarship? Who ever was, except a parcel of dry-as-dusts? Gow himself, as Auden shows, was puzzled by H. devoting all that time and brain to fifth-raters, and suggests as the reason what really amounts to vanity.

I have met Rosamond Lehmann once or twice at Grizel Hartley's. Excellent company, and very pleasant to look at. John Lehmann was in my Extra Studies. So (of course!) was Mure K.S. What a red-letter day you had at Oxford! What, by the way, about Provost J.C. Masterman for the Lit. Soc.? I am full, you see, of bright suggestions—generally met by you with bland declarations that they are inebriated pederasts, and—what is worse—bores of international calibre. I look forward to these dinners with what can only be described by that horrible word 'gusto'. Is there better company to be found? Not in the Ipswich Country Club or even among the governors of Woodbridge School, though I rather *like* grocers and sanitary inspectors. As Walt Whitman said in praise of animals, they 'do not make me sick discussing their duty to God', and though on occasions they do sweat, they don't 'whine about their condition'. The grocer retired some months ago, and had a month in Italy, where he enjoyed everything 'except all those old ruins'. The U.D.C. of Rome, he thought, deserved very little credit in view of the state of the Forum. The U.D.C. of Woodbridge (of which he is a member) would have cleared it up years ago.

26 May 1957 *Bromsden Farm*

The hour is late and I am far from bright. Thanks so much for sending back those items. Tomorrow from the office I will send you a typescript of Max's superb broadcast on George Moore, just given me by Lady B.—send it back sometime. Perhaps you listened to it? Anyhow it reads exquisitely.

A woman friend whom I consulted (she is a keen cricket-watcher) says she remembers the Grandstand at Lord's being rebuilt in the 1930's, only Father Time remaining of the old building. This supports my view, and you have not yet counter-attacked in any strength. With this same friend I dashed to Lord's on Monday and we were well rewarded. Tyson, I fear, is a spent force, but the batting was first-class—Walcott, Sobers and Close. The latter started off as though he'd already made 50 and I detected no mistake in his play. The W.I. fast bowler Gilchrist looks made of india-rubber. At the end of his prodigious run he leaps into the air, but alas, his length and direction were mediocre. They have made haste with that revolting new stand, and I daresay it *will* be ready for the Test Match—which unfortunately I shall miss. I plan to lie hidden in Yorkshire from June 7 to 28. In fact, dear George, I don't know *when* you'll get a proper letter from me again, for next week-end I have to spend at Blackpool (my second visit this year) with a hideous mass of booksellers. On Saturday I plan to escape for the night to a beautiful poetess (a good one) called Phoebe Hesketh, who lives in the country near Bolton. Perhaps I shall be able to write from there: I'll try.

I've long possessed a copy of the original edition of H.J.'s *Life of W.W. Story* and have often dipped into it with pleasure—and even with profit, though I have never steeled myself to reading it right through.

You're right on the beam in suggesting Masterman for the Lit. Soc. He was in fact elected two or three years ago but refused membership on the grounds that he would never turn up. The same, only more so, would I fear apply to Noel Annan, who would also be an excellent member. So go on thinking of other possibles. Not perhaps one of your good grocers. Some Frenchman said '*On nait demi-dieu et l'on meurt épicier*', so perhaps we shall all come to it.

What else of last week? On Tuesday Jonah dropped in for a cup of tea and gossiped happily for an hour. He hopes to finish his new book in a couple of months. That evening Eric Linklater turned up from his Ross-shire home and offered to take me to a theatre. I told him that what he (as a bucolic barbarian) needed was a spot of culture, but he said he'd prefer a 'leg show'. By the time I picked him up at his club at seven he had failed to get seats for *Grab me a Gondola* or anything else, so I reverted to culture and dragged him unwillingly off to the Arts Theatre to see Genet's play *The Balcony*, which takes place in a brothel. The theatre was half-empty, and when the lights went down a scruffy, unshaven Central European came on to the stage and announced that Miss Something had been taken suddenly ill, there was no understudy, and the part would be read by Miss Somebody Else. Anyone who asked for their money back could have it. No one did. Needless to say the part was the chief one—the brothel-keeper's pet—and it was read by a nice homely girl from Bagshot, desperately trying to follow the dialogue in a script the size of the telephone book. When she had to help the other woman to dress she fell behind through having to put the book down. The other actors were all appallingly bad, and the play pretentious and windy—rather like the reverse of a Maeterlinck medal—instead of 'moonshine' they repeatedly said 'sh-t' and 'bugger'. We stuck it to half-time and then repaired to the Ivy for an excellent dinner. Next day, fresh as paint, I travelled to Bath and took part in a Brains Trust at Monkton Combe prep. school (which is in *lovely* country). The others were Hugh Ross Williamson, Noel Streatfeild, W.E. Johns (whose *Biggles* books—he has written a hundred!—are enormously successful) and George Cansdale, recently Head of the Zoo. He brought along a python in a Gladstone bag, which delighted the boys. Tea-party, sherry-party, dinner-party, called at 6.45, and back to work.

Yesterday I drove to Reading University to see an excellent photographic exhibition concerning W.B. Yeats. When I get to Yorkshire I shan't *move*!

That M.B. talk on G.M. I listened to it *twice*—as they were sensible enough to repeat it—*and* cut it out of the *Listener* to preserve it for ever, and then of course lent the cutting to someone who hasn't returned it, and whose name I cannot remember. I can only hope that the Almighty does remember, and so directs my curses on to the right head, which I hope by now resembles that of the Emperor Nero, according to Suetonius, i.e. 'pustular and malodorous'. It (the M.B.) is *perfect*—and gave me the same degree and intensity of pleasure that some music, e.g. the Pastoral Symphony, does. I shall read it two or three times more before returning it—and let me tell you, Rupert, that to return it at all is proof of outstanding beauty of character. When they ask on the Judgment Day about my good deeds I shall say 'I returned M.B. on G.M.' and a few centuries of purgatory will at once be docked, which won't happen to the old man of Saxmundham:

> *Qui habuit ventrem rotundum;*
> He borrowed £5 from a master of hounds
> And flatly refused to refund 'em.

A favourite limerick of Tuppy Headlam's—composer unknown. I like the Gibbonian echo of line 2, where some imaginary indecency is 'veiled in the decent obscurity of a learned language.'

I have a horrible suspicion that you may be right about the Grandstand, but I *am* pretty certain that Father Time was *not* on the old G.S. I shall find out at the Test Match. The English Test side is rather *dull*. I have seen nearly all of them so often—Statham and Trueman with those immense and needless runs which waste so much time, and the batting of Bailey, which always recalls the writing of Professor Edith J. Morley of the Reading High School, or the Yorkshire pudding made by the hotel-cooks of southern England. But I want to see the three W's—the only time I saw Worrell, the shade of Trumper was a 'hover over the scene, smiling and nodding his head. And Ramadhin, whose bowling obviously costs him as much effort as breathing. Hutton put him very high last time he was over, on the odd and amusing ground that while it was hard enough to play a ball of which you didn't know the way it was meant to turn, it was still harder when the bowler didn't know either. He also said that he wished he had made the 200 he did make in the last Test in the first, because the W.I's are very temperamental and easily depressed by a big score against them.

Blackpool! I was once there on a fine August Bank Holiday. No sand was visible because of the people; there were eleven mechanical bands playing, fortissimo, different tunes along the front, and whatever lull there was in the din was at once filled by the hilarious yells of *homo sapiens*. If, say, Housman or Gow have to spend any years in Hell, old Nick need only plant them down at Blackpool on endless Bank Holidays. Gow will be forced to read Ethel M. Dell, Housman Galsworthy, for whom he had a mysterious but very strong hatred. I have just read Mottram's book about J.G. and wife—interesting but there *is* something baffling about him. It can't *only* be that he was a Harrovian. Why has all that perfectly genuine high-mindedness, humanity, perceptiveness, literary skill, etc so often a sort of *dreariness* about it? Did you know him at all? Why is there so much animus in so many of his critics? It cannot be only jealousy of his tremendous success. They always are particularly down on the *F. Saga,* which I shall always maintain is packed with interest of many kinds—historical, sociological, characterisational. What say they? Let them say.

Apropos of the Lit. Soc. I suppose these College dignitaries are very busy, though I should have thought they could always find some business in London. I liked Annan very much when I met him last December. Charles Tennyson, whom I came across at lunch yesterday, would of course be splendid, but alas, he is seventy-eight and has an invalid wife. Roger favours a man of law, but I don't know if he has one in mind. What rude things people say about grocers! I remember that French saying of yours being thundered at the Hagley congregation (in English) many years ago by the vast rector, who had the suitable name of Manley Power, but as far as I remember, the only effect was that the village grocer never darkened the door of the church again—like Neville Talbot, Bishop of Pretoria, girding at his flock for imagining God to be an angry old man with a beard—'like Mr Jones there', after which Mr J. joined the Anabaptists.

'The grocer who has made his pile—
Does he grow nicer?' 'No, Sir,

He alters not his ways nor style,
But grows a grosser grocer.'

Shakespeare or Milton, I forget which.

Your evening at the modern theatre gives me the shudders. There seem to be a great many degraded plays about. Are any of these Tennessee Williamses any good? It seems to be accepted that sour and confused writing is all right because that is what the times are. But isn't that a fallacy like 'Who drives fat oxen must himself be fat'?

2 June 1957 *Fisher House,*
Rivington, Lancs.

I write to you from the garden of my beautiful poetess, on a blazing summer's day. I have been for two long walks on the moors behind the house—very like my Yorkshire moors, with larks and curlews and plover—and now I am looking through tall trees at a small green hillock—a considerable protuberance, which I am told is described in Domesday Book as a 'toft and quillet of land'. Beyond that is a hill with the agreeable name of Anglezarke. It is all green and sun-drenched and infinitely agreeable—and not a moment too soon, for last week was a non-stop racket. On Monday I dined with an American thriller-writer. On Tuesday I gave a luncheon-party (six men) for the American poet Robert Frost, a wonderful old man of eighty. Twenty years ago I resurrected his poetry over here and got Jonathan Cape to publish it—but this was my first meeting with the poet. He was witty and charming and anecdotal and in every way delightful. After lunch I drove him back to the Connaught Hotel, where he wrote out a poem for me. We were in a large hotel sitting-room, and I suddenly realised that the only other people in it, at the far end, were my mother-in-law (to whom I hadn't spoken for three and a half years) and Adlai Stevenson (whose wife was my wife's first cousin, and whose books I publish). I decided that these two—in many ways the most interesting Americans alive—should meet, so I greeted my mother-in-law and got the two men talking very successfully.

That evening I dined with Elisabeth Beerbohm and a very amusing

American Jew called Sam Behrman (playwright and author of an amusing book about Duveen the picture-dealer). He is a fanatical fan of my Walpole book and said many flattering and gratifying things. Next day I lunched at the Travellers with a young man who is writing a life of Conrad and thought I could help him. At 6 I went for drinks to my friends the Jepsons, where I met Sam Behrman again—also David Cecil and Jenny Nicholson (Robert Graves's daughter)—all friends of Max, about whom there was much talk. Sam is going to write some pieces about him in the *New Yorker*. Just as I was leaving who should arrive but Mr and Mrs Boris Karloff! I had imagined him dead long ago, but no. He is an Englishman (né Pratt) of perhaps sixty, well preserved and so dark that he must have more than a dash of the tarbrush. I quickly discovered that his great interest is *cricket!* and we chattered happily of Surrey and the West Indies. He bemoaned the fact that he would have to miss one of the Tests to make a film. Who, outside a dream, would expect to discuss Ramadhin with Boris Karloff? On I sped, to dine with a nice man who edits the *Twentieth Century*. Thursday was filled with another lunch party, a visit to the Max exhibition (private view), a finance committee meeting at the London Library, and a champagne cocktail party at John Lehmann's. In the throng were T.S.E. with his new wife, thirty-eight years younger than he and very charming. They stood inseparably arm-in-arm in the most charming way, and the despairing lines of his face visibly softened as he talked of his new flat and his great happiness—very touching.

From all this you can imagine the relief of spending most of Friday in the train to Blackpool, where the whole of the Booksellers Conference (several hundred strong, with wives in tow) is lodged in an enormous hydro built like a pseudo-castle with every possible castellation, crenellation and whatnot. After a *dance* I staggered to bed, but the trams along the front are silent only from 12 to 6. Yesterday I attended the morning session of the conference, snatched some lunch, and came over here. Another session there tomorrow morning, back to London after lunch, to Eton on Tuesday, two days of desperate clearing-up in the office, and off to Yorkshire at 4 a.m. on Friday—blessed thought. I make no promises about writing, but have in fact so come to enjoy using you as my diary that you never know.

Did you hear of the would-be-psychiatrist who, when asked why he wanted to be one, said: 'I really wanted to be a sex-maniac, but I failed in my practical'? Now I must get ready for a Lucullan dinner-party in Bolton. What next?

7 June 1957 *Grundisburgh*

I have a horrid feeling that this *may* not reach you on Saturday in your northern fastness. All depends on the relevant postmen, and you know what a temperamental lot they are. I have been trapesing about all this week—Malvern for speech-day, then Oxford for a finance(!) committee, the members of which felt no doubt that no decision on those short-term mortgages could be arrived at without my help. But all *my* to-ing and fro-ing compared with yours is like the Vicar's journeys from the blue bed to the brown compared with those of Ulysses (apropos of which *must* I have another try at *Finnegans Wake* in my spasmodic efforts to 'keep up,' and not sink further into codgerdom?). It is yours to command and mine to obey. But how happy I shall be if you say I needn't!

Robert Frost sounds a good man, as I had already half gathered from references to him in the Press—and I have always admired Adlai as one of those really first-rate Americans. The first-rate in any case is rare, and perhaps particularly so in U.S.A. but—well old Abe Lincoln has always been one of my very favourite men. Has Adlai a pleasant voice? How important that is! The Yankee accent is, to me, always something of a barrier, e.g. when the excellent Dean of Christ Church (a Canadian) preached at the Abbey School a moving sermon about Pet'r. How hard he made it for us to take the apostle seriously. And possibly Adlai may come from one of those queer states which make such laws as that forbidding anyone 'to fire a pistol at a picnic except in self-defence', or, in another state, 'to eat scorpions or lizards in public.' The man who produced these in print vouched for their truth.

I read Behrman's immensely amusing Duveen book, which, too, I suppose, depicted the fantastic element in those unhappy, bored millionaires who fell to collecting pictures in order to get rid of the stuff which *would* go on piling up in their banks. B. must be a man of sound literary taste. Is he as right always as he is about your H.W. book? I have sent all my Wisdens—I had a complete set—to my nephew Charles to lighten his lot in N.Z. and I must confess to you that my lavatory reading lately has been your *H.W.* An essential for a book that is raised to this rare eminence is that one knows it and loves it already. Its influence is active and swift and benign, 'noble and nude and antique'. 'All occasions invite his mercies and all times are his seasons' was actually written by Donne of God, but it has other applications. Who wrote that invocation, which begins:

> 'Hail, Cloacina, goddess of this place
> Whose devotees are all the human race . . .' and ends,
> 'Soft yet consistent let my offerings flow,
> Not rudely fast nor obstinately slow.'

But perhaps your sensitiveness as an author and as a clean, decent, high-minded gentleman will strongly resent all this? Somehow I don't think so.

I found, to my great pleasure, that that Test Match really did quicken my old blood. The W.I. morale would have made them very hard to beat, if they had won in an innings, as looked very probable. Ramadhin's ninety-eight six-ball overs in one innings! And now at last, after three disappointing years, we shall see what God meant Cowdrey to be, and the time approaching when E. Blunden will write of him as he wrote of Hammond in that admirable book which arrived this morning, *bless* you. It may even succeed *H.W.* in the lavatory! I should like to have heard you with Boris Karloff; thank whatever gods may be for life's incongruities. That passion for cricket turns up in very odd places.

I enjoyed two days at Oxford, with the Roger Mynors, where was the beloved Mrs Alington—in excellent health and spirits, though nearly blind and lame as a tree (whatever that simile conveys to you). I had a good crack with my old pupil John Bayley of New College who writes novels and reviews and wholly unintelligible tomes about 'Romance', and is a very nice fellow. His wife Iris Murdoch was there, coruscating, but not offensively, with brains. I liked her, and promised to read her new novel, though I know that in three pages I shall be hailing the coastguard. Did you read of that pathetic and foolish young lady whose fiancé, swimming in the Serpentine with her, disappeared; she reported to the police, etc. 'I cannot find my boy-friend,' and could not get them to take it seriously, apparently not mentioning that she last saw him in the water. I called on another don, who was closeted with four or five young men to whom he was expounding *The Anglo-Saxon Chronicle*. He and I chatted lightly for a few minutes, while they contemplated me with that derision that one sees on the faces of amiable camels when one throws them buns. I nearly ventured on the Parthian shot as I left: 'Do not fall into the juvenile error of thinking that old gentlemen are as intellectually moribund as they look,' but I refrained. I like Oxford better than Cambridge, though the march of civilization has made a dreadful mess of its appearance in the last hundred years. At both places some of the young men are growing beards, and to my mind and taste a young chin with hair is as indecent as a young skull without it. I had a boy in my house who wore a wig; one evening I visited him when he was about to sleep, and on the pillow was an object like a shell-less egg or a very young horse-chestnut. It looked soft and damp—horrible.

Next week I give the prizes at Shrewsbury, telling them to keep the torch burning and hand it on. I shall speak about choosing a profession, and must say *some*thing fairly new, so you can imagine how grateful I am for your lovely anecdote of the would-be psychiatrist. Absolutely '*ad rem*'. If some of the parents don't like it, they must lump it. The days of prudery are over. Or are they? I expect I shall end by playing safe.

11 June 1957 *Kisdon Lodge, Keld*

Your splendid letter was brought up this steep hill yesterday (Bank Holiday) morning by a charming young couple who had been fagged by the village postmaster. He is also the warden of the youth hostel and so must be obeyed. I am taking your advice so closely to heart that I can scarcely put down two coherent words, so you must blame your advocacy for the ensuing rubbish. When I tell you that I have to-day re-read (after thirty-five years) and thoroughly enjoyed *The Prisoner of Zenda*, you will see how well the medicine is working.

How well, in this book, Anthony Hope got on with the story. There's no padding anywhere. Tomorrow I shall devour *Rupert of Hentzau.* I bought a lot of Oscariana with me, but so far have read only *Both Sides of the Curtain*, an account by Elizabeth Robins, the American Ibsen-actress and novelist, of her arrival in England in 1888, when Oscar was very kind to her. From her book I noted two plums (or anyhow sultanas) for your delectation. (1) When Mrs Kendal put on Ibsen's *Enemy of the People* she sought to soften the blow by introducing as curtain-raiser a recitation of G.R. Sims's *Ostler Joe.* How confused the audience must have been! (2) When Lady Ritchie was asked what Tennyson's reading aloud was like, she said 'melodious thunder'.

Now for your letter. You are hereby forever absolved from struggling with *Finnegans Wake.* When an American professor was sent for review a book called *A Key to F.W.*, he sent it back, saying 'What *F.W.* needs is not a key but a lock.'

The rigours of the 4th of June were softened by being able to listen to the Test Match in different people's cars. What a day's cricket! Apart from that I saw Jonah and lots of old friends. My elder boy got back from W. Africa the night before (his 21st birthday), so we were all present.

13 June 1957 *Grundisburgh*

I went to the Lit. Soc. yesterday, and sat between Sir Cuthbert and Tim. Sir C. was most affable. He is a dry wine, but very far from flavourless. I enjoy that stern unbending Toryism; his old eye gleamed and smouldered when someone mentioned the *New Statesman*, and I feel pretty sure that if he found it in his house he would eject it with the tongs. By the way, did you see that *disgraceful* apology(?) which the editor made at the end of Birkenhead's letter protesting at his references to his father? Surely even in 1957 journalistic licence doesn't countenance very damaging statements about a distinguished dead statesman's character and actions, and when his son denies them, reaffirms them and adds that the authority for them is incontrovertible but can't be given.

After dinner Tim took Roger and self to White's where we had an excellent crack. Roger had a good Rabelaisian story or two about Queen Victoria, and altogether was in good form. The sales of *Votes for Women* he says are steady but not tremendous. Don't half-a-dozen serial extracts in the Press tend to damp down the subsequent book's sales? I have met several people who said they weren't going to buy or even read Alanbrooke's book after those enormous *Sunday Times* extracts. Peter Fleming took your place at the end of the table. What a particularly pleasant chap he is. And how bad, and at the same time compellingly readable, brother Ian's thrillers are! The pattern of all four that I have read is identical. Bond does not attract me, and that man with brains on ice and pitiless eye who organises the secret service in London seems to be a monument of ineptitude. Everything about Bond and his plans is known long before he arrives anywhere. But I cannot help reading on and there are rich satisfactions, e.g. when Mr Big is crunched by a shark. Very good about food; he always details what any meal consists of. The young women are rather oppressively and monotonously bedworthy, but then of course he isn't writing for septuagenarians.

Coming out of the Garrick we met Dick Stokes and his brother (who, you remember, had the curious and interesting habit of driving his wife about in a small go-cart through the woods, naked). Old Cuthbert greeted his fellow M.P. quite genially; I had quite expected him to hiss like a serpent at the sight of a socialist, but, as he said in the car, S. isn't really a socialist at all.

To-morrow I go to present the prizes at Shrewsbury School and utter the inevitable platitudes, but I shall do a little cutting of the ground from under their feet by beginning with a quote from André Gide: '*Toutes choses sont dites déjà, mais comme personne n'écoute, il faut toujours recommencer.*' I recommend it to you as a very useful opening gambit (not necessarily in French!). It is never easy to know what will click and what will flop, though I don't understand Bob Boothby's surprise at an anecdote he told to a Paisley audience flopping (D. Stokes told me). A recent mayor of P. had had a holiday in Paris. When he returned and someone asked him what he thought of Paris, his reply was: 'I can tell 'ee, mon, f—ing's in its infancy in Paisley.' Nobody smiled and B. Boothby was deeply disconcerted.

18 June 1957
(the day on which
Napoleon looked forward to
'une affaire d'un déjeuner.'[1]

Grundisburgh

I knew there would be one of these insufferable heat-waves when them above knew I was going to go by train from Ipswich to Shrewsbury and make a speech in a school hall full to the brim with millions of the freest pores in these islands. However, though hot, it was about ten degrees cooler than it is today, and fifteen less than it will be to-morrow, when they know I train, and underground, and bus, and walk to the heights of Highgate Village to my brother's house. On Thursday I shall be watching Ramadhin, and Weekes, and Worrell—and yawning when Trueman bowls, or Bailey bats. (Do you realise that Trueman walks thirty-five steps from the crease to the end of his run and that four balls an over the batsman leaves alone?) And then of course on Friday come the thunder and rain.

Talking of thunder, Charles Tennyson corroborated 'melodious thunder' for his grandfather's voice—and hinted—only hinted for he is very loyal—that it must sometimes have been hard not to giggle at those readings; the old man's 'o's and 'a's were so very hollow and long-drawn-out. And, still on thunder, you know, of course, Haydon's superb 'feathered silken thunder' for the sound of the peeresses in their robes rising when the royal pair entered at their coronation. I have always thought it a gem of the first water.

How lovely to find you are still fond of *Zenda* and *Hentzau*. I rather doubt if even now I could read the end of Rudolf R. with entirely unmisty eyes. Are they still in print?

Your *Hugh W.* is still in the smallest room. My old friend Oliver Locker-Lampson, who, alas, went off his head, was full of whimsical ideas; one was to produce a series of books for reading in this place. They were to be called 'Lampson's Lavatory Literature', and were to be printed on soft paper with a good many blank pages. I am sure his amiable ghost would rejoice if his idea was taken up by one of our leading and more spirited publishers—perhaps one living not a hundred miles from Soho Square?

[1] i.e. the Battle of Waterloo.

By the way how *tremendously* good H.W's little character-sketches of Kipling and Winston are on pp. 296–298—so much so that I cannot help wondering whether—like E.F. Benson—memoirs from his hand wouldn't have easily outlasted his novels. These vignettes are nearly —*if not quite*—in the same class as Carlyle's. And the one of Winston was in 1928, but H.W. saw all the facets of his character that are now common knowledge. It is a brilliant page.

Thank you for that *mot* about *Finnegans W.*, also your letting me off trying to read it again. I can't remember who is the author of the Cloacina ode. Perhaps Gerald Kelly will know when I see him at Lord's. But I fancy he worships rather at the shrine of Priapus than that of the Lady C.

I think I did meet at Shrewsbury about the only famous man you don't know—though I may well be wrong about that. Father Huddleston, who was to talk in the chapel on Sunday. An amiable man. We did not talk about the S.A. colour-problem, but for some reason, obscure at the time, and now irrecoverable, about Sir Ernest Oppenheimer, of whom I know as much as a cow does of a clean shirt. At lunch I sat next to the Chairman, a genial Yorkshireman who was entranced by the story of the two Yorkshiremen watching Y. v. Lancs. One had unexpectedly to go home for an hour—and found his wife in bed with a neighbour. He was much annoyed and showed it to his friend when back at the match. His friend was sympathetic, but added: 'And I can tell 'ee some bad noos too. 'Utton's out' ('U pronounced like 'put on'). And now you will tell me Jelly used to tell that story at Private Business.

Last Sunday my nephew and I had lunch with one millionaire, and tea with another. Both were called Wills. Neither looked nearly as happy as I should if a millionaire. Or should I? Charles tells me they are a good deal fussed about the forthcoming report which will associate tobacco with cancer more definitely than ever before. And of course a generation is growing up many of whom, sensibly, don't begin smoking because they can't afford it.

Two splendid letters from you have been carried up the hill by the farmer in his jeep, and I have loved getting them. 'The first wet day,' I determined, 'shall be devoted to writing to George', but for a fortnight no drop of rain fell, and even now only a sharp shower last (Saturday) evening has broken the drought which is drying up the springs, ruining the farmers' hay, and delighting me. I can't tell you how deeply I am enjoying these enchanted days, which have been broken only (tell Pamela) by two delightful sales in sun-drenched gardens, at which I acquired a number of miscellaneous articles of great charm and beauty. Last night I got Friday's *Times* and the first day's score from Lord's. The second day I shall read of tomorrow evening in lofty detachment.

Since I last wrote I have read (besides *Rupert of Hentzau* and a brace of detective stories) six or seven long books about Oscar Wilde and his friends. The deeper one reads into a subject (particularly a complex one like this) the more interesting it becomes, or so I find. From one book—A.E.W. Mason's account of George Alexander and the St James's Theatre—I extracted this pleasing anecdote for you. The day after the first night of Barrie's play *The Admirable Crichton*, Mason ran into Squire Bancroft:

> I asked, having seen him at the performance, what he thought of the play. He was drying his hands on his towel in the lavatory of his club (? the Garrick) just before luncheon. He dried more slowly and shook his head with melancholy. 'It deals, my dear Mason, with the juxtaposition of the drawing-room and the servants' hall—always to me a very painful subject.'

So glad you enjoyed the Lit. Soc. I do hope you'll be able to get to the July dinner, since after that there is a break for summer holidays. Did I tell you that Peter Fleming is driving to Russia and back on one of these newly-allowed plans? He is to write some articles on the trip for *The Times* and is taking my son Duff as co-driver. I believe they hope to start in a few days' time.

I have a fine collection here of Nelson's sevenpenny series, including the two Anthony Hopes and three Sherlock Holmeses, on which I shall soon descend. I last read them all in 1939–1940, when I could fancy nothing else.

I plan to drive weeping back to London next Sunday (June 30), so write here this week, and to B.F. thereafter. I will resume proper letters directly I stop being all the things you said I was to be—and which I now am—brown, lazy, eupeptic, etc.

27 June 1957 *Grundisburgh*

I enjoyed Lord's. To my mind three days is right for 'a match at cricket'. The wicket was perhaps a bit too lively; several balls left the batsman no option but to duck. One black man seemed to receive one ball from Trueman plumb on the head. If not, how do you explain the hard crisp sound heard all over the ground? But I grant you the batsman was unmoved and didn't even scratch his head. Weekes was good; so was Cowdrey. I passed him and Bailey as they went in on Friday morning. I murmured 'Good luck'. Cowdrey said 'Thank you, sir'; Bailey said nothing. In five balls Bailey was out and in five hours Cowdrey had made 152. The god of cricket likes good manners. The black men are very temperamental; I expected to see Ramadhin cry when he missed literally the easiest catch ever in a Test Match. I much prefer Trueman as a bat to T. as a bowler.

His three sixes off consecutive balls were worth seeing, and never shall I forget the lovely sound of 25,000 people roaring with laughter when Weekes fell head over heels into the crowd and disappeared. Gerald Kelly was in good salacious form. I don't know that I much trust his judgments about people, but he is lively company and on the whole unmalicious. Like old Agate he mostly knows good stuff when he sees it.

For the last two days I have been among the girls—bumbling in and out of classrooms, listening to an anaemic, adenoidal lady with rheumy eyes declaiming the part of Lady Macbeth, watching Miss Biology Jones (this is how the H. Mistress distinguishes her from Miss Cello Jones, but the girls' affectionate name for her is 'Bilgy Rat') keeping sharp watch over the dissection of three crayfish. I took an ignorant but would-be intelligent interest in the three little virgins' work, but shied off just in time, as some little tension in the air told me that my questions were nearing those corporeal regions concerning which the crayfish, that prude of the piscine world, invariably purses his lips. I told one class about the young man after a job at the Lyceum, being tested by Irving and told to declaim a Shakespeare speech; he began 'Is this a *dadger*' etc., and Irving merely rang the bell and said 'Show this bedger out'. I remembered in time that Irving used a different first vowel in 'bedger'! I enjoy the visit greatly, but there are nervous moments—not the least nervous being at prayers where my chair, my hassock, and my little desk—or *prie-dieu*—are all of the lightest and most mobile character, and I remember how easily I get cramp when kneeling and how once I kicked my chair across the aisle.

There is a rich Victorian aura about that Bancroft story. Was he one of those bogus old splendids? I remember his reciting Dickens at Eton in, say, 1898. Very fine, no doubt, but does one become famous by recitation?

That Russian trip for your son and P.F. sounds exciting, if they are allowed to see what they want. I found the snapshot of Krushchef drinking soup in Finland disheartening. He looked so exactly like a pig. Of course soup *is* rather a severe test for anyone, with as many pitfalls to avoid as a golfer or an oarsman. How not to make a noise, or splash, or spill on the waistcoat, and of course if it is '*à la bonne femme*' the stuff is full of *strings*, very toothsome when they get to the mouth, but as hard to shepherd neatly as a flock of sheep. I took the letters of Horace Walpole away with me. Vilely edited. Several letters quite unintelligible if the *dramatis personae* are unknown, and no little parliamentary or literary imbroglio has any light shed on it. When I read that 'old Balmerino's windows have been stopped up because he talked to the populace' my interest is not aroused if I have no idea who B. was or why talking to the populace deserved punishment.[1] The editor was one C.B. Lucas—obviously an impostor.

[1] Lord Balmerino was one of the Jacobites imprisoned in the Tower before trial and execution, in 1746.

5 July 1957 *Grundisburgh*

No letter to answer this week, which *I hope* means that you found even more work awaiting you than you had expected, and it had to be tackled at once if you were not to be *spurlos versunken*. But there is always the horrid possibility that you may be laid up, which in St Paul's emphatic but not very lucid words would be 'very tolerable and not to be borne'.[1]

There has been some very repulsive weather here since I wrote to you—by which I mean those cloudless days with the thermometer in the eighties. Like Satan in *P.L.* I often say 'Sun how I hate thy beams', because I have always hated great heat. Even when young an evening party in June could be sheer agony, as I wondered whether damp patches would appear on my stiff shirt-front before the evening was out. I always shirked dances for that reason, though to my taste there were a good many others too. The silver lining to the cloud is that I don't mind the cold and never get one. Though I *feel* it rather more than I did, as the springs run down.

I am being restful at home *pro tem*, but next week I have to speechify about my nephew off to New Zealand for five years, and then face a million exam-papers. One by the way is on *The Knight of the Burning Pestle* which I have just read—*pitiable* rubbish it seemed, but that old bumble-bee A.W. Ward calls it 'highly diverting,' and apparently split his old ribs over a barber being brought to represent the giant Barbarossa. What a lot of *cant* was poured into all writing about the Elizabethan Drama by Lamb and Co. Much, surely, is not worth a moment's attention.

I have just begun Harold Nicolson's *Sainte-Beuve*, who seems, so far, one of those men no one will find any difficulty in disliking rather strongly, but perhaps I may alter this opinion later. The frontispiece is definitely daunting—and has a certain resemblance to another critic I am reading—Edmund Wilson, who slashes dogmatically about. Perhaps he too, like Ste-B., suffers from a constricted urethra.

I am in doubt whether to refer to N.Z. in my speech as 'Pig-island'. The book I read about N.Z. life tells the English visitor he mustn't

[1] George wrote St Paul but must have been thinking of Dogberry in *Much Ado*, III, 3: 'most tolerable and not to be endured'.

mind them calling him a 'pommy' and then he can call N.Z. 'Pig-island' so long as he does it with a smile. I doubt if the risk is worth taking; they might not like my smile. By the way why 'pommy'—and, for the matter of that, why 'limey' which the more bilious Yanks like Vinegar Joe Stilwell still call Englishmen?

7 July 1957 *Bromsden Farm*

The lovelier the holiday, the grimmer the return. My last day on the blessed moors (Saturday) was a happy one. I spent the afternoon (dull and raining) at an auction sale in the Temperance Hall of a neighbouring village, where I secured a gigantic writing-desk, stuffed with drawers and surmounted by a fine cupboard or bookcase, for £1. My sister's car (which I had borrowed for the holiday) luckily has a luggage-rack on its roof, and two village stalwarts lashed the heavier part of the desk to it with rope. My faithful farmer transferred it to his trailer and towed it up the hill-track behind his jeep. Hardly was it in place when the sun poured out hot and strong, and I sat outside the cottage for almost two hours, glorying in the heavenly prospect.

Next day (Sunday) I sadly packed up the cottage and started off in steaming hot sunshine. All went well until, between Wetherby and Doncaster, the fan-belt broke, and the car nearly caught fire. By ringing up an extremely efficient A.A. man in Leeds I managed to get a new fan-belt brought from some garage, but this entailed a wait of one and a half hours. At Doncaster (a loathsome town at best) I ran into a cloudburst—visibility nil and water up to the axles. Thereafter all the elements took a turn—thick fog, two more distinct cloudbursts, incessant thunder and lightning. Eventually I limped exhausted into London just before midnight. My flat was stifling, and from the mountains on my desk it was clear that everyone I had ever heard of had written to me while I was away. My excellent partner Harry Townshend had acknowledged all the letters, saying 'Mr H-D will write to you as soon as he gets back.' This might have been possible if my secretary hadn't been on holiday. Instead I was burdened with a pudding-faced 'temporary', who understood no word I said from Monday to Friday. The temperature was in the eighties all week, and ten yards outside my office-window gangs of half-naked men were riveting steel girders incessantly. Never has my hatred of London and publishing been so grim and concentrated.

When I got down here on Friday I found *another* fine letter from you: you've no idea—or perhaps you have—how much I look forward to this weekly treat. Yesterday was so hellish hot that I was incapable of serious effort, though I got through another enormous mass of arrears of correspondence and papers, and all is now up to date. To-day has been much cooler, and I have mowed, and clipped, and picked cherries, and eaten strawberries and raspberries from the garden. I once saw *The Knight of the Burning Pestle* at the Old Vic, with Ralph Richardson in it, and mildly enjoyed it. But then I was very young and a glutton for what I believed was culture. Now I should say that if any play has been produced only twice in three hundred years, there must be some good reason for it. My dictionary says that 'pommy' comes from 'pomegranate', and 'limey' from 'lime-juice'—but why? I must get a better dictionary. What else? Jonah is bringing in the manuscript of his new book next week. It is to be called *Georgian Afternoon.* Nothing is now left for the old pet except perhaps *Elizabethan Goodnight.* Also Diana Cooper is arriving in London to talk about her memoirs. My favourite American writer, Ray Bradbury, turned up last week, and London is stiff with competing American publishers.

No word from Russia, though I daresay you've seen a few brief but quite amusing pieces of Peter's in *The Times.*

Just before I left Yorkshire I read *The Hound of the Baskervilles* with great pleasure: a joy for ever. Forgive this scrappy and disgruntled letter: perhaps by next Sunday I shall be further back in my rut, and better supplied with gossip. Just now I am yearning for the moorland air and the quiet.

11 July 1957 *Grundisburgh*

I can remember so well what getting back to harness was in old days, and how irksome work looked in September, and after all your lot is much worse, for your holiday is much shorter, your work is in

London and I expect the human stresses that you encounter daily are much more tedious than those of any beak, if only because men (and women) are far more detestable on the whole than boys. And of course the heat—so far worse among streets than in the country, coming as it does from walls and pavements as well as sky. Before you started for home I was already thinking of you with deep sympathy, knowing that, unlike me, you couldn't merely wear a shirt and trousers—socks and tie both discarded. But I am sorry to see judges have been doffing their wigs. They cannot realise that, in many of them, *all* the dignity they have resides in the wig, and that without it they are indistinguishable from sanitary inspectors. The great Justice Holmes was the only Yank I know who saw the point of our judicial wig, viz how it raises a probably quite commonplace official from humdrum humanity to an impersonal figure of justice. Even little Darling, bewigged, no longer looked like a mischievous urchin.

Your journey home was a nightmare and your arrival in the great imposthume, as somebody, probably Cobbett, called it—the heat, the din, the new sec, the mountain of letters. Even on my short visits to London, it is the *people* who oppress one's spirits—their quantity, their complexions, their expressions, and you have, further, to deal with them, and must often feel about them as old Carlyle did—and too often his feelings were put down to his dyspeptic grindings, which, as Birrell pointed out, cannot have been all that bad, as he lived to eighty-six.

I have found out about Pommy and Limey from that admirable *Dictionary of Slang* by Eric Partridge, which you are sure to have. Too long to quote and anyway *all* the theories about the origin of both are fearfully silly. This dictionary is a very good bedside book, full of interest and oddities. I had no idea what an enormous vocabulary is devoted to, shall we euphemistically call it, 'the way of a man with a maid' and the relevant apparatus. I don't think Queen Victoria would have been amused.

I look forward to Jonah's book, and indeed to several others from the great firm. A man in the Ipswich club recently was speaking warmly of that book of Herbert Agar's you have just brought out. And it is rare that any book is mentioned in the I.C., so no doubt it is good. H.A. has a very intelligent face. Didn't he marry poor Barbie

Wallace who lost three sons in the war and one after it? They were all in my house and two of them were well above the average.

I am just approaching my hard work of the year—marking exam-papers and subsequently cooking the marks. It is a dreary routine, but at least one does get *some* fun out of what they write on English Literature. Fancy having to mark a thousand Algebra papers—but the silver lining to *their* cloud is that they can mark twelve or fifteen an hour and we only about six for the same pay. The *Art* examiners mark forty-five to fifty per hour, i.e. a glance or two at that number of drawings of a pot—also for the same pay. Justice? Faugh!

P.S. I am enjoying E. Blunden's poems very much. Surely they are the real stuff, their roots deep in English soil, and in each one the experience or the picture, whichever it is, stands out so clean and clear. I don't always follow his thought, but that is to be expected. My taste is for the country poems mainly; the air and even the smell of Suffolk is in many of them, it seems to me. Such a poem as 'The Scythe struck by Lightning' has the depth and richness of a little Rembrandt. (Am I talking fearful nonsense?) 'Hammond' is in that great tradition which insists that cricket is a much bigger thing than a game. What is it? Not exactly an art, though not far off. Can an artist be completely unconscious of what he is doing? Cardus wrote some admirable pages about Woolley, but I am told that W. himself thought them just rubbish. Odd that E.B. should put *Relf* among his heroes. I don't remember that R. had much personality as a cricketer, and *qua* skill was not more than Beta plus. No one ever *wept* while he was batting as they certainly did during a Trumper or Jessop innings.

I am re-reading FitzGerald's letters rapidly. They don't seem to me as good as they once did, or as they are usually supposed to be. Perhaps my taste has coarsened. It is interesting to find how absurdly bad he and Spedding and others found Irving's Hamlet, which C.E. Montague, Agate and Co all said was tremendous. Not very extra-ordinary perhaps. After all, Ruskin said *Aurora Leigh* was the greatest poem in the English language, and Coleridge said neither Gibbon nor Landor could write English, and that Tennyson had no idea of metre.

In an attempt to provide you with a less dreary letter I am reverting to my old plan of beginning on Saturday. Thank goodness Adam chose to come home rather than go to Lord's, which must have been pretty miserable. Moreover the motor-mower is still enough of a new toy to be welcome, and most of the grass has been cut by A. and the little Linklater boy who has come home with him.

Your excellent letter arrived this morning—with M.B. on G.M. faithfully returned. Many thanks. It is to be included in the forthcoming new edition of Max's *Mainly on the Air*. How I detest a practice which compels one to buy another copy of a book one already had, just for one or two extra pieces. Yesterday afternoon I went to the Royal Soc. of Lit. to hear S.C. Roberts's excellent lecture on Max, which was described in to-day's *Times*. It was first-rate and beautifully delivered: indeed when S.C.R. read extracts in Max's voice the likeness was too much for at least one lady, who almost burst into tears. The lecture, S.C.R. told me, is to be included in a collected volume of his essays during the next few months. Jonah was there, come straight from Lord's in grey top hat. I am now half-way through the typescript of his new book, which is delightful, and I think just as good as the others. I have told him I'll get it out in January. He is now worried because he has nothing more to write about, except religion, on which his views are not readily saleable.

Last week was much more bearable than its predecessor—cooler for one thing, and I suppose I'm growing used again to the hateful saddle. Edmund Blunden arrived on Wednesday from Siegfried Sassoon's. I gaily told him, months ago, that he could stay as long as he liked, and lo he is staying till November! So glad you're enjoying his poems: they are indeed the real stuff, and I'm glad to say this volume has had some excellent reviews, notably Betjeman in the *Daily Telegraph* and Alan Ross in the *T.L.S.*

Sunday night, 14 July

The death of old Lady Rothenstein (Will's widow) has brought to light (as I expected) the originals of Oscar's letters to Will, and perhaps to her. They are coming to me soon. Somehow, before I finish the job,

I must have one more shot at running to earth the *many* O.W. letters which I know are somewhere in America.

18 July 1957 *Grundisburgh*

Most interesting letter of your son's—an obvious writer in embryo. That '*hypnotically* straight road'—*le mot juste* calling up a picture of a passenger turning slowly into a hen with its beak on a line. And 'knifing' too. Clearly his father's son. The whole letter is very good reading. But Peter's health sounds a little sinister, or aren't the Russian medicos good at diagnosis? So many ailments start in the same way. I once had a boy in my house who got polio. A week later another boy had a temperature and a stiff neck and back and Dr Sprot (an ass) said, in view of the other boy, this 'must be regarded with grave suspicion'. No 2 was whisked home for a fortnight's quarantine, was perfectly well in two days and practically ran amok at home from boredom. I had, by the way, been told by Sprot that there might be a carrier in the house, and asked how we could find out. He replied with a wintry smile that there *was* a way, but he thought it was hardly practicable. I asked what it was. He asked how many people there were in the house. I said sixty-two. He said 'Well you would have to get sixty-two monkeys and inject the blood of the sixty-two people severally into them and one monkey will be paralysed and reveal the carrier.' I thanked him warmly for his helpful suggestion, but thought that as the monkeys could not be supplied under three months, we must regretfully think up something else.

I am back among my exam-papers after the London-New Zealand dinner yesterday, where I had to speechify about my nephew. It was a hot and hearty evening at Goldsmiths' Hall. I was introduced to a score of New Zealanders, who seemed to me immensely amiable and quite indistinguishable—rather as Chinese are, even though some were fat and others were thin. The famous Lord Freyberg was there and was charming about my speech but rather spoilt it by looking quizzically at me and adding 'Donnish, you know'. No doubt it was —the hand becomes subdued to what (for thirty-seven years) it works in, but I then gathered that all he meant was that I had tried to find the right words. And that, he added, was very good for the N.Z. audience, because in N.Z. nobody ever does that. And, you know, it wasn't really all that Max B.-ish. I essayed nothing like his label for Joad—'that mellifluous quodlibetarian'. Anyway it was a very friendly audience. I had some talk with Denzil Batchelor who seemed a pleasant chap. He too spoke and told rather too many cricket stories, not of the best vintage, including one about my uncle Alfred that was wrong in a great many ways—like that meat Johnson and Boswell had on the way to the Hebrides which the Doctor described as ill-killed, ill-hung, ill-cooked and ill-served, and no doubt in due course ill-digested. I sat next to the wife of Judge Aarvold who used to play Rugger brilliantly, and flirted in that shameless way common to the senile. She was very good fun, most amusing (and far from wrong) about the immense tedium of a day at a Test Match.

That sounds a good company at the Lit. Soc. I should like to have met Harold Caccia again. How nice of you—and characteristic—to hand on what I said of old Cuthbert—exactly what dear Dr J. used to advise: 'Sir, it increases benevolence.' And so many love doing the opposite.

My exam-papers are in full spate. I have just dealt with Harpenden, a co-ed school, and as usual the girls are much better than the boys, though one young lady paraphrased old Gaunt's 'this dear dear land' into 'this very expensive land' which is almost too up-to-date; and some of the boys who dimly gathered that the beak had said a 'pelting farm' was a 'paltry' farm, improved it into a 'poultry' farm. On the whole the percentage of candidates who get any good out of studying Shakespeare steadily falls—less speedily than the pound, but still steadily.

We have got to the heavy part of the summer, the foliage has, so to say, a middle-aged spread, and the trees which in May were Apollos are now Farnese Herculeses.

21 July 1957 — *Bromsden Farm*

Many thanks for returning Duff's letter so promptly. Ian Fleming rang up the other day to say that if on his return the boy can write a couple of short articles on his trip to Russia, the *Sunday Times* will print them. I've heard no more from the travellers, and have no idea when they'll be back.

My good resolve of starting my letter to you on Saturday was yesterday broken by my attendance at the Johnson Club dinner at Worcester College. Once again you were sadly missed, and indeed I fancy you would have enjoyed the evening more than most of the Gough Square ones. *Imprimis* the dinner was ample and first-class, secondly there was no paper; only a weakish speech by Harold Williams, welcoming the guests. These included J.C. Masterman (the Provost of Worcester), C.H. Wilkinson (the Vice-ditto), Basil Blackwell the bookseller, the Master of Pembroke (Oxon), and an aged American called Sherburn, who has just published an edition of Pope's letters in five vols—a lifetime's work. I took Simon Nowell-Smith, the ex-librarian of the London Library (who lives near here), and sat between him and Davin, the Assistant Secretary to the Clarendon Press, an aggressive but intelligent and incisive New Zealander. Before and after dinner we talked amiably in the J.C.R., a beautiful room with a barrel-shaped ceiling, from which, they say, Amy Robsart fell to her death.

Last week I had three business lunches—two with American publishers and one with a literary agent. I also took E. Blunden to Lord's on Wednesday, but we saw only an hour's poking and scratching by Richardson and Sheppard on a puddingy wicket before rain put a stop to it. (E.B. went again on Thursday and much enjoyed it. Have you, by the way, ever read his *Cricket Country*? If not I'll send you a copy.) On Wednesday evening I took E.B. to dine with the Day Lewises. It was a gay evening and I told too many stories. On Thursday I gave champagne in my flat to fourteen people, in honour of my American friend Ray Bradbury. They drank seven bottles, and I had a job to get rid of them. By the time I got down here on Friday I was all in. Nevertheless I managed to do a bit of the mowing that evening, and just as well too, since yesterday was too wet by far, and to-day I had time only for about half the rest before thunder, lightning, a cloudburst and hailstones the size of mothballs drove me in to Oscar Wilde. When I have composed another 165 footnotes I shall have brought him to his trials, poor man.

Yesterday a wild deer was sighted near the farm, and this morning the vegetable garden was full of strange footprints, but we haven't yet glimpsed the animal, and I long to do so: they are so graceful and they jump so beautifully. Do you know this poem? I won't tell you who wrote it, for fear of putting you off.

DEER[1]

Shy in their herding dwell the fallow deer.
They are spirits of wild sense. Nobody near
Comes upon their pastures. There a life they live,
Of sufficient beauty, phantom, fugitive,
Treading as in jungles free leopards do,
Printless as evelight, instant as dew.
The great kine are patient, and home-coming sheep
Know our bidding. The fallow deer keep
Delicate and far their counsels wild,
Never to be folded reconciled
To the spoiling hand as the poor flocks are;
Lightfoot, and swift, and unfamiliar,
These you may not hinder, unconfined
Beautiful flocks of the mind.

Good, isn't it? The 'unfamiliar' is part of their charm. I shall never forget the moment when, walking alone on the Wiltshire downs, I came face to face with a fox, and we stood staring at each other for a minute before he withdrew and I lost his bright colour in the grass. Birds' nests with eggs in them produce some of the same wonder and delight. I could easily turn and live with (selected) animals.

Alas, my promised visit to you is fading under the pressure of events, and any moment you will be overwhelmed with grandchildren, and my clock will have to tick a few more million times before its proud owner carries it off. Sometime soon I must spend a couple of days in Dublin, trying to get some sense out of Mrs Yeats, who never answers letters. And Arthur Ransome will soon be offended if I don't spend a day or two with him in rural Lancashire. And Diana Cooper's memoirs (now to be in two volumes) need their spelling, syntax and punctuation seeing to, and authors *will* send me manuscripts, and the

[1] By kind permission of Messrs Sidgwick & Jackson.

riveting outside the office window is loud and continuous—oh well, as Oscar said,

> He who lives more lives than one,
> More deaths than one must die.

25 July 1957 *Grundisburgh*

I look forward to seeing the younger generation pluming its wings for a flight in the *Sunday Times.* Will he consult Father about grammar and construction? Will infinitives split and participles hang? Humphrey never consulted me about *his* book, and I could have saved him from giving his great-uncles the wrong-coloured beards, and distinctions which they never achieved. Furthermore, though he is always writing articles—for papers even you have probably never heard of—he never, to my knowledge, deliberately learnt anything about style. I cannot think that to have had *Romola* read to him at Sunday Private by Cyril Butterwick helped him much towards the quite lively style which he has. I am pretty sure that what he has got most from is old Shaw's music criticism—by Corno di Bassetto. Do you know of any better model? I always delight in his two vols of *Dramatic Opinions and Essays,* and so, I believe, did Max B. What a bright, sharp, nimble sword the English language was in his hand! And (did I say this last week?) there are, as Serjeant Buzfuz said, critics, 'erect upon two legs and bearing all the outward semblance of men and not of monsters,' who don't think the Inquisitor's speech in *St Joan* superb.

That Johnson Club dinner sounds good fun. I always like Masterman, though I don't know him at all well, and that absurd old C.H. Wilkinson too. Lord Rosebery, when very old, told someone that only the determination to outlive Mary Drew kept him alive, for high among the terrors of death, according to him, was the certainty of being written about by M.D. She couldn't write interestingly for some reason—probably because she had no humour.

I envy you your wild deer—nothing so lovely ever roams the glebes of Suffolk. Who wrote that lovely poem? 'Phantom, fugitive . . . printless as evelight, instant as dew (I was *mouthing* it and wrote, if you please, 'due'!). I like it. But why 'kine' in these days? What is wrong with cows? Though I remember Arthur Benson telling us 'cows' would *not* do in poetry. That, however, was in 1899. And you remember Dr J. protested against the vulgarity of 'blanket' and 'knife' in *Macbeth*. I wonder why you don't tell me the author's name. Is he a *bête noire*? I once had a similar meeting with a fox to yours—a red-letter moment. I still recollect the piercing intelligence of his eye—all curiosity and vigilance and a general air of being equal to any occasion. I bet Chaunticleer would never have outwitted him as the Nonnes Preeste recorded, and as half the school population of England have been writing about this week—damn them! I am about half-way through my oakum-picking, but the worst is yet to come—mere essay-answers on five different books, and to separate the wheat from the chaff is a really infernal job. These exams are full of surprises. Can you tell me why the papers on *The Devil's Disciple* are mostly v. bad, while those on *The Riddle of the Sands* are mostly v. good? Because I can't. No outstanding howler so far, but I like 'yhact' for 'yacht,' and there are some good names—Grut, Seex, Allbless, Gbow, Jaglorn, Jellinek, Pedgrift, nicely sweetened yesterday by Flowerdew and Lillies.

Your visit, alas! but I know how pressed you are. We will *somehow* get the clock up to London in the coming months, probably when they put the railway fares up. My brother-in-law (Ld Leconfield) meets any grumbling about inflation with what *he* calls the comforting thought that the value of money has *always* depreciated since William the Conquerer (when a pig cost threepence).

27 July 1957 *Bromsden Farm*

You won't get much tonight, for I am full of sleep after a long bout of gardening. The Russian travellers are due home on Monday; Eton breaks up on Wednesday; and soon the house will be stuffed with untidy, large, noisy but charming children. If you look at *Cricket Country* again you will find two oblique references to me. Somewhere, in a forgotten place of safety, I have an excellent photograph of E.B. and myself coming down the pavilion steps to open the innings in 1935 or thereabouts.

So glad you liked the Fallow Deer poem. It is by Drinkwater, and I thought his name might possibly put you off. He wrote other good poems, but made himself a joke and a nuisance, and is now, I fancy, scarcely read. I knew him 1930-32, since Peggy Ashcroft had been in the original production of his play *Bird in Hand*, but I offended him (he was very touchy) and we met no more.

Sunday night, 28 July

Just now, as I was addressing an envelope to you, I thought how astonishing it is that by scrawling a few marks on a piece of paper I can get it delivered to you in Suffolk the day after it's posted. We take everything for granted nowadays, and complain if the miracle doesn't always work properly. Perhaps a long day of mowing has made me thus wonder.

My Canadian friend George Whalley (didn't you meet him?) came to tea with his wife and three children, otherwise a peaceful day, and now Tchaikovsky's Fifth Symphony is delighting me from a little box as I scribble rubbish to you. Miracles never cease.

Last week was oppressively hot in London, and I had a lot to do. On Monday Jonah and Evy gave a dinner-party of eight people in a private room at the Travellers' Club. The Duke of Wellington, Hamish Hamilton, Lady Harlech, Muriel Gore and Jonah's daughter Lavinia were the other guests. Very agreeable, but just now I have so much editorial work waiting at home that I begin to fret soon after the coffee is brought in. I particularly liked Lady Harlech—I expect you know her, elder sister of Salisbury and David Cecil.

On Tuesday I couldn't avoid a cocktail party on the third floor (walk up) in Harley Street. It was so hot and airless that I could soon feel sweat dripping down me. I talked to A.P.H., Gerald Barry and others, drank two champagne cocktails, and dashed on in pouring rain to the Garrick, where I gave dinner to Blunden and his wife. Wednesday was quieter, but Thursday left me breathless. In the morning I went with Diana Cooper to the Crypt of St Paul's to choose a place for Duff's memorial tablet. We were taken round by the Clerk of the Works (who would keep showing us where the bombs fell—and indeed I can't understand how the building stood it) and the accredited architect, Lord Mottistone, a very agreeable chap of about my age. (He is the son of Jack Seely and I remembered how once at the Beefsteak (or perhaps the Other Club) someone accused Duff of being the worst Secretary of State for War in our history. Duff answered: 'How dare you say that, with Jack Seely sitting at the table?') We had the Crypt to ourselves, and since in the Cathedral over our heads two bishops were being lengthily enthroned by the A B of C, there was much fine singing coming down to us. I'd never before been in the Crypt and was much moved by it all—the majesty of Nelson's sepulchre, the massive ugliness of Wellington's. 'You've no idea,' said the Clerk of Works, 'how difficult it is to fit in the hot water pipes among all these graves.' Mottistone would love to move forward the altar in St Faith's Chapel, 'but,' pointing to a splendid tombstone on the floor, 'Bishop Creighton's in the way.' We chose quite a good place for Duff, round the corner from Nelson, and I dashed back to make polite conversation to a Dutchman who markets our books in Holland. After lunch I had to make a tiny speech at the A.G.M. of the London Library, which was attended by maybe a hundred members. The only other speakers were T.S.E. and Harold Nicolson. That evening I dined with Sam Behrman and the Jepsons. On Friday morning I went to the Tate, and checked the texts of Oscar's surviving letters to Rothenstein. It was worth the effort, since I found the printed versions full of misreadings, and a new letter as well. Idiotically I left my umbrella behind, and the small metal tag they gave me in exchange won't keep much of me dry. Tomorrow the circus starts again. *Ora pro nobis.*

1 August 1957 *Grundisburgh*

Your life is simply Masefield's *Odtaa*[1]. Ceaseless activity! The very opposite pole to mine—eight hours a day for the last three weeks, I agree, but all of them in my chair. Let me say magnificently—all *my* activities are those of the spirit, though possibly you may think that is putting rumination and mild meditation and day-dream rather high! My first bout of drudgery nears its end. The last lap was tedious—young men and maidens to the number of two hundred pouring out

[1] One Damn Thing After Another.

not what they thought but what they had been told to pretend they thought about Falstaff and Wordsworth and Coleridge and Browning and Tennyson and Boswell and Johnson. Some of it was very dreary. The girls are the worst infliction because they have imbibed *all* the right things to say and their regurgitations are relentlessly copious. They know all their five books by heart, and have that disgusting habit of quoting twelve lines to prove a point where two would be ample. And I can *never* pass a quotation without verifying it and sometimes they take a long time to find. (Do you know that in my three-vol Wordsworth the Tintern Abbey poem is among the contents simply as 'Lines'. Isn't that frightfully silly?) The best (or worst) thing so far is a perfectly sound and knowledgeable reference to the 'bona roba', Jane Nightwork,[1] infinitely spoilt in one way, and infinitely improved in another, by her being called 'Florence Nightingale'.

I agree with you about the daily miracles—the post etc (I hope you ask 'has the *post* come' and not the 'mail'?). Wireless and TV still seem to me *sheer* magic. And though doctors don't go in much for wonder, I imagine the human body and its workings are the same. We too listened to Tchaikovsky. Very rich. I suppose the Leavises of the music-world have long put him on the scrap-heap—but who cares a rap about them? I literally *am* that figure of everybody's fun who knows nothing about music but does know what he likes. The truth is that *he* isn't absurd, but the remark is.

Mima Harlech is delightful and always was—also her sister, the lovely Mowcher. What *do* these Cecil nicknames mean—Fish and Linky *inter alia*?

Did you hear Winston last night? Very old. The words petered out at times and he often misread a word and corrected it. Why did he have to make sure of getting the great Coke right? Surely one of the names everyone knows.

I like your uncle Duff's retort about Jack Seely. I never met him but my Uncle Alfred didn't like him—'a bumptious fellow,' and indeed I heard someone else say he was the most conceited man in the world. But I believe he *was* very brave and that should count for something, as Bishop Gore said of Bishop Ingram's being a good man,

[1] See *Henry IV*, Part Two, III, 2.

after they had all been pouring contempt on his theology and utterances in general. I have never been into St Paul's crypt; it sounds very impressive. Is Donne there—a very tremendous man. 'If some King of the earth have so large an extent of dominion . . .'. Do you know that sermon? But I expect you have your favourites among them. I am not clever enough for much of his poetry, but, golly, he could write prose—as Housman said, a much more difficult job.

4 August 1957 *Bromsden Farm*

I imagine that this date means nothing to our children, but although I was only six in 1914 it tolls for me every year the death of the Golden Age, while September 3, which affected my life much more, passes almost unnoticed. I envy you and all those who had some grown-up years before the deluge, for the true *douceur de vivre* will not come again in our time.

It is said that Jack Seely recommended his soldier-servant for the V.C. saying: 'He's as brave as a lion: he goes everywhere I go.'

Yes, I do know that Donne sermon, and that particular sentence is in my commonplace book. Many of his poems are wonderful, even if one doesn't fully understand them. Try declaiming in the night-watches:

> At the round earth's imagined corners, blow
> Your trumpets, Angels, and arise, arise
> From death, you numberless infinities
> Of souls, and to your scattered bodies go.

Pull out all the stops, and the mice will marvel in the wainscot.

My two elder children have gone to Wales for the week-end, so we have only Adam with us. He missed a Distinction in Trials by thirty-five marks, but seems unmoved. Yesterday I got a note from Birley to say that Eton has awarded my elder boy Duff a 'Miss Goodall Bursary' of £100 a year for his three years at Oxford. It's most generous and will be an enormous help.

Last week I once again lost my precious little engagement-diary, on which my pell-mell life depends. For thirty-six hours I was helpless, unable to remember anything—and then a blessed taxi-driver brought it back. I rewarded him with 10/-, feeling that it should be £10.

On Monday I gave lunch to a friend from the country, signed some cheques at the London Library (a one-man meeting of the Finance Committee), visited Lady Emily Lutyens, who is very frail and thin but full of life and delight in her book's good reviews. That evening I dined with the Ray Bradburys and another friend at the Mirabelle restaurant in Curzon Street, which is probably the most expensive in London. Admittedly we had a very good dinner, with two bottles of reasonable wine, but the bill for the four of us came to £16!! Even our American hosts were a little shaken. How can *anyone* afford such prices out of to-day's incomes? Clearly it's impossible, and indeed most of the other customers looked as though they depended on expense accounts. I felt quite guilty for the next day or two.

Monday night, 5 August

This morning, before I was up, Comfort and Adam set out for a rag regatta at Wargrave, from which they didn't return till 7 p.m. This left me happily marooned for the day, but it also delayed this letter's departure till tomorrow. I divided the day placidly between Oscar and the garden, eradicating a large area of nettles under the walnut tree, and getting very hot even in its shade. All farmers were supposed to plant a walnut near their farmyard to keep off the flies. I now begin to think it was efficacious because all the flies in the neighbourhood are attracted to it, rather than repelled by it.

The rest of last week was comparatively calm, but the hideous and incessant clangour of the builders outside my window (the permanent closing of which makes the room suffocating) prompts me to spend as little time in the office as possible. On Thursday, for instance, I spent almost half the day in the Reading Room of the B.M., looking up things for my Oscar notes among the stuffy rustle of all those black clergymen and other *habitués*. Once in a way I enjoy such a diversion. If I could concentrate solely on Oscar for a month I could polish off the whole huge job: as it is, moving by fits and starts, heaven knows when I shall finish. Most of my considerable collection of reference books is in Soho Square and too heavy to bring down, so at week-ends I have to concentrate on what I can do here. This evening I have succumbed to a fierce *furor notandi* (if there is such a phrase) and have solved (or skirted) a few nasty cruxes (or cruces?). I've just read Evelyn Waugh's new book[1]. Short though it is, it should be shorter, but much of it is interesting, and it's straight fact lightly disguised as fiction. Have also read Stevenson's letters to Charles Baxter, and that old but still amusing skit, *The Green Carnation.* Also a rotten biography of Lord Alfred Douglas, not to mention sundry MSS and proofs. Are you going away? Or just resisting the invasions of grandchildren? Fleming has written three *Times* 'turn-over' articles on the Russian trip. They should appear this week.

7 August 1957 *Grundisburgh*

Another good instalment of your diary. How right you are about pre-Aug. 4 1914. I can of course remember it very well, and equally of course that we didn't in the least realise at the time that it *was* a golden age. In fact I am pretty sure that the real golden age was before the Boer War. At the time of the Diamond Jubilee there literally wasn't a cloud in the sky, whereas from 1902 onwards there were continuous though not loud rumblings about the German menace—and a good many strikes too. I remember an evening at Hagley when Leo Maxse shook us all to the core telling us all he *knew* about German plans, and how pleased he was after hearing that the Kaiser and Bülow had foamed with rage over one issue of the *National Review* and said that such a man as the editor oughtn't to be allowed to live. He also reported that the most encouraging news from Germany was that sodomy was about to be, not abolished, but legalised, as that must mean decadence pretty quick. How nice it would be if everything was as simple as that!

Apropos of the *National Review,* is it in that organ that the Lord Altrincham has been attacking the Queen and her entourage? I haven't seen it and, like James Forsyte, nobody ever tells me anything. In fact it becomes increasingly clear that if (a) you have no television, and (b) you never read the *Express* or *Mirror,* very soon you are cut off from all knowledge of what is going on. As I have often said before,

[1] *The Ordeal of Gilbert Pinfold.*

there is a great deal to be said for being seventy. Probably there always was, at least after 1897. I suppose *you* have never handled a golden sovereign? A beautiful coin! It rang with a note like the song of a bird, as Homer says the string of Ulysses's bow did when he twanged it. And what a lot of things it bought—including a *ton and a half* of coke. But that way madness lies. Carlyle—that very great and much underrated writer—declared that three hundred years of trouble were needed for the human spirit to purge and rebuild itself after the first blast from heaven, i.e. the French Revolution. So we're not far past the middle of that. I think that dyspeptic old genius—who, with Ruskin, really *was* made unhappy by the awful gap between rich and poor a century ago—would not have been noticeably blither now. Of course you know his Johnson essay—surely one of the noblest things ever written. But how Victorian are these naive enthusiasms!

Next week I go to Cambridge for a week. If the spirit continues to move you (this refers to the week after next) please send the results to me at the University Arms Hotel, St Andrew's Street, as we shan't finish before Thursday or Friday week.

I like your Seely story, but—well I prefer the A.J.B. attitude, recalling something that happened 'When I was Prime Minister, or something of that sort', or the Duke of Wellington. Wasn't it Tennyson who said a French hero's answer to the ass who said he was delighted to have shown the way to 'the great Duke' would have been '*Oui; on m'appelle le grand*'. That type of modesty is strictly English, I suppose. Foreigners from Tamburlaine onwards have never had it.

How good that you too spotted (when?) that great Donne sermon —'damped and benumbed, wintered and frozen, smothered and stupefied' (but, my dear, we mustn't admire *beauty of language* nowadays; that is hopelessly *vieux jeu*). Some criminal stole my volume of Donne's prose and I suppose now it is out of print. I must wander down the Charing Cross Road again soon.

I have just embarked on Aldington's biographical sketch of D.H. Lawrence and, after fifty pages, dislike both men about equally. It is a library book, but much greater strength of mind than I possess would have been necessary to prevent my twice writing 'ass!' in the margin. The Ipswich Library books are full of pencilled comments. The one I like best was on a volume of H. James's short stories. One reader had written 'Tripe', and another had prefixed 'Worse than.' *Sic transit*!

Congratulations on the Goodford Bursary. Do you remember Miss Goodford? It was impressive to see every day in chapel the daughter of the last headmaster but five (or are *you* right in calling it Goodall? If so, who in thunder *was* Miss Goodall?). Miss Goodford and her brother, both blind, used to watch cricket on Agar's by *ear*—just as Wilfred Rhodes does now—not, I am glad to hear, at all sorry for himself.

Your Mirabelle dinner gives me goose-flesh. I remember seeing old Agate at the Ivy doling out paper after lunching me and a Baconian solicitor from Birmingham, whom J.A. mocked at unceasingly. But I did not feel particularly compunctious, as it was *his* double brandies and cigars which inflated the figures. The weekly advertisements in the *Tatler* seem to show there is still plenty of money about. Is it all stock exchange profits, or is everybody living on capital?

11 August 1957 *Bromsden Farm*

I don't think you need waste any time on either the *National Review* (now a paltry rag) or Lord Altrincham. I only wish the Queen or the Duke of E. could hit back!

Your instructions about my writing to Cambridge are, alas, not wholly clear. After much thought I have decided that this letter should go to Grundisburgh and next week's to Cambridge: I hope that's right.

Why will you persist in reading books by the loathsome and fifth-rate Richard Aldington? You never enjoy them, and there's so much else. Rather the egregious Leavis any day.

The din in Soho Square is likely to continue for months: 'hammering' is altogether too gentle a term for the combination of circular saw, cement-mixer, and metallic crashing—sometimes one can't hear a word in the room. They start before 7 a.m. and go on for at least twelve hours.

The H.M. certainly wrote Miss Good*all*; blessings on her, however she spelt her name.

Fleming has driven to Scotland for the Twelfth. What did you think of his *Times* articles? My Duff is now struggling to cover the same ground without repeating what P.F. has said. He (Duff) has taken some first-rate colour-photographs, and he is trying to persuade the *Illustrated London News* to buy a page or two of them.

Last week was both shorter and quieter than usual. The silly season must now mercifully be upon us. One day I went book-hunting with E. Blunden to our old haunt, the barrows in the Farringdon Road. There are only half as many as there were twenty years ago, but we struck a sixpenny day and came back happily laden. In my time I have picked up wonderful bargains, and a large part of my library came from there.

In the past twenty-four hours I have read two detective stories and reviewed eight, besides adding a few Oscar footnotes to the pile. *Punch* have proved extremely co-operative, giving me an exact list (with dates) of all Ada Leverson's contributions. This has enabled me to date several letters and explain otherwise obscure references. I must confess that there are times when the sheer weight of work still to be done on the Wilde letters fills me with the gloomiest apprehension, but I love the job and must just plug on, doing as much as I can each day.

Next Tuesday I have been summoned to lunch with the Editor of *The Times*[1] in the Ritz Grill! Why? You shall have a full report next week. I've only met him twice, once at a dinner-party and once in the Athenaeum. We shall see.

If I go to Rapallo to see E. Beerbohm, it may be easiest to go next week: perhaps I shall spend my fiftieth birthday by 'the bluest and beautifullest of seas'. If my mission there is successful, I shall have *another* book of letters (Max's to Reggie Turner) to edit alongside Oscar. And at any moment the manuscript of Diana Cooper's memoirs will appear. How much can one do in a day? You've no idea how often I envy you your summer-house and your leisure. The latter is a blessing which youth squanders carelessly, and in the modern world it largely disappears until one reaches 'that unhoped serene that men call age'. So you see how enviable you are!

[1] Sir William Haley.

What a detestable month August can be! Today the garden is carpeted with thunderbolts, so to speak, and the thunder has that explosive suddenness and violence which led that lunatic (who ought to have been instantly set free) to exclaim 'God has shot himself'. If at lunch-time I hadn't run like Jesse Owens from summer-house to kitchen I should have been wet to the skin. Augusts in the nineties were not like that. 'The sunbrown harvest men with August weary'[1] is right off the bullseye in mid-twentieth century.

Your interpretation of my slightly half-witted directions was perfectly correct. I could not get out of my head that I was going to Cambridge on Monday when it was really Wednesday, i.e. tomorrow. *Next* Tuesday I shall be at the University Arms Hotel, surrounded by Americans.

I have finished Aldington on Lawrence. You are surprised at my reading anything by the man who in a competition for the post of Europe's prize sh-t would surely win hands down. Well, I will tell you why I do so. I can hardly read ten consecutive pages of D.H.L. without being invaded by boredom raging like toothache. But apart from so many people saying so, I am sure he is a genius—and in descriptive bits he can touch almost any height. And you know, one of the chief dangers of senectitude is a contented nestling in tastes and opinions formed many years ago, and of necessity steadily narrowing, so I quite often have shots at writers like D.H.L. and—dare I confess it?—Jane Austen!—to both of whom I am on the way to being allergic. And besides that I find getting angry (not with living people) is rather a tonic. And again—I often used to tell boys about Tolstoy deciding that Shakespeare was absurd, and the universal admiration of him merely showed that the world was mad, and while you and I (I said to them) read one book half through and decide the author is bad, he formed his opinion after reading all Shakespeare *seven* times, and had a right to his opinion.

But this is all very boring. And one opinion I shall never change, i.e. that whatever D.H.L. was as a writer, as a man, a member of the

[1] Should be 'sun-burn'd sicklemen of August weary' (*The Tempest*, III, 2).

human family, he was as near impossible as anyone could be—a dreadful compound of hatred and malice and arrogance and deliberate wrong-headedness. As for Aldington—but why should I take coals to Newcastle? You have got him docketed all right.

Goodall is no doubt the name—Provost a hundred and more years ago, one of those bland, learned, virtuous dignitaries who resisted any change of any kind, and in whose time that 'Long Chamber'[1] flourished at the memory of which, according to Strachey, 'aged warriors and statesmen would turn pale'. What a clever family you have. I shall keep an eye on the *I.L.N.* My five offspring were never within sight of a prize or a scholarship, though I fancy *theirs* may be. To date I have thirteen grandchildren, and rumour says that within a year I shall have sixteen. My daughters have no misgivings about the future of civilisation—in marked contrast to their father. Their view no doubt is the more praiseworthy one.

Peter Fleming's articles were very good reading, and had what I always think is a most enviable trait, viz making the reader think the author must be a very nice man. I gather from John Raymond and Co. that 'charm' is about the most damnable literary quality there is—'the logical and deathly end-product of the mandarin tradition' is his amiable reference to David Cecil's latest essays. What *is* the 'mandarin tradition'? It seems to me to be the pronouncements by the widely-read critics of the last generation on books they enjoyed and why they enjoyed them. Why all this rage? Half these angry young men, I suspect, in praising each other's stuff, are whistling to keep their spirits up.

What are they doing in Soho Square with all that hellish din? It would drive me mad. Don't, please, be driven mad—or wilt under Wilde. Remember that more than once Boswell seriously thought of abandoning the life of J., the burden of it being so great. I am taking the latest vol. of his journal to Cambridge. The reviews of it are very variable. Some, no doubt, detect traces of that deleterious element, charm. It is amusing to think what Macaulay could have added to his abuse of B. if he had known as much as we do of his character.

[1] The dormitory for junior boys in College at Eton.

This evening, contrary to my principles and practice, I attended a local cocktail party, at which I consumed two tumblers of what must have been very nearly neat whisky, so if this letter is illegible or incoherent, you must forget and forgive.

This dull grey wet weather I find most depressing. Will Italy be hot and sunny? I shall soon know, for on Tuesday morning I set out in great comfort on the Rome Express, first-class with sleeper at the firm's expense, and should reach Rapallo at 8.30 a.m. on Wednesday. Write this week c/o Lady Beerbohm, Villino Chiaro, Rapallo. I shall probably stay three or four days and then come home via Cagnes-sur-mer, near Nice, where some friends have taken a villa. Altogether I don't expect to be away more than ten or twelve days. This is my first visit to Italy, and I speak no word of the language.

Your fear of senectitude and hardening of the literary arteries seems to me morbid. Never did I know anyone less likely to congeal. Therefore I see no need to mortify yourself with Aldington, Leavis and company. I have always found *Don Quixote* unreadable, but there's plenty else to wear out my eyesight. If you haven't even begun to ossify (mentally) at seventy-four, you never will, and I should, if I were you, read for pleasure only. What cheek—it must be the whisky!

My son's efforts to market his Russian experiences have so far aborted: have you read Peter's article in the current *Spectator*?

The din in Soho Square is unabated. Building houses of steel and reinforced concrete is a grim and cacophonous business.

My lunch with the editor of *The Times* (in the Ritz Grill) was most enjoyable. He definitely *is* Oliver Edwards,[1] and his whole interest, outside his job, lies in books and reading. We gossiped hard about books and writers, and with the minimum of encouragement he told me the (most interesting) story of his life. I should say he has almost a genius for organising and running large institutions. I told him a bit about the Wilde letters, and within forty-eight hours he had had the files of *The Times* combed and the date of publication of the first volume of the *Yellow Book* established. There's nothing like harnessing the

[1] The name under which Sir William Haley contributed literary articles to *The Times*.

stars in their courses to work for one! In his letter he said he 'couldn't say how much he had enjoyed our lunch'. I answered ditto, and he is to lunch with me when I get back.

That afternoon E.B. and I drove out to Bushey to look at the books of a friend of his, recently deceased. E. was told he could take what he liked, but was too modest to comply, though with my assistance we pretty well filled up the car. On Thursday I dined with the Jepsons and worked on Max's letters till 12.30.

I look forward to the long train-journey with its excellent meals and time for reading. I am taking my bathing things and a panama hat. I haven't glimpsed the Mediterranean for something like twenty-five years—perhaps I shall never come back!

22 August 1957 *Cambridge*

I have had rather a sweaty week here, dealing with a million scripts, and staying in a hotel which has to be heated up for an army of Yankees. And there has been some species of scout jamboree which fills the dining-room with hairy-kneed, shiny-faced, wholly grown-up black men in shorts. Generally speaking rule 1 for shorts is that the wearer must be young, white, and well-shaped.

We have run up against some very loose and inefficient examiners —mostly women—whose marks have to be considerably doctored, and that delays us a good deal. However we get our own back by writing acid little reports on the bad examiners, and hope that they will be sacked before next year. The most depressing part of the whole business is the conviction that examination on set English books ought never to have been instituted. More than half the candidates merely retail what they have been told they ought to think. But this is all very shoppy. Let it cease.

But now you are sun-and surf-bathing without—I hope—a care in the world. Why don't you call on P. Lubbock at Lerici? He would love it. Tell him I urged you to. Be careful. Remember Shelley[1]; and tell me *all* about it next week.

[1] Shelley was drowned off the coast near Lerici.

26 August 1957 **11 a.m.**

I am starting this in the train on a blazing hot day at Ventimiglia on the Franco-Italian frontier. If, as I expect, you wrote to Rapallo, I haven't yet got your letter, for reasons which will speedily become apparent.

The first part of my journey passed off beautifully—a smooth Channel crossing, a happy chance meeting on the boat with Cecil Day Lewis and his wife (on their way to an Hellenic Cruise), two smashing meals on the Rome Express, and a fairly good night in my exclusive sleeper. When I detrained at Rapallo at 8.30 a.m. on a hot sunny morning I was surprised not to see Elisabeth B. on the platform. Nothing daunted I found a taxi and by means of almost the only two Italian words I knew (*Villino Chiaro*) managed to get there—only to find that Elisabeth was *away*! Some hideous misunderstanding, still not fully explained. The little Italian maid was most sympathetic, and knew a few words of French, but she had no idea when E. was coming back, the taxi-driver was asking for his fare, and it seemed to me the only thing to do was to push on to Cagnes-sur-mer, where I knew there was room for me, though my friends weren't expecting me for several days. So I left a note for E., giving her the Cagnes telephone number, and told the bewildered cabman '*Stazione*'.

Here my woeful lack of Italian was a great handicap. A request for a ticket to Nice threw the booking clerk into a frenzy of words, so I pacified him by asking for one to Genoa. Armed with this I sat on my suitcase on Rapallo station for one and a half hours, during which I chummed up with two Welsh girls and a female physiologist from New York City, none of whom spoke much more Italian than I did. Eventually I reached Genoa, where the main station is bigger and more modern than you'd believe. Lugging my three bags down corridors and up flights of stairs I finally found a ticket-clerk who spoke some English, and from him bought a ticket to Nice. There were then four blistering hours to fill in, so I left my luggage in the right place (found by tackling a policeman and saying '*Baggagio*' in a hopeless voice), had some coffee in a café and explored the city a little. It's enormous, with huge modern appartment blocks jostling the most squalid and picturesque of slums. But it was too hot to walk far, and soon everything shut for a long siesta. At the university bookshop I bought a little English-Italian phrasebook, just in time to learn that the Italian for lavatory is *ritirata.* Then I had a moderate lunch in a restaurant, some more coffee in another café, and at 3.20 literally *fought* my way on to the train. (Now this one has started again, so farewell legibility!) It was on its way from Rome to Barcelona and was already stuffed to bursting. For three and a half hours I sat on my suitcase in a crowded corridor (now we have stopped at Bordighera), reading a life of Oscar Wilde in French, while the temperature soared into the nineties. Eventually, three-quarters of an hour late, we got to Nice at 8.15 p.m., and the second taxi I tried agreed to drive me the eight miles to Cagnes. I had sent my friends a telegram from Genoa, but it took seven hours to arrive. (Now we're off again). The Cagnes villa is charming, built into the ramparts of the old walled city on a hill, in sight of the sea. (An Italian train official has just come in and made a long speech, of which I understood only one word—*Biglietto* (ticket). I smiled at him sweetly and he went away.)

On Thursday and Saturday I had heavenly bathes, but on Friday torrential rain fell all day. (Now we have stopped at San Remo, which would be unspeakable without the deep blueness of sea and sky.) On Friday night Elisabeth rang up in great distress over the misunderstanding and begged me to go back. I arranged to do so yesterday (Sunday), but on Saturday night I was seized with violent pains and diarrhoea, couldn't face the journey in such a condition, so put it off till to-day. I am recovered but feeble, and am eschewing the restaurant car in favour of a packet of petit-beurre biscuits. This train (bound for Rome) is due at Rapallo at 4.30—or so I gather, since no-one ever knows such things for certain, and I dare say I'll doss down in the Eternal City yet! I'll write more this evening. Too shaky now. R.

Tuesday, 27 August 1957 *Villino Chiaro, Rapallo*

My arrivals at Rapallo are clearly ill-fated. Yesterday I got there at 4—but once again no Elisabeth. I waited for a quarter of an hour, and then engaged the same taxi-driver as last week. When we got here, there was no one here either: the driver clearly thought me an idiot with a recurrent obsession and was unwilling to leave me. I persuaded him to go, well tipped, and soon afterwards E. arrived. Of course she had been told the train arrived at 4.20.

The whole place is exquisite: the little *villino* (all on one floor) right on the road: above it a huge wide terrace, with a tiny work-room in the middle of it: above again and behind, the *casetta*, a three-storied guest-house, an old peasant's house, with the disused Roman road behind. Everywhere Max's books and drawings, all exactly as they were. The garden is full of figs and grapes and oranges and olives. I am sleeping in the *casetta* where Max recorded his broadcasts. E. has all the records and last night played me the George Moore one. She is spoiling me with wonderful food and loving care. The only snag to the whole place is the road, on which endless vehicles of all calibres crash, roar and screech past. Doubtless one soon gets used to it. Below the road the blue Mediterranean stretches away, and at night the lights of Santa Margharita shine gaily across the bay. You can imagine with what joy and excitement I examine all the books, and the drawings in them, and all the other treasures. I shall go back to Cagnes tomorrow (my fiftieth birthday) and home a few days later. Send your next letter to Soho Square, since I probably shan't be at Bromsden till the week-end after next. I'll write again from wherever I am next Sunday, with the latest news of my journeyings on the Côte d'Azur. I did some Wilde work in the train yesterday, and here so much is germane. How I long for Max himself to be here, knowing all the answers to the questions that need so much research.

1 September 1957 *Grundisburgh*

What hideous adventures you record—with every appearance of cheerfulness. It must have been an immensely tedious experience, as it always is when modern organisation breaks down. One can't really doss down by the roadside as e.g. in Chaucer's day. All foreigners are immensely stupid in such circumstances. There must be *someone* in Rapallo who could talk English and put you on the right road; is there no British Consul there? The phrase-books leave out all that one wants. Percy Lubbock used to wonder how Max could stand the noise and nearness of that road—which I suppose was a little country lane when he first settled there. Anyway noise soon becomes tolerable, especially if incessant.

I read John Sparrow's review with great interest. He is severe on Watson, and I suppose that is all right *unless* that queer streak *was* in A.E. Housman, and I always understood—not knowing anything about it—that the 'homo' side of him was a matter of general acceptance. In which case all the cross pooh-poohing of attempts to grapple with and elucidate it are rather off the point and also rather unfair. I still think a lot of Watson's book is devilish interesting, whatever they say. And A.E.H. is one of those who somehow invite odd comment—some of it contemptuous, some patronising, some silly—e.g. John Wain, who says A.E.H. failed in Greats on purpose! It serves the old curmudgeon right really. No one has a right to be so arrogant and inhuman. But no one also has a right to say, as one ass did recently, that H. was less of a poet than Manilius ('Once in the wind of morning . . .' etc. Match me that in Manilius!). Critics are odd. Do you remember Walter Raleigh writing 'A wiser man than Macaulay, James Boswell'? Just trailing his coat, of course, for some reason.

I think I have had enough of Boswell *pro tem.* His absurdity is unvarying, and the unvarying grows tedious. And did anyone ever have venereal disease so often—and ultimately so luckily, for he was always cured. And the mystery of why so many people liked him and no one ever told him he was a B.F. Perhaps they did and he didn't mind. The Doctor of course did, but B. was full of family pride and surely wouldn't have taken it from anyone else.

Pamela and I went last week to *Look Back in Anger* in Ipswich. I wish you would tell me why it has had such success. I gather it is regarded as tremendously original, but surely a young man ranting away at the world and its conventions and absence of 'enthusiasm' etc. is about as old as anything can be—only another form of Byronism. We found the young man a good deal of a bore, but no doubt that is exactly what he would have hoped we should. They say the dialogue is very fine. Well, it is well enough, and never 'literary' etc. But isn't all that sprinkling of 'bloody's' and 'bitches' merely another form of pretentiousness? I am quite prepared for you to say I am quite wrong and out-of-date, and that it is first-rate stuff, etc. But when I remember the good Shaws and Galsworthys, it seems to me that we got more for our money, and also got *somewhere* by the play's end.

Monday, 2 September 1957 *Villa Lucie*
Cagnes-sur-mer
Alpes Maritimes

I meant to write to you yesterday, but in this lotus-land it is indeed always afternoon and later than one thinks. It is now 9.30 a.m. and I am sitting, dressed in shirt and shorts, on a vine-covered terrace on a hillside looking across to a very blue sea. Later today I will send you a postcard showing the position of this house below the battlements of the little mediaeval town, whose crooked winding streets (and open drains) draw in great numbers of sightseers. Luckily cars cannot get as far as this house—the street is too narrow.

My two days at Rapallo were idyllic. Perfect weather and such cosseting as you wouldn't believe: Max's last years must have been blissful. We ate all our meals (except dinner) on a little terrace covered with ripening grapes: Max called it the Vining Room: and on my birthday Elisabeth greeted me with a large silver tray on which she had arranged fifty flowers in a garland surrounding the figures 50 in scarlet geranium-petals. It looked quite lovely and I was much touched. She gave me several books that had belonged to Max, including one with a superb drawing in it (which I will show you). The whole place is saturated with Max's personality—he lived there for forty-five years, with gaps during the wars.

Eventually I spent another seven hours chugging back to Nice with the typescript of Oscar's prison-letters on my lap.

Sure enough there had been a muddle about my return ticket, and since I felt quite ready for a few idle days I was delighted to discover that I couldn't get a sleeper till next Saturday (the 7th), arriving London Sunday (8th).

My friends here have hired a tiny Renault, in which each morning I drive them to the beach—three miles away—for prolonged bathing and sunning. It's so long since I swam in the Mediterranean that I had forgotten how warm and clear and buoyant it is: one can keep afloat without movement. Most days I bathe again in the evening, after a considerable siesta. There are many books in the house, mostly French, German and Tauchnitz, including some Maughams, which I am re-reading with pleasure—*The Narrow Corner* (novel), *The Casuarina Tree* and *First Person Singular* (stories). Readability (extreme) is his great asset, for much of the prose is slipshod and many of the stories marred by a tiresome superiority and know-all cocksureness. I have also bought, and am enormously enjoying, Maurois's latest biography *Les Trois Dumas*. There isn't in fact much (all too little) about the mulatto general of Napoleon who sired the novelist, but *his* story is astonishing, and I have still to reach the *fils*, of *La Dame aux Camélias*. Maurois's French is easy to read, and the book exactly suits my mood. Occasionally I summon up a picture of the mounting piles of letters on my office desk, as a delicious antithesis to this remote and peaceful eyrie, where the postman brings me nothing—though we generally get *The Times* the same afternoon. I am sunburnt, mosquito-bitten and infinitely relaxed. I could always take a month or two of this sort of thing each year.

At Rapallo it was the greatest fun looking through Max's books, with their manifold inscriptions, marginalia, drawings, and (best of all) his touching-up of illustrations, often so skilfully done as to be almost invisible, but always exactly to the point. I should love to spend a week or two there, for I had time only to scratch the surface.

8 September 1957 *Grundisburgh*

Welcome home and all that! Reading not between the lines so much as the lines themselves, you have enjoyed your trip greatly in spite of those malicious logs dropped in your path by Fortune, who simply has no idea of what is cricket and what is not. And I hope you have got all the Max stuff you wanted. No, of course you can't have, but I am sure we may look forward to some very toothsome dishes from your *cuisine*. Do you communicate at all with David Cecil who is writing the life, or are you both driving on different lines? I hear of him from time to time from his and my old pupil John Bayley who has just published a formidable book called *The Romantic Survival*—the sort of book that always makes *me* feel thoroughly humiliated, because it is equally clear that the writer knows exactly what he means, and that I don't. And you too, I have no doubt, with such a book before you, resemble Pope's politician after coffee and 'see through all things with your half-shut eyes'. But when I meet a sentence like 'It is an inflexible application of the romantic egotism that the poet's universe must be purely his own' I know what the words say but seldom what they quite mean. You, as a Yeats expert, will perhaps be interested to read the W.B.Y. chapter. Bayley is a delightful chap who manages to be indubitably highbrow but nothing at all of a prig. His wife is Iris Murdoch whose brow is practically out of sight in the empyrean. I met her in his rooms at New College. A woman in college-rooms in my day would have meant a major explosion. So perhaps Tuppy H. wasn't entirely right in his complaint that *every* change was for the worse. The prurience of the Victorians was tremendous. They were convinced that for a girl to drive in a hansom with a man could end in nothing but rape. Their salacious imaginations, as you see, easily out-soared the facts of space and the exigencies of posture.

I wish I had known George Wyndham (Pamela's uncle) though John Bailey used to say that with all that charm and conversational gifts etc. you never got to know him any better, and after a delightful evening's talk on Monday, he might easily not recognise you on Friday. Anyhow charm to-day is *out*—practically a word of abuse. And if it often was bogus, well plenty of what has replaced it is bogus too, just as the Hemingway toughness is really just as sentimental as Kipling's strong silent subalterns.

To-morrow we have a governors' meeting at Woodbridge School and the chief item on the agenda is the HM's temerarious action in sacking the son of the Governor of Reading Gaol, and the Governor, who is 'strong upon the Regulations Act' like his predecessor, maintains that this action is agin 'em. Judging from the correspondence the HM has blundered into that major house- and head-master's error of putting on to paper things which he knows about the boy but couldn't prove; and of course if you want to burst any paternal blood-vessel, all you have to do is to imply that a boy of seventeen who spends forty-five minutes with a perfectly respectable girl and so is late for lock-up and climbs into the house is a criminal past reclaim.

But it is quite possible that the HM has more on his side than appears.

Sunday, 8 September 1957 *Le Train Bleu*

Since Sunday is my proper day for writing to you, and this train is at the moment stationary in the Gare du Nord, Paris, here goes!

I left the Riviera last night after a final week of heavenly weather—clear blue skies and warm waveless sea. Yesterday, my last day, was the loveliest of all, and I spent most of it in the water. The night before I dined out on a terrace looking across to the sea on which a full moon was reflected. This morning, after a goodish night in a sleeper, I woke to a blood-red sunrise, since when steady rain has fallen. Neither I nor my companion has hat, coat or umbrella, so what should have been an agreeable stroll through Sunday morning Paris (the train stops here for two hours) turned into a rush into a café opposite the station, buying the English papers *en route*, and a speedy return to the warm dry train. Last night's dinner was superb, and I have high hopes of lunch, which is due half an hour after we start again. My holiday, not having been arranged to last more than a few days, turned out to be the most restful and delicious for years—no mail, almost no work (though I've done a bit to Oscar and to Diana Cooper's MS), any amount of swimming and idleness and sleep. What horrors shall I find waiting for me in Soho Square this evening? However frightful, they will, I hope, be tempered by at least one letter from you. (Write to Bromsden this week. I shall be there on Friday evening.) I'm still reading and enjoying Maurois's book about the Dumas family, and you must certainly read it when it's translated, as it assuredly will be. Their lives (the Ds') are exactly like an exaggerated mixture of their works.

5 p.m. Mid-Channel

The lunch was so excellent and so large that the rest of the journey to Calais passed in a pleasurable coma. This boat is full to the scuppers, and we are lucky to have seats in the bar, and a sailor engaged to get us places in the train.

I can't remember how much I told you about Cagnes. It lies between Nice and Cannes, about three miles inland. Most of the streets are luckily impracticable for cars, and many are worn and very steep steps. The drainage system (if such it can be called) is truly mediaeval, and each narrow passage is bordered by two malodorous and flowing streams. A derelict cottage labelled CASA VERDE has had its appellation deftly changed by some wag to read CASA MERDE. Our villa was relatively unsmelly, and nicely placed on the hillside with three terraces and a garden of its own.

I think I shall finish this at Soho Square tonight and post it to-morrow, so as to surprise you on Tuesday morning. This bar is swarming with people buying cheap cigarettes.

Monday afternoon *Soho Square*

Alas for good resolutions. The train from Dover was unaccountably more than an hour late, and by the time I had got here and unpacked, I was ready for bed. To-day has been fully occupied in simply *reading*—not even answering—the huge pile of letters which has accumulated in three weeks. Your two were the highlights, and I will answer them properly next Sunday. I also found a number of birthday presents waiting for me, including three bottles of champagne from an author(!) and a fine cigar-case from the office staff. The trouble, I can see, will be to keep it filled.

September 13 (Friday!) 1957 *Grundisburgh*

Your picture of Cagnes is delightfully vivid. 'Casa Merde' gave me a good grin. I suppose the inhabitants are as impervious to smells as everyone must have been before Jonas Hanway was born (I never quite remember whether it was the W.C. or the umbrella that he invented, but I am in the summer-house, my reference-books are forty yards and more away over open country, and a thick prohibitive rain is falling). It is odd that the age when all such things were hideously primitive and obtrusive was the age of the Olivias and Violas, and Walter Scott's immensely refined heroines, whereas *now* it is the *ritiratas* which are refined and the ladies who are coarse, so they tell me. (How *proud* some of the young ones are when they utter words which would have made their grandmothers faint—like prep. school boys over their first 'damn'!)

I am now reading, believe it or not, *The Pilgrim's Progress*, not exactly for fun, but I have to set a paper on it for next year—only two questions of the essay type, but it is fatal not to know something about a book set, and I have not read it for half-a-century. A plebiscite at Columbia University placed it *top* of the list of 'the most boring classics,' which I find hopeful, as nobody supposes that Columbia University can be anything but plumb wrong about anything. Wasn't Dulles an alumnus? Still, I must admit that after forty pages or so, I did have the best night's sleep I have had *in years* (American!). I should hate to find myself on the same side as Dulles.

It is time we met again and had a long crack, feet on fender (there are no fenders in Suffolk). A monstrous suggestion to make to an overworked publisher—or would be if I didn't know you have that engaging and impressive trait of M.R. James, i.e. however busy he was, he was always ready for a talk.

15 September 1957 *Bromsden Farm*

No letter from you yesterday, to my sorrow. It's sure to arrive tomorrow after I've left, and I shall find it on Friday evening. Here, as in London, I found vast arrears of bills and letters, but in both places I am now pretty well up to date, except for unread MSS, which I feel increasingly disinclined to tackle. No word has been heard from Duff since he set out for Germany nearly a fortnight ago, to take some photographs for a retired Major living in Cornwall. Duff answered an advertisement of his in *The Times*, and I fear the expedition may cost a pretty penny, since D. apparently failed to get either an advance payment or anything in writing from the gallant gentleman. Comfort is beginning to worry at the lack of news, but I tell her that we should surely have heard if he was in trouble. Meanwhile, after all, the *Sunday Times* show signs of printing his article on Russia next Sunday. They also asked if they might print some of my introduction to the G.M. letters: naturally I agreed: so next Sunday's issue may prove to be the Hart-Davis Benefit Number. On the other hand it may not.

Last week was mainly taken up with full mopping-up operations, but was brightened by the enclosed letter,[1] which my natural boastfulness prompts me to send you: please send it back for my archives. Of course I accepted, with a mixture of pride and trepidation. It's an appalling baby to have to hold just now, but if I can cope with it I can cope with anything. And there's still a hope that the rest of the committee (the impish R. Fulford *et cie*) may revolt.

You and I, who agree so often about all literary matters, differ only in this: I take all precautionary steps to avoid reading Leavis and Aldington or witnessing such plays as *Look Back in Anger*, whereas you positively seek them out. This peculiarity of yours I take to be, not so much masochism, as some ridiculous idea that if you don't attempt all this nonsense you will quickly be out of the swim and on the shelf. I assure you, dear George, that there was never an unlikelier candidate for the shelf than you, with your ready sympathy and unresting interest in life and letters. Please let this idea sink in, and stop torturing yourself with these dreary excursions.

While I was away, Peter hit on an idea for his next book—an account of the siege of the foreign Legations in Peking during the Boxer rebellion of 1900, together with the story of the relief expedition etc. I encouraged the plan, which please keep for the moment under your hat.

Your praise of the Autumn List is particularly welcome, since the travellers complain that almost all the books in it are totally unsaleable except in the West End of London. Do they think I cater for Asia Minor?

I think that in some way Alfred Douglas was a cousin of George Wyndham, and must therefore have been related to Pamela, though perhaps, let us hope, only by marriage. Did I tell you I got three new Wilde letters from America last week? Quite good ones too.

I knew Ronnie Knox slightly during my short time at Oxford. He was then R.C. Chaplain to the University, and I remember a bare beautiful room in the Old Palace containing the minimum of furniture

[1] From Harold Nicolson, asking me to succeed him as Chairman of the London Library Committee.

and a barrel of beer. Of him I remember little, save that he was friendly and unalarming. When I, or perhaps someone else, asked him if he knew the egregious ex-priest Montague Summers (then living in Oxford), R.A.K. said that Summers lived with a little boy and a huge dog. Plenty of people had seen Summers and the boy, and Summers and the dog, and the boy and the dog, but nobody had ever seen all three of them together. Which I much enjoyed.

I have just finished the Maurois book on the Dumas family, which I loved. Edmund B. has taken his family to Belgium for a fortnight, so for the moment I mercifully have the flat to myself. Even the dearest guests can become a burden if there isn't much space, and one is constantly busy already.

20 September 1957 *Grundisburgh*

I hope you have heard from your son now. I hate gaps of that kind, and get a good deal of chaff from my family (wife included). It is in the blood. My father to his last day was convinced in the teeth of all experience that a telegram always announced a disaster, and naturally was a little peeved when, as often as not, it contained a S.O.S. for money from one of his sons. The optimism of the young is superb. *I* should be quite sure that the retired Cornish major is an impostor. I shall search the *S.T.* next Sunday.

I love your blunt refusal to see anything remotely laudable in my senile endeavours not to be left 'with the rear and the slaves'. But I can't help it. So many silly old men—contemporaries of mine—stick firmly, and, what is worse, complacently, in the mud of their ancient tastes and prejudices, all 'sealed of the tribe' e.g. of Sir A. Munnings. You will be derisively amused to hear that for the last two nights my evening book has been Colin Wilson's *Outsider* and my *bed*-book Trollope's *Prime Minister* which I hadn't read—a diet as it were of caviare and sago. And I find the sago far the more toothsome. Frankly I can't really see what *The Outsider* is all about, and my acquaintance with the young man's mentors—Sartre, Roquentin, Meursault, Krebs and Co is of the flimsiest possible. Household names to you I expect? Colin Wilson gives the impression of having read everything, but I gather from some of the reviews that, like the River Finn in my garden, the depth is not as great as it looks.

I revelled in the George Moore letters and wished they had gone on longer. I wonder what hers were like. Why have I got the feeling from his letters that I shouldn't have liked her very much—whereas one can't help admiring and liking Lady Emily L.? The picture of Lady C. in the Twenties gives her a pretty *hard* look.

I say, Rupert, the London Library! Have you as it is *any* spare five minutes in the week—and at this moment when the poor old institution is under fire from those marble-hearted fiends of the Inland Revenue. I beg you to *delegate* shamelessly from among your vast acquaintance. Lawyers no doubt are already active. Couldn't that admirable Somervell help? It couldn't surely take much to upset that sickening ass who said that the L.L. was a sanctum for the well-to-do, as it didn't bring Shakespeare to the costermongers. I have never belonged, as I never lived in London, but my grandfather was one of Carlyle's first associates in it. I once met old Hagberg Wright, who struck me as the rudest man I had ever seen—till I met his brother Almroth who easily dead-heated. But I have no doubt H.W. did fine work for the Library. How I do hate the recurrent evidences of a general trend to diminish, pare away, destroy all standards save those of the damned 'common man'. The last decades have given him confidence, and in any controversy his voice rings out loud and bold like that of faithful Chapman. I smell the same trend in your travellers' complaint about your list. At the same time it is very odd that pretentious stuff like Colin Wilson's should at once find a huge and hungry public. What *do* they think they get out of it? Anyway thank God for R.H-D and Co and all their works.

I have just finished reading 150 papers from Barbados on *Northanger Abbey*. Not very good—but I gave high marks to the candidate (I think a girl!) who, describing J.A's Bath, wrote 'They kept their balls in the Pump Room.' 'Held' of course would have done all right, but idiom is a little fragile in Barbados.

Here is a tiny and not very interesting mystery for you. Watson—following several others—says that Moses Jackson was a rowing and running blue at Oxford. Well, he wasn't. No Jackson of any sort ever rowed for Oxford. There was a hurdler S.F. Jackson (also of John's) in

March 1877. But Moses didn't go up till the autumn of that year, so it could not be he. I don't think this discovery throws a light of very startling novelty onto the relations of Moses and A.E.H., but the latter hated inaccuracy of any sort, and after all would spend half a morning crossing a 't' in Manilius, and no sane man can really say *that* is very important.

I met the Lord Woolton at dinner last week. A genial old boy, with a pleasant but intermittent little Lancashire burr. My cousin Oliver can mimic it to the life. He (Oliver) also told me that Winston never could resist ragging old Woolton, who (like a sensible man) never said much in the Cabinet. W., who knew his knowledge, say of Egypt, was not extensive, would say, if E. was on the tapis, 'Well, gentlemen, I thank you for your opinions; but I feel that in order to be sure that we have a wide and balanced view of the matter, we should like to hear what Lord Woolton thinks about it.' Mischievous old urchin!

22 September 1957 *Bromsden Farm*

Today has been hot and sunny, and once again the ever-growing grass has taken all my time. With us this autumn has brought more mists than mellow fruitfulness: not a single apple, pear, plum or damson (after last year's plenty), and only half-a-dozen shamefaced quinces to harvest. Have you any fruit?

Did not Sir John Harington invent the W.C.? See Strachey's admirable *Portraits in Miniature*. If so, perhaps Jonas Hanway was responsible for the umbrella. God bless them both!

A wise old Dublin lady, I was told last week, says that when she was young, people's class was a constant subject of discussion (Is he a gentleman? etc.), while their sex-lives were never mentioned. Now every sexual peculiarity is hotly debated, while the subject's U-ness or otherwise is rapidly becoming tabu.

At long last we have heard from Duff in Germany—a glum letter full of the boredom of driving two thousand miles alone and camping out in weather too dull for the photography which is the excuse for all this gallivanting. Anyhow he seems all right, and should be home this week—I hope perhaps in time for a dinner on Wednesday at the

Whitefriars Club, over which I am presiding, and after which P. Fleming is to talk on his trip to Russia.

If you seriously think that only a nightly tussle with Colin Wilson's pretentious rot can prevent your sharing the tastes and outlook of that foul-mouthed old Philistine Munnings, I suppose I can only leave you to your unnecessary mortification. After one glance through *The Outsider* I decided it was both unreadable and not worth reading. You'd better buck up: his next book appears tomorrow!

So glad you enjoyed the Moore letters. Wasn't Harold N's review in today's *Observer* fine. I agree with every word of it, except perhaps the 'usual astringency and taste'.[1] There have also been excellent notices in the *Daily Telegraph* and *T.L.S.* (the latter written by Joe Hone, Moore's biographer). As you doubtless saw, the *Sunday Times* (which is now too heavy to lift) printed a good chunk of my introduction (for which they promise twenty-five guineas), and postponed Duff's Russian piece on the grounds that father and son together would sink one issue.

Last week my secretary disappeared with flu, the Asian variety for all I know, and this delayed and complicated everything. On Wednesday I reluctantly agreed to dine with my father at the St James's Club—reluctantly because such evenings are generally a waste of silence and complaint. This one didn't begin too well, since we drank our sherry with a retired Civil Servant, who was slumped incoherently in a chair with a big glass. Just before we were due to go up to dinner your cousin Oliver arrived, at his most amusing, and dined with us gaily. My father perked up considerably, ordered grouse and champagne, and laughed heartily at O's many good jokes and stories. Of the retired Civil Servant O. said: 'He has been fighting a losing battle with Haig & Haig for years.' He mimicked Winston brilliantly and was altogether delightful. (As I daresay you know, his son Anthony is a partner in my father's stockbroking firm.)

Next day I lunched with Roger at Boodle's. He was very *affairé*, carrying piles of half-answered letters about with him, but very charming. We talked of the London Library, the Lit. Soc. and so on. At three I left him in Piccadilly, still carrying a mass of paper, on his way to a very necessary haircut. He won't be back from abroad in time

[1] Referring to my editing.

for the Lit. Soc. dinner. By all means let us have a preliminary crack. Will you come to Soho Square about six? I shall just have had (that afternoon) my first London Library committee meeting in or near the chair, so you may find me wild-eyed and wondering.

I haven't added a footnote to Oscar for *weeks*, and shall soon begin to feel overwhelmed by the work outstanding there if I don't get a move on. But how and when? I am reading proofs and manuscripts like mad already—now in the midst of Druon's next historical novel, *The Royal Succession*, which needs a certain amount doing to its translation before it can go to the printers. And soon Diana Cooper will turn up, expecting me to have transformed her MS., and I haven't—oh dear! Already newspapers and magazines are bidding high for the serial rights, but there won't be any book to serialise if I don't invent some free time to do it in.

26 September 1957 *Grundisburgh*

I think I told you how much I enjoyed the George Moore book, and I am glad to see the reviews—all that I have seen—noticed the great care and fullness of your notes as well as the really beautiful 'get-up' of the book. Do these things get rewarded in this world as surely as they will be in the next? I have noticed a tendency (not apropos of *this* book) to that line which invariably gets one of my many goats, the line briefly of 'Who is interested in George Moore now?' Am I right in feeling in these letters a slight but definite and recurrent touch of the *pathetic* about the old man? There are of course many glimpses of his naughtiness, but all the sting has gone out of his malice. I wonder why he had such a strong admiration of Edward VIII, and so firm a conviction that he had only to go to Ireland and there would be no more 'troubles'. I suspect that he was like many other men, great in some way or other, of one of whom it was said that he was right about everything except politics.

I hasten to tell you that we too have no fruit—hardly an apple, no plums, and our pears are playing their annual joke of falling off the trees while still as hard as bullets. Damson and quinces we never did have any truck with—*one* fig appeared and was solemnly presented to me. No law is more invariable than that a dry April and May means a wet August and September. Yesterday we had twenty-four hours' rain, but that typhoon or hurricane was *entirely* out of breath by the time it came here, and in sober fact:

> Each chimney's vapour, like a thin grey rod,
> Mounting aloft through miles of quietness,
> Pillars the skies of God.[1]

The weather pundit was quite sheepish about it on the air, as they had so confidently promised a rousing gale for all of us.

Of course you are right. I had quite forgotten Strachey's excellent paper. Hanway gave us the umbrella—and was stoned in the streets when he first produced it. And your old lady was quite right about class and sex. It is well worth remembering that Mrs Gladstone whispered in Gladstone's ear that she was about to have a baby. He was thunderstruck—and would have been still more so if he had known it was going to be Mary Drew—really rather a dreadful woman—scheming, bossy, conceited, humourless.

I am glad you have news of Duff. I shall keep an eye open for his article. I am quite sure it will be more readable than most of that portentous paper. How right you are on Colin Wilson. Unreadable. But *how* did he make everyone read him? You, as a publisher, must have an inkling. I haven't. Some of the reviewers surely rather lost their heads. As an antidote I read in bed Trollope's *Prime Minister*—about 940 pages—with great satisfaction for the best of all reasons. *You want to know what is going to happen.* Full of faulty art and psychology and all that, no doubt, but immensely readable—and what else matters?

I am glad cousin Oliver was in good form; he is very good value on such occasions. You didn't, by the way, say anything of my thrilling bit of research over Housman's friend Jackson. Can it be that you didn't think it thrilling? Incredible.

[1] From 'Dusk' by A. E. (George Russell).

I'm sorry I failed to applaud your detective work: well done, my dear Jackson! The author has had such a pasting in the press that I scarcely like to report such a thumping inaccuracy to him. The only ways in which good editing and production get any reward in this world are (a) by creating, through good reviews, that intangible (which is said to be an asset until you try to cash in on it) called 'goodwill,' and (b) by tempting authors to try and get their books similarly handled. When new writers turn up out of the blue I always ask them why they've come to *me*, and they nearly always say it's because the books look so nice. Nevertheless, shoddily produced best-sellers butter more parsnips!

Duff turned up exhausted at 10.30 last night. He had left Düsseldorf at 5.30 in the morning and driven three hundred miles before trans-shipping the car (a friend's) to Dover. With the resilience of youth he seems quite recovered today, except for a heavy cold in the head. I only hope he doesn't give it to Comfort, for she always takes *weeks* to shake one off. When I was young I caught cold almost weekly, but now I haven't had one for seven years. Let's hope I don't boast too soon. Duff's trip has cost him (or rather *us*) £65, and my hopes of recovering any substantial part of this from the Major in Cornwall are slender. Adam went cheerfully back to Eton on Tuesday, and we are daily expecting the usual letter asking for a collection of heterogeneous and unpackable objects to be posted immediately—a squash-racquet, a pair of roller skates and a pocket microscope.

I have *no* inkling of why Colin Wilson's rot suddenly broke loose, and certainly nobody was more surprised than his publisher, who had expected a minuscule sale and perhaps some *succès d'estime*. I daresay some of the bright boys will be gunning for C.W.'s next book. I have never read *The Prime Minister*, or indeed much of Trollope's mountainous *oeuvre*: I am keeping it until I am as unbuttoned as he is, but oh, when will that happy day arrive? I have just read a 400-page manuscript first novel about a rape in the suburbs of Philadelphia, and the awful thing is that it's very well done. As you say, no narrative is any good unless you want to know what's going to happen. That's why *Marius the Epicurean* and the later George Moore novels are no good: one couldn't, as they say, care less what is coming.

Last Wednesday I took the chair at a dinner of the Whitefriars Club (a dimmish sub-Fleet-Street affair) and Peter spoke about his trip to Russia. He is far from a polished speaker, but he answered questions well, and I think they all enjoyed it. The room in the Cock Tavern, Fleet Street, was hellish hot. The gossip is that P.F. is to be offered the editorship of *Punch*: there's probably no truth in it, and I doubt whether he'd take it on.

One day I had a drink with darling old Lady Emily Lutyens. At eighty-three she is frail but full of humour and interest in everything. She told me her fan-mail was keeping her busy, and she is conducting an immense correspondence with a passionate admirer in Karachi. She is thoroughly enjoying her old age, which makes it always fun to be with her. I only wish she could write another book, but I fear she has no more material.

For the first time since 1939 Peter has reared some pheasants—four hundred and fifty survived the hatching, they say—and now our garden is like a fashion parade of cock pheasants in fine plumage and all unconscious of their approaching doom. My Uncle Duff always preferred autumn to the other seasons, but I can't agree with him. Give me the cuckoo and the bursting buds of promise. I hate vests and sweaters and overcoats and fogs and cold. To cheer myself up I have bought Gordon Craig's memoirs, though I haven't yet had time even to begin the book. It should have lots of peripheral Wilde information in it. Craig's father, E.W. Godwin, decorated Oscar's house in Chelsea, and there are a number of letters to him. Last week I got hold of a water-colour painted by Oscar when he was twenty-two—a landscape, or rather seascape, in the West of Ireland. It might have been painted by any of our aunts, but his signature on the mount lends it a factitious interest. I'm having it photographed. Every day in the office I write up to a dozen letters about Oscar, asking for letters, information and so on, so, while my footnotes linger, my Wilde file bulges more and more.

Your son must be amassing a lot of valuable experience—much more than he would have in my day—a bit of silver lining to the clouds of this century. I do hope that plethoric *Sunday Times* will open one of its thousand columns for him and so pay for it that, contemplating your depleted bank account, you may say with Ulysses 'though much is taken much abides'.

Meanwhile I further risk your derision by telling you I am reading a book of L--v-s's. It is a form of masochism—a word of which I know the spelling, but not the pronunciation and am by no means secure of the meaning. Anyway I am indulging that odd human propensity to bite on an aching tooth. But I hasten to add, I am also humbly and admiringly reading Verlaine and shall probably interlard my conversation next Tuesday (I am rather George Moorean about putting the right figure to the day of the week) with French aphorisms, e.g. (though not from Verlaine) '*Le déluge n'a pas réussi; il reste un homme*', which I happened upon recently. It suits my misanthropic mood, which is invariably strong at the time of party conferences. But I am (at last!) going to take the hint given by your invariable silence on such topics, and say nothing about politics, knowing as good Johnsonians should,

> How small, of all that human hearts endure,
> That part which laws or kings can cause or cure.[1]

Not that the second line passes any more sweetly into the ear than Browning's 'Irks care the cropful bird' etc.

Is editing *Punch* much catch? I doubt it nowadays. My daughter and other of the young praise it, but there are a humiliating number of jokes in it that defeat me—mostly the captionless pictures—and when explained the joke puts no strain on my ribs. ('Old, Master Shallow'!) Is there still a plump head waiter at the Cock? And did you have lark pie or am I confusing it with the Cheshire Cheese? And shall you be at the Johnson Club on Oct. 17? Because I shall.

I agree with you about autumn—a sad month October, all its beauty rich with decay, the dead leaves, the shortening, ever more

[1] Johnson, 'Lines added to Goldsmith's *Traveller*'.

slanting sunshine—no, I can't understand liking out of doors as in the spring. When the day is shut out one's spirits rise, but no thanks to the season. How grim the next five months must have been in, say, William the Conqueror's time, and how much he must have welcomed 'the simple bird that thinks two notes a song'.

6 October 1957 *Bromsden Farm*

If I (fond, impious thought) were a psychiatrist, I should doubtless feel certain that, for all your protestations, you have for some time been sub-consciously shying away from our meeting on Tuesday. First you repeatedly referred to its date as the 9th; then, when I pointed this out, you ended your letter of last Thursday with a reference to 'Tuesday week'! It is on *this very next Tuesday* that in fact I shall expect you at Soho Square. It's possible that E. Blunden may be there: I don't yet know his movements: but you will like him anyhow.

I daresay that if you succeeded in fighting your way through the forty pages of to-day's *Sunday Times* you came on my Duff's long-awaited article: not at all bad, I thought, and they seem pleased with it. The boy is delighted, and this early success will certainly strengthen his determination to be a journalist. He goes up to Oxford (Worcester) next Thursday, but I have a feeling that three years there will seem too long to him: we shall see. Adam has got flu at Eton—one of seventeen in his tutor's—but doesn't sound too bad. My daughter got leave from her rich employers in Upper New York State and spent last week-end most enjoyably with the Caccias in the Embassy at Washington. She was particularly impressed by the multitude of servants—a circumstance unknown to most young people of to-day. Which reminds me that in my childhood Sir Lionel Phillips, a South African millionaire friend of my father's, had *seventy* gardeners at his house in Hampshire. Somewhere I have a snapshot of myself, aged two, sitting on the lawn there, beside Robbie Ross.

Meanwhile I am correcting the proofs of Jonah's new book, *Georgian Afternoon*. This is the third time that I have read most of it, and I'm enjoying it as much as ever: there is a good case to be made for its being the best of the three, if one can compare them at all: certainly it has much more *variety* than either of its predecessors: I shall await your verdict eagerly.

Have you ever tried to burn substantial lavender-bushes? Yesterday we uprooted some ten-year-olds which had grown too big, but the splendid bonfire we made of them keeps going out. A preliminary crackle and flame soon turn to smoke and fizzle: I shall have to try again next Saturday.

Alas, I can't manage the Johnson Club on the 17th. I hate to miss you, but the paper doesn't promise to be a rib-tickler.

Despite what I wrote in my last letter, I have read enough Trollope to know for certain that you are right about him, and that one day I shall enjoy his whole panorama to the full.

I gather that the somewhat totalitarian election at the London Library has passed off with some show of unanimity (one name only put forward: approve or else . . .). Last week I was accosted on the stairs by Esmond de Beer. He said he was delighted I was the new chairman, though he would have preferred Veronica Wedgwood. Naturally I agreed heartily.

Last week I was visited by an old Oxford friend (hitherto penniless) who told me he had just inherited £900 a year from his uncle. 'Hadn't he any children?' I asked. 'He had one daughter,' said my friend, 'but she was electrocuted by an electric iron at Beersheba.' He went on to tell me that this girl was a dipsomaniac who married a commercial traveller in whisky, and together they emigrated to Israel. Ironically enough, the only job the husband could get was in charge of the waterworks at Sodom! They saved his salary, and every three weeks went up into Jerusalem for a blind. Which only goes to show that truth is stranger . . . it's an ill wind . . . etc. Would you believe it?

9 October 1957 *67 Chelsea Square*
S.W.3

There is something faintly but decidedly absurd about this, but as you know very well, there is about a great many of the things that are worth doing. And I just want to show those foolish persons who think that I can have nothing particular to say to you to-day, are wholly without understanding. It may be in the blood.

I was particularly pleased to meet Edmund Blunden again. One gets in his company the same—what shall I call it?—easeful satisfaction that one used to get from Monty James. It comes—doesn't it? —when great kindliness of heart accompanies great distinction of mind. I remember M.R.J's cordial listening to a story which I knew he knew, and on another occasion to a man making assertions about the history of some cathedral which were so wrong that they *had* to be corrected, but how gently and beautifully M.R.J. did it. And now *I* am telling *you* about impressions E.B. made on me which you can't possibly want to hear. (As for my chuckle-headed messages to you about the Lit. Soc. date, 'Old, Master Shallow' is the only defence. I kept on confusing it with another gathering *next* Wednesday, though all the time it was securely in my book.) How unfailingly enjoyable these Lit. Soc. evenings are—the only fly in the amber being that so much excellent talk with A. and B. means that one can't have the same with C. and D. Harold N. was delightful, as was John Sparrow. I am not sure you ought not to have put me next to old Dunsany instead of shouldering all the burden yourself, but of course you would do that.

And the evening ended in the glow of Peter's kindness in taking me to this very door. He and Bernard F. insisted on waiting till they had actually seen the door open to my key—rather as debutantes were escorted home in Edwardian days with 100% protection of body and soul. Their belief that I am hardly to be trusted to look after myself in London is as benevolently obvious as it is justified. Cyril Alington once told me that in his study one morning he twice heard the same remark outside. It was 'Thank you; I think now I can manage for myself.' One was made by his father *aetat* 88, the other by his youngest son *aetat* 3. Both were being helped down the stairs.

I delight in your exact and generous appreciation of E.B., and I need hardly tell you that your feelings were warmly reciprocated. So glad Peter and Bernard saw you home so carefully: you're most precious and valuable to us all, you know: and you'd be surprised at the number of Lit. Soc. members who have referred to you as a fine acquisition. I do hope we succeed in getting Jonah in: he would love it so. I'm afraid Tommy thinks him a bore, and maybe others do too, but he's a pet, and *literary* as well, which is more than some of the members and candidates are.

E.B. is not in the Lit. Soc. because he lives (alas) in Hong Kong and is very shy of gatherings. H. Nicolson would, I fear, be vastly bored by the Johnson Club—but then aren't we all? Nevertheless it's surely a *good thing*.

On Wednesday I went to the opening of a new bookshop in the City at 11 a.m.—lots of authors and publishers, with champagne flowing. Then I lunched at the Ivy with Neville Cardus. He was as sympathetic and amusing as ever, but he is now so deaf that one has to shout, and since he whispers conversation is a bit of a strain. Then to a meeting of the Royal Literary Fund. Thursday was even busier. Two long sessions with Jonah, going through his proofs and persuading him not to write 'in the case of' all the time; lunch at the Travellers' with Allen Lane, the head of Penguin Books; a visit from a leading American librarian; drinks with Nancy Cunard; after which I had to preside at a dinner of my old club the Society of Bookmen because their new chairman had flu. After all that I was almost too exhausted to sleep.

Yesterday I took time off from the garden for writing and reading—the whole of an engaging gossipy book about Barrie in the theatre, 100 pages of Matthew Arnold's letters (humour was not his strength), a charming new book called *Tea with Walter de la Mare*,[1] a chunk of Gordon Craig's reminiscences, and part of a detective story. To-day has been digging and a huge bonfire. I much enjoyed the profile of Humphrey, but could have done with more about his father.

[1] By Russell Brain.

Well, if one must be likened to something in the vegetable kingdom, I suppose an oak-tree is about the top specimen.[1] At all events no one could ever describe a pumpkin, however giant, as 'branch-charmed by the earnest stars'.[2] I wonder who does those 'profiles'; I thought this one was definitely good—well-written, and perfectly accurate in its facts—which, I suppose, they have the sense to get from the victim?

And of course it immensely pleases me too to hear that the Lit. Soc. does not disapprove of your last candidate. All men love praise. Some pretend they don't. They lie—though of course there is that superb double-barrelled snub which the world's leading curmudgeon (Housman) spat at the scholars who commended him: 'You should be free to praise me if you did not praise each other'. Apropos of whom, I have just been reading John Wain's *Preliminary Essays*. A pretty good young man, isn't he? A few coat-trailing sillinesses but, as Johnson said of some woman, he has 'a bottom of good sense,' and his brilliant flashes are neither too many nor self-conscious. And, in its way, I have never read a more brilliant bit of comparative criticism than his demonstration of the superiority of Wordsworth's 'Lucy' to a Housman poem on a similar theme. Do read it and tell me if you agree with me that it is frightfully good.

I do hope Jonah's candidature will go through. I too have heard him called a bore, but always referring to him as he was thirty or forty years ago. He isn't the first Balliol scholar to have been called that, and as I used to take pleasure in telling my pupils, the young are very often much greater bores than the old. Anyway I am blowed if Jonah is a bore now. Those two books could not have been written by a bore.

I didn't know E.B. lived in Hong Kong, but suspected he might dislike gatherings—like Henry James when John Bailey asked him if he would be Chairman of the English Assocn. Do, for your own pleasure, look up his letter (P. Lubbock's 2 vol Edition. Vol. II p. 279).

[1] George had been so described in the *Sunday Times* profile of his son Humphrey.

[2] Keats, 'Hyperion'.

He was having that painful bout of shingles at the time, and couldn't use a pen; he apologises for having to reply 'as I can and not at all as I would,' and then dictates a perfectly beautiful letter of courtesy, and humour, and understanding, and masterly English—the finest flower of civilisation, you might say. I once told Percy that this letter was my favourite; he agreed about its excellence.

But probably all this is perfectly familiar to you. When is your James-Wells correspondence coming out? It should be of the greatest interest—the contact of two first-rate minds at absolute odds about art and life and everything else. It is difficult to understand V. Woolf's inability to see anything good in H.J's writing, or so she said to Lytton S. By the way J. Wain is refreshing about L.S's impertinence in deriding Clough—a much better man than himself. That is of course the (probably, in the end) fatal flaw in Strachey, viz that through his not having any basis of principle or belief, his satire often gives an effect of *tittering*. Don't you feel he is always showing his superiority both to his subject and to hoi polloi? But of course one must face the fact that Max B. greatly admired his writing, and there wasn't much M.B. didn't see through.

Poor luck yesterday. In the bus to Ipswich I noticed a small child of extravagant plainness, its face, like that of Sulla in Plutarch, resembling 'a dish of mulberries sprinkled with flour'. I was recalling that lovely remark of Groucho Marx when someone said he hated to see a small boy crossing the street, 'I hate him anyvay.' This child sensed my feelings and retaliated suddenly by being sick—only just missing me, but in such cases a miss is as good etc. Shortly after the bus ran, rather wildly but with a good deal of splintering of glass, into a tree. Later on, after I had got out, I heard that a lady's shopping basket, into which she had thrown her cigarette, had caught fire. It must, in fact, have been the very opposite of 'The Celestial Omnibus'.

19 October 1957 *Bromsden Farm*

Raking and burning leaves today made me think of Laurence Binyon's fine poem, 'The Burning of the Leaves', written in his old age. Do you know it? If I could find my copy I'd write it out for you, and for my own pleasure, but so far it eludes me. I love bonfires, don't you? Everything about them is most satisfactory.

Just now I took down *Ego 8* (*your* one), opened it at the page where a G.I. describes Bedford as 'a cemetery with traffic-lights,' and read on happily. Surely these volumes will survive—or is our pleasure in them bound up with our knowledge of most of the people and events?

Did you hear that Eisenhower lost interest in the satellite as soon as he found it wasn't pitted like a golfball?

The London Library occupies much of what I must call my thought. Did I tell you that what it needs is an *additional* £12,500 a year? Last week I had an idea so simple that it can scarcely succeed: namely, that if I can persuade the English publishers to *give* their new books to the Library, instead of selling them as now, the Library will at once be £3500 a year better off. I feel fairly confident of cajoling *most* of the publishers. Then I plan to raise £100,000 in cash, which would bring in another £3500 a year. That would leave us £5500 short—which would be more than covered by an increase of two guineas in the subscription (there are 4000 paying members). As a first attack on the £100,000 I have applied to the Pilgrim Trust, which luckily meets in November. If they would give us a substantial sum in annual instalments, we might even get off paying rates, since one of the reasons for the failure of our first appeal was our inability to prove that we are supported 'wholly or in part by annual voluntary contributions'. I'm sure my only hope of persuading the publishers is to beard each important one in his office—about forty of them! There's a certain irony in trying to collect all this money when I'm at my wits' end to pay my sons' fees at Eton and Oxford. I hope all this doesn't bore you. Please keep it all to yourself. Do you know any rich people who might contribute? Now I must go to bed. Last night I slept uninterruptedly for ten hours, and I'm hoping for much the same tonight. Then, after more raking and burning, I'll return to the charge.

Sunday evening, 20 October

Another nine hours' sleep left me feeling quite limp this morning—there's nothing like prolonged rest for relaxing one to the point of total immobility—but a further bout of raking and bonfire has set me up.

I fear the James–Wells correspondence, when it appears early next year, may disappoint you: what there is is good stuff, with James coming out on top after the row, but so few letters (especially of Wells's) have survived that the book is scrappy and rather unsatisfying.

Surely the great thing about Lytton Strachey was his style and literary artistry: I'm sure that's what Max so much enjoyed. But as a historian, or critic of anything after the eighteenth century, he is worthless, I should say. The only thing is to enjoy his books as purely literary essays, and give them pretty good marks.

Last week I dined out three nights running—with a publisher and party at the Garrick, with the Ransomes at Putney (an hour's journey each way), and with the Jepsons in Bayswater—all agreeable but exhausting. Next Friday I am nipping up to Yorkshire for two days on the moors, and to shut up the cottage for the winter. So write to Soho Square and I'll send you a line from my hilltop, which I have never before seen in October. My heart leaps up at the thought. Oh for several months there! Then I should surely get something on to paper. As it is, I can hardly keep pace with the chores and engagements, so that Oscar is neglected, and that mass of miscellaneous information about his life and times, with which an editor's head *must* be brimming, grows dull and gets forgotten, and will have to be painfully regained. I know it was silly to take on so big a job amid my bustling life, but it's exactly the sort of job I like, and can do, best. Soon perhaps I'll be able to break the back of it. Unfortunately my tidy mind is worried by tasks unfinished. You mustn't mind my pouring out all this tiresome nonsense to you: there must be, alas, much rough to very little smooth. I do hope you'll be at the November Lit. Soc. I can't face Dunsany without my oak-tree!

23 October 1957 *Grundisburgh*

This should catch you before your northern trip. How pleased old Agate would have been at one perceptive reader spotting the permanent value of the *Egos*. They are everlastingly readable and full of little plums like the one you quote on Bedford. It always seems very odd to me that he should have so much admired Arnold Bennett's *Journals* and modestly hoped that the *Egos* might be *almost* as good. The A.B.'s are full of entries like 'Long and interesting talk with F. Swinnerton,' and little or nothing more.

I forget whether you knew A. Bennett. A good man, I always think, with all his limitations and blind spots. You knew, of course, that it was G.M's *A Mummer's Wife* ('squalor and sordidness turned into poetry') that showed A.B. what could be done with the Potteries. (Some day you can produce *one* of your anthologies 'Things told me by G.W.L. which I knew already'. Only less damning than the one M.R.J. *could* have compiled 'Stories told to me by A. B. and C. which I had originally told them'.)

Bonfires, *yes*, superb; the smell, the noise, the spectacle. One of the human tests surely—i.e. a man who does *not* love them must, in some way or another, be a poor creature. And what a sense of humour they have, viz just when the smoke is thickest and one is poking and prodding, the wind suddenly and momentarily changes and one retreats rapidly, but not rapidly enough, choking, eyes smarting, smut-bestrewn (which sounds like a line of Hopkins), a figure of fun. I don't know the Binyon poem; please send a copy when found. I ask brazenly, because I know that you, like me, frankly enjoy copying out something you really like. But wait a moment. You won't have any time, with the L.L. now on your back. How typical it all is—you personally bearding one publisher after another—suave and tireless and resourceful. The result, I suppose, of having a profile rather like Wellington's, and an energy entirely like Napoleon's. The £100,000 ought to be exactly the sort of thing to appeal to a rich American. But perhaps they are all buttoning their pockets against a slump. A jumpy lot to be leaders of the modern world. I wish I knew some rich people. The richest man in Suffolk is Sir C. Fison, and if only the L.L. dealt in chemical manure rather than in books, hopes might be bright. Shall I attempt with him a bold flight of fancy or analogy on the lines of books being manure for the mind? At the moment Ipswich is all bye-electing, and the air is thick with platitude, recrimination and mendacity, none of which, they tell me, changes a single vote, though Hailsham's oratory was the most popular. What rot it all is!

Sleep! Yes, but I suppose *in the end* all those hours are restful? I have long outgrown all that stuff about eight hours and beauty sleep, etc. and hug the recollection of Horder's dictum that many people sleep much too much. Though I grant you a post-prandial snooze is not eschewed as rigorously as it might be.

I agree with you, *toto animo*, about Strachey. His style is perfect joy, and it is only when one has come across a fairer and kindlier handling of one of his victims that one is resentful of his tittering, however mellifluous. And with all his admiration, Max said some pretty sharp things about Bloomsbury—though mainly about those sillies who crabbed 'beauty' and intelligibility.

Did you look up the James letter to J. Bailey? I should hate to think you were too busy to enjoy its rich savours. Don't you like that positively granite refusal to compromise the tiniest jot of artistic principle that underlies all the honey and flowers so lavishly poured out by the most courteous of men? Of course he and H.G.W. were not talking the same language. But what an artist H.G.W. *might* have been—'"Wasn't it them Greeks as used to be so clever?" "*Used* to be," said the young man with dark scorn.' Was ever so much sociology packed into so few words?

I shall be at the November Lit. Soc. Put me next to Dunsany. One must earn one's keep.

P.S. Can you imagine Mrs Sidney Webb ever enjoying a bonfire? Or Mrs Humphry Ward? H.J. would have, so long as he didn't have to build it.

27 October 1957 — *Yorkshire*

I entirely agree about Arnold Bennett's journals, though our disappointment may be partly due to the prudish timidity of their editor, old Newman Flower. According to Hugh Walpole, N.F. was so appalled by much of what he found in the journals that he published only brief extracts, and those the safest. Perhaps we shall one day be given the whole works. I did know A.B. slightly, and liked him—most people did.

I still haven't run that Binyon poem to earth, but shall hope to copy it out for you next Sunday. Knowing exactly where ninety-nine out of every hundred of my large collection of books are, I am entirely baffled when one goes astray—and this is only a pamphlet. I dare say that the bonfire H.J. enjoyed most was the one at Lamb House, to which he consigned the great mass of the letters he had received from everybody (it scarcely bears thinking of), retaining only a few choice exhibits. He seemed to think that this indiscriminate holocaust would also destroy all the letters *he* had written to everybody, but naturally they had all been kept; my friend Leon Edel has already examined more than seven thousand, and still they come.

Last week began with a dinner-party, in (of all places) the Artillery Mansions Hotel, of three booksellers and five publishers, to discuss privately the troubles of the trade. I need hardly tell you that, though some agreed on the diagnosis, no two could begin to find a remedy acceptable to both.

On Tuesday evening I had sausage-rolls, cakes and coffee at the Royal Photographic Society, among a mass of hideous and unknown persons, whose skill with a camera has, I hope, compensated them for other things. Thus refreshed we all trooped upstairs to a lecture by Alvin Langdon Coburn. Does the name ring any bell? He is an American of seventy-five, who came to England in 1905 and has lived here ever since. He was a remarkable pioneer of photography—being an artist who happened to use a camera rather than a photographer trying to take artistic pictures. A great hero-worshipper, he managed to photograph most of the leading writers, artists, musicians, etc. from 1905 to 1912, and published the results in two remarkable books, *Men of Mark* and *More Men of Mark*. I'll show them to you on your next visit. In 1907–8 Henry James asked him to take special photographs for frontispieces to the big New York Edition of H.J.'s works, which he did. It was through this that, perhaps eight years ago, I got in touch with him, and we then published a new edition of Stevenson's *Edinburgh* with Coburn's photographs. (Have you seen that book? If not I'd love to send you a copy.) Anyhow I got quite fond of the old boy, and long ago promised to attend this lecture, which was to celebrate his fifty-year-old membership of the R.P.S. What I didn't know till I met him among the sausage-rolls was that his wife had died ten days before, after fourteen weeks of great pain, during which he nursed her alone in their little house in North Wales. She died on the forty-fifth anniversary of their wedding. He told me about it quite simply, and said that his faith was sustaining him. Incidentally he is a terrifically big bug in Freemasonry. The lecture was dullish, but in the circumstances rather touching. Afterwards I escaped fairly soon.

On Wednesday I attended, as Vyvyan Holland's guest, a dinner of the Saintsbury Club in the Vintners' Hall. A long succession of most potable wines, Laver was in the chair, and Douglas Woodruff made an admirable speech about Saintsbury, wine and letters. It seemed unprepared, and gave the effect of a fine artist improvising on the piano.

On Thursday afternoon I attended a conference in the Chambers of the London Library's leading Counsel—none other than Mr Geoffrey Lawrence Q.C., the saviour of Dr Adams! He is a small neat man, with a quiet, well-modulated, exact voice, and (it seemed to me) unusual clarity of mind. We discussed our coming appeal before the Lands Tribunal (probably in January) and I rather enjoyed it.

After all this (and entertaining E.B. in the flat in the intervals) you will realise with what joy and relief I drove off at dawn on Friday and got here at lunchtime. Since then the weather has steadily worsened, and the wind on this hilltop almost blows one over. But I have a roaring fire and an Aladdin lamp, and would like to stay here for months.

31 October 1957 *Grundisburgh*

What disservice these mealy mouths do us all! Like the premature Alanbrooke reminiscences, an emasculated Bennett *Journal* merely stops, or at best postpones, the full and (probably immensely) interesting publication of the whole lot. You will see, but I shall not, the full story of the abdication as told by Baldwin. I forget where it is deposited, but it will not be published till all concerned are dead. An idle biographer too can queer the pitch; I remember how cross old Agate was about O. Elton's inadequate life of C.E. Montague, which, he said, merely prevented a good life being written, and gave no good picture of C.E.M. I was pleased to see from various reviews that

R.H-D's outstanding merits as an editor are getting general recognition. And there will soon be a third string to your bow, as the Lord Leconfield, who frequents the London Library, speaks very highly of the new chairman.

Yes, how horrible to think of that bonfire of letters at Lamb House—almost as bad as the destruction of Byron's memoirs. Why do men do these things? Because any amount of stuff in the letters to H.J. must have been vastly interesting and not in the least personal to him.

Coburn? No, the name rings no bell. Cameron is the only name I associate with photography—apart from Lewis Carroll photographing small girls naked, John Everard doing ditto to larger girls, and so acting with horrible appropriateness up to his name (to show how far we have travelled from the days of Q. Victoria, let me tell you it was a young lady who told me this fourth-form ribaldry). I look forward to seeing *Men of Mark* and Stevenson's *Edinburgh*. I like to think of you among the sausage-rolls. They ought to be much better than they are; the pastry is always too dry, and the sausage lacking in flavour. Someone should start a revival—a golf-club perhaps could become famous for its sausage-rolls—like Westward Ho for its curry, Rye for its buttered eggs, and somewhere I forget for its potted shrimps (Lytham-St Anne's?).

The only lack in your letters is that you don't *always* specify the fare at your dinners and lunches. This should always be done—as, indeed, you once stated, and are the only man I know beside myself who knows exactly what old Heythorp had for his Last Supper. (And there are thin-witted, pince-nezed, flute-voiced men with Adam's apples bobbing up and down like the glass ball in Victorian lemonade-bottles, who presume to look down on Galsworthy!)

You will be contemptuous or cross, or both, when I tell you I have just read John Osborne's *The Entertainer*. My dear Rupert, I feel (almost) scared—like Douglas Jerrold in convalescence, reading *Sordello* and terrified that, though physically mending, his mind had gone; he handed the book to a visiting friend, and when he saw him completely baffled, ejaculated 'Thank God' and sank back into refreshing sleep. *The E.* is utter, hopeless, outrageous rubbish, and yet T.C. Worsley in the *N.S.* uses words about it like 'brilliant', 'dazzling', 'gripping', 'masterly' etc. My only hope is that it looks and sounds quite different on the stage. In the study it is puerile. I suppose the enormous increase in the numbers of those who *can* read accounts for the popularity of so much rubbish; discrimination is still to come. They tell me the young flock to concerts, and Humphrey is always infuriated by the wild applause of every item, good bad and indifferent. Quite different somehow from what is meant by a catholic taste—like old Saintsbury's who saw the good in Paul de Kock as well as in Milton. Not that he liked everything. I seem to remember his always having a down on Byron, but it was the B. of *Childe H.* and not of '*Donny Jonny*', as B. called it himself.

You didn't, I suppose, ask G. Lawrence about Dr Adams. I once asked the late Mr Justice Lewis about Greenwood, and he said it was quite certain Greenwood poisoned his wife (he was a junior for the prosecution) but got off because his daughter swore she had drunk from the relevant bottle of Burgundy. She disliked her father but wasn't going to have him hanged. I must go to another trial; I always enjoy them. Not a murder perhaps, though I have seen one or two very decent murderers in court—and one in Whitechapel, pointed out by Dick Sheppard, to whom he had confessed. He was never caught, and according to D.S. was a very good fellow. I like to listen to judges, especially the sort of judge whom somebody once described as 'belonging to the great traditional line of judges. He was slow, he was courteous, he was wrong.' (Quoted by J. Agate, who added 'the exact opposite of me, who am rapid, rude, and right.')

P.S. Poor old Dunsany. It gave me quite a turn. Not that he need be pitied.

3 November 1957 *Bromsden Farm*

More bonfire-work yesterday, but last night's heavy rain extinguished everything. Rain fell almost incessantly during my week-end on the moors, but I was warm and cosy and busy and blissfully cut off from the telephone and other intrusions. Never on any account disclose my Yorkshire address to anyone, particularly not to dear Roger:

if he discovered how comparatively near it is to him he wouldn't rest until he had disturbed my solitude in the friendliest way. I *still* can't find the Binyon poem, but it's worth waiting for. It was one of the only two poems my dear old Egyptologist uncle-by-marriage Walter Crum ever copied out. The other consisted of this extract:

> The solemn peaks but to the stars are known,
> But to the stars, and the cold lunar beams;
> Alone the sun arises, and alone
>   Spring the great streams.[1]

Friday was E.B.'s sixty-first birthday, and I invited some twenty of his family and admirers to a buffet lunch at Soho Square (sausage-rolls and all). It went with a swing and I'm sure pleased him. By the way, I've just discovered that he would dearly love to be a member of the M.C.C. Is there anything we can do, any string we can pull, to get him in? He plans to return finally to England in 1961, when he will be sixty-five. His cricket writings, in prose and verse, are, as you know, first-rate, and his knowledge and love of the game you have witnessed. Please give the matter your careful attention.

I see that all my efforts to wean you from deliberate mortification of the wits have failed: *The Entertainer* indeed! What a misnomer! All seem agreed that only Olivier's virtuosity keeps the play on, and I can see that he welcomed a change to shine in something so far from his normal playground. When I was a student at the Old Vic, the performances of Shakespeare alternated with those of Opera. Every night the stage-door was besieged by lunatic girls with autograph books. One night, as I was signing my quite unknown and worthless name, I asked the girl whether she came to the Opera too. 'Oh, yes.' 'What's the Opera company like?' I asked. 'Oh', said she, 'just like the Shakespeare company: it doesn't matter whether they're good or bad; we clap them just the same.' Such, I fear, is the mentality of much of the great new reading public which universal 'education' has brought forth.

By the way, I see that a new book (possibly the last) by one of my favourite living authors has just appeared: *Last Tales* by Isak Dinesen: order it from your library at once. And then her two earlier volumes,

[1] From 'In Utrumque Paratus' by Matthew Arnold.

Seven Gothic Tales and *Winter's Tales.* Sometimes she writes under her own name, Baroness Blixen. She is an elderly Dane, reputed to take drugs—but a smashing good writer. My Uncle Duff thought that one of the stories in *Winter's Tales,* 'The Young Man with the Carnation', or words to that effect, was one of the best short stories ever written. She certainly makes most modern practitioners look pretty thin. I hope you don't know her books already: it will be such fun for you coming to them fresh.

Poor old Dunsany: I bet he's boring the wings off the angels with disquisitions on rock-salt and the semi-colon. I now feel rather smugly satisfied at having endured his last Lit. Soc. appearance (and incidentally touched him for a pound which he had owed me for more than a year). We now have *three* vacancies, and so far *seven* candidates. This time last year I was interested only in your candidature: this year it's chiefly Jonah I'm concerned about: Dunsany was all for him, but perhaps the younger members won't be.

Last week produced *six* new Oscar letters, one of them twenty-two pages long, though he didn't get as much on his pages as we do on ours. My son Duff lectured on Russia (with coloured slides) to the Literary Society at Eton on Friday and thinks it was a great success. Yesterday he shot with Peter, who was taking time off from his mother's humiliating litigation. How silly can people be? There are surely many more enjoyable ways of spending large sums of money.[1]

THE BURNING OF THE LEAVES
by Laurence Binyon[2]

Now is the time for the burning of the leaves.
They go to the fire; the nostril pricks with smoke
Wandering slowly into a weeping mist.
Brittle and blotched, ragged and rotten sheaves!
A flame seizes the smouldering ruin and bites
On stubborn stalks that crackle as they resist.

[1] Mrs Fleming, aged seventy-three, was being sued by the Parsee Marchioness of Winchester for, among other things, the 'enticement' of the ninety-three-year-old Marquess.

[2] By kind permission of Mrs Nicolette Gray.

The last hollyhock's fallen tower is dust;
All the spices of June are a bitter reek,
All the extravagant riches spent and mean.
All burns! The reddest rose is a ghost;
Sparks whirl up, to expire in the mist: the wild
Fingers of fire are making corruption clean.

Now is the time for stripping the spirit bare,
Time for the burning of days ended and done,
Idle solace of things that have gone before:
Rootless hope and fruitless desire are there;
Let them go to the fire, with never a look behind.
The world that was ours is a world that is ours no more.

They will come again, the leaf and the flower, to arise
From squalor of rottenness into the old splendour,
And magical scents to a wondering memory bring;
The same glory, to shine upon different eyes.
Earth cares for her own ruins, naught for ours.
Nothing is certain, only the certain spring.

7 November 1957 *Grundisburgh*

First of all, will you and your lady dine with us on *Thursday Nov. 21 at 67 Chelsea Square*? It is the house of Alexander and Mrs Hood (my daughter) who have lent it to us for a day or two while they are in New York. If that day is impossible what about Tuesday the 19th? Not *quite* so good as the 21st but very, very far from bad. I have an inkling that Mrs R. does not come to London during your working week, and if I am right, will you yourself come? *Moreover,* we shall have your clock with us, and you could take it to S. Square with you after the dinner (long after). It all seems *to me* a good plan, but (like the late Field-Marshal Robertson) you may 'think different'. Let me have a p.c. with 'Oh well, yes, I suppose so' or 'Good God, no!' on it; you won't be writing a letter this week-end as we meet on Tuesday. Is the ritual of my calling on you before the Lit. Soc. intolerable?

Because that is what I should love to do. But it may well be that if I didn't you would be doing some important and profitable business.

I like the Binyon poem *very* much. It has all the smell and the noise and the spectacle of *the* bonfire (do you remember how cross Wordsworth was when someone referred to his writing a poem to *a* daisy instead of *the*?). And the reflections which rise therefrom. There is a grim note in the last two lines, for it is hard sometimes to believe that the mess *homo sapiens* is making of his affairs may not some day soon be found irreparable. Even so spring will return—like 'the august, inhospitable, inhuman stars, glittering magnificently unperturbed'. I imagine even Khrusch will take some time before annexing those stars which are over two million light-years away.

The other favourite of your Egyptologist uncle was also one of Charles Fisher's (killed at Jutland 1916). The very last time I heard the stanza declaimed—or even mentioned—was in 1912 on the top of Glaramara—'Thin, thin the pleasant human noises grow' . . . Old Mat laid them dead sometimes, though at others—! What do you, what can anyone, say about:

> Look ah! what genius—Art, Science, Wit,
> Soldiers like Caesar, Statesmen like Pitt;
> Sculptors like Phidias, Raphaels in shoals,
> Poets like Shakespeare—beautiful souls![1]

I mean, isn't that the writing of a complete and incurable *ASS*? By the way, another tiny fragment Charles Fisher was fond of was from old Daddy:

> So have I, not unmoved in mind,
> Seen birds of tempest-loving kind
> Thus beating up against the wind.[2]

Where did I read recently (Humphry House?) a strong commendation of at least three stanzas in a very old favourite of mine, the hideously

[1] Matthew Arnold, from 'Bacchanalia: or The New Age'.
[2] Wordsworth, 'To a Highland Girl'.

named 'Extempore Effusion on the death of James Hogg'?[1] Granted that

> On which with thee, O Crabbe forth-looking,
> I gazed from Hampstead's breezy Heath . . .

is lacking in thrill, what about 'The rapt One' . . . etc., and 'Like clouds' . . . ? What does E.B. think of them? He gave me the impression the other day of knowing practically all the poets have written. Of course he ought to be a member of the M.C.C. and I have written this very day to Harry Altham (the Treasurer) to find out if there are any ways and means. I am not immensely optimistic, as they are pretty rigid about their rules and regulations, and the austere shade of Lord Harris still broods morosely over the Committee Room. Some years ago there was an attempt to get Cardus in; I did what I could, but to no avail. But N.C. would, I suppose, be found by many much less likeable than E.B. Another difficulty is that many excellent cricketers are practically illiterate, and have no realisation of the obvious truth that it is the poetry of and in the game which keeps it alive. Tom Richardson had as little poetry in him as Achilles, but the sight of him bowling in 1896, or rather the mere thought of it, set N.C. writing stuff with the glow and quality of

> Stand in the trench, Achilles,
> Flame-capped, and shout for me.[2]

Isak Dinesen. I must confess that she is to me what the Holy Ghost was to the Corinthians. Why have I never heard of her? I shall order her stories at once.

[1]Nor has the rolling year twice measured,
From sign to sign, its steadfast course,
Since every mortal power of Coleridge
Was frozen at its marvellous source;

The rapt One, of the godlike forehead,
The heaven-eyed creature sleeps in earth:
And Lamb, the frolic and the gentle,
Has vanished from his lonely hearth.

Like clouds that rake the mountain-summits,
Or waves that own no curbing hand,
How fast has brother followed brother,
From sunshine to the sunless land!

[2] By Patrick Shaw-Stewart (killed in action 1917).

I do hope Jonah gets in. Apart from him, you must tell me on Tuesday how to vote. Old Dunsany had a striking career, and I suppose was, in his prime, a considerable man. So was Herbert Spencer, but that didn't prevent Carlyle describing him as the greatest ass in Europe, and in the American class as a bore.

How frightfully tiresome that law-suit must be for Peter. I never met his mother, but his father was one of the best of my Eton friends. What a caddish business cross-examining is, but I suppose it is all part of the game, and both judge and jury discount it. Asquith was a balanced and kindly man, but an old lawyer-friend told me he was a brutal cross-examiner—shouted, if you please, at the witness, which is hard to believe. Old Russell, of course, was a mere bully at the job, which I should have thought his skill made unnecessary. How heartening to remember the slightly squiffy subaltern who met his recriminations at the club after the subaltern had bogged his whist-hand: 'All right, all right, old cock! But remember ye're not in yer bally old police-court now!' Very salutary for the Lord Chief Justice of England.

I have been re-reading some of those delightful essays of G.M. Young which you gave me. How tragic that he should have collapsed. Writers of real quality are rare. His picture of old Gladstone is masterly. What a pity the 'noble old foghorn' was before the days of wireless and gramophone. Nobody believes in spell-binding who didn't see or hear the spell-binder. Tell a young man about W.E.G. or about Chatham and 'Sugar'[1], and he laughs with the implication that it wouldn't have impressed *him*.

Note I. Don't bother to write unless you can't come or face seeing me at 6.30 on Tuesday. I will assume you can if I don't hear.

Note II. Did you know geese are very fond of music? They flock into the corner of their pen when my wireless is on. They were clearly indignant at Schubert's symphony being unfinished.

Note III. How thin and slick and *indistinguishable* many of Haydn's symphonies are! Didn't he write too many?

[1] Alderman Beckford, when opposing the tax on sugar, had been interrupted by laughter. Pitt the Elder followed him and began his speech 'Sugar, Mr Speaker'. A hoarse laugh. 'Sugar, Mr Speaker', thundered Pitt. In the dead silence that followed, 'Sugar, Mr Speaker' he whispered in his most dulcet tones. 'Who will laugh at sugar now?'

Let us have a standing arrangement that on Lit. Soc. nights you will come to Soho Square at *six*, or as soon after as suits you. Press and pull every bell: they have just been mended and we must keep them in practice. I'd love to dine with you in Chelsea Square, but alas Comfort cannot get to London: her teaching keeps her tied here all term-time, and some child or children in the holidays. So may I come alone? Tuesday 19th would suit me much better than the Thursday, if you can manage it. Tell me this Tuesday. All this and the clock too!

E.B. (who may be present at S.S. on Tuesday) does indeed know almost all English poetry by heart, and not only the greatest. He is a firm Wordsworthian—and so am I. Inspired by your references I have just re-read the 'Extempore Effusion': those three stanzas are superb. Many other great poets have written as many bad poems as W.W. (Tennyson for one), but has any other managed to hide away tremendous lines and stanzas in mediocre poems? What about:

> My former thoughts return'd: the fear that kills;
> The hope that is unwilling to be fed;
> Cold, pain, and labour, and all fleshly ills;
> And mighty Poets in their misery dead.

And then back to that egregious old leech-gatherer. Did the old gaffer realise that these matchless lines were any better than the lame verses that surround them? I doubt it. I have never known a poet or writer who had any idea which was their best work: each poem or other work is inextricably bound up with the mood and circumstances of its creation.

I fear your championing of E.B. will make no impression on the dragons of the M.C.C., but it's angelic of you to try. It was I who asked you years ago to try and get Cardus in. His deafness doesn't seem to stop his hearing music, only other people's conversation.

I so agree about Haydn and his symphonies. As Sarah Bernhardt said, when asked by a reporter what she thought of the ten commandments, 'Zey are too many.' I can't tell one from another and am bored by all.

Sunday morning, 10 November 1957

More bonfire this morning with Adam, home for Long Leave, very tall, pale, long-haired and with a sniffling cold, but charming as ever. He wants to specialise, God help us, in Science! Duff has got flu at Oxford, but is confident of turning out next Saturday for Coleridge's Old Boys v. the Field.

Last Monday I was Stephen Potter's guest at a dinner at the Athenaeum, at which he spoke on English and American Humour. Menu enclosed: it tasted slightly better than it sounds, and was helped by a decent bottle of claret each. If you and I had been set down to invent a list of A. members, respectable, even distinguished, but deadly dull, we should scarcely have improved on the enclosed list. My other neighbour was an agreeable retired Treasury official with a deaf-aid (they all looked like that) called Sir Frank Nixon. During the speech he passed me a note asking me to a party, but I politely refused.

On Thursday I dined with the Haleys at their flat in Ashley Gardens—very richly furnished. At dinner I sat next to an immensely forthcoming neighbour of yours—Lady Albemarle. She spoke of you as a recluse, and I see your point. According to *Who's Who* she seems to run everything. Lord A. was there, also Hartley Shawcross and wife: she very attractive, but he rather supercilious. Also Joseph Harsch and wife: he an ace American radio-commentator. Good stuffed veal, and first-class cold chestnut pudding. The H's are teetotal but the wine was good and ample. Sir William talked about the B.B.C. and *The Times*, of which next day's first edition arrived at 10 p.m.

14 November 1957 *Grundisburgh*

That was again a wonderfully pleasant evening, and the appearance and demeanour of Sir Cuthbert were positively *chirpy*—there is no other word for it. I cannot help feeling that for the general friendly atmosphere the Secretary must be largely responsible. (Apropos of Sir C. my father always maintained that after a certain age many old men were rather *pleased* by the deaths of their contemporaries, if not great friends. Dunsany? Hush!) I was glad to meet E. Link later again;

his discourse was full of flavour. He has sent one of his boys to Eton and another to Winchester, after long and shrewd consideration of their respective characters. It all sounded very sensible; though the Ancient of Days' impish propensity for upsetting human plans may send all agley.

I thought poor Peter F. seemed in rather low spirits and no wonder. I have a feeling his mother may come in for some harsh treatment, or at least comment, by the judge Devlin. According to my brother-in-law, old Winchester is and always was a horrible man—though anyone remotely 'enticeable' at ninety must compel some respect. M.R.J. loved to tell how some old King's don over a century ago had to give up his Fellowship when they found out he was married. Well he was only, so to speak, married in the sight of God, and was reported by a friend as saying '. . . and let me tell you, sir, that it's a damned lugubrious thing to be turned out of one's fellowship for fornication at the age of eighty-four.'

In your last letter you commented on what poor critics poets are of their own poetry. I would add 'and often of anyone's'. Are you familiar with *The Oxford Book of Modern Verse* chosen by Yeats? I don't know it well and in fact rather left it when I found his *wicked* omissions—including some of the best of his own early stuff. And what of Auden's *insufferable* comments on Tennyson, which so infuriated D. MacCarthy, and good Dame Sitwell's contempt for Emily Brontë's 'Cold in the Earth', which actually led to Q, in his senility, omitting it from the new *Oxford E.V.* (though I *believe* he left in 'Meet we no angels, Pansie?'—but I may be wrong). What does surprise me is how many of FitzG's alterations to Omar are *not* improvements, because his palate, though eclectic, was a fine one. And am I right in thinking Henry James's re-writings were often unfortunate?

I have not yet heard from H.S. Altham about E.B. and the M.C.C. Of course there should be a possible entry for such people; it needn't be any larger or easier than the secret way into the Capitol (was it?); but you must know how sticky these old foundations are. (A pupil of mine was almost relegated to outer darkness once because, at the age of about twenty-five, he played a round at St Andrew's in sand-shoes.)

I never go to London without finding all those *faces* deeply depressing. 'Zey are too many.' A trainload in the rush-hour—silent, hurrying, mud-faced, wrapped either in private worries or in the evening-paper, but not *interested* in either, not really alive in any full sense—don't they devitalise you? My brother-in-law says if you live in London you don't notice them. I suppose they all have got to that point and so look as they do: Suffolk faces are often hideous, but they *are* faces: these aren't.

Give my regards to E.B. I never meet him without feeling a better, nicer, wiser man. I don't say even then that I am particularly good, nice, or wise, but, well, my uncle once heard a preacher enlarging on the miracle in the valley of Hinnom, and describing how when God breathed upon the skeletons they were 'elevated to the condition of corpses'. Consider me as having reached the corpse stage.

N.B. Dinner Nov. 26 (Tuesday) 8 p.m., don't 'dress', 67 Chelsea Square. Agenda: (1) to eat drink and be merry (2) to tire sun with talking (3) to add to the public stock of harmless pleasure (4) to meet Sir Terence and Lady Nugent (5) to meet Lord Leconfield (6) to take home cottage pendulum clock and till further notice to hear in every tick of it a message of affection and goodwill from your host and hostess.[1]

17 November 1957 — *Bromsden Farm*

I'm sure you're right about Cuthbert, and that the death of a contemporary, better still of a junior, is the breath of life to him. Did you realise that Eric L. was far from sober when he arrived? Not that liquor makes him tiresome—only loud, vehement and repetitive. I think I told you his eldest daughter had lain unconscious for seven weeks after a road accident. Clearly E's arrival in London was the signal for tension to be released in alcohol. After leaving the Garrick he collected some friends from the Savile and spent most of the rest of the night in some frightful nightclub. Next morning he woke when the bar opened, spent three hours over lunch, and arrived at Soho Square at 4 p.m. very merry indeed. Somehow I propelled him to some nearby

[1] I still (1979) do.

binders, where by means of astonishing will-power he managed to make a creditable shot at signing sixty copies of a limited edition of his new book. With great difficulty I found a taxi and sent him back to the Savile. Next morning he turned up, very sick and sorry, but bearing a letter from his wife to say that the child had at last spoken, and there was hope that her brain wasn't affected. You can work out the moral of this story if you're clever enough.

Yeats's *Oxford Book* cannot be taken seriously, except as a gloss on W.B.Y. Great writers are almost the worst critics, being egoists and usually interested only in their own work.

I entirely agree about the London street faces, and try not to look at them more than I must. Certainly a pretty girl stands out like a good deed in a naughty world.

Since I saw you I have been to lunch in the inner sanctum of *The Times*. Bidden by Lord Astor of Hever to a 'small intimate party', I found myself one of twenty-two men, including the Archbishop of York (who, as Bishop of Durham, so tenderly supported the Queen through her coronation). I was between old Mr John Walter (whose ancestors founded the paper and used to live in that very house). He is eighty-four and almost stone-deaf, so that was, as they say, tough sledding. On my other side was dear Laurence Irving, who made up for Walter. Food and drink were good and plentiful. The other guests were mostly directors of the paper and big business executives—all very unexpected, inexplicable, novel and amusing. Haley was of the party, but I scarcely got a word with him.

Yesterday Duff came over from Oxford and went on to Eton, where he played the Field game for F.J.R.C's old boys against the School (who won 5–0). At the same time Comfort disguised herself in black face and gipsy clothes to tell fortunes at the village fête. This left me happily alone, and at last I got back on to my Oscar Wilde treadmill. It took me some time to *get* back after so long an interval, for to do this sort of writing properly one must be steeped in the period and all its details. Often a neat footnote seems to have put paid to some event or individual, but then it or he crops up again and must be cross-referenced. Don't imagine I don't like it all, but it's hellish difficult to fit into the maelstrom of my ordinary life. E.B. leaves for Hong Kong at the end of the month—sorry to go, I fear.

I am greatly looking forward to the 26th, and only hope I shall end up in a fit state to carry proudly home my precious clock.

I have just read the latest novel of a man whom I consider one of the best living novelists—R.C. Hutchinson: have you read anything of his? If not, try this one: it is called *March the Ninth*, and though not his best is still jolly good. If you like it, then try *Shining Scabbard*, *One Light Burning*, and *The Unforgotten Prisoner*. He is an Englishman of roughly my age, and all his best books are about some European country to which he has never been: apparently his imagination has to be kindled by being far-flung. His long novel of the Russian Revolution, *Testament*, is astonishingly good, and he always writes beautifully. Here's another treat in store for you!

20 November 1957 *Grundisburgh*

That is an epic passage about E. Linklater. I had not realised the situation at the L.S. but merely noticed that he had plenty to say and that it was worth listening to. I am glad his daughter mends, but I see now he has just lost his father (or mother was it?). I expect, like most Scots, he is pretty good about the bludgeonings of fate. The Savile sounds a more convivial spot than it was forty years ago when I was a member, and some older man described it—I am sure unjustly—as 'the home of seedy prigs'. I didn't—being a very shy young man—much like its custom of a communal dining-table, and you took your chance about your neighbour. I lunched there only once and found myself next to Ray Lankester who talked of nothing, as far as I remember, but the criminal folly of the club management in having no fires just because the month was August. I had vaguely hoped I might go home with some valuable light thrown on the next world. Doesn't Max B. write somewhere of the importance of *not* meeting great men in the flesh? And what about Charlotte Brontë's horror on seeing Thackeray munching and enjoying potatoes! And many surely must have had a shock to see how dirty Tennyson's hands were.

I have a pleasant little malicious triumph coming next Saturday when the Revisers and Setters of English Literature papers in the

G.C.E. meet. The Revisers comment on our papers and, as you might expect, often, in our opinion, pick holes which aren't there. The Chief Reviser has objected to a judgment on Keats in a paper set by me, and an explanation of a Shakespeare phrase. Well the judgment is that of Bridges and the explanation taken word for word from a note of C.H. Herford, both of whom, I imagine, knew what they were talking about every bit as well as this amiable old bumble-bee.

I suspect I am steadily becoming more curmudgeonly and narrow in this matter. There are five Dickens novels I love, but last week I re-read (after half a century) *Bleak House* and am now in *The O.C. Shop*, and I find his obvious and admitted defects outweighing the genius; and as for the humour—well now, do *you* go chuckling about Soho Square whenever you think of Mrs Jellyby, and Mrs Pardiggle, and Messrs Chadband and Turveydrop, and Mrs Jarley and Dick Swiveller? B. Darwin does, I am sure—just as *I* do about Pecksniff and Mrs Gamp and the Wellers and Mrs Nickleby etc. Why is this? Why do I, in my bones, *know M. Chuzzlewit* (for all Macaulay called it 'dull and frivolous') to be *leagues* ahead of *Bleak H.*? Why do I love reading about Mr Squeers and don't a bit want to go on reading about Quilp? These are questions 'spirit-searching, light-abandoned', as one of the literary ladies said to Martin C.—and the worst is still to come, for little Nell is still alive.

P.S. What does G.M. Young mean by 'the ribbon-development' of George Moore's English? I am always coming across these brilliancies and so often failing to see that their point is all that sharp. On the other hand, almost everything G.K.C. says of Mr Pickwick gets me, so to speak, where it tickles. E.g. on that old suggestion that the idea of Mr P. was really Seymour's: 'To claim to have originated an idea of Dickens is like claiming to have contributed a glass of water to Niagara', and his play on the idea of Mr P. always being 'taken in'. Isn't his book on Dickens of quite extraordinary merit? It always seems so to me.

Please give E.B. my warm regard to take back to Hong-Kong *if you think he would like to have it.* Such things do fail sometimes. One of the least attractive episodes of old Gladstone's career was after his last Cabinet had said good-bye to him, practically all of them in tears.

He himself wasn't, and used to refer to them as 'that blubbering Cabinet'. I sometimes wonder whether George Meredith was right in saying W.E.G. was a man of marvellous aptitudes but not a great man. But who told me recently of A.J.B. in a company who were all telling of the most frightening moments in their lives? Battle, and fire and flood, crag and torrent, etc cropped up again and again. A.J.B. knew nothing of any of these, but merely recorded Mr G. looking at him in the House, *and his eyes widened.* But that brings me to La Rochefoucauld: 'Why have we memory sufficient to retain the minutest circumstances . . . and yet not enough to remember how often we have related them to the same person?' I have a suspicion that I heard the A.J.B. story with/from you.

24 November 1957 *Bromsden Farm*

Stay me with flagons, comfort me with apples! A glance at the enclosed will show you what I mean—but more of that later. I've always understood that it was *Frank Harris* who, on being taken to the Savile Club at a time when the conversation and the cellar were famous, said: 'The worst thing about this club of faded prigs is that you can't get a decent glass of wine.' ('faded' is better than 'seedy', don't you think?) I expect you know that the S.C.'s present premises in Brook Street were formerly the home of 'Lulu' Harcourt. When Max was asked how he would describe the *décor*, he said: '*Lulu Quinze*'. And I'm certain I've already told you of J.B. Priestley's superb remark, 'The *Savage* Club is the place where dirty stories go when they die.'

It's so long since I had time to read Dickens that I'm in no position to debate with you. The last I read was, funnily enough, *Bleak House*, about five years ago, and I loved it. All the same, *Martin Chuzzlewit* is my favourite too: when shall I have time to enjoy it again? By the way, if you haven't read Humphry House's book *The Dickens World*, do get it from the library.

The best description of George Moore's later prose compared it to one of the large French rivers—wide, placid, seemingly endless, no current, occasional felicities on the bank, shallow, and *just* moving.

This applies to *The Brook Kerith*, *Héloise*, *Aphrodite in Aulis*, etc. I suppose that by 'ribbon-development' G.M.Y. meant to indicate an endless projection without apparent plan or meaning, as opposed to a single building designed compactly as a work of art—but I agree that it isn't a wholly happy phrase. You have never before told me that story of A.J.B. and W.E.G. So there!

Last week was gruelling. Those two dinners alone, on consecutive nights, almost laid me out. Food and drink were on both occasions first rate. Lionel Fraser (although a teetotaller and non-smoker) was a perfect host, and it was amusing for once to mingle with all the riches of E.C.4.

The Trinity Hall evening was cosier, beginning at the High Table in their lovely little hall, and ending in the Combination Room with a horseshoe table and a little railway for the decanters. I was lucky to sit between the only two representatives of the humanities, my host Graham Storey and Brooke Crutchley, the Printer to the Cambridge University Press. Later, when we were scattered among the Professor of Metallurgy and other such terrors, conversation became tougher. When at last I got to bed at 12.45, my hostess's hot water bottle had filled my bed with water. Luckily I know her very well and she was still up to produce a complete new set of bedding. (The same thing once happened to me in the icy house of the Geoffrey Keyneses. I daren't wake them, and spent the rest of the night in my underclothes, bath-towel and goodness knows what.)

On Friday I lunched with Cecil Beaton at his exquisite house in Pelham Place (butler and all). The other guests were Nancy Cunard, Mrs Ian Fleming and W. Somerset Maugham, older and more lizard-like than ever. His stammer is as bad as ever, and he now clicks his fingers with annoyance when he can't get the word out, which adds to the confusion. When he came in, Cecil said: 'Willie, you look so sweet I shall kiss you'—which he did. The food was again delicious, but I am getting surfeited—comfort me with apples.

29 November 1957 *67 Chelsea Square*

Yes, that *was* an evening! It is odd and pleasant to commend one's own provender, but really we were all guests together enjoying the hospitality of Alexander and Diana from overseas via Janek and his admirable wife, who beam all over when told what we and the others thought of the little banquet.

The Reviser who found fault with C.H. Herford's explanation of a Shakespeare phrase climbed gracefully down—or at least as gracefully as is within the power of a seventeen-stone man with a broken hip-joint. But he stuck to it that a dictum of Garrod's about Keats was devoid of meaning—almost seeming to regard it as on the same level as the Frenchman's rendering of 'Bacchus and his pards', i.e. '*B. et ses compagnons*'. He had apparently learnt English via the mining stories of Bret Harte. By the way in last week's *Spectator* the man Amis described 'St Agnes' Eve' as that 'sugary, erotic extravaganza'. It is not really much good setting up as a judge of poetry if *all* your five senses are blunted. (More or less apropos, I often remember one of the sisters in *Quality Street* in charge, mildly, of some school; she hated teaching Algebra 'where you always have to be proving that x is equal to y, and you know all the time that it isn't'. I love that kind of touch in Barrie—e.g. his telling of the first time he saw Plum bat, when he made 1, 'but in the second innings wasn't so successful.')

That may well have been Frank Harris at the Savile (of course I should have realised that you would know it!). 'Faded' *is* better than 'seedy'. I have never really had a London club. *You* wouldn't regard my present one, the Royal Empire Society, as anything but an omnium-gatherum of hearty and earnest bores, who used to quote Kipling, and like to listen to addresses about Ghana and then refresh themselves with egg salad and blancmange. But it is very cheap and has quite good arm-chairs and is v. near Charing X.

You *hadn't* told me J.B.P's remark about the Savage Club. I like it. I am drifting through Hesketh Pearson's *Dickens* and steadily sharing your opinion of it. Surely to say that Sam Weller is as abysmally *un*funny as Touchstone is a foolish trailing of the coat. How tremendously important *tone* is in all writing: isn't it that mainly which makes one hate or love the man behind the pen? E.g. Max B.—but

I believe there *are* those who don't like that courteously twinkling eye. I think I confessed to you once that I *couldn't read The Brook Kerith*, and God saw to it that I never should, because my copy was burnt in the Hagley fire. But it did go on and on, and I never got used to the absence of any typographical help. I do hope that idiotic fancy for having no capital letters will never take root; perhaps it *has* died out? Wasn't it e.e. cummings who started it?

I am glad you enjoyed Cambridge. I always find dons very friendly folk, and they nearly always talk very good sense unless you run up against some conscientious eccentric like Provost Sheppard. It seems to me one of the odder anfractuosities of the human mind to want to kiss old Maugham, but one never knows. Surely the expression on his face must have been ultra-Graham-Sutherlandish—especially as there looks to be every chance that he may well not realise his ambition of leaving the record sum ever made by a writer, with Agatha Christie in the very centre of the big money. That hot water-bottle *contretemps* is very disheartening. Twice it happened to me long after everyone was in bed. A doubled bath-towel under and another above the sheet is effective unless the leak has really soaked the mattress, but apprehensions of rheumatic fever, pneumonia and paralysis don't permit a very refreshing slumber.

Bishop Henson couldn't bear his Dean, Welldon, and once at Eton when odd old sayings were being discussed (e.g. 'right as a trivet', what *is* a trivet etc) when asked if he had ever seen pigs in clover, answered 'Well, no, not exactly—though I have seen the Dean of Durham in bed'. You would have enjoyed his company.

Sunday, 1 December 1957 *36 Soho Square*

I had scarcely packed E.B. off to the Orient on Thursday when I was bowled over by my first cold in *seven years*, but so virulent a one that it seemed to contain all the malice of those seven defeated winters. I staggered to bed that evening, and stayed there, half-blind, half-dotty, every tube awash, all Friday and most of yesterday. This caused me to miss (1) St Andrew's Day (2) my week-end in the country (3) your letter. All the more fun next week-end!

To-day I am up in a feeble sort of way, and tomorrow shall totter down to my overcrowded desk. I daresay I was generally overtired, and this enforced rest badly needed, but you won't, I fear, get much of a letter to-day.

I am madly in love with my clock, now installed in the little hall here, and doubt whether I shall ever move it: you will be able to inspect it on the 10th, before the Lit. Soc.

That *was* a superb evening in Chelsea Square—and what heavenly food! Thank goodness my cold didn't come on me a few days earlier. Today, in the fitful and to me unaccustomed way of convalescents, I have been reading alternately Harold Nicolson's *Journey to Java* (delightful), Gordon Craig's excellent memoirs which I never finished, Priestley's *Thoughts in the Wilderness*, the newly-published original four-act version of *The Importance of Being Earnest*, a detective story, the new Isak Dinesen, and Tony Powell's latest—enjoying them all by turns and then switching. But in truth I have no energy yet, for reading, writing or aught but delicious drowsing.

4 December 1957 *Grundisburgh*

Apropos of that evening at 67 C.S. it is quite possible that we shall again have another week, as A.H. and my daughter are insistent that that admirable cook *enjoys* dinner-parties, the simple fact being that she is an artist, and to have nobody in the house is like depriving a painter of his brushes. Well, I give you fair warning, *you* will always be among the guests. Old Anne Talbot was immensely pleased with her company at table and in taxi!

I have Harold N's *Journey to Java* on my list, also J.B.P. (what a lot of people he seems to irritate ('No, sir, what made your head ache was the sense I put into it!'). I bought and read for the journey a very wretched detective story by Philip Macdonald called *X v Rex*. The murderer who has done in innumerable policemen is *first* mentioned two pages from the end and is without point or substance. Surely P.M. used to be good (*The Rasp* etc). Is the new Agatha any good? Like Haydn, she has written too much. I am glad to be told by the Penguin 'blurb' that she enjoys her food (does Ngaio Marsh hate the stuff?) and plenty of it must be at her command, but she ought to stop now and think upon her latter end.

8 December 1957 *Bromsden Farm*

Flushed with the satisfaction of having compiled fifty Oscar footnotes this week-end, I sit down late to answer your two fine letters. Despite Agatha Christie's phenomenal success of late in the theatre, I fear she won't leave a quarter of old W.S.M.'s haul. He made a great deal of his money in America (where the rewards are greater) and has mostly lived in France, paying no income tax of any kind.

I'm happy to say that last week's avalanche has subsided into a faint catarrhal trickle. The clock continues to charm me, and, as you proudly boasted, it keeps perfect time. Did you abandon the strike because you didn't want it or because the expert said it was past repair? If the former I feel inclined to try and get it into action.

So sorry you won't be at the Lit. Soc., to which I shall come hot-foot (or perhaps coldfoot) from the University rugger match. Tomorrow I go to see the Queen Mother present the second Duff Cooper Memorial Prize to Lawrence Durrell for his book *Bitter Lemons*, which I haven't read. On Wednesday I have to go out to luncheon, cocktails and dinner. On Thursday I take the chair again at the London Library—and so it rackets on.

Philip Macdonald *was* good and *is* bad. The new Agatha C. is no more than Beta plus. I am well back in the swing of the editing now, and only wish I had more time for it.

Last Thursday I was taken to the first night of the Stratford *Tempest* at Drury Lane. Gielgud spoke beautifully, as always, and Caliban wasn't bad, but except for the flashes of poetry it's a boring play, and I found my eyes closing more than once. In the audience I saw my former wife Peggy, looking very young and beautiful. Thank God I no longer have any ties with that intolerable profession the Theatre!

The Oxford term ended yesterday, and this morning I drove over to fetch Duff home. His kit filled our large station-wagon to the roof.

I don't think he did much work during the term and only hope he'll do some in the vac.

Have you been listening to George Kennan's Reith Lectures on the wireless? I've heard the best part of three of them and have been much impressed by his modesty, grasp, and general good sense. Duff has been to some lectures of his in Oxford—nothing to do with his Greats, but clearly the most interesting ones in Oxford—and thought them excellent. Peter Fleming says his (G.K.'s) book on the Russian Revolution is first-class.

The other day, thinking of you, I took down *Earlham* from the shelf and read its opening chapters in bed, delighted to find their spell as potent as ever. It is surely a lasting piece of literature: when I've finished it again I shall write to P. Lubbock. You've no idea how I envy your being able to read exactly what you feel like *when* you feel like it (exam-papers permitting). The lack of such freedom is my chief objection to my own life, though I daresay forbidden fruit tastes all the more delicious for being forbidden when one *does* get a chance at it.

12 December 1957 *Grundisburgh*

Good news *qua* both cold and clock. I won't swear it (yes I will, because P. has just come in and is sure that) no one has ever looked at or wound up the strike as she never cares for it; but of course there it is, governed by the second weight, and if it needs a little doctoring, any good clock man can do it. Our friend in Ipswich says the mechanism is a very simple affair—compared e.g. with one of those gold, butter-smooth watches of about the size and thickness of a shilling bit. It gives me a feeling of nice fat satisfaction that the clock at last has come home.

When we were at 67 Chelsea Sq. I found a dozen Maughams on the shelf and read a lot of the plays and stories. Very efficient, very readable, but—well there is a vacuity somewhere, moral and spiritual very likely. (But on the whole one should try not to talk like a bishop!) You must be my Goethe and put your finger on the spot. The bishops on the whole did better than the rest of their lordships in the homosexual debate. Odd that nobody pointed out what seems to me the real flaw in the law, i.e. that it can't be enforced (two consenting adults being normally pretty good at covering their tracks), and so practically any detection is keyhole work, undertaken with blackmail of some kind in view. That wise man, old Warre, was always very emphatic that to make a rule you can't enforce is not only futile but damaging.

The Rugger match was what we used to call 'suction pie' for the ebullient Cantabs. I am no Rugger fan, though I played the game for two terms at Cambridge, but I have always known how comparatively easy it is for a strong lot of forwards *on the day* to muck up a brilliant lot of backs. If they played five matches C. would win four. But yesterday was the fifth. I suppose you bellowed with Oxonian glee at the close, and hurled your cushion into the arena? The first O. and C. match I ever saw, I sat next to R.S. Kindersley, a staid old colleague of rigid respectability. But he had been a great player (in Vassall's team), and as a fast close match proceeded, the blood rose to his head, and, ignoring the sensibilities of the many parsons and occasional ladies within earshot, he endeavoured to nip in the bud any bit of brilliance by a Cambridge player with the simple stentorian advice: 'Poot him on his arrrrse!' There are too many women in the crowd nowadays. Tuppy used to complain of this in a penetrating voice, pointing out that most of them were in hopes of seeing a player deprived of his shorts. But these are deep Freudian waters.

What did you think of L. Durrell? His Cyprus book was good, if a bit over-written. The speeches sound to have been rather good. The critics were very enthusiastic about Gielgud's Prospero. I am immensely amused at your finding the play boring, because, to read at any rate, all the plays have always seemed to me bad *as plays*—though over and over again the poetry simply knocks one endways. But the action, the plot, the whys and wherefores are so often supremely absurd. One dislikes agreeing with D.H. Lawrence, but can't always help it. Surely

> When I read Shakespeare I am struck with wonder
> That such trivial people should muse and thunder
> In such lovely language

hits the bullseye?

Really the serious questions we have to set about the behaviour of Orsino and Olivia, and Bassanio and Portia, when it is hardly ever quite rational. But when they speak, you just don't mind *what* they do. I have just finished a lot of G.C.E. *Richard II* papers. Nearly all very bad. A leading scholar from Clayesmore brightened my morning by calling Bushy Blushy, and Bagot Bandot, but on the whole I think they have sent me the sweepings of the asylums. One boy, describing Richard's death, says that 'when he refused to eat his dinner, there was a bit of a mix-up, and when it was over he was found to be dead'.

Has Duff *got* to work at Oxford? Because if he is reading masses that he likes on his own, and seeing a good lot of intelligent people, and talking till 3 a.m., that is of course what the University was for, in old days, for any number of young men. But in these days—any way my views on education are subversive and immoral—almost George Mooreish. One thing I know, and that is that there is much to be said for being seventy-five if the education and 'culture' of the future is what Hogben and Co want it to be.

I don't listen to the wireless as our reception is so bad, but I have read every word of Kennan's lectures, and devilish good I thought them. But do you fundamentally see *any* hope? The thing that sticks in *my* gorge—and incidentally in that of Arthur Bryant—is 'Why are the Russians set on building a thousand submarines—more than twice as many as the rest of the world put together? And if and when the hydrogen bomb is abolished what are they going to do with these submarines?' Who *is* Kennan? Because his English for lucidity, point, and balance is in the same class as Hensley Henson's or Hal Fisher's or Inge's. Entirely different and every bit as good (and why the hell, Dr L. and Co., may we not enjoy *both*?) is of course *Earlham*. I am delighted with what you say of it, and *mind you write to P.L.* He would love it, I know. Will you, by the way, do something which I do about six times a year, and that is read *aloud* the last scene in *Earlham*. Your voice will get husky (as mine does—and also did M.R. James's and Hugh Walpole's) and I am sure you will arrive at exactly the conviction that I do, i.e. that with all its deep emotion there is not the smallest touch of the precious—sentiment if you like but no sentimentality. But what a lot of people don't know how to read! Tuppy, oddly, was one, but he always did everything much too fast. You can't read P.L. as if he was Phillips Oppenheim, and after all let us face the fact that most readers resemble Jock Dent's Tommy in an *Ego* who, after a glass of vintage claret, called for a 'pint of wallop'.

I have just finished my *Twelfth Night* papers. I was pleased to find the following answers to the Q. 'What is a pedant?'—a clown, a criminal, a chap who kept order in church, a salesman, an ornament for the ear, a yellow pole with ribbons, a tramp, a kind of dog. Some of them are not so very wide of the mark. And I have one gem for you. 'Viola couldn't have married Olivia as she was a girl, and not, as Olivia thought, a boy eunach.' What a pity E. Blunden is in China.

We are coming to Eton on Saturday week for ten days or so and should immensely like to lunch with you again. I believe both Sundays are bespoken, but otherwise the day that suits you suits us. I want to get again the 'aura' of that book-lined study of yours.

15 December 1957 *Bromsden Farm*

First, and most important, Comfort suggests Saturday, 28 December (Holy Innocents' Day!) for your promised luncheon visit. Does that suit? Send me your Eton address and I'll write there next Sunday, reminding you of the exact way here.

Now to your letter. I imagine that Willie Maugham's money will go to his daughter Liza, his only child, now married to John Hope and living a mile or two from here. But the old villain is quite capable of leaving a wayward and capricious will, and since he seems quite likely to outlive us all, we may never know. I have known him, rather more off than on, for twenty-six years, but I dare say 'acquaintance' is nearer the mark than 'friend'.

The rugger match was without exception the most *exciting* I have ever seen in more than twenty years, and what more can one ask? The crowd is usually generous to what seems to be the under-dog, and when Oxford got the ball five times from the first five scrums, and clearly had Cambridge confused and disorganised, few believed it could last. Then Oxford scored their well-deserved try (a score of 9–0 at half-time wouldn't have seemed unfair), and hung on to this frail lead for the rest of the game. Their tackling was *superb*—never seen better—and tension rose when Cambridge several times got within feet of the Oxford line. The last ten minutes were excruciating, and then I did indeed lend my voice to the mighty roar that echoed round Twickenham. I do wish you could have seen the game: you'd have been thrilled.

The Duff Cooper prize-giving went off beautifully on Monday. The room was looking lovelier than last year, with a silver Christmas tree above the parade of champagne-bottles, and the number of people (eighty to ninety) made less of a crush than last year's hundred and twenty. The Q.M. looked quite lovely in silver: her beauty and immediately irresistible charm are amazing. I explained the simple drill to her, and she was wide-eyed as a little girl who had never done such a thing before. After Durrell had been presented to her and they had taken up their positions, she whispered to him: 'I'm terrified. Are you?' which did much to calm his palpable fright. David Cecil made a tip-top speech, brief, poetical and entirely to the point. Then the Q.M. gave Durrell the prize and said some charming words about Duff, at which Diana's lovely eyes filled with tears. Then Durrell briefly said thank-you, and the ceremony was over. Champagne was briskly circulated, and the Q.M. talked to many, I think rather enjoying the informality.

Kennan has mostly been what the Americans call a 'career diplomat' and was U.S. Ambassador in Moscow until the Russians turned him out. One is so accustomed to U.S. ambassadors being millionaire business men that Kennan's choice of words and serene commonsense make him a peak in such company. This evening I forbade myself to listen to his final lecture, so as to write to you instead. Although you miss a few good things by not being able to listen to the radio, you also miss temptation to waste hours on twaddle. I seldom switch on except for music, which I find an agreeable background to footnote-writing. And if it takes one's fancy one can stop work and listen for a bit.

I have obeyed your orders and read aloud to myself the closing scene of *Earlham*: it is indeed most moving, without one false note. I shall write to P.L. when I have re-read all.

On Wednesday, after a cocktail party in South Kensington, I tooled out to Putney to dine with the Arthur Ransomes. On Thursday I presided at the London Library committee and delivered an interminable report on what had been done since the last meeting. Most of the members of the committee who were still sentient expressed their approval, particularly R. Mortimer. Altogether I spoke for more than an hour, and as the meeting broke up Rose Macaulay burst in, looking like a wall-painting of a mummy, and said: 'Am I late? Do tell me all that has been said.' I was too exhausted to comply, and I fear she thought me churlish. The old pet is really quite useless on committees now, bless her.

19 December 1957 *Grundisburgh*

We will do the *28th* with great pleasure. I remember we turn left at the top of that long incline after leaving the Long Mile, but am rather vague after that—and snow will be falling, and darkness will cover the earth, and gross darkness the people. And I have always been one of those whose instinct for missing the way is unfailing. Pamela is better when by herself, but I invariably muddle her. So in the more derogatory sense the Holy Innocents' Day is the right one for us to be groping our way to you in darkest Oxfordshire.

Your vignette of the Rugger Match makes my mouth water. But you know I still have a strong childish strain in me, and will confess to you that though, now, I rather wish I had gone to Oxford, I still *hate* seeing Cambridge beaten, especially when they are expected to win. I should like to have seen you yelling *à la* Kindersley. Twickenham is the only place where the clock manifestly takes sides. If one's side is clinging to a tiny and precarious lead, the minute-hand, to my certain knowledge, flatly refuses to move. I bet you noticed that last week.

That Duff C. ceremony as described by you must have been lovely. I always thought the Q.M. quite charming on the three occasions on which I met her. Once when she visited Eton the senior beaks were presented to the King and Queen. H.K. Marsden was next to me. He had taught Maths to the K. at Osborne (or Dartmouth?). The Queen graciously told him that the King remembered him and mentioned it to her. All she got was the menacing reply: 'Then he must have been talking during the service' (which they had attended) and of course the old dervish forgot to add 'Ma'am'.

Jan Crace's[1] target at the moment is *Macbeth* in modern dress. All that modern dress stunt always seems the wildest rubbish to me. When all the behaviour and speech in the play are archaic and of their time, doesn't modern dress merely distract one's attention or make for laughter? Does Duncan wear a Homburg hat and spats as Edward VII did on a visit? And what *is* the right twentieth-century fashionable dress for a witch? And do you or do you not find it intolerably incongruous that a contemporary field-marshal should soliloquise about sleep knitting up the ravelled sleave of care? Enough.

Your power of work is really terrifying. An *hour's* speech at the L. Library! And how many hours went to its making? My processes are—to compare small with great—like those Housman said were his when he had to compose an address or inscription (in English: Latin he claimed was quite easy)—one day spent staring at a blank page and longing for death; a second one jotting down phrases and crossing them out, feeling rather sick—and so on. But in his case no one would guess at the hideous history behind the majestic pageant of his prose.

Why is there no *Earlham* in modern prose anthologies? Perhaps there is. I don't really know any. I *knew* you would react as you did to the last pages. Bless you!

22 December 1957 *Bromsden Farm*

Delighted you can both come on Saturday. We shall expect you, in your oldest clothes, about 12.45. I enclose a brief résumé of the route.

Not only did the Twickenham clock dally at the end of that match, but the referee dallied still longer.

Shakespeare in modern dress is rubbish. Its advocates pretend that the process enables the audience to appreciate the words without being distracted by fancy dress, but in fact the effect is exactly contrary. When I had my viva at Balliol in 1926 I was questioned about the

[1] Eton master.

modern-dress *Hamlet*, which was then a novelty and clearly tickled the dons. My answers were so vague that I wonder they ever let me into the beastly college at all.

When I said 'an hour's speech' at the London Library I didn't mean a set oration. In fact I just sat at the head of the table and talked for an hour from a half-sheet of notes, which hadn't taken long to jot down. So, you see, I unconsciously dramatised and heightened a very ordinary task into something that sounded admirable. (It's true that one of the committee wrote to me next day: 'Thank God we've got a chairman at last,' but truly I hadn't much to surpass.)

I was much saddened by the death of Michael Sadleir. He was always very sweet and generous to me (as to most people) and I shall miss him. In fact I fancy he was ready to go. After a recent operation on his tongue (which must have been for cancer, though they never said so) he began to fail. They then said he was suffering from anaemia and gave him blood-transfusions, which probably killed him, for he died of a thrombosis. I went to his memorial service at Windsor on Friday: there would have been many more people if they had held it in London. John Carter drove me down there.

Last week wasn't too bad: one huge hideous cocktail party at the Hultons', one delicious dinner-party at the Jepsons', a mass of Christmas shopping and other nonsense. Tomorrow I return to London till Tuesday evening, and then five days peacefully here, with your much-looked-forward-to visit in the midst. Both the boys will be here, unless they're out shooting.

Today I read solidly from breakfast to supper—the papers, a grim French novel (which I may publish in translation) and a long manuscript, so I don't feel very fresh or bright. Glad to see Harold Nicolson picked the George Moore letters as one of the best books of the year, and only hope his words will sell a few more copies. So far only a thousand have been, as they say, 'shifted'.

No word from E.B. I fear the lecture tour in India on his way back to Hong Kong must have exhausted him. I go on sending him an airmail letter each Sunday. What on earth do you do about Christmas presents for all your descendants? Or does Pamela cope with them all? I have *nine* godchildren, ranging in age from twenty-seven to six months, and their needs baffle me afresh each year. What a nuisance the whole thing is—except that it brings you within driving distance. Now I must go to bed. A happy Christmas to you all. See you on Saturday.

29 December 1957 *Bromsden Farm*

This pleasurable habit has proved too much for me, so I propose to steal a march on you with this brief note. Your visit, I scarcely need say, was as usual pure pleasure, and I only hope Pamela's cold wasn't accentuated by it. Your hat has been recovered at the Brunners', and tomorrow Comfort will retrieve it and post it to Grundisburgh. Going hatless in Cambridge you will be mistaken for an undergraduate or an emancipated don, but I hope you won't catch cold thereby.

After tea yesterday I took C and A to the local cinema, where we saw a good but well-nigh interminable programme (more than three and a half hours), which included a spirited rendering of *Robbery Under Arms*—a book which I have never read and now feel absolved from attempting.

Looking through Emerson for an elusive quotation, I came on this excellent analysis of literary reputation. I expect you know it, but never mind:

> There is no luck in literary reputation. They who make up the final verdict upon every book are not the partial and noisy readers of the hour when it appears; but a court as of angels, a public not to be bribed, not to be entreated, and not to be overawed, decides upon every man's title to fame. Only those books come down which deserve to last. All the gilt edges and vellum and morocco, all the presentation-copies to all the libraries, will not preserve a book in circulation beyond its intrinsic date. It must go with all Walpole's Royal and Noble Authors to its fate. Blackmore, Kotzebue, or Pollok, may endure for a night, but Moses and Homer stand forever.

Isn't that splendid? Old Edward Garnett used to put the same sentiments into shorter space—'Everything finds its own level in the end'—

but I am charmed by Emerson's rhythms. I shall read more of him.

Peter looked in to-day and bewailed missing you. He is writing—or thinking of writing—a Strix piece about nicknames, and would like to rifle your store: perhaps he can wait till January 14.

This afternoon I did a modicum of gardening, but the wind was keen and I soon returned gratefully to the fireside. These five days, for all their solid meals, seem to have passed in a twinkling, and I have not done all I hoped to do—work, I mean. I shall think of you sorting out the Revisers, and hope that by Sunday I shall have some amusing items to recount. Meanwhile a happy new year, with many meetings.

31 December 1957 *Royal Hotel*
Cambridge

How *very* good of you to be so prompt about my wretched hat, and I hope Sir Felix took the episode kindly. I have in fact a *cap*, luckily, which is more convenient in a small car, so I am not, when I emerge, the sport of every wind. But my career as Mr Pooter continues. This morning I was rather sharply diverted from the ladies' lavatory which I was trying to enter, having not seen the notice, and this is a hotel we have not been at before. Food and bed quite good, but the tables in the dining-room are too close together, and apparently anyone sits anywhere, so while I was waiting for a colleague, the place at my table was filled by a stranger, whose nurse some thirty years ago had omitted to impress on him that porridge should be eaten silently.

Yesterday I dined in Trinity and my neighbour was a Russian mathematician with very little English. It is apparently a Russian habit to swallow or soften the final consonants of a word—an awkward habit I thought, when he asked me to pass the toa, and was slow to grasp that he must mean toast, and not toad or toes. N.B. If and when you dine at Trinity, the Madeira should not be missed.

Pamela thoroughly enjoyed that visit. Neither of us could believe that it was 4 before we left. *Robbery Under Arms* was my favourite book over sixty years ago, and I am furious at having forgotten the name of Captain Starlight's horse. As good a horse as I ever came across, though

I was fond of what H.G. Wells called 'that soundly Anglican' horse Black Beauty and wept inconsolably when he/she died.

That is fine Emerson—an oddly under-rated writer *me judice*. Perhaps there is too much bread to the butter. Do you remember his description of genius, 'that stellar and undiminishable something'. As near as anyone ever went I think? Old Samuel of course had the same belief in the judgment of the public (when given time) as opposed to that of the intelligentsia, and 'Few things are more risible than literary fashions' hits a nail neatly and finally. Among my colleagues are nice sensible Oxonians who do not draw a very attractive picture of Bowra, A.J.P. Taylor, Rowse, Trevor-Roper or, in fact, any of the louder Oxford voices. I liked Bowra at that Johnson luncheon, but they say he now indulges relentlessly in monologue, which of course does not go down well in a community where all want to do the same. Rum places, universities. Gow told me that Housman attended *one* lecture of Jowett's, but when the great man mispronounced one Greek word he attended no more. Nevertheless B.J. was a better man than A.E.H. The conversation of both was largely composed of usually unnecessary and uncalled-for snubs, but J. was much less conceited and thin-skinned and morose.

APPENDIX I

LYTTELTON ON GLADSTONE[1]

It seems to me almost impossible for anyone—it certainly is for me—to hold forth about Mr Gladstone at Hawarden without an apology. For what can I, what can anyone say of his achievements and character that can have any freshness of interest? All stones have been turned, all avenues explored, and all the other clichés of investigation and summing-up, of eulogy and condemnation, have gone their weary round till they slide over one's mind without entering it. These thoughts occurred to me when I was honoured by an invitation from my old friend and colleague and distant relative, Charles Gladstone, to address you to-day; and I must tell you frankly that the misgivings with which I accepted would probably have won the day if Sir Philip Magnus's excellent book had come out a month earlier than it did. What line is now possible? What vein is not worked out?

At one time I thought that something could be made of Mr Gladstone's correspondence with my grandfather, which was mainly on the Greek and Roman classics, or ecclesiastical matters, or the Canterbury Settlement in New Zealand, but after a very brief glance at it, the Valley of Hinnom rose to my lips, 'Can these dry bones live?' In Holy Writ the answer was 'Yes', but only through a miracle; and an equally tremendous one would have been necessary to clothe these ancient topics with interest. Then, Mr Gladstone paid his last visit to my home, Hagley, in 1895, but here again hope was disappointed. There was, of course, a huge cheering crowd from Birmingham and its neighbourhood, all Conservative supporters, but, 'We don't care about that, we want to see the old chap', was the general attitude, voiced by one of them. The rector's sermon, to which Mr Gladstone closely listened, his hand behind his ear, was punctuated by scrabbling noises amid the ivy outside the window, and triumphant announcements such as 'I can see 'is 'ead' from the apex of a perspiring pyramid

[1] A lecture delivered at Hawarden on 24 June 1955.

of hoisters remain in my memory; but all these things must have been common incidents wherever he went during his last years, and, you will agree, are thinnish material for an address. In many audiences the fact that, with my brothers and sisters, I had been patted on the head by Mr Gladstone might give me a unique though transient distinction, but certainly not in this company. He gave each of us a new shilling, and I spent mine, I seem to remember, on percussion caps. Boys of twelve have no sense of values. I ought, of course, to have treasured it as religiously as many did the chips which flew from the great man's axe.

Some members of that Hagley party attempted a record of his conversation. But Boswells are born and not made, and I cannot see you being very grateful for the information, unpublished and almost first-hand though it is, that Mr Gladstone was most interesting about Cromwell, and said that Charles II was a very bad king. Nor did the discovery, made by more than one lynx-eyed young spectator, that Mr Gladstone did *not* chew every mouthful thirty-two times demand or deserve very lengthy mention—though I am not sure that Mr Gladstone himself might not have made some weighty and useful observations on the common and deplorable gap between principle and practice.

But into a period of gloom there came at last a tiny point of light, so it seemed to me—though I grant that to you it may well seem too tiny to be visible. It was this. From what I can gather this annual address has been given in the past by men of distinction, by politicians steeped in Parliamentary history and tradition, by public men who had heard and seen Mr Gladstone, by relatives and friends who had known him; and it occurred to me that there was perhaps an opening for the views of a completely ordinary man who comes into none of the categories just mentioned. It is true that for the ordinary man to pass judgment on anyone like Mr Gladstone is to measure Niagara with a pint bottle, but that is always the penalty of greatness. Bunyan writes *The Pilgrim's Progress,* and three hundred years later the University of Columbia decides that it is the most boring book in the world. Mr Gladstone himself could not have objected; it was the ordinary man whose judgment he valued, and he would certainly, with his invincible optimism, have expected that nearly sixty years after his death the ordinary man would be sufficiently educated to take some interest in his country's past, and to catch some glimpse of his own vision.

You may think that one of my name is sure to be packed with the prejudices of a congenital pro-Gladstonian; but I would remind you that the atmosphere in which one is brought up produces rebellion as often as acquiescence, and in my undergraduate days the British Empire seemed to be at its zenith, Ireland and Europe were reasonably quiet, Kipling's imperialism was fashionable, Dizzy's shares were high, and to the short wind and immature sinews of the twenty-year-old mind Morley's *Life* was a long grind. So one rather took both Morley and Mr Gladstone for granted until Monypenny and Buckle's still more portentous *Life* of Dizzy forced on one, as vigorous partisanship always does, the conviction that anyone so invariably wrong-headed, unprincipled, absurd, and dominant as Mr Gladstone apparently was, must be well worth studying. No one, surely, who has read Sir Philip Magnus's book will dispute this. But even after digesting that, and a quantity of other Gladstoniana, one ordinary man, at least, is much puzzled by the extraordinarily diverse views of him taken throughout his long life, and still rife half-a-century after his death. Dizzy, concealing beneath a sphinx-like demeanour the queerest blend of British prose and Oriental poetry, is admitted to be a man of mystery, but Mr Gladstone? Where can be the mystery there? Ask the next man. He doesn't know what you mean; it is all quite clear to him. Mr Gladstone was a hypocrite, a pompous, incoherent, hysterical gas-bag, a self-deceiver, a little Englander, a bore, a demagogue, an egoist and so on. Practically any fool's cap will fit, any mud stick. But before this list is half finished the next man but one, red with indignation, will thrust the other aside to tell you the real truth. Mr Gladstone was a far-sighted idealist, an unrivalled orator and debater, a man of burning sincerity and deep humility, magnanimous, courageous, a genius of finance, an indefatigable worker in great causes, living every moment of his life 'as ever in his Great Taskmaster's eye'. The first will probably be strongly pro-, the second anti-Dizzy; the fires of that old antagonism are still aglow beneath time's ashes, and spring into life at the slightest breath. But apart from that it is not easy to explain the passionate violence of the anti-Gladstonian's dislike. Many of them were women, from Queen Victoria down to the woman who, with unfeminine accuracy, hit him in the eye with a piece of gingerbread, or the one who sent a wreath for the grave of the heifer which knocked him down in Hawarden Park, or the Irish lady who derived some obscure and imbecile satisfaction from getting hold of the morning paper before anyone was down and obliterating Mr Gladstone's name wherever it came.

And as one reads, one passes from a page on which is recorded some act of generosity on his part, or some entry in his private journal of astonishing and moving humility, to another page where is set down with a sort of giggling malevolence that an Anglican dean has alleged that Mr Gladstone is in the pay of the Pope, and has presided in person at a Black Mass, that his expensive and disreputable ways have made it impossible for Mrs Gladstone to have a maid, or alternatively, have driven her mad, that he has proved himself mad by ordering quantities of hats—and so he had; they were straw hats for Mrs Gladstone's orphanage—that he presided solemnly over the distribution of chips after felling a tree, that he had his hot-water bottle filled not with water but with soup, that he drank sherry and ate grilled chicken at 6 a.m. and followed this up with a breakfast at which the fat boy in *Pickwick* would have blenched, that his oratory and Hitler's were very similar, that his Quixotic rescue work on the London streets was all humbug—so the silly spiteful tale goes on till one feels that Tennyson's famous line should be turned upside down to 'we needs must hate the highest when we see it'. The orator, every one of whose countless speeches manifestly aimed at animating public life with the lofty ideals and moral considerations which to him were the spirit of private life, was to many a mere tub-thumping agitator. 'Oh dear, I do hope he won't make a disturbance,' said a village dame who heard Mr Gladstone was coming to an old friend's funeral, and similar misgivings were often expressed in very high places, and in very much the same words.

There was, there is, as his niece, Lady Frederick Cavendish, wrote in her diary, 'something about Uncle William which irritates'. One may perhaps surmise that the educated part of a generation which had read Darwin was growing and has continued to grow more sceptical about the Impregnable Rock of Holy Scripture, and less patient with a point of view about mundane matters which confidently (at least in public) seemed to claim divine guidance and approbation, especially when the claimant shewed equal or greater astuteness than his opponents on the lower levels. You remember, of course, Labouchere's famous gibe about the ace of trumps. Then Mr Gladstone, it must be admitted, was vehement, and vehemence rouses counter-vehemence. When he took up a cause it filled his head and heart. His overwhelming conviction that it was right, backed by an impressive panoply of knowledge, a limitless vocabulary used with all the resources of a master of thrust and parry in every kind of verbal controversy, must have been very hard to withstand. One is aware of a vague feeling that so tremendous an all-round equipment of emotion and reason was somehow not fair. It was easy enough afterwards to pick holes, to sneer, to be slightly ashamed of having been carried away, as anyone knows who has ever been swept off his feet by powerful oratory. It is not merely the greatness of the issue, the cogency and clearness of well-marshalled argument, or the enchantment of language, used as Beethoven uses an orchestra—but the power, indefinite but unmistakable, which emanates from the presence of the speaker. The late John Bailey used to tell of an occasion when he heard Mr Gladstone speaking to a huge audience at, I think, Manchester. He was a good deal heckled, but at last the moment came for his peroration. The majestic eagle spread his ample pinions and took the air, and a spell-bound silence fell upon the audience. And then a little man interrupted. Mr Gladstone made no pause, nor even looked at him. He merely stabbed twice with his forefinger in the little man's direction—that was all, but, as John Bailey said, you could almost see the mortal blow go home and the stricken victim fall.

Now, they say, Mr Gladstone's speeches are unreadable. Very well, but whose speeches of as long ago as his are not, uttered as they all were by a speaker, to an audience, on a topic, all three of which are dead? Burke? Schoolboys read his because examiners set them, and rich mines of political wisdom they indubitably are. Not to listen to. Even his contemporaries couldn't do that, for, as Goldsmith wrote, 'He thought of convincing while they thought of dining'. In fact he was called 'the dinner-bell', so unanimous was the stampede from the Chamber when he rose to speak. People will read such speeches as

Lincoln's at Gettysburg, of which the subject is elemental and not transitory—the death of the fallen in the cause of freedom. It is one of the great utterances of all time, and was thought at first a pitiable failure, fashionable American oratory then being of a dreadful opulence—and it is about the length of one Gladstonian sentence. Long-windedness was a common charge, but why against Mr Gladstone only? Nearly all were long-winded in those spacious days, when there was far less entertainment than we have for eye and ear. He did, of course, qualify, refine, parenthesise a great deal, in search, his admirers said, of exact accuracy, or, according to his detractors, to leave himself a loophole for subsequent evasion. Sometimes his refinements were engagingly comical, as when he said to the tenants of Hawarden, 'It is within the power of any man to make money by keeping poultry, and, if I may say so, from eggs'.

And perhaps I may be allowed to quote a delightful parody from the *Quarterly Review* of exactly a hundred years ago:—'Suppose the Prime Minister and the Chancellor of the Exchequer were each to be asked what day the session would be over, Lord Palmerston would reply that it was the intention of Her Majesty to close the session on August the 18th. Mr Gladstone would possibly premise that inasmuch as it was for Her Majesty to decide upon the day which would be most acceptable for herself, it was scarcely compatible with Parliamentary etiquette to ask her Ministers to anticipate such decision; but, presuming that he quite understood the purport of the Right Honourable gentleman's question, of which he was not entirely assured, the completion of the duties of the House of Commons, and the formal termination of the sitting of the Legislature being two distinct things, he would say that the former would probably be accomplished about the 18th of August, and that such day would not be unfavourable for the latter, and, therefore, if the Sovereign should be pleased to ratify that view of the case, the day he had named would very likely prove to be that enquired after by the Right Honourable gentleman.' It is like a paragraph from a Henry James novel and, like that, demands from listener or reader patience, an appreciation of verbal niceties and of the speaker's scrupulous search for exactitude. I hope it is not *lèse majesté* to suggest that Queen Victoria possessed other qualities in greater abundance than any of these—she whom he served with so deep a sense of her position as Queen, and so little of her nature as a woman. He never could follow Mrs Gladstone's shrewd advice, 'Do pet the Queen'.

The melancholy story of their incompatibility need not be told again. The anti-Gladstonians put much, if not most, of the blame on Mr Gladstone's lack of a sense of humour, which, as a foreign critic has acidly observed, the English seem to regard as one of the seven deadly sins, forgetting how often the failing is found in many of their greatest men from Milton and Burke down to Peel and Wordsworth. Mr Gladstone—a pure-bred Scotsman—has always been denied a sense of humour, but those who knew him best do not at all accept this. Lady Oxford's rather subtle verdict was that he had plenty of humour but often was in a mood when the humour did not seem the chief aspect in a situation, an incident, or a story. Sometimes, very unexpectedly, it did. Once at some gathering his eye was caught by one of the guests' flamboyant waistcoat. He commented on it, and was told it was of Armenian material and workmanship. His eye twinkled, and after a few moments during which, the narrator says, one had the impression of some vast machinery being set in motion, a joke emerged—and not a very bad joke either. 'I have said much in recent times of Armenian atrocities but this is the first time I have ever actually seen one.' The odds against his being in the mood when the word atrocity produced a joke must have been very long. But when Robert Browning, highly amused, told him how Dizzy publicly praised some British paintings for the very merits on the absence of which he had in very recent conversation heartily derided them, Mr Gladstone glared: 'You call that funny? I call it devilish.' One Dizzyite calls this Dizzy's delightful irony. To Mr Gladstone it was just a lie. He used irony very little and hated cynicism. When anarchists had been busy abroad Dizzy said he hoped they would not murder the ambassador M. Waddington—a sentiment Mr Gladstone would certainly have shared, but not Dizzy's reason, which was that it would make assassination ridiculous. Paradox and nonsense were alien to his mind, and the Oscar Wilde witticisms in Dizzy's novels must have sounded to Mr Gladstone's ears the merest crackling of thorns under a pot. 'Every woman should marry and no man'; 'I rather like bad wine; one gets so bored with good'; 'I should like to die, eating ortolans to the sound of soft music.' Was Mr Gladstone so very wrong?

Light reading was not for Mr Gladstone. He said that when exhausted he found 'hard close-grained stuff more refreshing than light literature'. History, Theology, Dante, Homer (whose name according to Dr. James, late Provost of Eton, he pronounced 'Oomy'): such did for him what the Wodehouses and Agatha Christies do for lesser men. He seems to have attended the theatre fairly often, but I don't know what was his taste in plays. John Morley found his views on Shakespeare rather naïve. 'He is too healthy, too objective, too simple,' he wrote, 'for all the complexities of morbid analysis.' This appears to be rather borne out by what happened when he listened in a theatre-box to a recitation of an Ibsen play. According to Bernard Shaw, the audience were on the edge of revolt, but 'the situation was saved by Mr Gladstone toppling forward with a loud choking snore over the front of his box, and being pulled back by his heels just in time'. But I doubt if Shaw on Mr Gladstone was entirely trustworthy.

But it is, of course, on his Parliamentary activities and on the qualities of character and the motives which men thought they saw, or imagined, behind them that the great flood of obloquy falls. On the Eastern question, the Sudan, the Transvaal, Home Rule, his Midlothian campaign, many amiable and intelligent men were apparently sure, not merely that he was wrong, but that he was clearly wicked and worthy of detestation. Traitor, murderer, arch-villain, crazy old fanatic, vindictive fiend, unprincipled maniac, viper (that was from His Holiness at the Vatican), Ananias, Tartuffe, Judas, Satan—such were the choice terms showered on him; and at various times he was cut dead, threatened with violence, spat at, hissed in the street, hooted in the Lobby, and had his windows broken by the mob. His motives were confidently and repeatedly alleged to be personal ambition and egotism, vindictiveness, rage, hatred, or mere hypocrisy. Charges of opportunism (he called it his sense of timing), vote-catching, clinging to office and so on may be discounted as the common coin of party intercourse, but it was not only his enemies who saw in him a more than normal capacity for self-deception. It is not a very rare human weakness, and an easy enough charge to bring against any man, especially one who, with almost inhuman earnestness and persistence, pursues a course of which we don't approve, precisely at the moment and in the circumstances which best suit him and his party. Sometimes what was expedient seemed to chime in too felicitously with the suddenly-revealed will of God, as when, soon after Dizzy had 'dished the Whigs', by first defeating, and then improving on their Reform Bill, Mr Gladstone's new-found enthusiasm for disestablishing the Irish Church brought his party—many of whom did not care a rap about the Irish Church, but the electorate apparently did—a resounding triumph. Mr Gladstone tried to be unworldly; all admitted that, in fact 'not a man of the world' was one of Dizzy's black marks against him, and the Queen adopted it. So no doubt it was an unpleasant surprise to find that in the Parliamentary battle he did not rely wholly on the armour of light. He had nearly all the mundane weapons, and one which he wielded with unrivalled skill was the ability to use words as a sort of smoke-screen, behind which he could safely, brilliantly, and infuriatingly retreat from an awkward position. Mr Goschen once understood from Mr Gladstone that a Bill of his would have priority in the new session. It didn't, and he was very angry. But Mr Gladstone shewed him that, according to Hansard, he had promised only that the Bill should be 'in the forefront of the new legislative programme', and triumphantly pointed out that a forefront was a line and not a point. And Mr Goschen was no doubt angrier still.

Dizzy, on the other hand, deceived many people, but certainly never himself. How could he, when he was on the stage, behind the scenes, and in the audience all at once, watching with a connoisseur's enjoyment every word and movement of his own performance? His dealings with the Queen read now as sheer comedy; how much genuine feeling and truth there was behind all the make-up and rodomontade and tinsel, who can say? No one knew better than he did what rubbish he was talking when he told the Queen she was the head of the literary profession, or Titania in a sea-girt isle, or that English history could show no character approaching the Prince Consort's except Sir Philip Sidney. It was effective no doubt, but whatever may be said about Mr Gladstone's over-punctilious formality, and his lengthy and complicated explanation of Government measures, did not his attitude shew deeper respect not only for her position as Queen, but for her understanding, than Dizzy's unblushing exploitation of her femininity?

An over-simplification, no doubt, as almost any forthright judgment must be about the most bizarre and inscrutable figure in English politics. Fierce partisanship is still rife. The pair were well matched and finely contrasted. One writer says they had nothing in common except that both were politicians, authors, and good husbands, but looking a little deeper, one sees more resemblances. Each had immense courage, and each, not always, but usually, was unresentful of injury or insult, and spoke fairly of all opponents except the other; and while Dizzy was obviously a superb actor, Parnell told Mary Gladstone that her father was the best he had ever seen.

But their differences were very wide and deep. Can anybody imagine Mr Gladstone as a young man begging the Prime Minister for a place in his Government, and subsequently denying flatly that he had done so; or delivering as his own a funeral speech taken word for word from a French oration; or charging his opponent, falsely, with indulging in personal abuse, and, when courteously asked for chapter and verse, pretending that he was too busy to find it? Surely these are as unimaginable as to think of Mr Gladstone dyeing his hair, or wearing rings outside his gloves, or composing an unactable tragedy, and writing to his wife that he saw no use in writing tragedies unless they were as fine as Shakespeare's. On their respective political achievements opinions have always differed and still do. The ordinary man's is of no particular value, but perhaps he may ask two questions which refer to what many still regard as Mr Gladstone's chief aberrations. Seventy years ago all Conservatives, many Liberals, and literally all the leading men of letters, historians, scientists and philosophers were unanimous that Mr Gladstone was wrong about Home Rule for Ireland. Where is that unanimity now? Then they saw England's future in the light of the bland fortissimo assurances of 'Land of Hope and Glory'. 'Wider still and wider shall thy bounds be set.' Was that a truer or wiser vision of the world's future than the one which saw the only real hope of peaceful civilisation to lie in freedom and self-government for all nations? We don't know the answer to these questions yet, but those who share Dizzy's view that government is a question of expedients, and deride the idealistic Gladstone's conviction that it is a matter of morals, must face a third question—What has government by expedients made of the world today? But the mills of

God grind slowly. No one knew that better than Mr Gladstone, and though, with all who think and feel, much that has happened since his death would have appalled and saddened him, I do not believe the central fortress of his being would have been shaken.

So what nonsense the climax to Lytton Strachey's brilliant character-sketch of him, in *Eminent Victorians*, surely is! The explorer of Mr Gladstone's mind and spirit is depicted as wandering in a maze, and then 'with the last corner turned, the last step taken, the explorer might find that he was looking down into the gulf of a crater. The flame shot out on every side, scorching and brilliant, but in the midst there was a darkness'. A darkness indeed! How blind these clever men can be! To Strachey Mr Gladstone's rock-like simplicity of heart was naïveté; in the matter of faith, child-like was the same as childish, and his motives in the Gordon tragedy were remorse, rage, and jealousy. And another clever fellow, only four or five years ago, denied Mr Gladstone any greatness at all of mind or soul. Words seem to have completely lost their meaning. We see a man who devoted an outstanding intellect, all his long life, to the service of the State; who won the deep admiration of numberless good and distinguished men, and the devoted allegiance of a host of common men. What were the mainsprings of this career? On numerous occasions he appeared to court, and succeeded in winning, marked unpopularity—this self-seeking demagogue! And when he was 'the people's William', what was it that won their adoration? What bait did he dangle before their eyes? The answer is simple, but in 1955 has an odd look. He made no appeal to their pockets or stomachs. He tried to make them 'feel the issue of the moment as part of the eternal duel between good and evil'. He believed in them and made them believe in themselves. And we know from many sources, which really cannot all be vitiated, that he would have preferred a life in the Church, that on about twelve separate occasions he wished to abandon politics, and that he was kept to that uncongenial grindstone by a sense of duty, based on what he could ascertain of the will of God. If all this does not spell greatness, English vocabulary needs an overhaul. Flawless? Of course not. As Dr Johnson said, 'Depend upon it, Sir, a fallible being will fail somewhere,' and no one was ever more humbly conscious of that than Mr Gladstone. Of course there are flaws. But flaws in the marble did not prevent Michaelangelo from making the statue of David out of it.

And the more the ordinary man learns of him the more surely admiration warms and deepens. It takes a little time, for there is an aloofness about the great. Mr Gladstone, we read, was not good at casual conversation. He never gossiped, and trivialities of small talk often elicited no response, and sometimes an alarming one, when some poor little nut you had tremulously offered was steam-hammered into nothingness. You couldn't be quite sure what would please or amuse him. One who mildly said that the rising generation at Oxford was not interested in Parliamentary debates must have been startled by a tremendous condemnation of 'this plague-spot on the body-politic'. With the possibility of such explosions, some picked their conversational way with rather gingerly steps as in a minefield. Sometimes even your sleep was invaded by that formidable presence. Lord Houghton actually fell out of bed and broke his collar-bone in escaping in a dream from Mr Gladstone, who was pursuing him in a hansom. I don't know how psychiatrists would explain that, but I suggest that, at any level of consciousness, flight from Mr Gladstone may well have seemed the only possible course for one who had the largest collection in England of erotic literature.

And then, finally, we look at the great man at home, and our last hesitations crumble. It is not an austere picture. We see him out of doors in shirtsleeves, tree-cutting—an energetic but not perhaps a strikingly skilful woodman, and rather an absent-minded one, who once felled a tree among whose branches a son was sitting; then in the garden playing French cricket with his sons, or on a picnic 'frisking with Mrs Gladstone in the heather', the perfect wife surely for him, for in the sunshine of her gaiety any formal trappings withered like weeds. But without the smallest loss of dignity, even when they stood on the hearth-rug, their arms round each other's waists, singing what I believe was an ancient costermonger's ditty. Or there might be music, and he would join in Negro melodies, for in his youth, we are told, no one sang romantic songs better. Occasionally he played whist—badly, like all great men—or chess, or backgammon. And at any time when he could be enticed out of his library, the Temple of Peace, he could be 'incomparable'—I quote John Morley—'in conversation, sitting on a low stool, playful, keen, and versatile'. Family discussion was animated; there was no deferential acquiescence in pronouncements which in the Commons would have been hailed as inspirations from one or other of the unearthly powers. They were often, in fact, met by spirited shouts of 'A lie, a lie!'—which he took with a beaming smile. He was never angry. It is a very happy picture, and one nearly —not quite, perhaps—understands Lord Clarendon's nickname for him: Merrypebble. Did he call him that to his face? We shall never know, and some things even the wildest fancy just refuses to face.

I should like to have said something about Mrs Gladstone, the beloved Aunty Pussie, for it is no great flight of fancy to see her radiant influence in all this home life. But I could have said no more than what everybody who knew her has said. She was adored, and adorable. Sixty-five years ago, at Hagley, she gave me a drum, not because I had been good but, characteristically, because I had been naughty, and she thought that to punish a child of seven by locking him up in a room for several hours was wrong and stupid. The drum is no more, but Aunty Pussie has never moved from the corner which she took in my heart on that day of wrath and tears. Her great consort is not quite in that place, but he is not so very far off. And not only because he once patted me on the head.

APPENDIX II

THE TRUE SON OF VIRTUE[1]

by George Lyttelton

On the walls of the dining-room at Hagley before the calamitous fire of 1925 was displayed the whole gallery of ancestral Lyttelton portraits. There was the great legal light of Edward IV's reign, swollen to Falstaffian proportions by his preposterous robes, with the bad lord on one side of him and the mad lord on the other, and directly opposite the portrait of him who was pointed out to us children as the good lord. It was only a head and shoulders, so there was no opportunity of judging, later on, how far Horace Walpole was right in saying he had the figure of a spectre, or, according to another writer, that every limb was a blemish, every movement a disgrace. Doctor Johnson's adjective for his face, 'meagre', was perfectly just. The large curved nose gave it a distinct likeness to the Duke of Wellington's, without the strength, or the 'air of cold command', but the head was well enough poised, and by no means, as Chesterfield described it, 'hanging upon one or other of his shoulders as if it had received the first stroke upon a block'. A mild, remote, colourless figure he seemed to us, markedly inferior in interest to his handsome scamp of a son. Why, and how, we asked, was he the good lord? Was he always in church? Was he a missionary?—these being our simple criteria of goodness. No, came the answer, no, he was not a missionary, he was a statesman and a poet—and a very good man. Later we discovered that he was not a very good statesman nor a very good poet; and as to being a good man, well there seemed to be several who didn't think so, who in fact spoke and wrote of him, not with the passing irritation of the Athenian voter towards Aristides, but in words edged with genuine dislike and contempt.

Horace Walpole clearly thought him a solemn ass and derided both

[1] Delivered at a luncheon of the Johnson Club at Brown's Hotel, Dover Street, on 15 April 1953.

his wits and character, regarding them as overrated by a coterie, Mrs Montagu and her maenads, as he called them. Horace's anti-Lyttelton feelings seem at first sight proved by a letter in which he wrote that the sight of the river at Oxford gave him particular pleasure from remembering that two Lytteltons had been drowned in it; but as the letter was written to Richard Lyttelton, it is, so to speak, a dig in the ribs and not a stab in the back. Still, a good deal of the fun he pokes at Lyttelton has an acid flavour—and something more. A man need not be called double-faced for expressing to an author a different opinion about his book from what he gives to a third person when the author isn't there, but it is hard to acquit Walpole of this charge, unless he had his tongue in his cheek when he told Lyttelton that his *History of Henry II* was a book not to skim but to learn by heart, and that his style would fix and preserve the language. To another he writes 'How dull one may be if one will but take enough pains for six or seven and twenty years'. (Of Lyttelton's conversation 'I have heard him discuss points of midwifery with the solemnity of a Solon' and 'Sir George'—as he was then—'came here to expectorate with me as he called it'.)

Another to whom Lyttelton appeared far from good was Smollett, but he may be discounted, partly because his temper was always on the boil, partly because Lyttelton, to whom he had sent his tragedy, responded kindly but tardily by advising him to devote himself to comedy—and which of the *genus irritabile* would forgive that? Lyttelton did in fact put in a good word with Garrick for Smollett's play, but Smollett may not have known that, as, in the words of his biographer, 'the play never struggled on to the stage'. Even so his savage burlesque of Lyttelton's 'Monody on the Death of his Wife' seems well below the belt even for a literary feud. But later Smollett did make some amends, and perhaps it was only in his rages that he was what Handel called him, 'ein tam fool'.

But why is Doctor Johnson's Life of Lyttelton so grumpy and sour? All kinds of explanation have been given, but most of them do not hold much water. Lyttelton was a Whig, but so was Burke, and who has praised Burke more nobly than Johnson? Lyttelton, when young, wrote pastorals, but escaped, as did Pope, with a mild growl or two. Lyttelton was religious, and wrote a treatise on Saint Paul which

Johnson actually praises, saying 'infidelity has never been able to fabricate a specious reply to it'. I doubt myself whether infidelity has ever tried very hard to do so, for its main theme is that Saint Paul was entirely sincere, which I never heard of anyone doubting. Then again, though Lyttelton had learning, it was too bookish for Johnson's approval. 'That man sat down to write a book to tell the world what the world all his life had been telling him.' (But that cap fits many a literary head a good deal more closely than 'poor Lyttelton's'.)

For the grounds of Johnson's personal antipathy to Lyttelton we have mainly to explore the realm of fancy, or, what is often much the same thing, the recollections of Mrs Thrale. She says that Johnson told her how he and Lyttelton had been rivals for the affections of Miss Hill Boothby, and that she could see from his Life how he still resented her preference of 'that fellow Lyttelton'. Her tale bristles with improbabilities, as Croker showed, and, though the old Johnson never minded laughing at the young Johnson, does not somehow ring true. The same lively lady tells us of Johnson's visit to Hagley, when he stayed with William Lyttelton after the good lord's death. 'He was enraged', she writes, 'at artificial ruins and temporary cascades, so that I wonder at his leaving his opinion of them dubious. Besides he hated the Lytteltons, and would rejoice at an opportunity of insulting them.' Johnson himself wrote of his visit: 'We made haste away from a place where all were offended'; but Mrs Thrale softens the grimness of this by suggesting that the causes of offence were no more than that Mrs Lyttelton made Johnson play whist against his will, and Mr Lyttelton may have further annoyed Johnson by declining to supply him with materials for the Life of his brother. This Life has that chilliness of tone which suggests that a writer is treating of a subject which does not much interest him, or a man whom he does not rate very high, but does not strike me as essentially unjust. No one could quarrel with Johnson for saying that Lyttelton's letters 'have something of that indistinct and headstrong ardour for liberty characteristic of the young', or that his poems 'have nothing to be despised and little to be admired—that the shorter ones are sometimes sprightly and sometimes insipid'. It is all perfectly true. There is one good example of that grave irony which gives so much enjoyment to readers of the *Lives of the Poets*, and, I suspect, to the writer. Lyttelton took immense care and a portentous time over his *History of Henry II*, and, says Johnson, 'one Andrew Reid had persuaded him, as he had persuaded himself, that he was master of the secret of punctuation, but before the third edition', Johnson goes on, 'Reid was either dead or discarded, and the superintendence of typography and punctuation was committed to a man, originally a comb-maker, but then known by the style of Doctor. Something uncommon was probably expected, and something uncommon was at last done; for to the Doctor's edition is appended what the world has hardly seen before, a list of errors in nineteen pages.' That is fair enough. But the same cannot be said of the statement, perilously like a sneer, that after his wife's death 'Lyttelton solaced himself by writing a long poem to her memory'. Probably grief that did not prevent the griever from marrying again two years after did not arouse much sympathy in the widower of Tetty.

And then, as always in any discussion about these two, arises the question 'Which was Chesterfield's "respectable Hottentot"?' The present company no doubt is solid in support of Doctor Birkbeck Hill's claim to have wiped this blot off the social and convivial reputation of Doctor Johnson. (The respectable Hottentot, you remember, threw his soup and wine anywhere but into his mouth, and mangled his meat.) You all probably know the pros and cons, with which I will not weary you. But there is one point which, as far as I know, has had no explanation, though some seems called for. In one of the four letters of Chesterfield's used by Doctor Hill to establish his proof, the man described—in almost identical terms with those in the other three letters—is called by Chesterfield 'a near relation of mine'. Well, if he was that he was certainly not Lyttelton—still less, of course, Johnson. But if the expression was what would now be called 'camouflage', what was the point of it in a letter to his son? I can throw no light on the small mystery. Still, though Boswell denies that Lyttelton was violent in argument (as the Hottentot was) just as strongly as he does that Johnson, though his table manners had their weak spots, was an untidy feeder, a collateral descendent must admit that the Hottentot was probably meant for Lyttelton, and must extract what comfort he can from the epithet which preceded it.

Of Lyttelton's politics Johnson says little, and I shall say less. Can the dry bones live of domestic politics two hundred years ago?

Certainly not to me. The dust lies thick upon Lyttelton's speeches, though some of them were praised at the time, even by Walpole. It still remains a nearly insoluble mystery how an absent-minded scholar, particularly weak at arithmetic, and apparently never quite clear about the difference between prices and duties, between discounts and premiums, became Chancellor of the Exchequer. Must he not have felt, when about to introduce his budget, as George du Maurier did in his nightmare on finding himself billed to sing 'The Lost Chord' at the Albert Hall? There is no sign that he did, though something may lie behind Johnson's dry remark that 'the office required some qualifications which he soon perceived himself to want'.

Lyttelton's literary remains consist of both prose and poetry. The two chief prose works, the *Persian Letters* and the *Dialogues of the Dead*, are both derivative, Lucian, Montesquieu, Fénelon and Fontenelle having already blazed the trail. The *Persian Letters* are still readable enough, though they suffer from comparison with the grace and humour of Goldsmith's very similar *Citizen of the World*, written some years later. In places they are surprisingly indelicate, almost Decameronian, to come from the pen of one whom Thomson called the true son of virtue; Lyttelton is said to have expressed regret for this in later life, but there is no extant evidence of his doing so, and it may be an invention of his biographer, who admits, with a frankness that somehow does not disarm, that his main object in writing the life was to please the Lyttelton family. The *Dialogues of the Dead* had many admirers, among whom were *not* Johnson and Walpole, who decry them for exactly opposite reasons. Johnson calls them nugatory and says that the names of his persons too often enable the reader to anticipate their conversation, while Walpole, who amiably changes the title to *Dead Dialogues*, says that the persons all talk out of character. Both are really right. The sentiments of, for instance, the goddess Circe are exactly what one would expect, but certainly not the polished and balanced phrases in which she clothes them. I am afraid Walpole's amended title is pretty near the truth.

What of Lyttelton's poetry? One is tempted to summarise it, as one might so much eighteenth-century poetry, in the form of a prescription or a recipe. Take a taste for romantic scenery, a decorous affection for a young lady, a profound admiration of Milton and Pope, a pinch—not more—of irony and demure playfulness, several slabs of moral sentiment, and serve cold with a rich sauce of poetic diction. There is, I think, the savour of genuine feeling in some lines of his Monody on his dead wife, but the Miltonic echoes are too blatant. 'Where were ye Muses . . . ?' 'Nor where Clitumnus rolls his gentle stream', 'the light fantastic toys', and so on. The worst of these is in the poem 'Blenheim' when he takes Eve's unsurpassable tribute to Adam—'With thee conversing I forget all time', and applies it, almost unaltered, to the Duke of Marlborough talking to his Duchess. How right Johnson was about pastoral trappings when employed by almost anyone except Milton: and how hard it is today to recapture the thrill which presumably our ancestors felt when Philomel was urged to resume her song or pour her plaint—or to sympathise when a man claims, as Lyttelton did, that his grief for his lost wife *must* be far greater than Petrarch's for Laura, because Petrarch was not married to Laura, or to realise the charm of that wife when she is summed up as 'though meek, magnanimous, though witty, wise,' which all may read today who leave Hagley Church by the west door.

It is when Lyttelton is considered not as a statesman or poet, but as a patron of literature, or more simply and broadly, as a friend, that his special virtues really do begin to emerge. As a patron he would of course not be likely to get a very warm word from Johnson, but his relations with authors, and indeed with men in general, do reveal a character of outstanding generosity and good nature. A man who could remain unruffled under the savage contempt of Pitt and restore him to amiability before the end of the sitting, who bore no long resentment against a cousin who referred to him in Parliament as '*hominem detestabilem atque imbecillum*', who could keep without a break the friendship of Pope and Garrick and Bolingbroke and Shenstone, and ask and return a favour from Swift, who never ceased to defend and help Archibald Bower, regarded by everyone else as a detected impostor, whose letters contain hardly a hint of a grudge cherished or a slight resented—such a man must surely be credited with far more than ordinary magnanimity.

His kindnesses to authors were very numerous. The best known of his beneficiaries were Thomson and Fielding, both of whom wrote of him with especial warmth. The placid and indolent Thomson was, through Lyttelton's good offices, appointed surveyor-general of the Leeward Islands, a post which brought him, after paying a deputy to do the work, about £300 a year. He was often at Hagley, where a little shelter called Thomson's seat still marks his favourite spot in the park, 'the British Tempe' as he called it, whence he surveyed, not the Leeward Islands, but what he called 'the bursting prospect', or, more prosaically, a view over some ten midland counties.

Lastly there is Lyttelton's old schoolfellow Fielding, who, in dedicating *Tom Jones* to him, declares that it owed its inception to Lyttelton's suggestion, and its completion to his assistance. The characters of Lyttelton and another friend and patron, Ralph Allen, are blended to produce the flawless but unexciting Squire Allworthy, and in a breathtaking sentence in the dedication Fielding says that to associate his book with Lyttelton is a guarantee that there will be in it 'nothing inconsistent with the stricter rules of decency, nor which can offend the chastest eye'. I wonder how the good lord swallowed that. In fact one is left wondering about him. To have gained—leaving out smaller fry—the friendship of Pope and the enmity of Johnson surely argues a character of some force, substance and quality, but I confess, it eludes me. I have read the eight hundred prosy pages of his idle, unrevealing, inaccurate and immensely dull biography; I have read pretty well all that he wrote—except the *History of Henry II*—and much of what others said and wrote of him. But it is no good. His public and poetic life and words are there for all to note; so are the gaunt visage, the ill-compacted frame, the unlovely voice, the jerky movement. But what manner of man was behind this façade, I have still no clear idea. Horace Walpole was right. There *is* something spectral, something puppet-like about him. And yet this spectre has achieved one solid, splendid and indeed all but unique distinction. He and Fulke Greville are the only Chancellors of the Exchequer who are represented in *The Oxford Book of English Verse*; and surely the shared distinction is likely to remain for ever unique. It is of course possible that the song which, a few years ago, Doctor Dalton told us he had in his heart may yet emerge in words. But even if it does, I feel fairly confident that the anthology (if any) into which it finds its way will be more akin to *The Stuffed Owl* than to one which skims the cream of English poetry of the last six hundred and fifty years.

INDEX